Data Communications, Networks, and Systems

Data Communications, Networks, and Systems

Thomas C. Bartee
Editor-in-Chief

A Division of Prentice Hall Computer Publishing
11711 North College, Carmel, Indiana 46032 USA

Publisher: *Richard K. Swadley*
Publishing Manager: *Joe Wikert*
Managing Editor: *Neweleen Trebnik*
Acquisitions Manager: *Charlie Dresser*
Manuscript Editor: *Don Herrington*
Keyboarding: *Katia Forêt*
Cover Artist: *Jean Bisesi*
Designer: *Scott Cook*
Compositor: *Shepard Poorman Communications, Incorporated*
Indexer: *Sharon Hilgenberg*

Production Assistance: *Claudia Bell, Michelle Cleary, Mark Enochs, Bob LaRoche, Joe Ramon, Linda Seifert, Dennis Sheehan, Bruce Steed, Suzanne Tully, Mary Beth Wakefield, Phil Worthington*

Contents

2 Carriers and Regulation

3 Modems, Multiplexers, and Concentrators

4 Protocols 129

5 Integrated Voice/Data Networks 153

6 Baseband Local Area Networks

7   Broadband Local Area Networks   247

8   Computer and Communications Security   267

9   Local Area Network Standards   *311*

Preface

THIS BOOK CONTAINS THE LATEST INFORMATION in the important area of digital communications, networks, and systems. The book begins with communications media, progresses through government regulations, describes the latest components and system strategies, and finally concludes with such important topics as security, standards, and error control.

In order that the most current and accurate information be included, each of the chapters of this book has been prepared by an expert in the given subject. Also, each chapter includes introductory material so that readers can learn basic facts about each subject at the same time that they are obtaining up-to-date material concerning the various areas covered.

The first chapter presents an overview of the most used transmission media in data transmission. Many media have been used in data communications systems but twisted pairs, coaxial cable, optical fiber, waveguides, and radio (including satellite transmission) are all widely used and are herein discussed. At the same time as the characteristics of these media are given, some history, background, and observations on the good and bad features of each are presented. Dale N. Hatfield, the author, has a considerable background in communications systems; he was formerly Deputy Assistant Secretary of Commerce for Communications and Information, Chief of the Office of Plans and Policy at the Federal Communications Commission, and Deputy Administrator in National Telecommunications at the Department of Commerce. The editor of this book has contributed the changes in this latest version in order to accommodate Mr. Hatfield's busy schedule. This chapter is exceptionally clear and it contains much useful and practical information.

Management and engineers must always be concerned with the regulatory aspects of common carrier usage in communications and this chapter, written by Walter Hinchman, is an excellent introduction to the subject. The chapter briefly delves into some of the history of communications law and then describes the forces that are shaping the structure and regulation of common carrier operations. The chapter includes some information on current regulatory rules, industry structure, and service offerings including the role of the Federal Communications Commission (FCC) in present regulations, all areas which Walter Hinchman, as a former Chief, Common Carrier Bureau of the FCC, Assistant Director, Office of Telecommunications Policy at the White House, and Chief of the FCC Office of plans and services, is ideally suited to explain.

When communications systems are assembled, there are three types of basic components which play a major role in the systems. These are called *modems, multiplexers,* and *concentrators.* These system components are in most systems so system planners and designers must take their characteristics into careful consideration. We are fortunate in having a recognized authority in this field, Professor Raymond Pickholtz, former Chairman of the Department of Electrical Engineering and Computer Science at George Washington University, and the winner of many awards in the communications area prepare a carefully written and up-to-date introduction and survey of this area. There is a wealth of information in Chapter 3, ranging from formulas for, and graphs of, operational performance values to some knowledgeable comments on design strategies. The general information given in this chapter should be of value to almost anyone.

In order to make computers, terminals, and communications systems components work together, it is necessary to use *protocols.* These protocols provide the procedures for interoperating in communication systems; there is a long history of protocol development in the data communications area. An introduction to protocols may be found in Chapter 4, along with some carefully worked-out examples of widely used present-day protocols. John McQuillan, the author of this chapter, is well-known in this area and has participated in many IEEE and ACM seminars and courses. He was responsible for pioneering work on early networks at Bolt Beranck and Newman. The value of his experience is clearly shown in this chapter.

Chapter 5 describes Integrated Voice and Data Networks. A wealth of background material is explained including the Private Branch Exchange (PBX), voice and digital communication techniques, packet switching and fast circuit switching, etc. The Chapter is written by Richard S. Kagan, an award winning engineer who, after working at Bell Telephone Labs went to ROLM, where he worked on local area networks. He is now European Director of Business Development for Echelon Corporation which develops intelligent, distributive control systems.

The next two chapters treat the subject of Local Area Networks (LANs) in some detail. There are three basic system approaches to local area networks at present. The PBX is in Chapter 5 and the other two are described by a proponent of that particular approach in Chapter 6 and 7.

Baseband Local Area Networks, described in Chapter 6, use coaxial cable, twisted pairs, or fiber optics, and communicate using digital signals in "conventional" digital form. (Fiber optics are described in Chapter 1.) These systems have been very successful commercially and the details of their operation and advantages can be found in this chapter. Basic information on the advantages and disadvantages of different approaches to LAN networks, including the media selected, access techniques, security considerations, network topology, etc., is given. Some learned comments on performance evaluation are also included. The material clearly shows the accumulated experience of David Potter. Mr. Potter, formerly Vice President of Interlan Incorporated, also participated in the development of several LAN systems in this area with other major companies (for example, DEC and Xerox).

Broadband Local Area Networks, the subject of Chapter 7, also use coaxial cable, but the cable is of a different type. This type cable has been extensively used in closed-circuit television systems. The digital information is, in this case, used to modulate a carrier, as is explained. Since the cable used can carry broadband frequency signals, it is possible to use the same cable for several digital signals at the same time and also include audio and video signals. This permits the construction of multifunction systems which can be used for teleconferencing. Connections to and from broadband systems are more complex because of the modulation and demodulation equipment required and because of the type of coaxial cable used; however, the use of system components that were developed for video systems makes for cost reductions. Chapter 7 covers these details fully and gives some interesting operational features. John Summers, Associate Technical Director of the Information Systems and Technology Division of the MITRE Corporation, a major developer of broadband systems, uses his expertise and clear writing ability to present the information concerning broadband systems.

When networks of computers and users are formed, quite often some system of security measures must be taken to protect the users and system operators from intruders, both from within and from outside the network system. Chapter 8 goes into this subject, giving the rationale behind security measures and discussing the techniques used to provide security. This is a fascinating subject that is still in its infancy and one that is the subject of much press coverage as systems continue to be broken into. Stephen Walker and William Barker, the authors of this chapter, are well-known in the security field. Steve Walker is now President of Trusted Information Systems Inc. and a member of the Defense Science Board Task Force on Defense Data Networks and the Foreign Applied Science Assessment Center Panel on Computer Science. William Barker is the Principal Communications Security Analyst for Trusted Information Systems. He spent 12 years in cryptographic work for the Government and then five years managing development of cryptographic equipment in private industry.

In order to interconnect computers, terminals, and other components of various types and manufacture, and to provide interconnections between networks, it is desirable to have standards for system operation. These standards also aid suppliers of components and systems since they then have a target to build to. This further facilitates the assembling of systems by users and also makes it possible for manufacturers to expand their markets. Chapter 9, on local area network standards, explains what standards are now being worked on by various committees and provides the organizational structure of those agencies participating in this important endeavor. This information is useful to both systems and component developers and potential users as it makes it possible to ascertain the current state of this area and the sources of information. The two authors are John Carson, a Professor of Management Science at George Washington University, and David Wood, a Consulting Scientist at MITRE.

The last chapter in the book, on error control, deals with a most important subject. No matter how careful the design, any communications system will have to contend with errors, and some systems are even designed to have an error rate which can be "tolerated" in order to improve certain other system parameters. Since errors which occur must be handled in some way, much research has gone into developing techniques for handling errors and many system strategies have been formulated and used for dealing with this problem. There are several basic strategies, however, and several types of coding for communications which align themselves with these strategies. From the first, this has been a subject which included considerable mathematics and this chapter treats this subject accordingly; however, the math is carefully laid out so that the material can be learned in stages. There is even some previously unpublished material in this chapter that is primarily concerned with coding for satellite systems. Joseph Odenwalder, the author of this chapter, is an Assistant Vice-President at Linkabit Corp. His work in the error-control field is well-known and highly regarded.

Photographs and biographies on each of the contributors will be found with the chapter he has authored.

The material in this book can be read in order, that is, from the front to the back of the book, but it is possible to read most chapters independently. I would like to take this opportunity to thank Katia Foret for coordinating the preparation of this book. Several authors have also expressed their gratitude for her assistance on their chapters.

Thomas C. Bartee

Transmission Media

Dale N. Hatfield

Dale N. Hatfield is the owner of Dale N. Hatfield Associates, a consulting firm specializing in engineering and regulatory matters in the common carrier, mobile radio, satellite, cable television, and local distribution fields. He is a former Deputy Assistant Secretary of Commerce for Communications and Information. During the 1970s he served as Chief of the Office of Plans and Policy at the Federal Communications Commission and, subsequently, as Deputy Administrator of the National Telecommunications and Information Administration in the Department of Commerce.

Mr. Hatfield is a frequent speaker before industry groups and has testified on numerous occasions before both Houses of Congress. He is currently a Visiting Lecturer in the Masters Program in Telecommunications at the University of Colorado where he teaches a course in telecommunications policy and regulation. He has served as a consulting member of the IEEE Committee on Telecommunications Policy and, in 1973, he received a Department of Commerce Silver Medal for contributions to domestic communications satellite policy. Mr. Hatfield holds a B.S.E.E. from Case Institute of Technology and an M.S. in Industrial Management from Purdue University.

1.1 Overview

In its most basic form, a communication system consists of a transmitter, a receiver, and a *channel* of some type for connecting the transmitter and the receiver. The purpose of the system is to convey information from transmitter to receiver over the channel. The distance between transmitter and receiver may range, from a few feet (in the case of a computer sending information to a nearby printer) to millions of miles (in the case of data being sent back to earth from a space probe deep in outer space).

1.1.1 Analog and Digital Signals

The information to be conveyed and reproduced by the communications system can be continuous (for example, the position of a gear or a distance) or discrete (for example, whether a switch is open or closed). The information is sent through the channel using signals which can be electrical, light intensities, radio signal frequencies, etc. An *analog signal* is a signal that varies continuously between a maximum and a minimum value. At a given instant, an analog signal can assume any one from an infinite number of values between the two extremes. Examples of analog signals include the amplitude of a human voice, the frequency of a radio signal, the amplitude of an electrical voltage, etc. A *digital signal*, in contrast, does not take on a continuous set of values. Rather, at a given instant it takes on one from a limited set of values, each of which represents a symbol like a number or alphabetical character. Examples of digital signals include whether or not an electrical voltage is negative or positive, the status of a telegraph key (up or down), or the status of a key on a keyboard (e.g., whether the letter "A" key has been struck or not).

A communication system can be either analog or digital (or a combination of the two). That is, the information can be transmitted in either analog or digital form within the communications system. In an ordinary telephone loop, the signal consists of an electrical current which varies in amplitude in step with the variations of the intensity of the sound that are impinging upon the microphone in the headset at the transmitting end. The variations in electrical amplitude are converted back into sound (in the earphone) at the receiving end. This is an example of an analog transmission.

In a digital transmission, only a limited number of discrete or discontinuous signals are transmitted during each discrete interval of time. These discrete signals, or sequences of signals, can be used to send alphanumeric characters or quantized values of an analog signal at particular instants of time.[4] Typically, digital communications involves the transmission of a stream of "on" and "off" signals called *bits*. In the digital transmission of alphanumeric text, for example, each letter or number is encoded into or represented by a unique sequence of bits. These bits, in turn, can be transmitted in numerous ways. For example, they can be transmitted by a series of current pulses on a transmission line or by varying the amplitude, frequency, or phase of a radio wave.

1.1.2 Modems

It is obvious that analog transmission systems can be used to transmit analog signals and that digital transmission systems can be used to transmit digital signals. However, the opposite is also true. A digital signal, such as the output of a computer terminal, can be transmitted via a network designed for analog transmission by first converting the signal into a form that can pass through the network. The most important example of such a network is the ordinary switched telephone system. It was designed or optimized for the transmission of analog voice signals. In order to transmit digital signals over this network, the characteristic of one or more tones or carriers (amplitude, frequency, phase, or some combination) in the frequency range of ordinary voice signals is changed in a discrete manner from one signaling period to the next. In the most familiar case, that of personal (and larger) computers, this is done in a device called a *modem*. With the modem, at the sending computer, digital information is converted to analog form by the modem. The analog signal is then transmitted over the telephone system. At the receiving end, the voice-frequency analog signals are converted back into a digital signal that is suitable for an input to a computer. A modem at the receiving computer performs that latter function as well. The term "modem" is a contraction for "modulator/demodulator." The two modem functions just described are performed by the modulator and demodulator, respectively. Because of the ubiquity of the ordinary voice telephone network, it has always been used extensively for the transmission of digital information. This means that modems are extremely important devices in data communications and they are treated in detail in Chapter 3.

1.1.3 A/D and D/A Conversion

Similarly, a digital transmission system can be used to transmit analog signals. However, in order to do this, the analog information must go through a three-step process. First, the analog signal must be sampled at an instant of time. Second, the sample must be quantized; that is, it must be converted into the particular interval or level (out of a limited group of such intervals) that most closely approximates the amplitude of the signal at that instant of time. Third, and finally, this quantized value must be converted or encoded into a unique digital signal (e.g., sequence of bits) corresponding to the particular signal level. This process is known as analog-to-digital conversion. At the receiving end, the process must be reversed to restore the analog signal to its original form; this is called digital to analog (D/A) conversion. If the input analog signal is sampled frequently enough and if a sufficient number of different digital levels are used, a very accurate representation of the analog input signal can be obtained at the receiving end.

1.1.4 Data Communications

Data communications is associated with machine-to-machine communications, such as terminal-to-computer and computer-to-computer communications. Because these machines are inherently digital in nature, they communicate most readily with signals in digital form. Thus, the terms *data communications* and *digital communications* are sometimes used synonymously. Increasingly, however, all forms of information, including voice, video, and facsimile signals, are being transmitted using digital rather than analog transmission techniques. Indeed, significant portions of the ordinary telephone network now use such techniques, and there are presently substantial efforts at both domestic and international levels to evolve the entire network into an Integrated Services Digital Network (ISDN).[2]

1.1.5 Signal Regeneration

This increased emphasis on digital transmission stems not only from the rapidly growing importance of data communications, but also from its many other advantages. One of the most important and fundamental of these other advantages stems from signal regeneration. When analog signals are transmitted over long distances, the signal gets progressively weaker and noise and interference creep in. When amplifiers are employed to boost the signal, the noise and interference are amplified along with the desired signal, and the amplifier itself adds additional noise and distortion. Thus, the quality of the signal transmitted in the analog mode deteriorates steadily with the distance because of the cumulative addition of noise and interference.

In digital transmission, the bit sequences associated with the input signal are regenerated at repeaters spaced along the transmission path.* The repeaters only need to detect the signal and decide whether a one (1) or a zero (0) was transmitted. By spacing the repeaters close enough together and, in some instances, by employing error-correction techniques (refer to Chapter 10), the repeater can make this decision with very low probability of error even though the signal is also corrupted by noise and interference. Having reached the correct decision, the repeater creates a new uncorrupted signal. Because a new uncorrupted signal is regenerated at each repeater, the overall performance of the circuit need not deteriorate with distance. The overall performance is determined primarily by the terminal equipment as long as errors in transmission are properly controlled. Thus, constant high-quality performance can be achieved regardless of the length of the circuit. Other advantages that stem from the transmission of voice and other analog signals by digital means include ease of multiplexing, ease of sending network control information, the ease with which modern digital components (with their rapidly increasing performance and falling costs) can be incorporated into system designs, the efficiencies that result when digital transmission is combined with digital switching, performance monitorability, and the ease of encryption.[18]

1.1.6 Summary

Of course, the transmission media itself does not "care" whether the signal is carrying analog or digital information. Its characteristics remain the same although the effects of those characteristics on system performance can and do vary greatly depending on the particular transmission technique employed. The purpose of this introductory chapter is to describe the properties of various transmission media. Because this book is devoted to data communications topics, and because of the growing importance of digital transmission, the emphasis in this chapter will be on the characteristics of the different media when used for the transmission of signals in digital form.

When describing the capacity of a digital communications channel, it is common practice to give the number of bits-per-second (bps) the channel can carry. Early telegraph (teletype) channels which also were used for digital terminals carried 300 bps. If 10 bits were used for a single character, as was often the case because of start and stop control bits, 30 characters could be sent each second over such a system. As time passed the rates increased until several hundred to several thousand characters can be sent over most digital channels now.

When the telephone companies decided to digitize voice transmission they adopted a system where voice signals were sampled 8000 times each

---

*The term "bit sequences" is used here since it is common to talk in terms of two level (i.e., binary) transmission systems. However, systems with more than two levels are increasingly being used wherein each sampling element carries more information than does a basic binary signaling element (bit).

second and each sample was converted to one of 256 levels requiring eight bits for each sample. Thus, $8 \times 8000 = 64,000$ bits per second were sent for each voice telephone connection. The device which converts a voice signal in analog form to a digital signal is called a codec (coder-decoder.) Codecs normally generate 7 or 8 bits for each sample, we will continue to describe the 8-bit systems.

When coaxial cable, fiber, and microwave are used to transmit voice signals in the telephone system they are capable of carrying much more than 64,000 bps and so in order to economize on equipment and use the high-capacity channels efficiently 24 voice signals were combined on a single high-speed channel called a T1 carrier. An extra bit was used for each 24×8 bit "frame" (i.e., each sample from all 24 voice channels) to synchronize the system. The T1 carrier thus carried 1.544 million bits per second (Mbps) and this became a popular standard for specifying digital communications capacities. Users can buy T1 services from point-to-point from a number of communications companies.[12]

When 24 voice signals are combined on a single T1 carrier the signals are said to be *multiplexed* onto the T1 and at the receiving end the 24 signals are then separated or *demultiplexed* into the 24 original voice signals.[2]

The T1 system became very popular and variations on it are used internationally. The variations concern the use of the extra bit for synchronization (framing) and whether 7 or 8 bits are used for each sample, how the bits are integrated, etc. (Reference 19 treats this in detail.) The T1 has been expanded to a T2 at 6.312 Mbps, T3 at 44.736 Mbps, T4 at 274.176 Mbps, etc. The CCITT standards call for 8.848, 34.304, 139.264, and 565.148 for corresponding rates.

To give some further feeling for the bit rates for communications systems in common usage today, Table 1-1 shows the most used North American, European, and Japanese standard services.

The figures in the Table 1-1 are for services which can be obtained from telephone companies, etc., and the interfaces are standard so connection is straightforward as mentioned before.[33] The services can also be used for terminals, computer-to-computer connections, etc. as well as for voice communications (the original use).

The remainder of this chapter is divided into six sections, each corresponding to a different transmission media. Paired cable, coaxial cable, microwave radio (both terrestrial and satellite paths), and optical fibers are treated in detail because of their current and future importance. Other media, such as open-wire lines, nonmicrowave radio, and waveguides are mentioned briefly for completeness.

1.2 Open-Wire Lines

Open-wire lines were the original telephone and telegraph transmission media for both local and long-haul transmission. Open-wire lines consisted of

Table 1-1. Standard Rates for Digital Services.

	North American	European (CEPT)	Japanese
Level 1			
Bit Rate (Mbps)	1.544	2.048	1.544
Voice Circuits	24	30	24
Level 2			
Bit Rate (Mbps)	6.312	8.448	6.312
Voice Circuits	96	120	96
Level 3			
Bit Rate (Mbps)	44.736	34.368	32.064
Voice Circuits	672	480	
Level 4			
Bit Rate (Mbps)	274.176	139.264	97.728
Voice Circuits	4032	1920	1440
Level 5			
Bit Rate (Mbps)	Not defined	565.148	397.20
Voice Circuits		7680	5760

pairs of bare wire conductors that were tied to insulators attached to cross-arms on telephone poles. The wire itself was copper or copper-clad steel.

The major advantage of well-designed open-wire lines was their very low loss at voice frequencies. This attenuation, as low as a few tenths of a decibel* (dB) per mile at one kilohertz (kHz), permitted the transmission of voice signals over distances of hundreds of miles even before the invention of vacuum-tube amplifiers. Noise pickup and crosstalk were minimized by proper spacing of the wire pairs and by the transposition or reversal of each pair at regular intervals.[16]

Open-wire lines are rapidly being replaced by other media because of the limitations in the number of pairs that can be carried on a single-pole line, because of their susceptibility to damage from vandals and severe weather conditions, because of their high-maintenance costs,[9] and for aesthetic reasons.[30] Today, the use of open-wire lines is largely confined to previously established systems in extremely rural areas.

1.3 Paired Cable

A multipair cable consists of individually insulated pairs of conductors enclosed in a common protective sheath. Each wire pair is twisted together to

---

*The term *decibel*, abbreviated *dB*, is a unit used to express the relation between two amounts of power, P_1 and P_2. The number of decibels is equal to $10 \log_{10}(P_1/P_2)$.
Thus if $P_1 = 10$ watts and $P_2 = 20$ watts, the number of decibels is $10 \log_{10}(10/20)$, or -3.01 dB. To convert decibels to power ratios, simply divide by 10 and raise 10 to the resulting number. For example, 20 dB corresponds to a power ratio of $10^{(20/10)}$, or $10^2 = 100$; and -10 dB corresponds to $10^{(-10/10)}$, or $1/10$.

minimize and randomize the coupling of noise and crosstalk into each circuit. The twisted pair(s) used to connect most telephone headsets are examples of twisted pairs. Twisted pair(s) connected to telephones are often referred to as "loops." The loop to a customer is called a "subscriber loop." Large numbers of these twisted pairs can be combined in a single cable. Depending upon the application, a multipair cable can contain as many as 3000 such pairs.

Multipair cable is used extensively in telecommunications networks. It is used in the telephone network for wiring within buildings, in the portion of the telephone network between the customer's premises and the local central office (i.e., the subscriber or loop plant), and in the portion of the network that is between central offices in a metropolitan area (i.e., the trunk plant). Because of the extensive use of multipair cable as a transmission medium, it follows that the characteristics of multipair cable will have a major influence on the performance of the telephone network. This is important for two reasons.

1.3.1 Data Communications

First, it is important because the telephone network has always been used for data communications on both a dial-up and a dedicated line basis. When the demand for data communications services arose in the 1950s, the analog voice telephone network was already nearly ubiquitous and its technology well understood. The development of modems allowed use of the existing network by providing a means for converting digital information into signals which could be carried over a network that had been optimized for voice transmission. As will be described later, the extensive use of multipair cable places significant constraints on the use of the analog voice network for transmitting data. In order to organize the transition from an analog to a digital telephone system, three surveys of the subscriber loops in the (US) Bell system have been made and results are in the chapter by Ahamed and Lawrence in Reference 2.

1.3.2 Inside and Outside Wiring

Second, it is important because inside wiring, the loop plant, and the trunk plant, together, represent a large fraction of the total investment in the telephone network. There is today a strong incentive to adapt this existing plant for use with pure digital transmission. For example, when digital multiplexing was introduced as a cost-saving measure in metropolitan-area (T1-like) trunk networks in the 1950s, it was designed to use existing cable pairs. More recently, existing inside wiring has been adapted for use with digital local area networks (LANs) and the regular use of local loops for carrying high-speed digital signals has become more widespread. Again, it is clear that the characteristics of multipair cable will have a significant influence on the development of future digital services that are built upon the existing telephone network.

Inside wiring cables consist of insulated 19-, 22-, 24-, or 26-gauge copper conductors. In the outside plant, the conductors were originally paper-insulated and covered with a common moisture-resistant lead sheath. Plastic-insulated cable is now the most popular type cable used in the outside plant. The conductors again consist of 19- through 26-gauge copper wires. Various sheath materials are used depending upon the environment. In the telephone industry, two basic construction methods are employed for multipair cable installation—above ground on poles or below the surface. Two types of subsurface construction are employed, namely, "buried," where a cable is placed directly in the earth without any underground conduits and "underground," where the cable is installed in underground ducts. In general, cables may contain from 6 to 3000 wire pairs.[18]

1.3.3 Losses

Insulating the individual conductors and then placing them within a sheath greatly increased the number of wire pairs that can be carried by a single-pole line and it made buried and underground construction practical. The development of multipair cable created other problems, however. The much closer proximity of the two conductors greatly increases the capacitance between the two wires and, thus, significantly increases the attenuation. As noted before, open wire has a loss as low as a few tenths of a dB per mile at one kilohertz. In contrast, a 22-gauge multipair cable has a loss of approximately 1.8 dB per mile at the same frequency. This loss increases significantly with frequency. The loss is exacerbated by the use of smaller wire sizes and by shorter leakage paths. The twisting of the individual pairs within the cable sheath reduces the coupling between pairs but, as the frequency increases, this isolation decreases and crosstalk problems increase rather dramatically.

1.3.4 Data Rates

The net effect of these characteristics is to limit the maximum practical data rate that can be transmitted over such cable pairs. An indication of this limitation is graphically shown in Fig. 1-1. It illustrates the serving (transmission) distance capabilities of nonloaded cable pairs at various data rates for 22-, 24-, and 26-gauge wire.

The term "nonloaded" will be explained in a subsequent paragraph. Note in Fig. 1-1 that for 24-gauge wire, the distances range from 6000 feet at 1.5 Mbps to nearly ten times that distance at 2.4 kbps. In interoffice trunk applications, existing voice-frequency-grade cables are used to carry pulse code modulation (PCM) signals at a 1.544 Mbps rate by employing repeaters at approximately one-mile intervals. As explained earlier in the chapter, these repeaters regenerate the signal and thereby allow higher data rates to be carried over greater distances. Care must be taken to ensure that crosstalk among cable pairs is minimized.

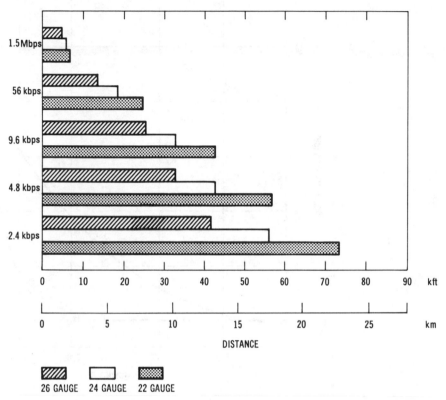

DATA RATE

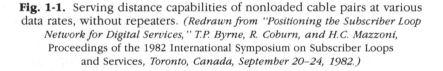

26 GAUGE   24 GAUGE   22 GAUGE

Fig. 1-1. Serving distance capabilities of nonloaded cable pairs at various data rates, without repeaters. *(Redrawn from "Positioning the Subscriber Loop Network for Digital Services," T.P. Byrne, R. Coburn, and H.C. Mazzoni, Proceedings of the 1982 International Symposium on Subscriber Loops and Services, Toronto, Canada, September 20–24, 1982.)*

In the loop portion of the telephone network, the maximum data rate is reduced even further by the presence of *loading coils* and *bridged taps*. Loading coils are employed in the network to improve the transmission of voice frequencies. Loading coils are simply inductors that are placed in series with the line at regular intervals. They have the effect of significantly reducing (and flattening) the attenuation at voice frequencies (i.e., between about 200 and 3500 Hz), but significantly increasing it at higher frequencies. This effect is illustrated in Fig. 1-2.

The invention of loading coils was crucial to the development of telephony because it allowed analog voice transmissions over much greater distances. Loading coils are typically used with loops that are longer than about three miles in length. However, loading coils have the effect of drastically reducing both the bandwidth and the maximum data rate that can be transmitted on a

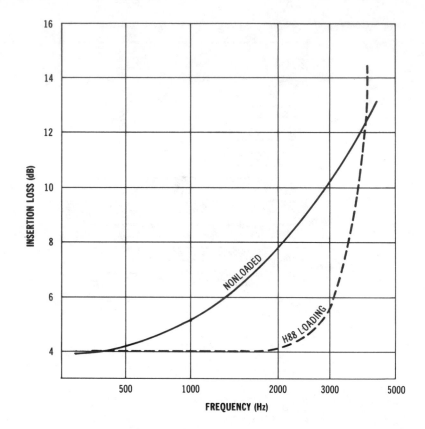

Fig. 1-2. Insertion loss characteristics of 12,000 feet of 26-gauge cable. *(Redrawn from Technical Staff, Bell Telephone Laboratories,* Transmission Systems for Communications, *Bell Telephone Laboratories, 1971, p.23.)*

multipair cable. Bridged taps are extra cable pairs that are connected in parallel with a particular loop. Such extra pairs were originally employed to provide added flexibility in the use of the loop plant. They allowed for the provision of party-line service as well as for the continued use of at least a portion of the loop if a subscriber discontinued service. The presence of such open loops does not cause a noticeable signal degradation at voice frequencies, but the added capacitance and discontinuity do cause serious impairments for high-speed digital signals. Loading coils and bridged taps must both be removed to allow the direct transmission of high-speed digital signals over multipair cables.

Electronic systems of various types have been used for decades in the telephone industry to extend transmission distances and to multiplex multiple voice channels on a single transmission medium. Since the bandwidth is generally a valuable commodity, these systems limit the individual voice-channel bandwidths to the range between 200 and 3500 Hz. These systems, now predominately pulse-code-modulation (PCM) systems* in new applications, are used extensively in the trunk network and increasingly in the loop network. The bandwidth of these electronic systems also limits the maximum data rates that can be achieved using the analog voice networks. Because of the increasing use of such systems, even those circuits covering relatively short distances may encounter them.

Data speeds up to 19,200 kbps (refer to Chapter 3) can be achieved over conditioned leased lines. Since a leased line makes more or less permanent use of a transmission path through the network, its characteristics, such as attenuation and delay distortion, can be chosen and adjusted more readily. This process is known as *conditioning* and several types are offered by the telephone company. Dial-up connections are subject to a much wider range of transmission variability because of the unpredictable way that calls are routed through the network. Dial-up calls are also subject to the greater noise levels that are produced by switching equipment, and these combined effects generally limit the maximum speed on dial-up lines to about 19.2 kbps and many 14.4 kbps systems exist.

1.3.5 Subscriber Loops

One further limitation of the telephone network should be noted. Subscriber loops normally consist of individual wire pairs in the multipair cable. Full-duplex two-way transmission of voice signals over a single pair of wires is achieved through the use of hybrids. At voice frequencies, adequate isolation between the two directions of transmission is relatively easy to achieve. Various methods are now under investigation to provide high-speed full-duplex digital transmission on ordinary two-wire loops. An example of a promising method is time-compression multiplexing (TCM).[11] In TCM, a burst of high-speed digital information is sent in one direction and, after a short period of time to allow for propagation delay and for echoes to die out, a burst of high-speed digital information is sent in the opposite direction. This process is continued in "ping-pong" fashion with alternating half-duplex transmissions. A net full-duplex rate of over 192 kbps can be obtained. Existing plant facilities can support such rates on unloaded loops of up to several thousand feet in length depending upon the wire gauge and other factors.[3]

To summarize, the basic electrical characteristics of multipair cable, plus the associated apparatus for optimizing its use in voice-frequency applications, have significant impact on the maximum data rates that can be transmitted using the ordinary analog telephone network. In addition, when multipair cable is utilized for direct digital transmission, data rates are limited to a maximum of about 2 Mbps, depending upon distance and other factors.

---

*Pulse code modulation refers to the process of sampling an analog signal at regular intervals and converting each sample to a unique value. Jayant in Reference 3 covers this in detail, including voice-quality considerations.

1.4 Coaxial Cable

A coaxial cable consists of a single-wire conductor centered within a cylindrical outer conductor or shield as shown in Fig. 1-3A. The two conductors are insulated from one another using various dielectric materials, including plastic (solid or foam) or gas (including air). In the case of the latter, the concentric arrangement is maintained by using insulating disks spaced at regular intervals. The outer conductor may consist of one or more layers of braided metal fabric, where flexibility is needed, or a solid metal tube, where greater shielding and/or rigidity is required. Depending upon the application, the outer conductor, in turn, may be surrounded by a protective jacket.

A coaxial cable has a number of important advantages as a transmission medium. The principal advantage of coaxial cable is the wide bandwidth that stems from its relatively low loss at high frequencies. Because of this wide bandwidth capability, coaxial cable can be used to carry large numbers of voice conversations, high-speed data, and large numbers of television channels. The other advantages of coaxial cable include an excellent isolation from external noise and crosstalk and its more predictable, controllable, and less frequency-dependent electrical characteristics, especially when compared with twisted pairs.

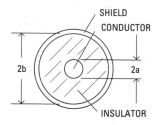

(A) Cross section of single cable lines.

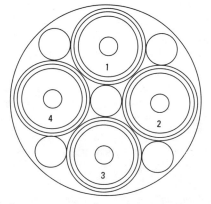

(B) Example arrangement (lay up) for a multiconductor cable.

Fig. 1-3. Coaxial cables.

In addition to its uses within communications subsystems (e.g., to connect a radio transmitter to an antenna) coaxial cable has been used extensively in the telephone network in certain high-traffic density portions of the long-haul toll network where it could be justified on a cost basis and, also, in areas where radio-frequency congestion precludes the use of microwave systems. In this application, several coaxial structures or tubes are normally enclosed within a single sheath (Fig. 1-3B) along with the ordinary wire pairs used for control and other purposes. A standard coaxial tube has an attenuation of slightly less than 4 dB per mile at 1 MHz. Normally, a pair of tubes is used for each duplex (bidirectional) long-haul application of transmission. For example, in the AT&T network, the number of voice channels per pair of tubes has risen from 600 channels in the L1 system to 10,800 channels per pair in the L5 systems. The latter system consists of ten working pairs plus a spare or protection pair. With ten working pairs, the total route capacity is 108,000 voice circuits. Frequency-division multiplexing is employed, and in the case of the L5 system, repeaters are spaced at one-mile intervals.[32]

Coaxial cable has also been used almost exclusively as the transmission media in the cable television industry. In this application, the cable is used to transmit multiple channels of television programming from a headend, where the signals are picked up over the air from broadcast stations or received via terrestrial microwave or via satellite transmission, to the homes and businesses of individual subscribers. Within the cable, the individual channels are transmitted on a frequency-division multiplex basis through a system of trunk lines, distribution lines, and subscriber drops. Cables with different characteristics are used in different parts of the network. Large diameter, rigid, and high-quality cable is used for the critical trunk lines while smaller diameter, more flexible, lower-quality cable is used in the less critical distribution and feeder portion of the network. Trunk amplifiers and, where necessary, distribution amplifiers are placed at regular intervals to maintain the signals at a suitable level. In a modern cable system, bandwidths of up to 400 MHz are achievable. Such systems are capable of carrying as many as 52 television channels. The cascading of analog amplifiers with attendant noise buildup limits the maximum individual trunk length.

Various arrangements are used to provide two-way, or upstream, as well as downstream, communications from and to the customer's premises and the headend. The cable itself is obviously a two-way medium, but the amplifiers in the basic system, as described, are not. The most common way to provide two-way service is to divide the available bandwidth into two parts; one for downstream communications and one for upstream. Separate amplifiers for each direction of transmission are required. In residential systems, the upstream signals are placed in the 5- to 30-MHz portion of the spectrum while the downstream signals are contained in the 50- to 400-MHz region. This unequal division of downstream and upstream capacity is referred to as a *lowsplit*. In some systems, a second cable is installed for institutional (e.g., nonentertaining programming) use. These systems typically divide the available channel capacity equally in both directions and they are referred to as *midsplit systems.* As discussed later, the midsplit arrangement is also used in private local area networks (LANs) that employ coaxial cable as the transmission medium. Some systems (both cable television and private LANs) use dual cables, one for each direction of transmission. The various techniques employed to provide two-way capability on cable television systems are treated in some detail in the "Data Communications Via Cable Television Networks."[14]

As noted earlier and described in much greater detail in Chapter 6, coaxial cable systems are also being used in private LANs on the customer's premises. In LANs, the coaxial cable transmission medium can be utilized in two fundamental ways: baseband and broadband. In the baseband mode, the digital signals are impressed directly on the cable while, in the broadband mode, the signals are first modulated onto a carrier and, then, are impressed on the cable using a radio-frequency (rf) modem. The latter mode evolved from a cable television technology base; multiple carriers can be carried on a frequency-division multiplexed basis in analogous fashion to that done on cable television systems. In the broadband mode, the headend receives the upstream or reverse-band channels and translates or converts them to downstream or forward channels. The forward and reverse channels can be carried on the same cable (e.g., midsplit) or on different cables, one for each direction of transmission. The modem at each user location transmits on the reverse channel(s) and receives on the forward channel(s). Various methods for accessing the capacity are available including polling, frequency-division multiple access, time-division multiple access, token passing, and contention.

In the baseband mode, the data rates on the cable are typically on the order of 10 Mbps. In the broadband mode, existing systems achieve aggregate data rates of up to 5 Mbps for each 6-MHz channel.[15] One major advantage of using broadband coaxial cable as a transmission medium in LANs is the ready availability of low-cost components developed for the cable television industry; however, baseband cable connections and interfaces are still less expensive.

1.5 Waveguides

A waveguide consists, simply, of a hollow conductor or tube. It may be rectangular, elliptical, or circular in shape, and it may be either rigid or flexible in construction. Electromagnetic waves at microwave frequencies can travel down such tubes. Like twisted-pair cable and coaxial cable, waveguides are used extensively within communications subsystems (e.g., to connect a microwave transmitter to an antenna). Unlike the other two media, however, a waveguide has not been used for longer distance communications. Considerable research effort was expanded, however, on millimeter waveguide systems for long-haul transmission in the early 1970s. AT&T, for example, announced its WT-4 millimeter waveguide system which had the capacity to carry nearly 230,000 two-way voice circuits using pulse code modulation. However, the technology has not been commercially exploited because of rapid developments in optical fiber technology. It is mentioned here only for completeness.

1.6 Optical Fibers

An optical fiber consists of a very fine cylinder of glass, called the *core*, surrounded by a concentric layer of glass, called the *cladding* (Fig. 1-4). The glass in the cladding has a lower refractive index than the glass in the core. (Light travels slower in the core than in the cladding.) When a light ray passes from a medium with a higher refractive index to a medium with a lower refractive index, the ray is bent back toward the original medium. Hence, if a ray of light is launched into a fiber optic core at an oblique enough angle, it is reflected back into the core by the cladding. The process is repeated as the ray travels down the core.[1] In other words, the difference in refractive index between the core material and the cladding material guides the light ray from one end of the fiber to the other.[3]

1.6.1 Cables

One or more fibers are often grouped together to form a fiber-optic cable. Such a cable may include coatings to protect the individual fibers, a steel wire or other member to add tensile strength, copper wires to carry electrical

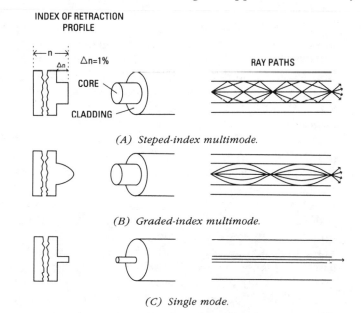

(A) Steped-index multimode.

(B) Graded-index multimode.

(C) Single mode.

Fig. 1-4. Optical fiber types.

power, a filling material, and a protective outer jacket of some type. Multifiber cables are often ribbon structured with multiple fibers between two strips of plastic. Cables of 12 ribbons of 12 fibers each are common. Fiber-optic cables have a number of important advantages that have propelled the technology from the laboratory to widespread commercial and military applications in just a few years. These advantages include extremely low losses, very wide bandwidths, extremely high isolation between parallel fibers (i.e., absence of crosstalk), immunity to inductive noise and interference, and extremely small and lightweight physical characteristics.

Optical fiber systems are used extensively in telephone networks of metropolitan-area interoffice trunk applications and many major long-haul intercity systems. Fiber systems are also being introduced at a slower pace in loop plants, primarily in the feeder portion of the network. Fiber-optic cables are often used as transmission media in LANs.

1.6.2 Performance Characteristics

The attenuation of an optical waveguide is a function of the wavelength (frequency) of the light and the characteristics of the glass. The attenuation or loss is caused by absorption due to impurities in the fiber material, scattering due to variations in glass density and composition, and, less significantly, radiation losses. Advances in materials and manufacturing have reduced light attenuation in optical fibers by a factor of nearly 100 in the period since the first low-loss cable was fabricated in 1970.[24] Fig. 1-5 displays a plot of the attenuation of a typical low-loss communications-type optical fiber as a function of wavelength. Even lower losses are possible (e.g., less than 4.5% per kilometer) and optical transmission over 100 km and greater distances can be obtained without using repeaters.[5] Long-haul fiber-optic systems currently under construction have repeaters that are, typically, spaced up to 35 km apart.[12]

In addition to overall attenuation, one other important performance characteristic of optical fibers is pulse distortion. The severity of the distortion depends on the type of cable. There are three basic types or categories of optical fibers: single-mode, multimode stepped-index, and multimode graded-index, as shown in Fig. 1-4. If its core is large enough in diameter, several different modes of propagation can be supported within the core of an optical waveguide. That is, there are a number of different zig-zag paths by which the entering light can reach the other end of the fiber. Rays that are reflected at very steep angles will travel a greater distance to reach the other end of the fiber than will the rays that are reflected at very oblique angles. Since the rays traveling by different modes travel different distances, the ones associated with the more oblique angles will exit the fiber sooner than those associated with steeper angles. Thus, short pulses of light, i.e., information bits, will be spread out or dispersed in time when they leave the fiber. This pulse spreading is cumulative with distance. This effect is referred to as modal dispersion and the intersymbol interference it produces limits the maximum

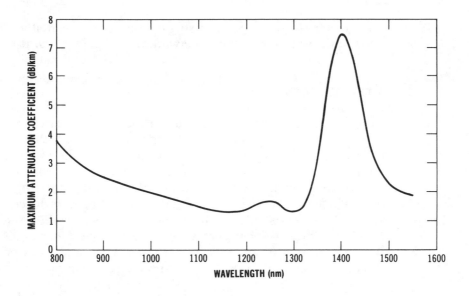

Fig. 1-5. Attenuation vs. wavelength for a typical low-loss silica-core optical fiber. *(Redrawn from* Alternative Transmission Media for Third Generation Interface Standards, *J.A. Hull, A.G. Hanson, and L.R. Bloom, U.S. Department of Commerce, National Telecommunications and Information Administration, NTIA Report 83-121, May 1983.)*

data rate achievable at a given distance, or, equivalently, it limits the maximum distance that can be achieved before repeaters are required.

The number of modes that can propagate down the fiber can be decreased by reducing the size of the core. If the diameter is reduced far enough and the index difference between core and cladding is small enough, only a single-mode will propagate. Thus, a single-mode fiber does not exhibit modal dispersion and such fibers are capable of much higher bit rates.

Another kind of pulse distortion also can be important, especially when single-mode fibers are used to eliminate modal dispersion and where much higher data transmission rates are of interest. This distortion happens because of *material dispersion*, the property of the fiber that causes a variation in the group velocity of light in glass as a function of wavelength. When incoherent light sources are used, such as a light-emitting diode (LED), material dispersion can cause pulse spreading. For example, an LED source, operating at 0.8 micrometers with a spectral width of 50 nm (10^{13} Hz), will cause a pulse spreading of about 5 ns/km, resulting in a modulation-bandwidth-length product of about 50–100 MHz/km.[13] Thus, any practical light source will experience a degree of material-dispersion-produced broadening as it travels down a fiber.

Fortunately, there is a particular wavelength, called the *zero-dispersion wavelength*, where all light over a narrow band of wavelengths travels at a constant speed, making extremely high transmission rates possible over long distances with practical light sources.[35] This occurs in the neighborhood of 1.3

micrometers in some popular single-mode fibers. Partially for this reason, most long-distance fiber-optic networks now operate near this wavelength.

1.6.3 Graded-Index Fiber

In a graded-index fiber, the refractive index does not change abruptly between the core material and the cladding. Instead, the refractive index changes continuously and smoothly from a maximum value at the center of the fiber to a minimum value at the outer edge. Since light rays travel faster where the index of refraction is lower, the light rays traveling near the outer edge of a fiber propagate faster than those traveling near the center of the core where the index is higher. This means that rays near the center of the fiber travel at a lower velocity than those rays near the outer edges of the fiber. Because the slower rays go a shorter distance and the faster rays go a longer distance through the fiber, all of the rays tend to exit the fiber at more nearly the same time. This reduces the pulse spreading and permits higher bit rates to be achieved on graded-index fibers than on their step-index counterparts. Good-quality graded-index fibers used in telephone applications are capable of transmitting 1000 Mbps at a distance of 1 km.[29] Stepped-index multimode fiber bandwidths are on the order of 10 MHz/km. As indicated before, the dispersion effect is cumulative with distance, so this means that at 100 Mbps, the repeaters for graded-index fibers could be spaced 10 km apart.[13]

For the reasons described earlier, extremely high data rates become possible with optimized single-mode fiber-optic transmission systems. Transmission rates over single-mode fibers of 8000 Mbps at a distance of 1 km are routine, and capacities as high as 200,000 Mbps at the same distance have been produced.[35] This indicates repeater spacings on the order of 80 km, with transmission rates in the 1000 to 2000 Mbps.[24] Single-mode, long-haul, fiber-optics systems can operate at approximately 400 Mbps in regular service with repeaters spaced at 26 km, or greater, intervals.[7] Recall that, in comparison, the twisted-pair transmission media required repeaters approximately every mile to achieve a transmission rate of 1.5 Mbps. To amplify this, Fig. 1-6 shows a comparison between twisted-pairs, cables, and fiber.

1.7 Radio

The media used for electromagnetic transmission can be divided into two basic categories: guided or unguided. The different transmission media described thus far in this chapter fall into the "guided" category and it is obvious that much greater control can be exerted over such systems compared to unguided "over-the-air" radio systems. Radio-based systems, however have the substantial advantage that they do not require physical rights-of-way between the points of communications. Such systems are a natural for communications

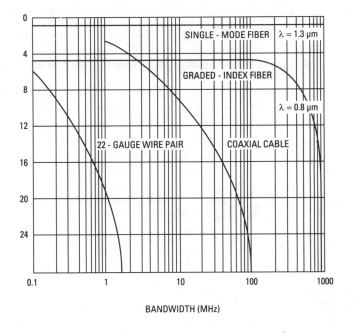

Fig. 1-6. Comparison of losses in various transmission media.

over barriers such as bodies of water, mountainous terrain, or those heavily forested or environmentally sensitive areas where guided media would be difficult to employ. Furthermore, radio-based systems may be the only practicable means of communicating when the end point or points are mobile.

With unguided radio-based transmissions, the received signal power is a function of transmitter power, antenna patterns, path length, physical obstructions, and many other factors. Indeed, the propagation of radio waves through the "over-the-air" media is affected by so many diverse factors, such as meteorological and even extraterrestrial phenomena, that no simple and universally applicable theory exists to explain it.[25] The use of theory must be supplemented by observations from previous systems and coupled with extensive data on phenomena that affect the systems, such as meteorological conditions and the sources of received noise and interference. This is in direct contrast to guided systems where the theory is much more useful in predicting exactly the transmission characteristics and the outside effects are generally less important. Table 1-2 provides a very brief summary of the propagation modes and systems, uses, and characteristics of various radio bands from 3 kHz to 300 GHz. (Reference 28 gives a complete breakdown of frequency allocations in great detail.)

The remainder of this section is divided into two parts. The first part consists of a very short explanation of the characteristics of the frequency bands below 3 GHz. The second part deals with frequency bands above 3 GHz. More emphasis is placed on these frequencies because of their greater importance to wideband data transmission.

Table 1-2. Radio Propagation Modes and Systems/Uses/Characteristics for the
Internationally Based Radio-Frequency Bands

Frequency Band	Frequency Range	Propagation Modes	Systems/Uses/ Characteristics
VLF	3–30 kHz	Earth-ionosphere Guided.	Worldwide, military and navigation.
LF	30–300 kHz	Surface Wave.	Stable signal, distances up to 1500 km.
MF	300 kHz–3 MHz	Surface/sky wave for short/long distances, respectively.	Radio broadcasting. Long-distance sky wave signals are subject to fading.
HF	3–30 MHz	Sky wave, but very-limited short-distance ground waves also.	3–6 MHz: Continental, 6–30 MHz. Intercontinental. Land and ship-to-shore communications.
VHF	30–300 MHz	Space wave.	Close to line-of-sight over short distances. Broadcasting and land mobile.
	30–60 MHz	Scatter wave.	Ionospheric scatter over 900–2000 km distances.
UHF	300 MHz–3 GHz	Space wave.	Essentially line-of-sight over short distances. Broadcasting and land mobile.
	Above 300 MHz	Scatter wave.	Tropospheric scatter over 150–800 km distances.
SHF	3–30 GHz	Space wave.	The "workhorse" microwave band. Line-of-sight. Terrestrial and satellite relay links.
EHF	30–300 GHz	Space wave.	Line-of-sight millimeter waves. Space-to-space links, military uses, and possible short-distance local distribution.

1.7.1 Frequency Bands Below 3 GHz

The frequency bands below 3 GHz include the very low-frequency (vlf), low frequency (lf), medium-frequency (mf), high-frequency (hf), very high-frequency (vhf), and ultrahigh-frequency (uhf) bands. In the vlf band from 3 to 30 kHz, signals are propagated in a guided mode between the earth and the ionosphere. This mode of propagation produces very stable signals and good coverage, but only a limited and specialized use is made of this band because of the high cost of the large transmitting facilities required, the very limited bandwidths available, and the susceptibility of the signals to atmospheric noise disturbances. Because of these factors, the vlf band is used mainly for global broadcast, for the transmission of both standard frequency and time signals, and for long-range navigation. The next highest frequency band, the lf band from 30 to 300 kHz, has many of the same characteristics as the vlf band and is used primarily for the transmission of both medium-range navigation and time signals. The next band, the mf band from 300 kHz to 3 MHz, contains the familiar am broadcast band. Signals in this band are propagated via surface waves for relatively short distances and by sky waves that are reflected by the ionosphere for much longer distances. The latter are affected by ionospheric conditions which, in turn, vary with time of day, season, and level of solar activity. In addition to am broadcasting, the upper portion of this band is used for intercontinental and ship-to-shore communications, including some low-data-rate teleprinter applications.

The next highest band, the hf band from 3 to 30 MHz, is used extensively for shortwave broadcasting, other long-distance point-to-point intercontinental communications, and for ship-to-shore communications. Use of surface-wave transmissions is limited to relatively short distances and nearly all communications made is via the sky-wave mode. Like the upper portion of the mf band, signals in this region of the spectrum are heavily dependent upon ionospheric conditions and reliable communications requires regular changes of operating frequencies.

Low-data-rate teleprinter operations in both government and commercial applications are still found in this band. However, with the exception of international shortwave broadcasting, many of these uses have been shifted to satellite and other more reliable and wider bandwidth systems.

The vhf band, ranging from 30 to 300 MHz, is used heavily for television broadcasting and in land, aeronautical and maritime mobile applications.[34] Propagation in this region is by space wave (i.e., the direct and ground or object-reflected waves) and is confined to almost line-of-sight distances. Frequencies within this band, and up to about 1 GHz, are ideally suited for mobile communications. Historically, data communications within this band has been very limited, and it was only after 1983 that the Federal Communications Commission removed data from a secondary status to voice in land mobile communications in the United States. Increased use of data transmissions, at rates up to about 10 kbps, occurs in land mobile and related applications.[10]

The uhf band ranges from 300 MHz to 3 GHz; television broadcasting has a substantial allocation in the lower portion of the band. Also, most of the land mobile frequency allocations are within this band and below 1 GHz. Land mobile channels are typically 25 or 30 kHz wide at uhf frequencies, similar to the channel widths in the lower land mobile bands. Thus, transmission capacity per land mobile channel is quite limited throughout their spectrum allocations.

Land mobile propagation suffers from *Rayleigh fading* due to *multipath effect* and the median signal level tends to follow a log-normal distribution with location as the intervening terrain changes. In addition, the signal level falls off much faster than in free space, typically falling off at about 40-dB per decade. Thus, the land mobile communications range varies substantially with frequency, power, antenna height, intervening terrain, buildings, foliage, etc., so that useful range is generally under about 40 miles.

Above 1 GHz, frequency uses are similar to those for the shf frequencies—point-to-point or multipoint, radar, and navigational purposes. These uses will be discussed with the shf band.

1.7.2 Frequency Bands Above 3 GHz

The shf band between 3 and 30 GHz is the real "workhorse" for radio systems in terms of traffic capacity. In the United States, there are microwave radio bands in the 4-, 6-, 10-, 11-, 12-, 13-, 18-, 23-, and 28-GHz regions of the shf range that are available for point-to-point use by private and/or common-carrier systems. Generally speaking, the total frequency allocation in each of these bands increases with increasing frequency and goes as high as 2000 MHz in the 28-GHz band. These frequency bands are, in turn, subdivided into individually assigned channels whose bandwidths range from as low as 10 MHz to as high as 220 MHz, depending upon the particular band and its use. Larger authorized bandwidths are usually associated with the higher frequency bands.

In the shf band, clear-path point-to-point communications is the norm. Frequencies in this range are generally unsuitable for terrestrial broadcasting or land mobile purposes, because coverage to those points with obstructed paths is difficult to achieve. This progressively worsens as the frequency is increased above the 1 GHz region, where the present television broadcasting and land mobile allocations end.

Normally, shf line-of-sight signals decrease or fall off at a rate of 6-dB per octave as in free space. However, in actual practice, the received signal levels vary considerably due to atmospheric conditions, especially on terrestrial paths. Generally speaking, the severity of signal fading increases with increasing frequency and path length. Fading is caused by both multipath and inverse path bending. The latter is produced by changes in the refractive index of the atmosphere which cause the path to become obstructed during abnormal conditions. This effect can be minimized by insuring adequate path clearance.

Multipath fading results from interference between a direct wave and another wave, usually a reflected wave from the ground or from atmospheric layers. Such fading can be in excess of 30 dB for periods that can be seconds or even minutes long. In addition, for frequencies above about 10 GHz, fading due to rain attenuation must be taken into account.

In the case of satellite-to-earth paths,[17] high elevation angles minimize path obstruction possibilities and atmospheric effects, including *rain attenuation*, due largely to the shorter paths through the atmosphere. Rain attenuation not only causes lowered received signal levels, but it can add noise temperature—up to the temperature of the rain itself, say 290 Kelvin to the receiving system noise temperature. This can have a greater effect than the attenuation on the quality of the received signal.[20]

Within a given frequency band, rain attenuation varies very little with frequency so that in-band frequency diversity is ineffectual. Widely separated ground stations can provide good space diversity improvements on earth-to-satellite paths[21] as the heaviest rains of concern tend to occur in relatively small cells where simultaneous heavy attenuation at both locations is unlikely.

The length of the individual links, or repeater spacings on longer transmission systems, varies from about 1 mile to 30 miles, depending upon the frequency. The shorter paths are generally required at the higher frequencies where multipath effects and rain attenuation are the greatest.

Most point-to-point microwave radio systems use frequency modulation (fm). The baseband signal consists of single-sideband, frequency-division multiplexed, analog voice channels. Progressive advances in technology have steadily increased the number of voice circuits transmitted per channel using fdm/fm until today, for example, 1800 and 2400 voice circuits are routinely carried on 20- and 30-MHz channels in the popular 4-and 6-GHz common carrier bands, respectively. More recently, single-sideband radios have been introduced that permit the transmission of 6000 voice circuits in the 30-MHz channels of the 6-GHz band.

In the last few years, there has been a rapid increase in the use of digital radio for microwave transmission. This growth has been driven by the increased use of digital switching in both public and private networks, by lowering multiplexing and demultiplexing costs, as well as by the other advantages of digital transmission described earlier. The maximum data rate that can be transmitted over a channel depends upon the channel bandwidth and the spectral density or transmission spectrum efficiency achieved. Presently, digital radios have the disadvantage of not utilizing the spectrum as efficiently as analog fdm/fm when fundamentally analog signals, such as voice, are being transmitted. Because of spectrum scarcity and regulatory requirements, digital radios must achieve a high level of spectral density. The most commonly used digital radios today achieve a spectral density of 3-bps-per-hertz of bandwidth using an 8-level phase-shift keying (psk) modulation technique. This allows the transmission of a 90-Mbps signal, for example, in the 30-MHz channels of the 6-GHz band. By using 64-level, quadrature amplitude modulation (QAM) spectral densities of 6 bps/Hz are possible. Such systems compare favorably in terms of spectrum efficiency with analog fdm/fm radios, but they fall far short of the new analog single-sideband radios. Digital radios with capacities of up to 274-Mbps per radio carrier are available for use in the 18-GHz band where wider bandwidth channels are available. As noted earlier, the required repeater spacings depend upon the particular band chosen and the geographic area. For the 18-GHz band, the required spacings are in the 2- to 3-mile range.

1.8 References

1. Andonovic, Ivan and Uttamchandani Deepak. *Principles of Modern Optical Systems*, Norwood, MA: Artech House, 1989.

2. Bartee, Thomas C. *ISDN, DECnet, and SNA Communications*, Carmel, IN: Sams, a Division of Macmillan Computer Publishing, 1989.

3. ———. *Digital Communications*, Indianapolis: Howard W. Sams & Co., 1986.

4. Beauchamp, K.G. *Computer Communications*, 2nd ed. New York: Chapman and Hall, 1990.

5. Bell, Trudy E. "Long-Distance Fiber-Optic Networks, Direct Broadcast Satellites, and Low-Cost PBXs Bring Increased Communications Capacity to Customers," *IEEE Spectrum*, January 1984, p. 53.

6. ———. "Long-Distance Fiber-Optic Networks, Direct Broadcast Satellites, and Low-Cost PBXs Bring Increased Communications Capacity to Customers," *IEEE Spectrum*, January 1984, pp. 54 and 56.

7. ———. "Long-Distance Fiber-Optic Networks, Direct Broadcast Satellites, and Low-Cost PBXs Bring Increased Communications Capacity to Customers," *IEEE Spectrum*, January 1984, p. 54.

8. Bellamy, John C. *Digital Telephony*, New York: John Wiley & Sons, 1982, pp. 64–80.

9. ———. *Digital Telephony*, 2nd ed. New York: John Wiley & Sons, 1991.

10. Bhargava, Amit. *Integrated Broadband Networks*, Norwood, MA: Artech House, 1991.

11. Bosik, B.S. and S.V. Kartalopoulos. "A Loop Access System for a Circuit Switched Digital Capability," *Proceedings of the 1982 International Symposium on Subscriber Loops and Services*, Toronto, Canada, September 20–24, 1982.

12. Briere, Daniel D. *Long Distance Services: A Buyer's Guide*, Norwood, MA: Artech House, 1990.

13. Duke, David A. and Donald B. Keck. "Single-Mode Fiber-Optic Features," *Telecommunications*, Vol. 17, No. 12, December 1983, pp. 34–38.

14. Estrin, Deborah L. "Data Communications Via Cable Television Networks: Technical and Policy Considerations," Laboratory for Computer Science, Massachusetts Institute of Technology, May 1982 (Paper MIT/LCS/TR-273).

15. ———. "Data Communications Via Cable Television Networks: Technical and Policy Considerations," Laboratory for Computer Science, Massachusetts Institute of Technology, May 1982 (Paper MIT/LCS/TR-273), p. 28.

16. Fike. John L., and George E. Friend. *Understanding Telephone Electronics*, 2nd ed., Carmel, IN: Sams, a Division of Macmillan Computer Publishing, 1990.

17. Gagliardi, Robert M. *Satellite Communications*, 2nd ed., New York: Van Nostrand Reinhold, 1991.

18. Harper, Charles A., ed. *Handbook of Wiring, Cabling, and Interconnecting for Electronics*, New York: McGraw-Hill, 1972.

19. Held, Gilbert. *Digital Networking and T-Carrier Multiplexing*, New York: John Wiley & Sons, 1990.

20. Inglis, Andrew F. *Satellite Technology, an Introduction.* Stoneham, MA: Focal Press, (Imprint of Butterworth-Heinemann), 1991.

21. Ippolito, Louis J., Jr. *Radiowave Propagation in Satellite Communications*, New York: Van Nostrand Reinhold, 1986.

22. Jordan, E.L., ed. *Reference Data for Engineers: Radio, Electronics, Computer, and Communications*, 7th ed., Carmel, IN: Sams, a Division of Macmillan Computer Publishing, 1985.

23. Keck, Donald B. "Single-Mode Fibers Outperform Multimode Cables," *IEEE Spectrum*, March 1983, p. 30.

24. ———. "Single-Mode Fibers Outperform Multimode Cables," *IEEE Spectrum*, March 1983, p. 32.

25. Killen, Harold B. *Fiber Optic Communications*, Englewood Cliffs, NJ: Prentice-Hall, 1991.

26. Kostas, D.J. "Transition to ISDN—An Overview," *IEEE Communications Magazine*, Vol. 22, No. 1 (January 1984), pp. 11–17.

27. Miller, Stewart E. and Ivan P. Kaminow, eds. *Optical Fiber Telecommunications*, San Diego, CA: Academic Press, 1988.

28. Personick, Stewart D. "Review of Fundamentals of Optical Fiber Systems," *IEEE Journal on Selected Areas in Communications*, Vol. SAC-1, No. 3, April 1983, p. 374.

29. Sibley, M.J.N. *Optical Communications: Optical and Electro-Optical Engineering Series*, New York: McGraw-Hill, 1990.

30. Technical Staff, Bell Telephone Laboratories. *Engineering and Operations in the Bell System*, Whippany, NJ: Bell Telephone Laboratories Inc., 1977.

31. ———. *Engineering and Operations in the Bell System*, Whippany, NJ: Bell Telephone Laboratories, 1977, p. 127.

32. ———. *Engineering and Operations in the Bell System*, Whippany, NJ: Bell Telephone Laboratories, 1977, pp. 328–329.

33. Turin, William. *Performance Analysis of Digital Transmission Systems*, Computer Science Press, 1990.

34. Whitaker, Jerry C. *Radio Frequency Transmission Systems: Design and Operation*, New York: McGraw-Hill, 1991.

35. Zanger, Henry, and Cynthia Zanger. *Fiber Optics: Communication and Other Applications*, New York: Macmillan, 1991.

Carriers and Regulation

by Walter R. Hinchman

 **Walter R. Hinchman** was Common Carrier Bureau Chief at the Federal Communications Commission from 1974 through 1978, and played a major role in crafting FCC policies that created a competitive environment for the U.S. telecommunications industry. Previously, he served with the President's Task Force on Communications Policy (1967-68), as Assistant Director of the White House Office of Telecommunications Policy (1970-72), and as Chief of the FCC Office of Plans and Policy (1972-74). Since leaving the FCC, he has been a telecommunications consultant to many organizations, including the U.S. Department of Justice during its successful antitrust litigation against AT&T. Mr. Hinchman is a 1955 graduate of the Ohio State University, where he majored in physics.

2.1 Historical Perspective

2.1.1 Origins of Common Carrier Principles

The business of transporting information (messages) for the public as a for-hire service has traditionally been termed "communications common carriage," and those who provide such for-hire services have been termed "common carriers." These terms, as well as many associated principles of operation and public responsibilities, initially developed within the transportation field (e.g., stagecoaches, railroads, bus and trucking companies, airlines, etc.), where such for-hire transportation services have existed for centuries.

In recognition of their importance to the general welfare, including both social and economic development, English common law imposed upon transportation common carriers certain public rights and responsibilities that are not usually applicable to other businesses. In exchange for the right to use public roads and/or rights of way, such firms were generally obligated to carry goods and people along their customary routes without discrimination in either access or price. While there were clearly many exceptions which reflected other social and economic discriminations that were generally acceptable within particular locales and time periods, this concept of nondiscriminatory service became an essential characteristic of transportation common carriage.

While these common carrier principles were evolving in the transportation field, somewhat similar concepts were evolving with respect to another group of services that was considered essential to the general welfare, i.e., the centralized distribution of such essential items as water, natural gas, and electricity. For a variety of reasons, including the very extensive use of public rights-of-way over private properties that were required as well as the general concern for public health and safety, there emerged a general consensus that these services would best be organized as either public or private monopolies within specified franchised areas. Moreover, to ensure that these franchised monopolies would not only provide a safe universal service throughout the franchise area but that they would do so at reasonable cost and in accordance with nondiscriminatory charges and practices, continuing public oversight of their operations was established. Such enterprises were termed public utilities and the public oversight of their activities came to be known as public utility regulation.

These parallel concepts of "public utility" and "common carrier" status and regulation were embodied in the statutes of the United States and its individual constituent states long before the development of telecommunications (e.g., telegraph and telephone) capabilities or services. Initially, telecommunications services were allowed to develop outside the ambit of the common carrier and public utility laws and concepts, even though they were provided in many instances as an adjunct to other common carrier (e.g., railroad) or public utility (e.g., electric power distribution) services. However, as these new telecommunications services grew in both socio-economic importance and complexity, similar concerns about their general availability at reasonable nondiscriminatory prices began to emerge. These concerns were heightened substantially by the widespread refusal of early competing suppliers of telephone services to interconnect their networks of subscriber lines such that a subscriber to the service from one company could communicate with another company's subscribers without having to subscribe to both services and replicate his own telephone instrument. The growing social, economic, and political power of one such company in particular, i.e., the American Telephone and Telegraph Company (AT&T), was a major concern. By the early 1900s, AT&T had managed to parlay its control of the original telephone patents by Alexander Graham Bell, plus the financial backing of the J.P. Morgan banking interests, into a position of enormous power within the evolving telecommunications industry. Through patent licensing agreements and direct ownership, the AT&T holding company controlled the dominant supplier of telephone services within most urban areas, which were, in turn, linked to one another by a network of long-distance lines that were also controlled by AT&T. By refusing to interconnect either the local or long-distance networks it controlled with the independent telephone companies serving more rural and suburban areas, AT&T posed the threat of establishing a nationwide monopoly over the emerging telephone business.

2.1.2 Early Telephone Regulation

Faced with the threat of an unregulated monopoly or what many perceived as "destructive" competition on either a statewide or nationwide basis, both State and Federal authorities sought to establish some public-interest control over telephone operations in general, and the operations of AT&T in particular. Since telephone service in this early period was predominantly local in nature, State legislatures were the first to respond to these growing public-interest concerns. In most instances, this response took the form of statutes which classified the suppliers of such services as "common carriers" and/or "public utilities," and extended the regulatory principles and jurisdiction already applicable to transportation and utility companies to this industry. In most cases, these statutes gave either explicit or implicit recognition to the concept that telephone and related services would be provided on a monopoly basis within designated franchise areas. In many of these legislative proceedings AT&T strongly supported the extension of such public utility regulations to its operations in the apparent belief that such regulated monopoly status would better serve its interests than either a competitive market environment or a potential antitrust action if it succeeded in eliminating such competition.

The Federal response to the growing social and economic importance of telecommunications, in general, and the control exercised by AT&T, in particular, was both slower in developing and somewhat more diverse than were the State responses. Although the Mann-Elkins Act in 1910 extended the jurisdiction of the Interstate Commerce Commission (which regulated the trucking and railroad industries) to the telephone industry as well, the ICC did not actively pursue this new authority. Prior to 1934, most Federal involvement with the telephone industry took the form of threatened antitrust action by the U.S. Department of Justice, acting under the antitrust statutes. In response to these threats, AT&T agreed in 1913 to end its efforts to acquire competing independent telephone companies, to allow independent telephone companies to connect into its long-distance network, and to dispose of its interest in the Western Union Telegraph Company, which it had acquired a short time previously. While these AT&T commitments did not preclude its acquisition of independent telephone companies with whom it did not directly compete (e.g., those outside the operating territories of the Bell System companies), and thus did not fully resolve the concerns of the independent telephone industry, they did effectively head off any further Federal consideration of antitrust action against AT&T for many years.

Between 1913 and 1936, AT&T continued its vigorous policy of acquiring many of the more attractive independent telephone companies, while at the same time consolidating its control over telephone equipment manufacturing through its ownership and policy direction of the Western Electric Manufacturing Company. As the newly-created Federal Communications Commission reported to the Congress in 1939, "By the end of 1936, the Bell System's control of the desirable telephone-exchange territory in the United States was substantially complete," and "Its manufacturing department, the Western Electric Company, enjoyed almost complete control in the field of telephone manufacturing."*

---

*Investigation of the Telephone Industry in the United States, A Report of the Federal Communications Commission on the Investigation of the Telephone Industry in the United States, as Unanimously Adopted by the Commission, 76th Congress, 1st Session, House Doc #340, June 14, 1939.

As a part of the broad social and economic reforms instituted by the Roosevelt administration in response to the great depression, Congress enacted the Communications Act of 1934. This Act was not the product of any single event or concern, nor was it addressed exclusively to the subject of common carrier communications.

A major impetus for the legislation appears to have been the serious problems of radio interference being created by the rapid, largely uncoordinated expansion of the new technology of radio broadcasting and the perceived need for more effective governmental coordination of these developments. Thus, a major portion of the Act deals with the licensing and regulation of various forms of radio systems, including those used for broadcast services and private systems, as well as those used for common carrier services. However, the Act did consolidate various common carrier regulatory activities that were previously carried out by the U.S. Department of Commerce and the ICC, and it established new standards of conduct for common carriers.

2.2 Legal and Regulatory Framework

2.2.1 Communications Act of 1934

The basic legal framework within which common carrier (and other) telecommunications services are provided within the United States is contained in the Communications Act of 1934 and the various statutes of the individual states.

The Communications Act established the basic division of jurisdictional responsibility between the Federal and State governments; created the Federal Communications Commission (FCC) as the organization to execute and enforce the provisions of the Act; and established the basic policies, definitions, standards, and guidelines for interstate common carrier operations and services, as well as various other telecommunications activities.

In principle, the Communications Act governs only *interstate* services and operations, while jurisdiction over all purely *intrastate* services and operations remains with the individual states. In practice, since it is frequently difficult and/or economically inefficient to establish a clear distinction between interstate and intrastate services and operations (e.g., the same user equipment and local telephone networks are typically used interchangeably for local, intrastate long distance, and interstate long-distance services), Federal jurisdiction has increasingly preempted State jurisdiction over many activities that might be viewed as essentially intrastate. For this reason, as well as the fact that the underlying principles of State regulation are essentially the same as those at the Federal level (despite significant variations in detail), the following description of the legal framework for common carrier operation and regulation will focus primarily on the Federal statute.

One of the most fundamental distinctions between communications common carriage and other business activities is the necessity of obtaining a special "license" prior to entering the business at all. For *intrastate* common carrier operations, this special "license" is generally termed a "certificate of public convenience and necessity," which the State Public Utility Commission will issue only after it determines that the "public convenience and necessity" will be properly served by the proposed operation and services. Since already-established carriers have the right—and the obvious incentive—to oppose the entry of new carriers into the market, the process of obtaining the required regulatory certification is generally costly, time-consuming, and uncertain.

Entry into the market for *interstate* communications common carrier services—as well as the expansion, contraction, or discontinuance of interstate common carrier operation—requires the issuance by the FCC of a similar certificate of public convenience and necessity. These requirements are spelled out in Section 214 of the Communications Act, which states in pertinent part that:

> "No carrier shall undertake the construction of a new line or of an extension of any line, or shall acquire or operate any line, or extension thereof, or shall engage in transmission over or by means of such additional or extended line, unless and until there shall first have been obtained from the Commission that the present or future public convenience and necessity require or will require the construction, or operation of such additional or extended line."

and further that:

> "No carrier shall discontinue, reduce, or impair service to a community, or part of a community, unless and until there shall first have been obtained from the Commission a certificate that neither the present nor future public convenience and necessity will be adversely affected thereby."

(In both instances, the term "line" is broadly defined to mean "any channel of communication established by the use of appropriate equipment.")

Established interstate carriers, as well as other interested parties, again have the right to challenge such authorization requests before the FCC, with essentially the same purpose, process, and effect as exist in State certification proceedings. In addition, where the transmission facilities or lines, for which Section 214 authorization is sought, involve the use of radio transmission (e.g., microwave, satellite, etc.), the applicant must also request and obtain a radio license from the FCC, which may trigger a separate set of challenges, based on radio interference as well as social and economic contentions, from interested parties. To successfully weather all these challenges and gain market entry, the prospective entrant must be prepared to expend substantial resources in demonstrating to the satisfaction of the FCC and/or State regulators the public benefits that are to be expected from such entry—and he must do so before any facilities may be constructed, services offered, or revenues obtained.

Once a prospective carrier obtains the requisite State certification or Section 214 authorization, and the radio licenses (if needed), the full panoply of statutory and regulatory rules, standards, and processes come into play. In order to offer any service for hire, the carrier must first file a "tariff" with the appropriate regulatory authority—State commissions for intrastate services and the FCC for interstate services. These tariffs must set forth in substantial detail the nature of the service offering (e.g., whether the service will handle voice, data, or video communications, whether it provides on-demand access to the intended recipients or only "dedicated" channels between specified locations, etc.); the terms and conditions under which it is provided (e.g., any restrictions on its use or its interconnection with other services or facilities of the same or other carriers); and above all, the charges that are to apply for each element of the service. Tariffs must be filed well in advance of their effective date (e.g., 90 days for a new interstate service offering or an increase in charges for an existing interstate service) and no service may be provided until the relevant tariff becomes effective. Once filed, tariffs are subject to challenge by concerned parties or by the FCC itself. On the basis of such challenges, the FCC may suspend the effective date of the tariff for up to five months and order an investigation into its lawfulness. The FCC may also reject a tariff filing which is clearly unlawful on its face or which is determined to be unlawful as the result of an investigation. If investigation determines the filing to be unlawful, the carrier must file a new or an appropriately modified tariff from which the unlawful elements have been eliminated and must begin the tariff review process anew. However, given the complexity of most interstate tariffs and the underlying justifications, the FCC seldom finds it possible to resolve the issue of lawfulness at once or even within the five-month suspension period allowed by the Communications Act. Thus, in most instances, an interstate tariff will become effective and service will be offered according to its terms without regulatory approval, even though it may later be declared unlawful and have to be withdrawn.

In the case of intrastate services and tariffs, the procedures often differ from those just described. For example, in some states, tariffs may be suspended for much longer periods, or even indefinitely, until the regulatory agency completes its investigation and renders a decision. The specific tariff filing, review, and implementation procedures vary widely among the various state jurisdictions.

The basic standards against which interstate tariffs are to be judged in ascertaining their lawfulness or unlawfulness, as well as the tariff filing and review procedures just described, are set forth in Sections 201 through 205 of the Communications Act.

Section 201 states, in pertinent part, that:

"(a) It shall be the duty of every common carrier engaged in interstate or foreign communications by wire or radio to furnish such communication service upon reasonable request therefore; . . . "

and further that:

"(b) All charges, practices, classifications, and regulations for and in connection with such communication service, shall be just and reasonable, and any such charge, practice, classification, or regulation that is unjust or unreasonable is hereby declared to be unlawful . . . "

Section 202 states, also in pertinent part, that:

"(a) It shall be unlawful for any common carrier to make any unjust or unreasonable discrimination in charges, practices, classification, regulations, facilities, or services for or in connection with like communication service, directly or indirectly by any means or device, or to make or give any undue or unreasonable preference or advantage to any particular person, class of persons, or locality, or to subject any particular person, class of persons, or locality to any undue or unreasonable prejudice or disadvantage."

Section 203 states that:

"(a) Every common carrier, except connecting carriers, shall, within such reasonable time as the Commission shall designate, file with the Commission and print and keep open for inspection schedules showing all charges for itself and its connecting carriers for interstate and foreign wire or radio communication between the different points on its own system, and between points on its own system and points on the system of its connecting carriers or points on the system of any other carrier subject to this Act when a through route has been established, whether such charges are joint or separate, and showing the classifications, practices, and regulations affecting such charges. Such schedules shall contain such other information, and be printed in such form, and be posted and kept open for public inspection in such places, as the Commission may by regulation require, and each such schedule shall give notice of its effective date; and such common carrier shall furnish such schedules to each of its connecting carriers, and such connecting carriers shall keep such schedules open for inspection in such public places as the Commission may require.

(b) (1) No change shall be made in the charges, classifications, regulations or practices which have been so filed and published except after ninety days notice to the Commission and to the public, which shall be published in such form and contain such information as the commission may by regulations prescribe.

(2) The Commission may, in its discretion and for good cause shown, modify any requirement made by or under the authority of this section either in particular instances or by general order applicable to special circumstances or conditions except that the Commission may not require the notice period specified in paragraph (1) to be more than ninety days.

(c) No carrier, unless otherwise provided by or under authority of this Act, shall engage or participate in such communication unless schedules have been filed and published in accordance with the provisions of this Act and with the regulations made thereunder; and no carrier shall (1) charge, demand, collect, or receive a greater or less different compensation, for such communication, or for any service in connection therewith, between the points named in any such schedule than the charges specified in the schedule then in effect, or (2) refund or remit by any means or device any portion of the charges so specified, or (3) extend to any person any privileges or facilities, in such communication, or employ or enforce any classifications, regulations, or practices affecting such charges, except as specified in such schedule.''

Section 204, which establishes the basis and procedures for Commission investigation of any interstate tariff, states that:

"(a) Whenever there is filed with the Commission any new or revised charge, classification, regulation, or practice, the Commission may either upon complaint or upon its own initiative without complaint, upon reasonable notice, enter upon a hearing concerning the lawfulness thereof; and pending such hearing and the decision thereon, the Commission, upon delivering to the carrier or carriers affected thereby a statement in writing of its reasons for such suspension, may suspend the operation of such charge, classification, regulation, or practice, in whole or in part but not for a longer period than five months beyond the time when it would otherwise go into effect; and after full hearing the Commission may make such order with reference thereto as would be proper in a proceeding initiated after such charge, classification, regulation, or practice had become effective. If the proceeding has not been concluded and an order made within the period of the suspension, the proposed new or revised charge, classification, regulation, or practice shall go into effect at the end of such period; but in case of a proposed charge for a new service or an increased charge, the Commission may by order require the interested carrier or carriers to keep accurate account of all amounts received by reason of such charge for a new service or increased charges, specifying by whom and in whose behalf such amounts are paid, and upon completion of the hearing and decision may by further order require the interested carrier or carriers to refund, with interest, to the persons in whose behalf such amounts were paid, such portion of such charge for a new service or increased charges as by its decision shall be found not justified. At any hearing involving a charge increased, or sought to be increased, the burden of proof to show that the increased charge, or proposed charge, is just and reasonable shall be upon the carrier, and the Commission shall give to the hearing and decision of such questions preference over all other questions pending before it and decide the same as speedily as possible.

(b) Notwithstanding the provisions of subsection (a) of this section, the Commission may allow part of a charge, classification, regulation, or practice to go into effect, based upon a written showing by the carrier or carriers affected, and an opportunity for written comment thereon by affected persons, that such partial authorization is just, fair, and reasonable. Additionally, or in combination with a partial authorization, the commission, upon a similar showing, may allow all or part of a charge, classification, regulation, or practice to go into effect on a temporary basis pending further order of the Commission. Authorizations of temporary new or increased charges may include an accounting order of the type provided for in subsection (a).''

Finally Section 205 authorizes the Commission itself, under certain circumstances, to "prescribe" (i.e., mandate) the charges, terms, and conditions for an interstate common carrier service, stating in pertinent part that:

"(a) Whenever, after full opportunity for hearing, upon a complaint or under an order for investigation and hearing made by the Commission on its own initiative, the Commission shall be of opinion that any charge, classification, regulation, or practice of any carrier or carriers is or will be in violation of any of the provisions of this Act, the commission is authorized and empowered to determine and prescribe what will be the just and reasonable charge, or the maximum or minimum charge or charges to be thereafter observed, and what classification, regulation, or practice is or will be just, fair, and reasonable, to be thereafter followed, and to make an order that the carrier or carriers shall cease and desist from such violation to the extent that the Commission finds that the same does or will exist, and shall not thereafter publish, demand, or collect any charge other than the charge so prescribed, or in excess of the maximum or less than the minimum so prescribed, as the case may be, and shall adopt the classification and shall conform to and observe the regulation or practice so prescribed."

The Communications Act contains numerous additional provisions relating to the carriers' liability for damages, procedures for resolving consumer complaints, intercarrier contracts and relationships, and similar matters. The Act also attempts to ensure that the Commission might have sufficient information of the type required to enforce the Act's provisions by authorizing the Commission to make "valuations" of the interstate carriers' property; to inquire into the management of such operations; to require annual and other reports; to prescribe accounting, depreciation, and record-keeping practices and procedures; and, more generally, to "perform any and all acts, make such rules and regulations, and issue such orders, not inconsistent with this Act, as may be necessary in the execution of its functions."

2.2.2 Case Law

As is apparent in all these provisions, while the Act expresses rather firmly the general obligations of interstate carriers, and the general authority of the FCC, it does so in many instances without a great deal of specificity. For example, there is no explicit standard for what constitutes "just and reasonable" or "unjust or unreasonable" carrier charges or practices; or what the "public convenience and necessity" specifically requires. Such matters are left, at least in the first instance, to the FCC's discretion. However, other provisions of the Communications Act, as well as other Federal statutes, both impose bounds on the FCC's discretion and involve other Federal authorities and statutory guidelines in the regulation of interstate common carrier services. Thus, Section 401 of the Communications Act provides that the Federal district courts shall have jurisdiction to enforce compliance with provisions of the Act; while

Section 402 provides that any party aggrieved by the Commissions's own actions may appeal such actions to a Federal Court of Appeals, which has authority to approve, reverse, or require modification of any commission action which it finds to be in violation of either the Communications Act, the Administrative Procedures Act (which generally governs the practices and procedures of all administrative agencies), or any of several other Federal statutes including the U.S. Constitution. Finally, all such judicial actions are themselves appealable to the U.S. Supreme Court, while the Congress itself retains the authority to modify or reverse FCC action, to issue new directives to the Commission and/or the industry, or to require specific changes in industry and/or regulatory structure and operation.

Given this combination of extensive administrative discretion, coupled with equally extensive review authority, the actual legal framework within which interstate common carrier services are provided differs substantially, at least in detail, from the basic framework enunciated in the Communications Act. Such deviations are embodied in an extensive record of what is termed "case law" (i.e., interpretations, extensions, and interpolations of the Act, of prior FCC and Court decisions, and of similar issues decided by other authorities), issued as a part of FCC and Court decisions in individual cases or proceedings. Such "case law" is seldom codified, at least in any format readily available to the lay reader; yet it is, to a significant extent, the working legal framework for common carrier communications. Thus, to gain any understanding of the current structure, operation, and regulation of the common carrier industry, or any insight into where it may be heading, one needs at least a general appreciation of not only the Communications Act itself, but also the body of case law that has evolved, particularly since 1934.

2.3 Industry and Regulatory Developments, 1934–1984

During recent years, a number of significant changes have taken place within the United States telecommunications industry and its regulations. While it is not possible to provide a comprehensive description and interpretation of all these changes within this chapter, a brief description of some of the major changes is essential to an understanding of the present and future environment for data communications.

2.3.1 Pre-1960s Market and Regulatory Framework

Until about 1960, telecommunications activities in the United States were organized along quasi-monopoly lines, with the various firms within the industry operating largely without competition within particular combinations of service classifications and geographic franchises. At the State and local level, Bell Operating Companies (BOCs) were the sole providers within most of the more urbanized areas of voice telephone services, while independent telephone companies enjoyed a similar monopoly status in the more rural areas. Voice telephone services between and among these franchised local exchange areas were provided as a joint undertaking by the local BOCs, the independent telephone companies, and the Long-Lines Department of AT&T which organized and managed the integrated network of Bell System interexchange facilities, of which it owned a minority share. So-called "record" communications services (e.g., telegraph and telex, the latter being a self-originated switched version of the former) were provided both intrastate and interstate as the residual *de facto* monopoly of the Western Union Telegraph Company, and were provided internationally on a somewhat competitive basis by the international record carriers (RCA, ITT, Western Union International, and several other companies serving regional markets). To the limited extent that "data" communications existed, it was accommodated either through the use of the dial-up telephone network (for relatively low-speed data) or through the use of dedicated, specially conditioned, transmission channels leased from either the telephone industry partnership or from Western Union.

In this market environment, wherein each supplier occupied a rather well-defined market niche in which it was essentially the sole source provider of both equipment and services, public regulation played a rather limited and often passive role. Carriers encountered little if any opposition from competitors or organized user groups when seeking regulatory authorization to add new facilities, and such authorizations were routinely granted. When particular users or the regulators themselves challenged carrier-initiated changes in the terms, conditions, or charges for their services, the effectiveness of such challenges was rather sharply curtailed by a lack of independent verifiable data concerning the existing and projected cost of providing such services, plus the inherent legal right accorded such carriers (at least at the interstate level) to institute such changes by merely filing the necessary tariffs with the Federal Communications Commission.

2.3.2 Key Decisions of the 1950s

While the changes that have occurred in this market and regulatory environment in recent years cannot be traced to any single factor or event, or even to a discrete set of such factors and events, one basic force appears to have provided much of the impetus for this change, while three Federal actions in the 1950s appear to have laid the foundation for it. The principal driving force appears to have been technological development, which both contributed to the capability of providing an ever-expanding array of new telecommunications products and services and also stimulated the demand for such new products and services by creating sophisticated social and economic structures that were increasingly dependent on information collection, processing, exchange, and distribution.

The principal Federal actions of the 1950s were: (1) a 1956 Federal Court of Appeals ruling that subscribers to telephone (and presumably other) tele-communications services had the right to use such services in any way that was "privately beneficial and not publicly detrimental"; (2) a 1956 agreement (Consent Decree) between the U.S. Department of Justice and AT&T whereby AT&T, in exchange for dismissal of a 1949 antitrust suit, agreed to limit its activities and those of its Western Electric manufacturing subsidiary to the field of regulated common carrier telecommunications services; and (3) a 1959 decision by the FCC to authorize private entities, such as railroads, gas pipelines, electric utilities, broadcast networks, manufacturers, or others with extensive communications network requirements, to establish private micro-wave systems to supplement or substitute for the long-distance telecommuni-cations services normally provided by interstate common carriers (primarily AT&T and its telephone industry partners).

The first of these decisions, in the case of *Hush-A-Phone Corp. vs. United States*, reversed an earlier FCC decision which had upheld the long-standing policy of AT&T and the telephone industry that only devices (e.g., telephones or other instruments) rented from the telephone companies themselves could be attached to their communications networks. The particular device in ques-tion (i.e., the independently manufactured *Hush-a-Phone*, a plastic cup-like mouthpiece which allegedly eliminated bothersome background noise when attached to an ordinary telephone handset) was relatively insignificant. How-ever, the principle enunciated by the Court in reversing the FCC and rejecting the telephone industry's long-standing policy against any such intercon-nection of so-called "foreign attachments" became the cornerstone for many subsequent decisions by the FCC and the Courts, dealing not only with equip-ment interconnection but with other tariff restrictions on the use (including resale) which a subscriber could make of the telecommunications services acquired from a carrier.

The subsequent effects of the second decision (i.e., the Department of Justice/AT&T Consent Decree) were both less direct and less discernible. However, when the FCC concluded in its 1971 Computer Inquiry that neither the sale of computers nor the provision of remote data-processing services fell within the definition of communications common carriage, the 1956 Consent Decree largely blocked the entry of AT&T and Western Electric into these burgeoning new markets, which were natural adjuncts to the provision of tele-communications services. This created significant opportunities for other firms to enter and prosper in these unregulated markets which, in turn, cre-ated both new demands for more sophisticated data-communication services and new demands for the interconnection of sophisticated data terminals with the telephone network. These developments, in turn, created further pres-sures for a change in both the telecommunications industry structure and its regulation. More recently, AT&T's continuing desire to enter these markets by eliminating or modifying the 1956 Consent Decree and the 1971 Computer Inquiry decision has become a major factor in its decision to accept divestiture of local Bell System operations in exchange for the lifting of these restrictions, as part of the settlement of a more recent antitrust suit.

The third major 1950s decision (i.e., the FCC authorization of private microwave systems) became the primary source of two separate but related regulatory developments that have had a profound effect on the telecommunications common carrier business. These were: (1) heightened regulatory concern about the regulation of AT&T's charges and practices and, in particular, about potential cross-subsidies between and among its various service offerings; and (2) a profound shift in Federal regulatory philosophy toward the concept of competition rather than regulated monopoly as the basic organizing principle for telecommunications common carriage.

2.3.3 Regulatory Challenges and Frustrations of the 1960s

To understand how and why these developments in regulatory philosophy occurred, it may be useful to review in some detail the FCC's efforts to implement the regulatory concepts embodied in the Communications Act. Prior to about 1960, the FCC employed a process of informal discussion and negotiation which it termed "continuing surveillance" as its primary means of common carrier regulation. Through frequent informal contacts with representatives of AT&T and other interstate carriers, the Commission and its staff were made aware of developments in technology and services, as well as carrier plans for new tariff filings, price changes, etc. Likewise, the carriers were made aware of the Commission's expectations and concerns about the same matters. As a result of this process, applications for authority to construct additional facilities, as well as tariff filings were largely a formality to implement the results of these informal "negotiations," and were rarely challenged or denied by the Commission.

In response to the FCC's decision to authorize the establishment of private microwave systems, AT&T filed, in January 1961, a bulk-rate tariff for its so-called "private line" services (i.e., dedicated intercity communications voice/data channels used primarily by large businesses and government agencies). Under this new "TELPAK" tariff, such entities could obtain from 12 to 240 such channels for as little as 15% of the prevailing single-channel private lines rates. AT&T acknowledged that the communication channels provided under the TELPAK tariff were identical to those provided under its other private line tariffs and that the facilities used were also identical. However, AT&T contended that the lower bulk-rate prices were justified on the basis of "competitive necessity" (i.e., to prevent certain large users from abandoning AT&T's private line services to establish their own private microwave systems).

The TELPAK tariff filing was vigorously challenged by Western Union (the only competitive supplier of private line services at that time) and Motorola (a large manufacturer of private microwave equipment), who contended that the bulk rates were not compensatory and, thus, were predatory. Moreover, the FCC itself was deeply concerned over the apparent offering of "like" services at differing rates—a practice explicitly forbidden by Section 202(a) of the Communications Act. The Commission first ordered AT&T to file an amended tariff to correct these defects, but when the amended tariff still did not remove these concerns, the Commission suspended it for the maximum allowable period (90 days), and launched a formal investigation (hearing) on the TELPAK tariff.

The fundamental issues raised in the TELPAK tariff investigation were new to FCC and, in many respects, to regulation in general. First, under what circumstances can essentially identical services be priced differently without violating the Section 202(a) prohibition against unjust or unreasonable discrimination in pricing "like" services? Second, what is the proper relationship between and among the costs and prices of the various service offerings provided by a multiservice carrier, as distinguished from traditional regulatory concerns which focused only on the overall costs and profits of such firms? The first issue dealt with possible discrimination between the users of essentially identical services and the second with possible discrimination between users of essentially different services (e.g., forcing one class of users to pay higher rates in order to offset losses resulting from below-cost rates to other user classes).

The FCC was unable to resolve satisfactorily either of these issues in its initial TELPAK investigation. The FCC concluded that the services provided under the TELPAK tariff were indeed no different than the individual private line services provided at higher rates under other AT&T tariffs, but it accepted AT&T's contention that some such price discrimination might be justified by "competitive necessity." The Commission thus allowed AT&T to retain the discount rates for the larger TELPAK channel groups (60 and 240 channels, respectively) on the grounds that private microwave systems would only be competitive, if at all, where such large tariff flows existed. However, the FCC stated that it was "unable to determine on this record that the rates for TELPAK are compensatory in relation to the costs of furnishing the services offered thereunder and, therefore, are unable to find that the other users of AT&T services will not be burdened by the application of such rates."

The FCC attempted to resolve this issue of potentially discriminatory "cross-subsidization" between and among service and user categories by expanding the initial TELPAK investigation, in Docket #18128, into a comprehensive examination of AT&T's practices with respect to cost assignment/ allocation and pricing of its various services. As a parallel effort, the FCC also launched the first-ever general investigation of AT&T's overall operations, costs, services, and tariffs in Docket #19129. These two investigations, both instituted in the early 1960s, were not completed until the mid-1970s. Moreover, despite the expenditure of enormous resources by the Commission, AT&T, and other interested parties, and the compilation of massive hearing records in both cases, the FCC was unable in either case either to verify the lawfulness, under the Communications Act, of AT&T's cost assignment/allocation and pricing practices (or its specific tariffs); or to prescribe specific costing and pricing methodologies (or tariff rates) of its own design which AT&T must follow. The FCC experienced similar frustrations in a lengthy series of individual tariff investigations throughout the 1970s. The Commission repeatedly concluded at the end of each such investigation that AT&T had not shown that the prices for the more specialized and/or discounted services which it provided to government and industry fully covered their relevant costs, or even what the relevant costs were. However, without the latter information, the FCC considered itself powerless to prescribe prices for these services, and generally felt obliged to permit AT&T to continue offering them so as not to disrupt service to their users.

Throughout most of the 1960s and 1970s, therefore, AT&T was providing most of its specialized and/or discounted services pursuant to tariffs which the Commission eventually found to be in violation of the Communications Act; in many instances, the services continued to be offered under these tariffs even after the FCC declared them unlawful, pending the filing of replacement tariffs by AT&T. This lengthy, frustrating, and essentially futile effort by the FCC to impose effective public-interest regulation on the services and charges of the principal interstate carrier that was subject to its jurisdiction became a major factor in the decisions by the FCC and, subsequently, by the Courts and the Congress, to encourage more competition as a substitute for regulation in this field.

2.3.4 Development of Pro-Competitive Policies

There were, to be sure, many other factors which contributed significantly to the shift in Federal policy and regulatory focus from the concept of regulated monopoly to that of increased competition as the organizing principle for the telecommunications business. Moreover, it should be recognized that this was neither an abrupt nor a recent shift in policy and regulatory philosophy. Long before most persons were aware of the FCC's existence, and long before other Federal authorities or the Courts began to appreciate the evolving issues in the field, the FCC had already begun the process of change—not necessarily through greater foresight, but through greater exposure to these issues and developments by virtue of its pivotal position with respect to the authorization and policing of such activities. As early as 1948, the FCC authorized the establishment of independent "radio common carriers," to compete with local telephone companies in the provision of mobile (i.e., vehicular) telephone services, in the belief that such independent competitors would likely spur the development and public benefit of this new technology which resulted from World War II activities. As the result of several decisions throughout the 1950s, the Commission had also authorized, first, the establishment of private microwave systems and, later, the establishment of so-called "miscellaneous" carriers for the limited purpose of distributing network television programs between and among television broadcast stations and cable television (CATV) systems. In both these situations, however, the principle thrust of FCC's reasoning had been to extend either the type or the geographical coverage of services considered to be of potential value to the public beyond the scope of services then available from the telephone industry monopoly; in short, the intent was primarily to augment rather than compete with traditional telephone industry services and operations.

In December 1963, just as it was becoming increasingly embroiled in the discriminatory pricing and cross-subsidization issues raised by AT&T's TELPAK tariff, the FCC received an application from Microwave Communications, Inc. (MCI) for authority to construct a common carrier microwave communications system between Chicago, Illinois and St. Louis, Missouri. The services which MCI proposed to offer via this system would be in direct competition with the private line voice and data services AT&T was then providing to large business and government users under its TELPAK and individual private line tariffs. This application was vigorously opposed by AT&T and its Illinois Bell and Southwestern Bell subsidiaries, as well as several other established carries. Grounds for this opposition included contentions that the Bell companies "fulfilled every public need" of which they were aware, that MCI's proposed microwave system would result in "harmful interference" to AT&T's existing microwave network, and that the MCI system would be unreliable. However, after lengthy hearings and related proceedings necessitated by the continued opposition of the established carriers, the FCC granted the MCI application in August 1969. This was the first major decision in which the FCC approved the entry of a new firm in the market for interstate telecommunications services whose explicit intent was to compete with AT&T and other established interstate carriers. But even this competition, in the Commission's view, was to be limited to the area of "specialized" or private line services, including both voice and data services, but excluding switched, on-demand, long-distance telephone services.

During the same 1960s time frame, the FCC was also called on to reexamine the issue of the interconnection of subscriber-provided terminal equipment to the telephone network, which had been addressed by the 1956 *Hush-a-Phone* decision. On this occasion, the issue centered on the refusal of the Bell companies to permit the connection of a new device, the *Carterfone*, which was designed to allow the dispatcher in a private mobile radio system to make an acoustical (i.e., audio) connection between a standard telephone instrument leased from the telephone company and the radio transmit/receive equipment used to contact mobile units, for the purpose of extending ordinary telephone calls to and from these mobile units. Taking its cue from the earlier Court decision in the *Hush-a-Phone* case, the FCC in the 1968 *Carterfone* decision declared AT&T's tariff provisions which denied such interconnection to be unlawful, in that they prevented telephone subscribers from using their telephone services in ways that benefitted them without harming either service to others or the telephone network operations or personnel. In this stance, however, the FCC decided that the ruling would not be limited solely to the *Carterfone* device but, more generally, to any type of customer-provided equipment. The Commission's intent was to shift the burden of proof from the prospective user of such equipment to the carrier, by requiring the latter to establish factual grounds concerning the potential harm to the telephone network before imposing such restrictions on any type of terminal equipment. The decision had the potential effect of opening the entire market for customer-premises telecommunications equipment (which had traditionally been the exclusive preserve of the telephone industry under the concept of sole end-to-end service responsibility) to competitive suppliers. However, the Commission's primary objective, in this instance, was simply to guarantee what it and the Courts perceived as a basic consumer right.

In addition to its substantive effect on both competition and consumer choice, the *Carterfone* decision signalled a significant shift in the FCC's procedural approach to such issues. In most of its prior actions, particularly those involving prospective incursions into the common carrier business, the FCC had limited the effect of its rulings to the specific equipment or service involved, and had given them rather narrow interpretations. But in the *Carterfone* decision, and in many subsequent decisions, the Commission now began to enunciate broad policies of general applicability. This shift was particularly beneficial to the subsequent development of competition, by significantly reducing the capability of established carriers like AT&T to both forestall competitive entry and substantially increase its costs through repetitive challenges and interminable regulatory proceedings directed at each individual entrant. Given the virtually unlimited resources and continuing near-monopoly revenue sources of the established carriers, and the inability of new entrants to offer any service or generate any revenues prior to FCC authorization, such case-by-case determination of each new entry application, interconnection issue, or other matter by the FCC could have had a very chilling effect on the development of telecommunications competition.

The next application of this new policy-making approach occurred in July 1970 when the FCC launched a rulemaking proceeding to determine whether and under what conditions other prospective carriers like MCI should be authorized to compete with the established carriers in the provision of interstate services. Whereas the authorization of MCI's initial microwave route required six years of controversial hearings, the Commission completed this general rulemaking proceeding in slightly less than one year. In what came to be known as the *Specialized Common Carrier* decision, the FCC concluded that

" . . . there is a public need and demand for the proposed facilities and services and for new and diverse sources of supply, competition in the specialized communications field is reasonably feasible, there are grounds for a reasonable expectation that new entry will have some beneficial effects, and there is no reason to anticipate that new entry would have any adverse impact on service to the public by existing carriers such as to outweigh the considerations supporting new entry. We further find and conclude that a general policy in favor of the entry of new carriers in the specialized communication field would serve the public interest, convenience and necessity."

The FCC's 1968 *Carterfone* and 1971 *Specialized Common Carrier* decisions established the basic pro-competitive philosophy that has been reflected in many subsequent FCC actions. This pro-competitive philosophy was given additional impetus and support by the 1970 Presidential recommendation for a competitive, open-entry policy concerning the establishment and operation of domestic satellite communication systems and services, which was largely adopted in the FCC's 1972 *Domestic Satellite* decision.

While a detailed and comprehensive review of all the regulatory and industry developments of the past decade is beyond the scope or needs of this text, some of the more significant highlights bear emphasizing. For example, despite the *Carterfone*, *Specialized Common Carrier*, and *Domestic Satellite* decisions of the 1968–72 period, as of late-1973, there had developed little actual competition in any of these markets. Effective competition in the market for customer premises equipment (CPE) continued to be restricted by the requirement written into AT&T's post-Carterfone tariffs that all independently provided CPE had to be interconnected with the telephone network only via an interface device which could itself be obtained only from the telephone companies—for a substantial lease charge. Competition in the market for specialized intercity services continued to be restricted as the result of disputes between the Specialized Common Carriers (SCCs) and the telephone industry about both the scope of the SCC's authorized service offerings and the responsibilities of the established carriers for interconnecting their facilities and service with those of the SCCs. In addition, telephone company tariffs continued to impose many restrictions on the use that a customer could make of the services acquired from the company, including general prohibitions against the sharing of such services among multiple users or their "resale" to other parties. Moreover, the threat of "cross-subsidization" between and among AT&T's various service offerings continued to serve as a significant deterrent to competitive entry and expansion.

In its 1971 *Specialized Common Carrier* decision, the FCC recognized that these newly authorized carriers would require interconnections with at least the local networks of the established telephone companies, which were operated as essentially franchised monopolies, in order to extend their intercity services to their customer's locations. However, the FCC did not prescribe specific interconnection arrangements for this purpose, but left such arrangements for private negotiation between the specialized carriers and the telephone companies. By 1973, serious disputes had arisen between AT&T and the specialized carriers concerning both the services that the latter were authorized to market, and the type of interconnections that the former was required to provide. AT&T contended that the specialized carriers were only authorized to offer dedicated intercity communication channels which terminated at both ends in dedicated customer-premises equipment, and refused to provide interconnection arrangements that could be used in any way to access the switched public-message telephone network, either at the local or long-distance level. The specialized carriers contended they were authorized to provide any type of "private line" services that AT&T itself offered, including services, such as foreign exchange (FX) or Common Control Switching Arrangements (CCSA), which accessed the public switched-message telephone network either at the local exchange or at other network nodes.

Both the FCC and a Federal district court ruled, in early 1974, that the specialized carriers' interpretation of their service authorizations was correct. The FCC ordered AT&T (as well as any other telephone company) to file tariffs providing for the type of interconnections required by the SCCs to offer

FX and CCSA, as well as other private line services. When the FCC concluded that the tariffs filed in response to this order were both overly restrictive and overly expensive, it suspended them and ordered negotiations between AT&T, other telephone companies, and the SCCs to be conducted under the Commissions's aegis. After several months of intensive negotiations, the parties reached agreement on what were described as "interim" interconnection arrangements and charges, which the FCC "accepted" as a satisfactory interim resolution of the issue.

During much of the same period of time, the FCC became engaged in a series of investigations of the AT&T price reductions for its private line services and its newly instituted Dataphone Digital Service (DDS), which was filed in response to the *Specialized Common Carrier* decision. These investigations began with a January 1974 FCC decision, which suspended for the maximum allowable 90-day period the revised Hi Density-Lo Density (Hi-Lo) rate structure for private line services that was filed by AT&T on January 4, 1974. The Hi-Lo tariff was presented as simply a cost-based repricing of AT&T's existing private line services to reflect alleged economies realized on AT&T's high density "routes" and/or high capacity network facilities between major population and business centers. However, both the specialized carriers and the FCC became concerned that the substantial price reductions offered between and among so-called Hi-D locations might simply represent a situation in which these services were actually being priced below their full cost of production, while the prices of some other services which were not subject to competition (e.g., private line services between Lo-D locations or even public message telephone services) were set above their full cost of production in order to cover any losses. In short, they were concerned that the Hi-Lo rate structure might constitute a case of potentially anticompetitive "cross-subsidization."

The issue of potentially anticompetitive cross-subsidization was not resolved, at least to the FCC's satisfaction, either by the Hi-Lo investigation or by any of several succeeding or parallel investigations of AT&T tariffs. In January 1976, after two years of hearing and investigation, the FCC declared the Hi-Lo rate structure to be unlawful, after concluding that AT&T had failed to demonstrate the alleged cost differences between Hi-D and Lo-D routes. The Commission ordered AT&T to file a new private line tariff, and to include in its justification for any similar price differentials a valid determination of the respective costs of providing the services over their respective routes.

However, to avoid interruption of services to the public, the FCC allowed these unlawful tariffs to remain in effect pending the filing of their replacement. When AT&T filed its new tariffs, now termed the Multi-Schedule Private Line (MPL) Tariff, the Commission's initial review produced the same concerns about inadequate cost justification and potential cross-subsidization. In May 1976, the Commission suspended these tariffs, again for the maximum allowable period, and instituted another investigation. In October 1979, following three more years of hearings and investigation, the Commission again concluded that AT&T had not provided an acceptable cost justification for the

MPL rates, and thus found the MPL tariff "unjust, unreasonable, and unlawful in violation of Section 201(b) of the Act and our *Docket No. 18128* Decision." However, the FCC again felt compelled to allow the tariffs it had declared unlawful to remain in effect, so as to avoid interruption of services upon which users had come to rely.

The Hi-Lo and MPL tariff cases are but two of several examples of tariff investigations throughout the 1970s in which the FCC, despite strong concerns about possible cross-subsidization between those services in which AT&T enjoyed *de facto* monopoly status and those in which it was subject to at least potential competition, and despite vigorous efforts to ascertain the facts, was unable to satisfactorily resolve the issue. AT&T has steadfastly maintained that the FCC employed improper standards for cost determination and pricing in repeatedly finding its tariffs unlawful, while the Commission has been equally adamant in asserting that AT&T's cost determination and pricing practices were consistently biased to favor its competitive service offerings at the expense of the users of its monopoly services. Whatever the merits of these respective positions, it seems quite clear that the FCC's unbroken frustration, in its efforts to carry out what it perceived as its regulatory responsibilities *vis-a-vis* AT&T, contributed significantly to its growing conviction that competition, rather than regulatory oversight, would be a more effective protector of the public interest in the telecommunications business. Moreover, this record of regulatory frustration clearly became a major factor in subsequent public and private antitrust actions against AT&T which led to the ultimate break up of the Bell System.

The relationship between the FCC's actions concerning carrier-to-carrier interconnection and AT&T's competitive tariffs, and its evolving pro-competitive philosophy, is fairly direct and readily discernible. While the relationship between other significant concerns and actions of the mid-1970s and this pro-competitive philosophy were much less direct, their ultimate effect was much the same. As noted previously, despite the 1968 *Carterfone* ruling that telephone network subscribers could connect essentially any terminal device to the telephone network so long as it did not impair service to others or otherwise result in "public harm," the post-*Carterfone* tariff requirement that all such connections be made only through costly interface devices that could only be leased from the telephone company served as a significant constraint on both user choice and on the competitive marketing of customer premises equipment. In 1969, the FCC launched an investigation looking toward the establishment of alternative, less costly, and less intimidating arrangements for CPE interconnection. Following several years of inconclusive comment and discussion among the principle parties involved, the FCC acted in late 1975 and early 1976, over the strong objections of AT&T and other telephone companies, to adopt and implement a Federal certification program. Under this program independently supplied CPE, once certified by the FCC to be harmless to the telephone network based on design and manufacturing standards, could be directly connected to the telephone network without benefit of any "interface" device. While the primary thrust of this FCC action was to relieve telephone subscribers of the burdensome interface device requirement, and thereby provide for greater user choice of CPE, the indirect effect was to open the CPE market to full competition.

In a similar vein, the FCC acted in 1976 to strike down AT&T's historical prohibitions on the resale and sharing of its service offerings. This action resulted from a complaint by one major user, the American Trucking Association, and was addressed primarily to the rights of such users to use the telecommunications services acquired from AT&T in any manner that was "privately beneficial but not publicly harmful"—the *Hush-a-Phone* standard. However, it too had the effect not only of encouraging additional competition, in the form of new "resale" carriers, but also of discouraging the bulk-rate (i.e., discounted) pricing of services where these bulk rates did not reflect actual costs. Briefly stated, the ability of another entity to subscribe to services at bulk-rate prices and then resell them individually in competition with the underlying carrier's own individually priced services, forced the underlying carrier to raise its bulk-rate prices to a profitable level. For example, this FCC decision succeeded, where all other FCC investigations had failed, in convincing AT&T to abandon its bulk-rate TELPAK tariff. Since such bulk-rate competitive tariffs had long constituted one of the more serious threats to competitive market entry, the decision had a beneficial effect on such competition.

2.3.5 Divestiture and Deregulation: Keywords for the Future

By the late 1970s, the transition from a public telecommunications policy based on the concept of "regulated monopoly" to one based on unrestricted competition was essentially complete. While this transition began with some rather cautious and tentative actions by the FCC, it was given significant boosts by two decisions of the Washington, DC Court of Appeals in 1977 (Execunet I and II). These decisions reversed FCC rulings that the specialized carriers were limited to the offering of private line services. Congress subsequently rejected legislation sponsored by the telephone industry that would have rolled back many of these pro-competitive decisions.

Since about 1979, with this widespread consensus on the potential benefits of competition fully established, the FCC's philosophy has shifted increasingly toward "deregulation"—i.e., the elimination of regulatory processes and controls for *all* industry participants, including "dominant" carriers to the maximum extent possible. This new philosophy was first evidenced in the FCC's 1980 Second Computer decision, in which the primary thrust was not simply (or even at all) to open up some heretofore "protected" telecommunications equipment or services market to new competitors, but rather to facilitate AT&T's entry into the equipment and information-processing markets previously denied to it by a 1956 Consent Decree between AT&T and the U.S. Department of Justice. This deregulatory philosophy, coupled with the pre-existing pro-competitive philosophy, provides the principle thrust for most current FCC, judicial, and legislative action concerning the telecommunications business, in general, and common carrier communications, in particular. The following listing includes the major FCC decisions made between 1960 and 1990 that have both contributed to and reflected these changes in policy and regulatory philosophy, and in the common carrier industry structure and operation.

Use of Recording Devices. Docket 6787
    Report of the Commission: March 24, 1947
    Order: November 26, 1947

Jordaphone Decision. Docket 9383
    Decision: May 5, 1954

Hush-A-Phone. Docket 9189
    Order: May 13, 1949
    Decision: December 21, 1955

Telegraph Investigation. Docket 14650
    Memorandum Opinion and Order: May 25, 1962

Telpak Investigation. Docket 14251
    Order: April 12, 1961
    Tentative Decision: March 20, 1964
    Memorandum Opinion and Order: December 21, 1964
    Memorandum Opinion and Order: May 3, 1965
    Memorandum Opinion and Order: November 9, 1966

Carterfone. Docket 16942
    Order: October 21, 1966
    Decision: June 27, 1968

Specialized Carriers. Docket 18920
    Notice of Inquiry: July 17, 1970
    First Report and Order: June 3, 1971

Computer Inquiry I. Docket 16979
    Notice of Inquiry: November 10, 1966
    Final Decision and Order: March 18, 1971
    Memorandum Opinion and Order: March 30, 1972

Domestic Satellite Carriers. Docket 16495
    Notice of Inquiry: March 2, 1966
    Supplemental Notice of Inquiry: October 21, 1966
    Report and Order: March 24, 1970
    Further Notice of Inquiry and Proposed Rulemaking:
        September 25, 1970
    Memorandum Opinion and Order: March 17, 1972
    Second Report and Order: June 16, 1972
    Memorandum Opinion and Order: December 22, 1972

Hi Density-Low Density Rate Structure (Hi-Lo). Docket 19919
    Memorandum Opinion and Order: January 11, 1974
    Order: October 22, 1974

Interim Decision: September 18, 1975
Decision: January 22, 1976

Resale and Sharing. Docket 20097
Notice of Inquiry and Proposed Rulemaking: July 5, 1974
Report and Order: July 16, 1976
Memorandum Opinion and Order: March 14, 1977

Dataphone Digital Service. Docket 20288
Memorandum Opinion and Order: December 16, 1974
Memorandum Opinion and Order: July 2, 1975
Memorandum Opinion and Order: January 22, 1976
Memorandum Opinion and Order: February 18, 1976
Final Decision and Order: January 17, 1977
Memorandum Opinion and Order: June 20, 1977

General Rate Investigation. Docket 19129
Phase II: Final Decision: February 23, 1977
Reconsideration of Phase II: February 24, 1978

Cost and Ratemaking Principles. Docket 18128
Memorandum Opinion and Order: August 7, 1969
Memorandum Opinion and Order: October 29, 1969
Memorandum Opinion and Order: January 16, 1970
Memorandum Opinion and Order: October 1, 1976
Reconsideration Order: June 13, 1977
Second Order on Reconsideration: February 24, 1978

Equipment Registration. Docket 19528
Notice of Inquiry: June 16, 1972
First Report and Order: November 7, 1975
Second Report and Order: March 18, 1976
Third Report and Order: April 13, 1978
Memorandum Opinion and Order: February 5, 1979

Wide Area Telephone Service (WATS). Docket 21402
Notice of Inquiry: September 27, 1977
Final Decision and Order: December 18, 1978

Digital Termination Systems. CC Docket 79-188
Notice of Proposed Rulemaking: August 31, 1979

Multi-Schedule Private Line Tariffs (MPL). Docket 20814
Memorandum Opinion and Order: May 20, 1976
Final Decision and Order: October 4, 1979

Second Computer Inquiry. Docket 20828
Notice of Inquiry: August 10, 1976
Tentative Decision and Further Notice of Inquiry: July 6, 1979
Final Decision: April 7, 1980
Reconsideration Order: December 1980
Further Reconsideration Order: October 1981

MTS/WATS Market Structure. CC Docket 78-72
    Notice of Inquiry: March 23, 1978
    Supplemental Notice of Inquiry: August 30, 1979
    Second Supplemental Notice of Inquiry: April 16, 1980
    Third Supplemental Notice of Inquiry: August 25, 1980
    Fourth Supplemental Notice of Inquiry: June 4, 1982
    Order: December 23, 1982

Competitive Services Rulemaking. CC Docket 79-252
    Notice of Inquiry and Proposed Rulemaking: November 2, 1979
    First Report and Order: November 28, 1980
    Further Notice of Proposed Rulemaking: January 16, 1981
    Second Report and Order: August 20, 1982
    Fourth Report and Order: October 19, 1983

Interim Cost Allocation Manual. CC Docket 79-245
    Notice of Inquiry and Proposed Rulemaking: September 28, 1979
    Notice of Proposed Rulemaking: June 26, 1980
    Report and Order: January 6, 1981
    Order on Reconsideration: May 15, 1981

Uniform System of Accounts Proceeding. CC Docket 78-196
    Notice of Proposed Rulemaking: July 31, 1978
    First Supplemental Notice of Proposed Rulemaking:
        August 13, 1979
    Second Supplemental Notice of Proposed Rulemaking:
        October 7, 1981

Third Computer Inquiry. CC Docket 85-229
    Decision: May 15, 1986
    Reconsideration: January 14, 1988

AT&T Price Cap Regulation. CC Docket 87-313
    First Report and Order: March 16, 1989
    Second Report and Order: September 19, 1990

While many of the significant changes that have occurred in the common carrier industry can be traced, either directly or indirectly, to FCC actions—and more fundamentally to technological developments—the most significant change of all resulted from antitrust action by the U.S. Department of Justice. On January 4, 1982, the Justice Department and AT&T announced a proposed settlement of an antitrust case initiated against AT&T by the Department in 1974. Under the terms of the settlement, AT&T agreed to divest all of its local telephone operations, in exchange for the right to retain its equipment manufacturing subsidiary (Western Electric), its intercity network facilities and services, and the Bell Telephone Laboratories—plus the right to expand into new markets for information-processing equipment and services. This settlement was reached after the Justice Department had presented its case and the presiding Judge had rejected an AT&T motion to dismiss, but before AT&T had completed presentation of its counter arguments. The settlement thus terminated the case without a finding of either guilt or innocence; although in denying the AT&T motion to dismiss, the Court ruled that the Justice Department case, thus far, had demonstrated "that the Bell System has violated the antitrust laws in a number of ways over a lengthy period of time."

While the AT&T antitrust settlement agreement itself required only the divestiture of AT&T's "local exchange" operations and services (traditionally, those operations performed and services provided within an individual city or community of interest), the actual reorganization plan developed by AT&T and approved by the Justice Department and the antitrust court expanded the concept of "local exchange" in a manner that would significantly affect future market and industry structure and regulation. Specifically, the concept of local-exchange areas encompassing individual communities was replaced by the concept of Local Access and Transport Areas (LATAs), encompassing both intracity and intercity operations extending over very large geographic areas—in some instances, entire states. Under this plan, the 23 regional Bell Operating Companies* divested from AT&T were awarded all the Bell System facilities and service operations within these expanded LATAs, with AT&T retaining only the so-called inter-LATA facilities and services.

The significance of this expanded definition of local exchange operations and services, and expanded role of the "local" Bell Operating Companies, results from several associated factors. First, since the primary rationale of the antitrust settlement was said to be the separation of "natural monopoly" local-exchange operations from "potentially competitive" interexchange operations, the expanded LATA definition correspondingly expands, by orders of magnitude, the geographic and market areas within which the divested companies or sympathetic State regulators could contend that "natural monopoly" conditions do or should prevail. Moreover, since these expanded LATAs have generally been defined so as not to extend beyond the boundaries of individual States, the authority of State regulatory authorities in reaching such determinations is substantially increased.

Quite apart from any such "natural monopoly" rationale, the expanded LATA concept by its own terms has significantly reduced the overall scope of the potentially competitive market for intercity services, and has confined much of this competitive activity to the relatively small number of high-volume routes and high-capacity network facilities required to handle "inter-LATA" traffic. While all inter-LATA carriers are eventually to be afforded equal access to intra-LATA services, under equal terms, conditions, and charges, it remains to be determined whether or not there can be effective inter-LATA competition when it is both confined to such a limited portion of the overall end-to-end operation and is subject to common arrangements and charges for the remaining portions.

---

*In the process of divestiture, the ownership of these 23 operating telephone companies was reconsolidated under 7 regional holding companies, each of which acquired an approximately equal share of the pre-existing Bell System assets.

2.4 Post-Divestiture Industry and Regulatory Developments

Following the 1984 breakup of the Bell System, there have been significant changes in the interests, alignments, and activities of the U.S. carrier industry—and in the policies and practices of its regulators. Predictably, the divested Regional Bell Operating Companies (RBOCs) have become more closely aligned with other Local Exchange Carriers (LECs), while AT&T is frequently aligned with its long-distance competitors in opposition to LEC and RBOC plans and actions. Also predictably, the RBOCs have attempted in every available regulatory, judicial, and legislative forum to obtain relief from the various restrictions that were imposed on their activities by the Bell System divestiture agreement—despite their continued near-monopoly status in the local exchange market and their prior participation in the abuse of such market power that led to the divestiture.

What was not so predictable has been the extent to which regulators and legislators have been receptive to and supportive of these RBOC efforts, and the extent to which these authorities have been willing to promote RBOC entry into competitive markets while simultaneously abandoning longstanding efforts to impose more effective regulation on such monopolies.

Many of these public officials have expressed concerns about the continued economic viability of the RBOCs, the continued availability of universal telephone service, and/or the continued competitiveness of U.S. telecommunications firms in world markets, as the grounds for their deregulatory proposals and actions. Quite understandably, the RBOCs have both promoted and attempted to exploit such concerns. To this end, they have repeatedly petitioned the divestiture court to waive or rescind the prohibitions against RBOC equipment manufacturing, and the direct provision of interexchange telecommunications services or information services. They have also sought amendments to the 1934 Communications Act, or regulatory decisions, that would effectively override these judicially approved—but Bell System designed—divestiture restrictions. To date, the divestiture court has granted only limited relief, and efforts to amend the Communications Act have not been successful.

In the regulatory arena, however, both the RBOCs and AT&T have been more successful. As noted in the previous section, the divestiture agreement itself vastly expanded the area in which the RBOCs could claim regulatory protection on "natural monopoly" grounds. This essentially limited interexchange competition to inter-LATA trunk lines, while imposing common, levelizing exchange access costs on all such competing interexchange carriers. Citing threats of bypass, loss of alleged subsidies from long distance services, and the potential reduction of universal local telephone services, the RBOCs (and other LECs) initially pressed for and received favorable regulatory decisions to impose significant "exchange access fees" on both exchange customers and interexchange carriers. At the same time, they sought and received substantial rate increases from State regulatory commissions. Consequently, rather than the poor financial condition some had anticipated, by the late 1980's most RBOCs (and other LECs) were reporting significantly higher earnings levels.

These increased earnings, coupled with the holding company structure of the RBOCs, may have further fueled their desire to enter new markets. Quite naturally, they also fueled demands for more effective regulatory control of both customer and carrier exchange access fees, and local exchange rates. However, all these developments have occurred during a period when "deregulation" has become the guiding principle for both elected and appointed public officials at all levels of State and Federal regulatory, legislative, and executive organs. Consequently, rather than renewed efforts to impose traditional regulatory controls on rates and earnings, these developments have only promoted searches for new, less "regulatory" solutions. In most instances, the preferred alternative has been even greater reliance on "competitive market forces," despite the absence or extremely limited scope of such forces in many market segments. To this end, the FCC in its Computer III decision decided to relieve AT&T and the RBOCs of the Computer II requirement that customer-premises equipment and enhanced services be marketed only through fully separated subsidiaries. Instead, they may rely on merely "accounting separation" and Comparably Efficient Interconnection (CEI), including the establishment by RBOCs of Open Network Architecture (ONA). However, the Court of Appeals subsequently vacated this decision and remanded the issue to the FCC for further proceedings; thus at this time the Computer II requirements still apply.

Where the evidence that competitive market forces cannot provide safeguards is overwhelming—as in the case of local exchange services and access, and AT&T's public message services—the FCC and State regulators have embraced the new concept of "price cap" regulation. Under this form of regulation, carriers are not required to demonstrate that their rates cover only relevant costs, including a specified return on invested capital, as did the traditional regulatory concepts embodied in the Communications Act and most State statutes. Instead, carriers must only demonstrate that new rates do not differ by more than some prescribed amount from existing rates, where the prescribed difference is determined by a formula which reflects changes in inflation, productivity, and other factors. At this point in time, there is no track record on which to judge either the effectiveness or the enforceability of price cap regulation. However, there is significant concern among competitors, legislators, and former regulators that it will prove even less effective than the admittedly weak traditional forms of rate regulation.

2.5 Current Industry Structure and Regulatory Framework

Both the industry structure and the regulatory framework for what has heretofore been considered the common carrier communications business are in a high degree of flux, as are its service offerings and prices. The pro-competitive actions of the FCC and the Courts throughout the 1970s, coupled with continuing technological developments both within and dependent upon this business, have created an environment in which new firms are continuously entering the business. The more recent actions by the FCC designed to "deregulate" the business are also changing many of its public obligations, to the extent that it is somewhat misleading even to refer to it any longer as a "common carrier" business. With the breakup of the Bell System into seven regional holding companies (providing essentially intrastate services) and a national holding company (providing essentially interstate services), the market power of what has long been the dominant force in the business has been substantially reduced, providing further opportunities for competitive entry and expansion.

Given this high degree of industry and regulatory flux, any attempt to provide a comprehensive list of existing common carriers, service offerings, tariffs, or Federal and/or State regulations would be both futile and promptly outdated. As a result of recent FCC rulings, resale carriers are no longer required to obtain Section 214 authorization for the lines they acquire, or file tariffs covering their service offerings; this effectively eliminates any comprehensive public record of such activities. It should also be noted that the distinction between facilities-based and resale carriers, which has never been sharply delineated, has become increasingly less so as many facilities-based carriers now engage in extensive cross-leasing and resale of their respective facilities and services as a normal operating practice. Such extensive cross-leasing, coupled with recent FCC and Court decisions lifting prior restrictions on the services that can be provided via previously authorized facilities, has also eliminated most distinctions between so-called "miscellaneous," "specialized," and "satellite" carriers. The FCC has also authorized satellite vendors to "sell" rather than "lease" satellite transmission facilities and to do so via private, individually negotiated, contracts rather than public tariffs. The requirement for other "nondominant" carriers to provide cost justification for their tariff filings has also been eliminated.

The net effect of all these regulatory and industry developments is an environment in which essentially any existing or prospective supplier of almost any type of interstate communications service can do so with a minimum of regulatory constraints. Moreover, through extensive leasing and resale of the facilities and services of other entities, such service offerings can be extended throughout large geographic areas for a relatively small capital investment.

The principal distinctions now being maintained by the FCC are between so-called "basic" and "enhanced" interstate services, between equipment and services, and between "dominant" and "nondominant" carriers, The basic vs. enhanced services distinction adopted in the Commission's Second Computer Decision is intended to segregate, for regulatory purposes, the supply of those services which involve merely the electronic transportation of information from those which involve manipulation or processing of the information content. According to the Computer II decision, only the former is subject to conventional common carrier regulation, while the latter can only be offered by telephone companies under separate accounting (in the case of AT&T, separate subsidiary) arrangements, on a detariffed unregulated basis.

Similarly, the distinction between equipment vs. service offerings, also adopted in the Second Computer Decision, is intended to separate what is considered to be a fully competitive equipment manufacturing and sales market from a common carrier services market in which competitive forces are not yet deemed fully adequate to police against cross-subsidies and related anticompetitive practices. As with enhanced services, telephone companies may only offer equipment on a detariffed basis through separate accounting procedures or, in the case of AT&T and the divested Bell Operating Companies, separate subsidiaries.

The third current regulatory distinction, between "dominant" and "nondominant" carriers, is intended to segregate those carriers (primarily AT&T and the newly divested Bell Operating Companies) which enjoy sufficiently extensive and intensive market power to effectively dictate prices and interconnection/access conditions from those who do not. Again, the Computer II decision held that only the former should be subject to conventional regulatory constraints, such as full Section 214 proceedings and tariff justification, or more recent regulatory innovations, such as the requirement of separate subsidiaries for enhanced service and equipment offerings.

As a result of these distinctions, most of the detailed provisions of the Communications Act are currently applicable only to the telephone companies, in general, and the former Bell System companies, in particular; although the FCC retains the authority to investigate any interstate carrier's practices or prices in response to a complaint or on its own initiative, as well as the authority to reimpose any Communications Act provisions it should deem necessary.

While each of these regulatory distinctions is clearly applicable—in some cases, principally so—to the data communications business, there are, in fact, relatively few regulatory or industry constraints on the provision of data communications services at this time. For low- to medium-speed data communications (e.g., 300–9600 bits/sec), capable of being carried by analog voice-communication channels, virtually any of the private line or switched public-message voice services of the numerous facilities-based and resale carriers may be used. Due to the widespread coverage of the traditional telephone networks, these have enjoyed a significant advantage over other carriers' services for occasional data communications needs; however, with essentially unrestricted sharing and resale opportunities, virtually any carrier can now handle such traffic on a nationwide basis.

For more specialized, higher-speed, data communications services which require either broader bandwidth or specially conditioned channels, there are fewer options, even though the market is fully open to competitive, largely unregulated, entry and operation. Several facilities-based carriers currently offer a wide range of both dedicated (i.e., private line) and switched data-communications services at speeds from 9600 bits/sec up to several million bits/second, all essentially unregulated. Several resale carriers offer packed-switched (as distinguished from dedicated or circuit-switched) public data-communications services under similar conditions. Other than the indirect effects that might result from local-telephone exchange-access charges or the competitive repricing of underlying transmission facilities/services, there is little reason to expect any significant change in the structure or regulation of this market. Moreover, with the growing number of technological alternatives to existing networks and services, actively encouraged by current policy and regulatory philosophies, even such indirect effects are much less likely to occur.

Data communications services have received relatively little regulatory attention in the past, except for occasional issues concerning interconnection, potential cross subsidies, and potential co-mingling of regulated "basic" and unregulated "enhanced" services. There is little reason to expect anything but less attention under current deregulatory philosophies. The principal threat that such services might be subjected to increased policy or regulatory scrutiny arises from the increased fungibility of voice and data networks and services. To the extent that competitive data communications services were to begin handling significant amounts of public-message voice telephone traffic, particularly so as to "bypass" the local telephone networks whose basic public telephone services are considered socially essential by many policy makers, such services could be subjected to many of the access charges/surcharges and bypass prohibitions currently applicable to competitive intercity voice services. The same result could also occur if predictions of a transition to all-digital networks for both voice and data services prove correct.

Modems, Multiplexers, and Concentrators

Raymond L. Pickholtz

Raymond L. Pickholtz is professor in, and a former chairman of, the Department of Electrical Engineering and Computer Science at The George Washington University. He received his Ph.D. in Electrical Engineering from the Polytechnic Institute of Brooklyn (now New York) in 1966. He was a researcher at RCA Laboratories and at ITT Laboratories. Dr. Pickholtz was on the faculty of the Polytechnic Institute of Brooklyn and of Brooklyn College. He was a visiting professor at the Université du Québec and the University of California. He has published scores of papers and holds six United States patents.

Raymond Pickholtz is a fellow of the Institute of Electrical and Electronic Engineers (IEEE) and is a recipient of the IEEE Centennial Medal. He was an editor of the *IEEE Transactions on Communications*. He is the editor of the Telecommunications Series for Computer Sciences Press. In 1990 he was elected President of the IEEE Communications Survey.

Dr. Pickholtz is president of Telecommunications Associates, a research and consulting firm specializing in Communication System disciplines.

Dr. Pickholtz wishes to add the following acknowledgements: "I have benefitted from discussions with **Dr. S. Quereshi on modems and with Mr. S.N. Weiner on STDMs. Dr. Quereshi and Mr. Weiner are both with** Codex Corporation. I also wish to thank the many manufacturers who supplied technical data on their products. Finally, I wish to thank Ms. Katia Foret for her diligent work in helping to prepare this second edition. The concern of inadvertently leaving any person out of any listing prevents the specific mention of anyone except where credit is given in the text for use of photographs or where specific mention is made as examples."

3.1 Introduction

The components of a data communications network that have the most intimate contact with the physical telecommunications transmission facilities are the *modems, multiplexers*, and *concentrators*. Modems are devices which permit data access via the ubiquitous and world-wide telephone voice network. Multiplexers and concentrators are used to aggregate data traffic and to reduce per unit cost of transmission facilities. The nature of the hardware circuitry and the degree of intelligence and special features that have been introduced into these devices over the past decade have been drastic and revolutionary. In the past few years and through the 1990s, digital transmission will become available through the Integrated Service Digital Network (ISDN), customer access to T1 lines (1.544 Mbps in North America and Japan, 2.048 Mbps in Europe) and possibly Fast Packet Switching, Asynchronous Transfer Mode (ATM) and Switched Multimegabit Data Service (SMDS). These new services will displace some modem applications and will alter the nature of multiplexer applications, but the principles involved will remain valid. In this chapter, we will describe the basic principles of operation and the special techniques that have made it possible to utilize existing transmission facilities with unprecedented efficiency and reliability.

3.1.1 Modems

"Modem" is a contraction of the words *MO*dulator and *DEM*odulator, which represents the principal transmitter and receiver operations, respectively, in a point-to-point transmission system. In actuality, these terms are misnomers in a digital communications environment, since the notion of modulation has its roots in analog communications. A digital signal is transmitted by selecting one of a *finite* number of symbols, *waveforms*, for transmission; the rate in symbols sent per unit time is called the *baud* rate. The transmitter function (Fig. 3-1) is then to convert a finite string of logical data symbols (usually binary digits or bits) into a sequence of physical symbols representing the data. The receiver function is to make a correct sequence of decisions on the sequence which will permit the recovery of the data.

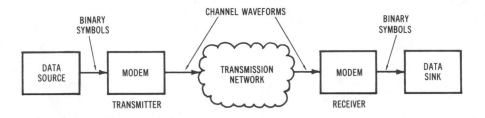

Fig. 3-1. A one-way point-to-point data link.

The attributes of the channel through which the symbols are transmitted dictates the nature of the physical symbols that are used to represent the data. In this chapter, we will focus on the use of voice-grade telephone channels which were designed originally to transmit analog voice signals in the frequency band of 300 to 3000 hertz. Thus, the signals used in modems must be tailored to fit into this band and must operate with the various constraints, impairments, and limitations that are associated with this channel.* The characteristics of the telephone voice channel are discussed in Section 3.3, and the special techniques of modulation, demodulation, equalization, and noise immunity that are currently used to maximize the use of this channel are described in Section 3.4. In Section 3.2, we will confine ourselves to a general description of the various classes of modems, their interfaces, and their uses in data networks.

3.1.2 Multiplexers and Concentrators

When data communications began to proliferate in the 1960s, it became apparent very quickly that the major cost in providing long-distance interconnections was the cost of transmission. This was, and continues to be, a major issue, whether we use private leased facilities (usually from a common carrier, such as AT&T, Sprint, or MCI), or whether we use the public network, such as public switched network telephone facilities.

Data communications tends to be bursty and nonsymmetric. That is, there are significant latent periods when little or nothing is sent, and the volume of data sent to one direction (say, from a computer) may be very much larger

---

*The word *modem* has taken a generic meaning so that we now have satellite modems, microwave modems, optical modems, etc., for describing techniques which interface directly to these media.

than that sent in the other direction (say, to a computer by a keyboard entry terminal used for queries). Furthermore, many devices, such as terminals, can, at most, generate data which is only a small fraction of the capacity of a voice-grade telephone channel. Similarly, workstations, files servers, and even Local Area Network (LAN) traffic rarely can fill the capacity of a T1 or T3 line. Now, since the cost of the channel per unit time is independent of the data rate (up to capacity), there is a large incentive to devise techniques by which: (1) many low-speed devices can share a channel and (2) the bursty and statistical fluctuations common to data communications are smoothed so that the transmitted aggregate data rate corresponds to the average rather than the peak rate generated by the devices. Both of these objectives (and other incidental ones) are achieved by the use of multiplexing.

As an illustration of the first need, suppose that a telephone channel, using a modem having a capacity of 4800 bits per second, is employed to support the transmission of sixteen co-located 300-bps terminals (Fig. 3-2A). Then, as shown in Fig. 3-2B, a multiplexer will save both the cost of lines and multiplexers. Of course, the crucial economic inequality is that two multiplexers,

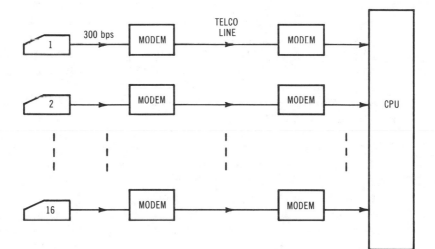

(A) Individual modems and lines.

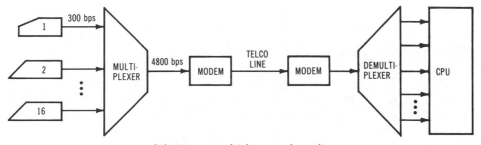

(B) Using a multiplexer and one line.

Fig. 3-2. Using multiplexers to save costs.

two 4800-bps modems, and a telephone company (TELCO) line must cost less than thirty-two 300-bps modems, and sixteen TELCO lines! However, this is invariably true with present-day tariffs and equipment costs. Furthermore, if the terminals are active only 5% of the time (a typical number), then by the use of buffering and a systematic framing structure and protocol between the multiplexer and the demultiplexer, we could use a "statistical" multiplexer which will, in principle, handle up to 320 terminals with an aggregate *average* rate ($320 \times 300 \times 0.05 = 4800$ bps) with only one TELCO line! Again, the question is whether such a "smart" multiplexer has a smaller incremental cost than the additional lines and modems that would be required to support 320 terminals, and the answer is usually yes. Finally, because such intelligent multiplexers usually come with programmable microcomputers that have a memory of 64K words and more, it is possible to achieve further efficiencies of about 2:1 by data compression and, in addition, perform some intelligent functions, such as automatic speed recognition for heterogeneous terminals, protocol intervention, system diagnosis, error control, and a variety of user programmable functions.

Inherently, a multiplexer is a concentrator in that it combines a large number of individual data lines into a single line. Traditionally, the word concentrator was used in data communications to denote devices which not only performed multiplexing to one output port, but which had a resident programmed and/or programmable processor that would perform switching and routing to several output ports as well as handling data compression, code conversion, error control, protocol functions, etc. Indeed, "Concentrator" and "Communications Processor" are often used interchangeably.

The role of the concentrator and the front-end processor is to relieve the central processor of the routine communications tasks of interfacing with the transmission network. With the present generation of intelligent statistical multiplexers having the capability to perform many of the tasks previously relegated to concentrators, the traditional concentrator has migrated upward to function as a sophisticated switching node in a large data network and to provide, in addition to the multiplexing functions, switching, network management, and complete like-protocol handling. Many of the details and applications of multiplexers and concentrators will be described in Sections 3.6 and 3.7.

3.2 Modem Types and Interfaces

In the early 1970s, there were about one-half million voice-band modems in use in the United States, mostly low speed (less than 300 bps), and mostly manufactured and installed by the Bell System (predecessor of AT&T and Bell Telephone operating companies). There are now millions of modems in use and scores of independent manufacturers supplying a wide variety of modems with speeds of 300, 1200, 2400, 4800, 9600, 14,400, and 19,200 bps, and possessing a diversity of special features that range from simple handshaking and bandsharing to sophisticated multiplexing, data compression, unattended autodial, and diagnostics.

3.2.1 Modems

Modems are classified as either asynchronous (no clock) or synchronous, which requires synchronizing the data stream to a clock. Asynchronous modems usually operate at speeds below 2400 bps, sending a character at a time. Modems operating above 2400 bps are invariably synchronous.

The speed at which modems operate is given in terms of *bits per second*. The symbol rate that is transmitted into the channel is given in *bauds* (symbols/sec.) and is either equal to the bit rate, as in modems operating at 1200 bps, or below (less than) the bit rate, depending on the modulation used. Modulation is discussed in detail later in this chapter.

Some modems are acoustically coupled into the telephone lines via a telephone handset transducer, while others are line drivers that operate at baseband (without modulation) directly into a metallic circuit. The following is a list of these modem types along with their speeds.

- Low speed (600 bps)
- Medium speed (1200, 1800, 2000, and 4800 bps)
- High speed (9600 bps, 14,400 bps, and 19,200 bps)
- Wideband (over 16,900 bps)—group band modems
- Short haul or limited distance
- Line drivers (modem eliminators)
- Acoustic couplers (telephone couplers)
- Touch-Tone™* modems

Modems are additionally classified in terms of their mode of transmission— point-to-point or multidrop, half duplex or full duplex, 2-wire or 4-wire—and also in terms of the types of lines they are to be operated on—dial-up lines, leased (telephone) lines, or nonloaded metallic wire (twisted pairs leased from the TELCO or self installed).

Half duplex (HDX) implies that the modem will operate in both directions but only one direction at a time, so the modem must be "turned-around" by going from the transmit to the receive mode. *Full duplex* (FDX) means that the modem will operate in both directions simultaneously.

Two-wire lines are most commonly used in connecting to the (dial-up) public data network; the transmit and receive signals are propagated together on a single pair of wires so the transmit and receive signals must be separated by a hybrid transformer (balanced bridge). Most of the long-haul part of the network uses a *4-wire* format. That is, there are two independent channels for transmitting and receiving (see Fig. 3-3). This arrangement creates conditions

---

*Touch-Tone is a trademark of American Telephone and Telegraph Co.

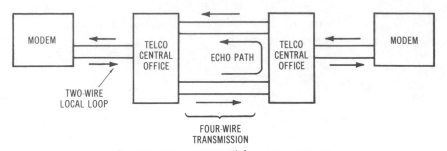

Fig. 3-3. Two-wire and four-wire circuits.

for *echoes*. On voice communications over long distances, these are handled by introducing "echo suppressors" whenever the echo delay (due to distance) exceeds about 150 milliseconds. Echo suppressors are "added attenuation" in the nontalking direction. For modems operating in full duplex, the echo suppressors must be disabled. More sophisticated full-duplex modems employ "echo cancelers" which adaptively cancel echoes.

Multidrop modems usually operate on leased 4-wire lines with a master modem polling many remote tributary modems in turn. Only the master modem and the polled modem communicate during any transmission internal. The polling cycle time is very sensitive to the time it takes for each modem to get ready to send upon being polled. Therefore, such modems should require no more than about 10 ms to respond. This is the interval between when the request to send (RTS) is received from the data terminal equipment (DTE) and when the clear to send (CTS), to which the modem responds, is sent back to the DTE. The ideas are illustrated in Fig. 3-4. It is possible to have polling through the dial-up network, but this exacerbates the response time problem, because dialing and connect time can exceed 20 seconds per poll.

The majority of modems are stand-alone, although a significant number of printed-circuit (PC) board modems and even large-scale integrated (LSI) chip-set modems are available to original equipment manufacturers (OEM) for insertion into modem racks, terminals, multiplexers, concentrators, and personal computers. The stand-alone modems are completely equipped with a power supply and are packaged with front-panel lights and a standard interface. A photograph of a recently introduced modem, the Codex 2234, is shown in Fig. 3-5. This modem has a built-in Automatic Call Unit (ACU) which can dial automatically. It operates at either 300 bps, 1200 bps/2400 bps asynchronous or 1200 bps/2400 bps synchronous and is compatible with many modems currently in use, such as the Bell-type 212 or V.22 bis. A plug-in modem card for the IBM PC or PS/2 with some of the same features is the 48720 or 48721, shown in Fig. 3-6. Both of these modems also permit switching the line from data mode to voice mode, and vice versa, and they use a standard interface which, in addition to passing data and control from a terminal or personal computer, may be used to pass autodial instructions.

Most modems built for the U.S. market are compatible with those made by the manufacturing arm of AT&T, and are designated as "Bell-type modems." The most common of these modems are listed in Table 3-1.

Table 3-1. Common Bell-Type Modems

Type	Data Rate (BPS)	Transmission Mode	Data Application*	Modulation
103 A,E,F,J	0-300	HDX or FDX	A	FSK
113 A,B,C	0-300	HDX or FDX	A	FSK
202 B	1200(on DDD) 1800(on Leased)	HDX	A	FSK
212 A	300 or 1200	FDX	A	QPSK
201 A,B,C	2400	HDX	S	QPSK
208 A,B	4800	HDX	S	DIFF, 8-PSK
209 A	9600	HDX	S	DIFF, 16-QAM

*A = Asynchronous; S = Synchronous

The Bell-type 103 modem is a full-duplex (FDX) unit which uses frequency-shift keying (FSK) and bandsharing in two separated portions of the voice telephone band. In the "originate" mode, the transmitter sends a 1270-Hz tone for a mark (binary "1") and 1070-Hz tone for a space (binary "0"). It simultaneously receives marks and spaces in the high band at 2225 Hz and 2025 Hz, respectively, for the reverse data path on the same voice channel. The "answer" modem at the other end reverses the roles so that it receives in the low band and transmits in the high band. This convention of originate and answer must be established to allow proper full-duplex operation. Some types of Bell-type 103 modems are frequently used for low data-rate (<300 bps) polling on multidrop lines, and newer versions have about an 8.5-ms turn-

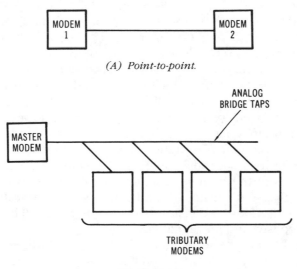

(A) Point-to-point.

(B) Multidrop.

Fig. 3-4. Point-to-point vs. multipoint modem configurations.

Fig. 3-5. The Codex 2234—a stand-alone modem. *(Courtesy Codex Corp., Division of Motorola, Inc.)*

around time. Acoustically coupled modems frequently operate as an "originate" type 103 modem.

The Bell-type 113 is essentially the same as the type 103 (in fact, they are totally compatible) and is either originate only (113 A,C) or answer only (113 B).* The Bell-Type 202 is a half-duplex (HDX) device which also operates with FSK at a rate up to 1200 bps on dial-up lines and 1800 bps on leased lines. The Bell-type 202 has been used in multidrop leased lines for polling, since the turnaround time can be as low as 10 ms. Bell-type 202 modems have a low data-rate reverse channel at 5 to 75 bps. The Bell-type 202 has also been used for acoustically coupled modems, but because of distortion and other limitations of the telephone handset, the 1200-bps data may be only marginally acceptable. The Bell-type 212A was developed to provide full-duplex operation at 1200 bps and it requires the use of Quaternary Phase Shift Keying (QPSK), which is described later in the chapter. Bell-type 212A modems have the ability to operate either at 300 bps or 1200 bps. They are compatible with the type 103/113 devices and will automatically switch speeds to perform an asynchronous to synchronous conversion.

The Bell-type 201 series are half-duplex synchronous modems that operate at 2400 bps using differential 8-PSK (described in Section 3.4) and are used extensively on 4-wire multidrop applications, since they have a very short turnaround time of about 8 ms (this is the delay between the "request to send" command and the "clear to send" response). The type-208 and type-209 series operate at 4800 and 9600 bps, respectively. The principal applications of these higher data rates have been to support multiplexed data and high-speed transfer file and graphics communications. There have also been applications for transmitting compressed (2400 bps) speech and data simultaneously, and for digital facsimile.

It must be stressed that the listing in Table 3-1 is not exhaustive, even for the Bell-type modems, and that most manufacturers make modems which are

---

*Both have the ability to receive as well as send. "Originate" and "Answer" refer only to the convention described above.

Fig. 3-6. The modem card for an IBM PC. *(Courtesy Codex Corp., Division of Motorola, Inc.)*

compatible with the Types 103, 113, 212, but not necessarily with the others. In fact, at the higher data rates of 4800 and 9600 bits per second, virtually all modems have at least the option of compatibility with the CCITT international standards that are designated as V.27 (which is also U.S. Federal Standard 1006) and V.29 (Federal Standard 1007). Even at 2400 bps, CCITT V.22 bis, is coming into use for FDX operation on dial-up lines. These modems do not necessarily correspond to any Bell-type and are described later in the chapter.

The maximum theoretical transmission rate on voice-grade lines is probably around 30 kbps, but the techniques required to get even close to that figure would be very costly at this time. With the use of special modulation techniques, sophisticated automatic equalizers, and the phase-tracking circuitry described later in Section 3.4, modern modems are now available that will work at 14.4 kbps and 19.2 kbps. The Codex 2680, Racal Milgo (1451PA) and the AT&T Paradyne 2698, for example, have developed 14.4 kbps modems, but they are not compatible and there are no standards yet at these rates.

3.2.2 Interfacing Modems

The physical interface between modems and DTEs have been standardized so that all stand-alone modems provide a 25-pin RS-232C/V.24 interface. This interface actually constitutes the lowest or physical-layer protocol used internationally and promulgated by the International Standards Organization (ISO) for its Open Systems Interconnect (OSI) reference model for computer networks. The RS-232C was introduced as a standard by the Electronic Industries Association (EIA). The Consultative Committee on International Telegraphy and Telephony (CCITT) promulgates international standards, and V.24 is essentially the same as RS-232C.

The physical interface protocol specifies pin connections, their functions, and their electrical characteristics, such as voltage levels for logic, impedances, maximum cable length, etc. Fig. 3-7 illustrates where the interface applies and gives a listing of the principal pins and their functions along with the EIA RS-232C and CCITT V.24 designations. Many of the pins in any given modem may not be used since they are assigned to functions, such as secondary signals or special functions, or are unassigned in the standard. The manufacturers provide details on how the standard is executed for their particular product. The transmit data (to the DCE or modem) and the receive data (from the DCE) is binary serial, with binary "zero" being a positive voltage and binary "one" being a negative voltage (the magnitudes must lie between 3 and 25 volts). CCITT V.28 is the equivalent electrical specification. This range departs from standard TTL logic, so that impedance matches must be applied. The other most commonly used pins refer to the control signals for handshaking operations between the DTE and the DCE. Although not specified in the

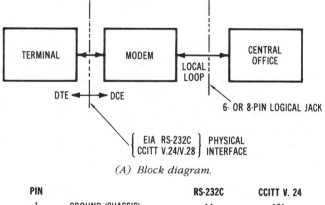

(A) Block diagram.

PIN		RS-232C	CCITT V. 24
1	GROUND (CHASSIS)	AA	101
7	COMMON (SIGNAL GROUND)	AB	102
2	TRANSMIT DATA	BA	103
3	RECEIVE DATA	BB	104
4	RS (REQUEST TO SEND)	CA	105
5	CS (CLEAR TO SEND)	CB	106
6	RY (MODEM READY)	CC	107
20	TERMINAL READY	CD	108
22	RI (RING INDICATOR)	CE	125
8	CO (CARRIER ON/OFF)	CF	109
21	SIGNAL QUALITY	CG	110

(B) Pin designations.

Fig. 3-7. Physical interfacing of modems for voice-grade lines.

standards, the most common 25-pin physical connection is called a DB-25, with the male on the DTE side and the female on the DCE side of the modem. In 1987 the EIA issued a revised version of RS 232 called RS 232D which specifies the D-connector and provides for communications testing.

Other interfaces for modems include the 37-pin EIA RS-449, RS-422, and RS-423, which were introduced to accommodate the increased functions then expected to develop in new equipment. With the advent of inexpensive microprocessors, however, it was possible to avoid having a single pin dedicated to a binary control function (e.g., RTS, CTS, etc.). The increased costs of large connectors, with their associated clumsy cables, have induced the introduction of a smaller 15-pin connector, which accomplishes a much larger repertoire of commands and responses by using sequences of binary data to designate many control signals—rather than a simple electrical high or low. This new standard is called CCITT X.20, for asynchronous operation, and CCITT X.21, for synchronous data. Further details are available in *Technical Aspects of Data Communication* (see reference 20) or directly from the CCITT "blue book."

3.3 The Voice-Grade Channel

The voice-grade channel for telephone use has evolved during the past 100 years into a worldwide and ubiquitous network approaching one billion telephones in every corner of the globe. They can each access the other through a vast network of trunks (involving wire pairs, cables, microwave and millimeter wave radio, fiber-optic cables, and satellites) and connected via a complex of switching systems (from the step-by-step electromechanical switches to modern stored-program-controlled electronic digital switches). Because the network is in place, because the addressing and internal signalling has been standardized, because the economy of scale has kept the price of a call at a reasonable level and, finally, because it is literally possible to access virtually any place on earth with existing equipment, this network was viewed from the onset of data communications in the early 1960s as an excellent candidate for providing data communications over long distances.

3.3.1 Background and Problems in Data Transmission

Unfortunately, telephone networks evolved with the objective of providing good (telephonic) quality *analog* voice communication and it was not designed for, nor did it take into consideration, the needs of data communications until fairly recently. The fine tuning of transmission facilities to accommodate voice meant that the emphasis was placed on sectioning the transmission medium into neat 4000-Hz units with filters that emphasized flat attenuation over each 4000-Hz band, without regard to phase delay. (Voice quality is relatively insensitive to variations in phase delay across the band; data and image transmission are not.) Even the twisted-wire pairs in cables are conditioned, by the use of "loading coils" spaced about 6000 feet apart, to flatten the attenuation vs. frequency response at the expense of degrading the differential delay of the frequency components in the voice band of 300 to 3300 Hz. This is illustrated in Fig. 3-8. In addition, for long distances, the 2-wire to 4-wire conversions are susceptible to undesirable echoes which are suppressed by attenuating the reverse direction when one party is talking.

For transmission of higher-speed data, these effects are most undesirable. Even when leased lines are used specifically for data transmission (Table 3-2), the same kind of voice-quality channel is provided, albeit loading coils and echo suppressors may be removed. For example, in the United States, arrangements are made through a tariff to provide a voice-grade leased facility called a 3002 channel specifically for data communications using voice-band facilities (see reference 2).

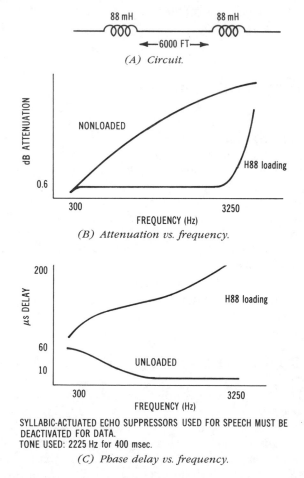

(A) Circuit.

(B) Attenuation vs. frequency.

SYLLABIC-ACTUATED ECHO SUPPRESSORS USED FOR SPEECH MUST BE DEACTIVATED FOR DATA.
TONE USED: 2225 Hz for 400 msec.

(C) Phase delay vs. frequency.

Fig. 3-8. Loading coils and echo suppressors on DDD telephone lines.

Table 3-2. Bell (AT&T) System Series Equipment for Data Transmission

Series Comments	Characteristics
100 (subvoice-grade lines)	Low Speed (0–300 bps) Serial
200 (voice-grade lines)	Medium Speed (1200–9600 bps) Serial
300 (group band and T1 lines)	Wideband (19.2, 40.8, 50, 230.4 kbps, 1.344, 1.544 Mbps)
400	Parallel
500 (submultiplexed T-carrier)	DDS (2.4, 4.8, 9.6, 56 kbps)
600	Acoustic Coupler, Special-Purpose
800	ACU, DAS, Channel-Terminating Units
900	Test Equipment

A typical frequency response curve of the attenuation is shown in Fig. 3-9, which indicates (by the dashed lines) that there is a wide range of attenuation responses possible, depending on how the line is routed, variations in time, etc. If a fixed equalizer is used which compensates for the variation in frequency, one can only hope to have a *compromise* equalizer which adjusts to the *average* line. A compromise equalizer also attempts to keep the relative phase delay constant over the band. At rates of 2400 bps or below, a fixed

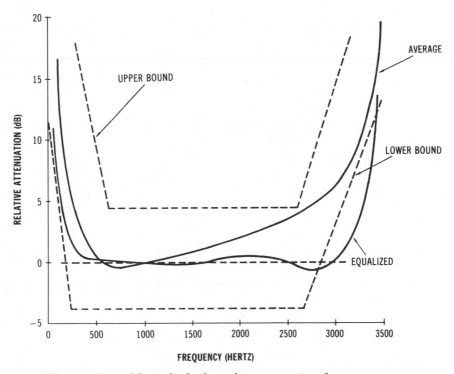

Fig. 3-9. Typical leased telephone line attenuation-frequency curve.

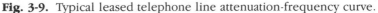

compromise equalizer, or a manually adjustable equalizer, may be all that is required to operate satisfactorily with properly designed modulation. At higher rates, the effect of improper frequency response, even to a minor degree, manifests itself in gross intersymbol interference (discussed later) which can render the data received useless. Also, since line responses vary over time (seconds and minutes) due to environmental conditions, power-supply variations, etc., it is impossible to maintain the desired response for data even with an adjustable equalizer which "tweaks" the particular line at setup. For this reason, at data speeds above 2400 bps, when using voice-grade lines, special automatic and adaptive equalizers must be used to adjust and track the line variations.

In addition, at the higher data rates, a more sophisticated modulation than the frequency-shift keying (FSK) discussed earlier must be used to get more bits per second for each hertz of bandwidth. Finally, at high speeds, careful attention must be paid to the many other impairments on real lines, such as noise, phase jitter (caused by frequency conversions in the analog multiplexer chains in the network), echoes, phase and gain "hits" (sudden changes in the amplitude and phase of a carrier signal), and harmonic distortion caused by nonlinear effects in amplifiers.

3.3.2 Conditioned Lines

In order to alleviate some of these problems, telephone administrations offer (for an additional monthly fee) to condition leased lines so that the lines are somewhat more tightly controlled for the requirements of data transmission. For example, so-called C-conditioning insures a tighter control of the attention and (envelope) delay (distortion) than the basic 3002 line. These controls are illustrated in Fig. 3-10, which shows the control on attenuation (solid lines) and the differential delay (dashed lines) across the voice band.

Table 3-3 summarizes the delay constrained for C1, C2, and C4 conditioning, and Fig. 3-11 shows that all the other impairments on the basic (3002) line are not controlled by conditioning. For very high data rates at 14.4 and 16 kbps, or in areas where the basic lines are very noisy, D conditioning may be necessary (at additional cost) to control the signal-to-noise ratio and harmonic distortion. Since C conditioning is essentially a compromise, or at most a fixed

Table 3-3. Delay Tolerances for Voice-Grade Conditioned Lines

μs Differential Delay (Freq Range, kHz)		
C1	**C2**	**C4**
<1000 (1.0–2.4)	<500(1.0–2.6)	<300(1.0–2.6)
<1750 (0.8–2.6)	<1500(0.6–2.6)	<500(0.8–2.8)
(Unconditioned)	<3000(0.5–2.8)	<1500(0.6–3.0)
		<3000(0.5–3.0)

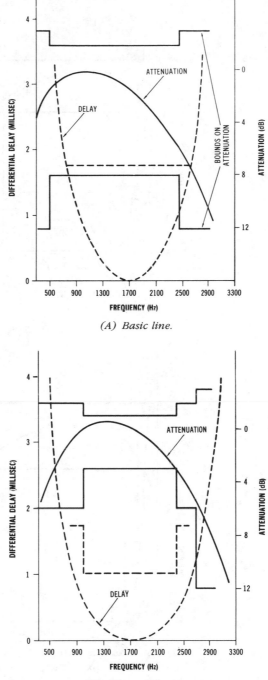

(A) *Basic line.*

(B) *C1 conditioning.*

Fig. 3-10. Conditioned lines. *(cont. on next page)*

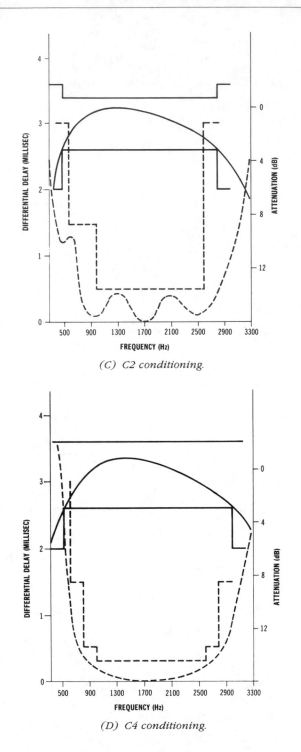

(C) C2 conditioning.

(D) C4 conditioning.

Fig. 3-10. (cont.)

	INTERNAL PRACTICE	CONTROLLED TO TARIFF SPECIFICATIONS	
	BASIC LINE	C COND.	D COND.
• ATTENUATION DISTORTION	✓	✓	SAME AS BASIC
• ENVELOPE DELAY DISTORTION	✓	✓	
• SIGNAL-TO-NOISE RATIO	✓		✓
• HARMONIC DISTORTION	✓		✓
• IMPULSE NOISE	✓		
• FREQUENCY SHIFT	✓	SAME AS BASIC	SAME AS BASIC
• PHASE JITTER	✓		
• ECHO	✓		
• PHASE HITS	X		
• GAIN HITS	X		
• DROPOUTS	X		

Fig. 3-11. Line conditioning.

manually adjustable compromise equalizer, many modern modems operating at or below 4800 bps have a built-in compromise equalizer and frequently do not require conditioning.

3.3.3 Intersymbol Interference, Eye Patterns, and Line Errors

In data transmission, the objective is to transmit symbols (one every T seconds) so that the receiver modem can make a proper sequence of decisions, even though noise and timing errors (which can cause an error in deciding the correct symbol) are always present to some degree. It is *not* necessary to preserve the fidelity of the waveforms that are sent, as in analog transmissions, but it is necessary to avoid confusing a symbol with another one. The principle potential source of this confusion is caused by *intersymbol interference* (ISI), which is due to the fact that a short finite-duration (T seconds) pulse transmitted into a band-limited channel will emerge as a time-dispersed signal that lasts more than T seconds. This is illustrated in Fig. 3-12. The dispersion is caused by the fact that the frequency components making up the input pulse are differentially attenuated and, more importantly, differentially delayed so that at the output of the channel, the frequency components do not reconstitute the input pulse. And, since some components are delayed more than others, the output will be spread or dispersed over a much longer interval than T. The trouble with this is that if we want to put other (different) pulses into the channel every T seconds, so that we can signal at a 1/T baud rate (symbols/seconds), then, at the output of the channel, the dispersed responses from all of these will interfere with one another. This is the effect of intersymbol interference.

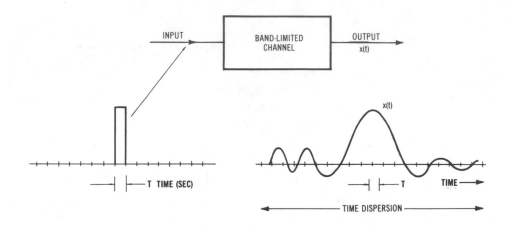

Fig. 3-12. Dispersion in a band-limited channel.

It is conceivable that, if we *knew* each symbol and *how* it is affected by the channel *separately*, we could devise a scheme for canceling or subtracting out the effects of the *other* pulses while we are examining any one for decision. The trouble is (1) we do *not* know what the symbols are at the receiver (for otherwise what would be the purpose in sending them?) and (2) the channel response, even if it were measured and known once, would change as we were using it. As an illustration, in a typical telephone channel, the pulse dispersion is of the order of 10 ms. Therefore, to avoid intersymbol interference by brute force, we can put no more than one symbol into the channel every 10 ms or, equivalently, operate at 100 baud.

Fortunately, in data transmission, it is not necessary to preserve the fidelity of the symbol, only to identify it from others. Thus, intersymbol interference (ISI) can be avoided if we arranged the response of the channel to go through zero (or, in practice, a very small value) every T seconds while maintaining a high value at its "main-bang," as shown in Fig. 3-13.* This will ensure that the other symbols occurring every T seconds will not be interfered with. There is a hitch however, and that is that the timing must be very good and the channel must not change. The evaluation of the effects of intersymbol interference, which is the principal practical barrier to high data transmission on band-limited facilities (such as telephone lines) is to observe the effects of the *superimposition* of a large string of symbols at the output of the channel called the *eye pattern*.

"Ideal" eye patterns are shown in Fig. 3-14. Each represents *all* of the *possible* waveforms that *could* appear over three symbol intervals (in this example). That is, if the data sequence is a random pattern of binary symbols (. . . $a_{-2} a_{-1} a_0 a_1 a_2$ . . .) where the "a's" are randomly chosen to be +1 or −1 (to represent binary "1" and binary "0", respectively), then the eye pattern is the *collection* of possible waveforms superimposed.

---

*There are conditions on the frequency response due to the Nyquist interval which guarantee this condition provided that the bandwidth is BW $\geq 1/2T$. The most common of these is the "raised cosine" spectrum often used as a compromise equalizer.

$$y(t) = \sum a_k x(t - kT)$$

That is, if the data string is, say, 30 bits long, then there are $2^{30} \cong 10^9$ possible waveforms superimposed to represent the eye pattern. The important point in Fig. 3-14, however, is that, if the channel response is perfectly time-domain equalized, as in Fig. 3-13, then when the receiver samples precisely at a symbol sampling time which is an integer multiple of T (say, mT), then $x(mT - kT) = 0$, except for $k = m$ and $y(mT) = a_m$. If the symbol a_m was +1, it will be received as +1; if it was −1, it will be received as −1 *without* ISI.

The "lined and crosshatched" areas represent all the other waveforms that could result from all possible data patterns. *At the sampling times, the values are exactly what was sent regardless of the other data.* In an ideal, perfectly equalized eye, the full noise margin is realized, which is the range from the decision threshold to the peak signal level(s). If, however, the timing is offset, then the full noise margin is not realized. Thus, the quality of transmission performance in the presence of both noise and timing "jitter" depends on having both a fully equalized eye *and* a wide margin against timing. Figs. 3-14A and 3-14B contrast two perfectly equalized channels with different tolerances against timing jitter.

Fig. 3-15 shows an eye pattern which results from a poorly equalized channel. The noise margin is reduced, the eye is skewed, and its maxima do not line up with the symbol timing, so the residual timing margin is low. In the extreme, the eye pattern is completely closed, and the ability to discriminate symbols is nonexistent even without noise. All of these effects are caused by ISI, which gets worse with increasing symbol rate, since, even if we were able to time-domain equalize the channel, as in Fig. 3-13 for symbol rate 1/T, if we doubled the rate using that channel, it would no longer be equalized since $x(mT/2)$ would no longer be zero at integer values of m. As stated earlier, the total dispersion on a typical telephone channel is about 10 ms. Therefore, if we try to operate at 1200 baud, we must control the values of $x(t)$ at 10 ms $\times$ 1200 = 12 points. If we raise the rate to 2400 baud, we need to equalize 24 points in the time domain. At higher rates, or when special signalling is used to increase the number of bits/baud, as in 9600- and 14,400-bps modems (see

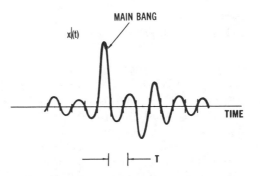

Fig. 3-13. A channel response with no intersymbol interference.

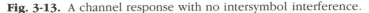

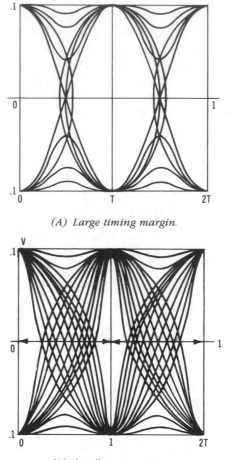

(A) Large timing margin.

(B) Small timing margin.

Fig. 3-14. ''Ideal'' binary baseband eye pattern.

Section 3.4), then we may be required to equalize over 15 ms or more, so it is not uncommon to have to control 60 or even 128 points in the response.

3.3.4 Adaptive Equalizers and Adaptive Echo Cancelers

The modern method for achieving time-domain equalization is to use a transversal filter (tapped delay-line structure), as shown in Fig. 3-16. The unequalized baseband signal is applied on the left, propagates through the delay line towards the right and symbol-delayed versions are available at the taps* for

---

*This is the so-called T structure where the delay increments, T, are the reciprocal of the symbol rate, 1–T baud. Many modem equalizers use the T/2-structure with delay increments of T/2, which requires twice the number of taps but offers significant advantages.

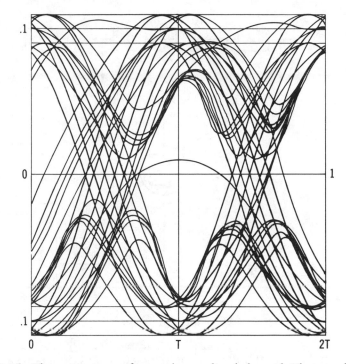

Fig. 3-15. The eye pattern of a poorly equalized channel. The eye diagram has ISI and timing error.

multiplication by a set of N-weight coefficients, C_0, C_1, . . . C_{N-1}, before being summed. It can be shown that in order to control N points on the channel response, it takes about N taps. The most commonly used algorithm for controlling the taps, which converges to an equalized response (or an open eye), is the so-called Linear Mean Squared (LMS) Steepest Descent algorithm, which for the nth tap gain is an iteration from time K to time K + 1:

$$C_n(k+1) = c_n(k) - s(e_k \cdot r(t - nt + kt))$$

where e_k is the "error" at time kT between the (partially) equalized output z(t) and either the Training Sequence, T(t), or the output data, d(t); i.e.,

$$e_k = z(kt - T(kT)) \qquad \text{(during training)}$$

or

$$e_k = z(kt - \hat{d}(kT)) \qquad \text{(during tracking)}$$

The equalizer operates first in a training mode, whereby the transmitter sends a predetermined "pseudo-random noise" (PN) sequence which is also known to and generated at the receiver. The resulting error, e_k, is multiplied by the delayed received signal r(t − nT − kT) to determine the magnitude and

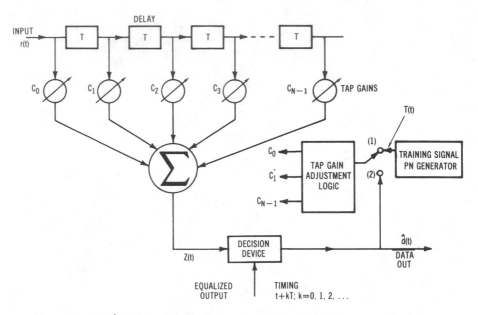

Fig. 3-16. Tapped delay-line automatic and adaptive equalizer.

polarity of the adjustment to the corresponding tap. s is a fixed constant which scales the "step-size" of each adjustment in order to ensure smooth convergence. After the training mode is completed (about 20 ms for 4800-bps modems to several hundred milliseconds for 14.4 kbps modems using a very large number of taps), the equalizer automatically switches to the tracking mode in position (2) of Fig. 3-16 and derives its reference from the reconstructed data, $\hat{d}(t)$, available by making decisions on the equalized signal, $z(t)$. Since the reconstructed data now is derived from an equalized signal with a high noise margin, it is good enough to be used in place of the training PN sequences to derive the error, and the equalizer will now adaptively adjust to the slow changes in the channel. This is an example of decision feedback which is used in many other forms in digital communications. An LMS equalizer is stable, fast, and digitally implementable with either LSI chips or a special-purpose digital signal-processing (DSP) microcomputer. Even a general-purpose microcomputer will work, if it is fast enough. Fig. 3-17 shows some actual oscillograms of the effects of automatic equalization. An excellent review of the current status of adaptive equalization is found in *Adaptive Equalization*,[22] and good treatments of the theoretical foundations are reported in *Digital Communications*.[11,21]

In modern high-speed modems, which are implemented almost entirely by digital processing, four adaptive equalizers are usually required to handle the modulated (nonbaseband) signal, and the tap gains may require complex multiplication (four real multiplies). The adaptive equalizer then consumes the largest amount of processing resources in the modem. Without it, however, operation or voice-grade lines above 2400 bps would not be possible.

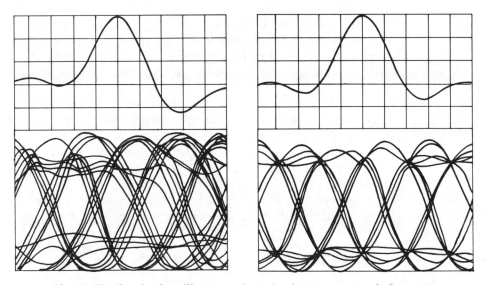

Fig. 3-17. Sketch of oscillograms of received eye pattern and after auto-equalization. *(From "Common Carrier Data Communication" by R.W. Lucky; Chapter 5 in* Computer-Communication Networks, *F.F. Kuo, ed., Prentice Hall, 1973.)*

An impairment with fundamentally the same effects as intersymbol interference due to pulse dispersion is the *echo*. Echoes are caused by reflections at mismatches in the transmission medium. In voice-grade facilities, the primary point of mismatch is at the hybrid circuits which convert 4-wire to 2-wire. Echoes are particularly troublesome in full-duplex data communications since echo suppressors (voice- or signal-actuated switches) cannot be used. The echoes involved when satellite lines are part of the channel can cause significant deterioration of the error performance of a modem and, because of the very large delays (greater than 250 ms), special techniques are required. One of the most promising of these techniques is that of the *echo canceler*. An echo canceler is an adaptive filter which selectively eliminates echoes. It operates on the same principle as that of an adaptive equalizer using a tapped delay-line transversal filter whose coefficients are adjusted by a Linear Mean Squared Steepest Descent algorithm (described before). The error for driving the algorithm is obtained from the difference of the echo simulated by the transversal filter and the actual echo. There has been much work and many field trials of adaptive echo cancelers at Bell Telephone Laboratories and at COMSAT Laboratories. Some of the newest modems operating at 9600 bps and higher have echo cancelers. An excellent introductory article on the subject is *Echo Cancellation in the Telephone Network* by Stephen Weinstein.[27]

3.3.5 Error Statistics

In the final analysis, a modem has value only if it delivers data at the specified rate with an error rate which is acceptable. The error rate referred to here is the "raw error rate" before error coding for detection and/or correction is applied. For alphanumeric natural-language text, an error rate of 10^{-5} to 10^{-6} is usually acceptable. In other applications, or where several communication hops are required, the acceptable bit error rate (BER) may be required to be better than this.

In real applications using telephone lines, it is usually not possible to calculate or predict this BER due to trunk differences that have different noise, phase, jitter, bits, and other impairments as discussed above. In practice then, one must be content to disclose that a certain percentage of lines or connections will yield performance that is better than desired. The 1970 Bell System connection survey for using data modems on telephone lines provided an experimental basis for such statements. An example of the results of this survey is shown in Fig. 3-18. Other surveys are continuing all over the world.

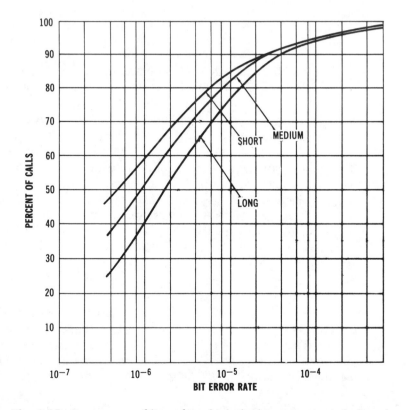

Fig. 3-18. Percentage of lines for which the bit error rate is below the abscissa for short- and long-distance connections operating with a modem speed of 1200 bps. *(From "High Speed Voice Data Performance on the Switched Telecommunication Network" by M.D. Balkovic, et al;* Bell System Technical Journal, *Vol. 50, No. 4, April 1971.)*

3.4 Digital Modulation and Demodulation

3.4.1 The Need for Modulation

Most communications, and, in particular, the voice-grade channel, will permit signals to be transmitted in a limited band of frequencies. Therefore, any information-bearing signal must be such that most, if not all, of its power spectral density lies within this band. The voice-grade channel has a usable bandwidth of about 3 kHz (300 to 3300 Hz), so that any signals that are used must lie in this band. The most convenient way of ensuring this is to use sinusoidal signals of the form

$$A(t)\cos(2\pi ft + \theta(t))$$

where,
  f is the carrier frequency,
  A and θ are the amplitude and phase, respectively, which may be time varying.

The modulation of a sinusoid thus consists of varying either the amplitude or the phase with time, as required, with the information or data signal sequence.

Note that frequency modulation technically can be viewed as a special case of phase modulation, since the rate of change of $\theta(t)$ represents a change in frequency. Any change in the parameters of a sinusoid will spread the spectrum occupied by the generation of sidebands around the carrier frequency. The amount of total spectrum occupied by a digital modulation of the sinusoid depends proportionately on the symbol rate or the rate at which the parameters are disturbed. As we will see later, the bandwidth occupied may be much less than the bit rate if each symbol represents several bits. The simplest situation is where each bit of data causes a potential change in only one parameter of the sinusoid—say, the frequency. This is discussed next as binary frequency-shift keying (FSK). In order to operate at rates above 2400 bps within the constraints of the voice bandwidth, it is necessary to use sinusoidal signals whose parameters of amplitude and phase can take on more than two values during any symbol interval; this will be shown subsequently under the discussion of PSK and QAM.

3.4.2 Binary Frequency-Shift Keying

Binary frequency-shift keying (FSK) is very easy to generate (modulate) and detect (demodulate). Consider sending $A\cos 2\pi f_0 t$ for a binary "0" and $A\cos 2\pi f_1 t$ for a binary "1." If the data rate is **R** bps, then a frequency separation of $f_0 - f_1 = (3/2)R$ is sufficient to allow reliable discrimination at rate **R**/second. For example, if we use 1270 Hz for a "0" and 1070 Hz for a "1," then $f_0 - f_1 = 200$, and a rate **R** of 300 bps can be supported. The sidebands generated as this speed will spread the resulting signal over approximately $2 \times 300 = 600$ Hz. This is the basis of the Bell 103- and 113-type modems discussed earlier in this chapter. Since the voice bandwidth is considerably larger than 600 Hz, another FSK signal can be bandshared for the reverse direction on the same channel, as shown in Fig. 3-19A. The shaded areas indicate the signal power density of the originate (high band) and answer (low band) transmitted.

Demodulation of binary FSK is particularly easy, since the information is contained in the rate of zero crossings. A commonly used demodulator is to count the average number of high-frequency clock pulses (several megacycles) that occur between zero crossings. If the count is high, it represents a large interval between zero crossings, and the low frequency (mark) is decided; the reverse for a space. This kind of detection is called ''noncoherent'' since the reception is independent of the phase of the signal. The result of this simplicity in generation and detection is that FSK modems, where they can be used, are very inexpensive and are available for as little as $100, or less, in pc-board form.

FSK modems suffer from extravagant use of the bandwidth so that, at rates above 1200 bps on voice-grade lines, other modulation types, such as *phase-*

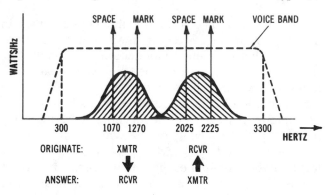

(A) Spectrum of the Bell 103/113-type FDX 0–300-bps FSK modem.

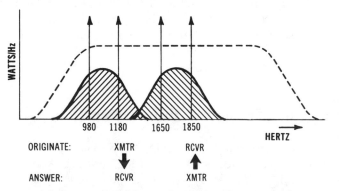

(B) Spectrum of the V.21 FDX 0–300-bps FSK modem.

Fig. 3-19. Signaling frequencies and

shift keying (PSK) and *quadrature amplitude modulation* (QAM) must be used.

3.4.3 Phase-Shift Keying and Quadrature Amplitude Modulation

3.4.3.1 Phase-Shift Keying (PSK)

In order to squeeze more bps into a given bandwidth (W, Hz), it is necessary to use a larger alphabet of symbols so that each symbol, as it is transmitted, carries more than one bit. For example, if four symbols are available, then each can be associated uniquely with one of the four binary pairs (dibits) 00, 01, 11, 10. The bandwidth occupied by a signal is proportional to the *symbol* rate. Therefore, for a given symbol rate and a given bandwidth, we can increase the information rate in bits per second by having each symbol represent several bits. In general, if we use one of **M** symbols every **T** seconds, then we have a symbol rate of 1/T baud and an information rate of R = $\log_2$M/T bits per second. Thus, R/W is proportioned to $\log_2$ M and we can get more bps/Hz by increasing **M**.

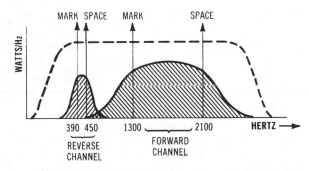

(C) Spectrum of the V.23 HDX 0–1200-bps modem with a 75-bps FSK reverse channel.

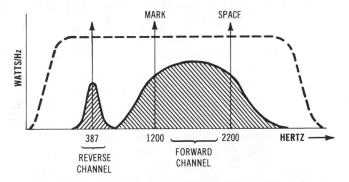

(D) Spectrum of the 202-type HDX 0–1200-bps FSK modem with 5–150-bps on/off keyed reverse channel.

spectra of asynchronous FSK modems.

The simplest set of symbols which can be characterized by changing a single parameter of a sinusoid is called phase-shift keying (PSK). For M-ary PSK, the waveform in a symbol interval (O, T) is

$$Sk(t) = A\cos(2\pi f_0 t + 2\pi k/M); \qquad k = 0,1, \ldots M{-}1, m0 \geq t \geq T$$

where,
   A is the amplitude,
   A^2 is proportional to the power,
   f_0 is the "carrier frequency,"
   $2\pi k/M$ is the phase depending on the parameter k.

It is convenient to represent the M-possible PSK signals as a set of points on a circle of radius A. For example, if M = 8, then for every three bits of data (tribit), a different phase is selected uniformly along the circumference of a circle of radius A. This is illustrated in Fig. 3-20A. The carrier frequency, f_0, is chosen typically to be around the middle of the band and sent so that no harmonics will interfere with the in-band signalling tones used between switching centers.

A common choice (and a CCITT standard for many modems) is 1800 Hz $\pm$ 1 Hz. A potential problem with straight PSK, as described, is that, since phase must be measured relative to a reference, pure PSK would require either the separate transmission of a phase reference or else a mechanism for unambiguously extracting a phase reference from the modem signal waveform itself. Neither of these alternatives is desirable nor necessary. Instead of the information tribits being encoded directly into phases, the tribits are used to effect a *phase change* from the previously transmitted phase.

This technique is called *differential phase-shift keying* (DPSK). Using this method, the previous symbol waveform becomes the phase reference for demodulating the current set of tribits. The particular differential-PSK signal constellation used for transmission of 4800 bps in the Model 208 modem is shown in Fig. 3-20A. Fig. 3-20B shows the signal spectrum centered about the carrier at 1800 Hz when the symbol rate is 1600 baud (1600 symbols/second $\times$ 3 bits/symbol = 4800 bps). The nominal bandwidth occupied by the sidebands is 2 $\times$ 1600 = 3200 Hz, centered at 1800 Hz, so that the signal barely fits into the voice band as shown. The result is considerable ISI, so that an adaptive equalizer is necessary. The tribits are chosen so that adjacent phases differ by only one bit (Grey code) and, since an automatic equalizer is used at this rate, the data is scrambled or randomized in a clever way (described in the following) so that the equalizer doesn't adjust to some periodic pattern in the data and so that the signal spectrum is evenly spread across the band. The relationship of the scrambled tribits and the corresponding phase changes for the 208 modem and for CCITT V.27 modems (also 4800 bps) are shown in Fig. 3-20A. Note the Grey coding. The CCITT constellation is the same except that it is rotated clockwise by 22.5 degrees so that 001 corresponds to a phase change of 0°. A significant advantage of not having a phase change of 0 is that phase changes always take

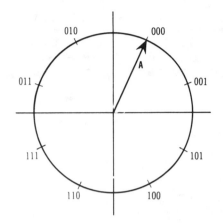

(A) Differential phase-signal constellation for 208-type modems (CCITT V.27 modems are offset −22.5°).

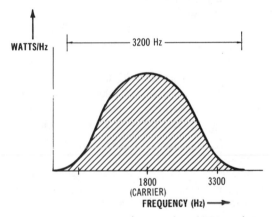

(B) Power spectrum of a 1200-baud PSK modem.

Fig. 3-20. Differential 8-PSK-208-type and CCITT V.27-type modems.

place at the symbol rate, and this fact is used to extract a symbol clock directly from the modulated signal.

For modems which operate at 2400 bps, differential 4-PSK (sometimes called DQPSK, with Q for *quaternary*) is used. Again, an 1800-Hz carrier is used at 1200 baud, but since only four phase changes are possible, we have 2-bits/symbol × 1200 symbols/second = 2400 bps. At 1200 baud, the signal spectrum is nominally 2400 Hz and fits easily with the voice band so that adaptive equalization is not necessary. In fact, this speed is often a fallback mode for higher-speed modems when the channel is poor. Manual equalization is frequently all that is required, but even if adaptive equalization is used for improved performance, it requires few taps and the training time is very short. There are two signal constellations, as shown in Table 3-4, used for

Table 3-4.   Differential Phases*

| Dibit | Phase Change (Degrees) | |
	Alternative A	Alternative B
00	0	45
01	90	135
11	180	225
10	270	315

*Differential phases for 2400-bps modems under CCITT V.26. (Bell-type 201 was alternative B.)

2400-bps QPSK modems. As before, alternative B has the advantage of mitigating the extraction of symbol timing from the signal.

Since the bit rate can seemingly be increased for a given symbol (and hence a given bandwidth) by increasing the *number* of phases, why not keep going? That is, why not use 16 bits (4 bits) or even 256 (8 bits) phases so that at 1200 baud we would get $4 \times 1200 = 4800$ or $8 \times 1200 = 9600$ bps, respectively? The answer is that impairments on the channel, such as noise, phase jitter, harmonic distortion, and intersymbol interference eventually prevent the reliable discrimination of the symbols and cause an intolerably large error rate. For Gaussian noise alone, using only *binary* signals with optimum detection, the relationship between the bit error rate (BER) and the signal-to-noise ratio is given in Fig. 3-21 for various modulations. For example, a signal-to-noise ratio greater than 10 dB (a factor of 10) is necessary to achieve a barely acceptable BER of 1 in 10^5.

For larger symbol alphabets where the objective is to achieve a larger number of bps/Hz, it becomes necessary to increase the required signal-to-noise ratio as the number of symbols used increase. This observation is shown quantitatively in Fig. 3-22 which is plotted for various modulation schemes. Each curve corresponds to a particular modulation, and the (hidden) parameter is the symbol alphabet size. For example, as we move up on the PSK curve, we have **M** equals 2, 4, 8, and 16 possible phases. All curves are shown for a fixed BER of 10^{-6}. Thus, if we use 4-PSK, we could get about 2.5 bps/Hz at a BER of 10^{-6}, provided the signal-to-noise ratio is at least 17 dB (about 50:1). These curves cannot be used directly on real channels, such as voice-grade lines, since they do not take into account impulse noise, phase jitter, intersymbol interference, harmonic distortion, amplitude hits, etc. All of these exacerbate the problem so that either a much larger signal-to-noise ratio is required in a specified bps/Hz or, more likely, is given a limitation or impairments as there is a practical limit on the bps/Hz.

Notice that FSK is poor in its use of bandwidth and that is why it is not used for higher data rates. DPSK, which is used as discussed earlier for 2400- and 4800-bps modems, is better, but quadrature amplitude modulation (QAM), discussed next, is still better. Single-sideband (SSB) is no longer used

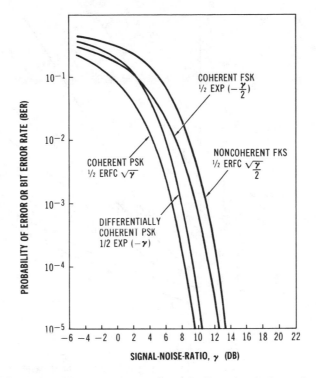

Fig. 3-21. Bit error rate vs. signal-to-Gaussian noise ratio.

on voice-band modems. There is an absolute theoretical limit (due to Shannon) and that limit implies that it is *possible* to achieve that performance even at bit error rates lower than 10^{-6} (in fact, an arbitrarily small BER). For example, at 30 dB, this limit gives approximately 10 bps/Hz, which translates to about 30 kbps or a 3 kHz channel, but techniques for doing this are not economically feasible at this time.

The first serious impairment we encounter in the use of multiple-PSK is phase jitter. The effects of various impairments on QPSK is shown in Fig. 3-23. Without impairments, there would be only four possible points in the received constellation. Over a large sequence of data, each symbol, as received, will experience a perturbation due to noise, distortion, phase jitter, etc., and will be seen in a randomly different position. The diagrams are called *scatter diagrams* or *two-dimensional eye patterns* and are used for diagnostics, by presentation on an oscilloscope. It is seen that phase jitter ultimately limits the number of phases that can be used or, equivalently, the number of signal points that can be placed around a circle. If the rms phase jitter in degrees is close to the angular spacing of phase points, then the ability to discriminate them at the receiver is greatly impaired, and the error rate quickly becomes unacceptable.

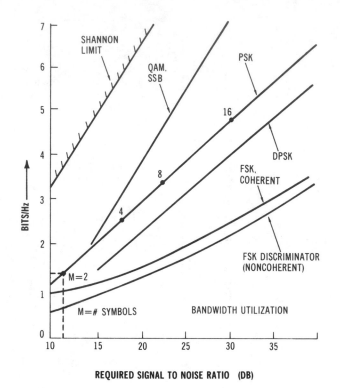

Fig. 3-22. Bit-per-sec/Hz vs. signal-to-noise ratio for a BER = 10^{-6}
in Gaussian noise.

3.4.3.2 Quadrature Amplitude Modulation (QAM)

The solution to the problem of phase jitter, given that we cannot expand the circle due to power limitations, is to place the additional symbols on other concentric circles so that any pair are sufficiently phase separated. To guard against the other impairments, the signal points must be as far apart from one another as well. The general method of setting up a signal constellation in a plane is called *quadrature amplitude modulation* (QAM), since it establishes each signal point in the plane by specifying the *amplitudes* x and y along the *quadrature* (perpendicular) axes. A sinusoidal signal of fixed frequency, with amplitude and phase parameters, can be related to a sum of properly scaled cosine and sine waves called the *in-phase* and *quadrature* components, respectively, by the trigonometric identity:

$$A\cos(2\pi f_0 t + \theta) = x\cos(2\pi f_0 t) - y\sin(2\pi f_0 t)$$

where,

   x = Acos θ,
   y = Asin θ.

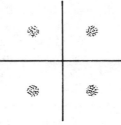

(A) Gaussian noise.

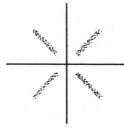

(B) Harmonic distortion.

(C) Phase jitter and frequency translation distortion.

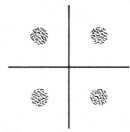

(D) Noise, attenuation, and intersymbol interference.

Fig. 3-23. Scatter diagrams—effects of various impairments
on QPSK as received.

Thus, to generate any point (x,y) in the 4 × 4 signal or V.29 constellation shown in Fig. 3-24, we need only to amplitude modulate a cosine with x and a sine with y, as shown in Fig. 3-25.

The 4×4 lattice is used in Bell-type 9600-bps and V.29 modems; both use a 1700-Hz carrier frequency operating at 2400 baud giving $2400 \times 4 = 9600$ bps. The V.29 is now used by virtually all manufacturers. The method for obtaining the coordinates (x,y) of the signal points is also different for these constellations. The V.29 constellation consists of four points on four concentric circles of relative radius $\sqrt{2}$, 3, $3\sqrt{2}$, and 5 and there are eight possible phase changes, as shown in Fig. 3-26. The assignment of the quadbits to each of the sixteen signal points is cleverly done to minimize the effects of impairments. Grey coding is used to keep adjacent signal points differing by as few bits as possible, and the differential phase is switched among the four quadrants to minimize intersymbol interference and to insure that phase-reference errors do not propagate.

The logic of quadbit assignments Q_1, Q_2, Q_3, and Q_4 (with the first appearing first in time) is given in Table 3-5. The last three quadbits, Q_2, Q_3, and Q_4, determine the phase change and the first quadbit, Q_1, determines one of four amplitudes, depending on its value and the absolute phase. Fallback modes are provided for 7200 and 4800 bps without changing the symbol rate of 2400

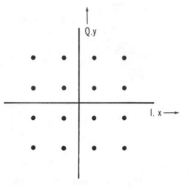

(A) 4×4 QAM, 9600 bps.

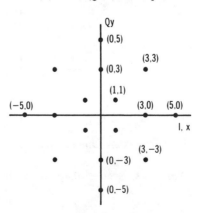

(B) V.29 QAM, 9600 bps.

Fig. 3-24. QAM signal constellation used

baud by using the last three bits as a tribit and setting $Q_1 = 0$ for 7200 bps and by using only Q_2 and Q_3 as a dibit, as shown in Table 3-6 (for 4800 bits with fixed amplitude = 3). At 4800 bps, this assignment is identical to V.26, alternative A QPSK, as given in Table 3-4. A summary of the characteristics of V.29 and other CCITT synchronous modems is provided in Table 3-7.

3.4.3.3. Error Coding and Trellis-Coded Modulation

Modems for voice-grade lines have, up to now, not usually been equipped with forward error-correcting (FEC) coding capability. There have been only rare applications when FEC equipment, as an add-on device, has been used for data transmission via voice-band modems. For example, when a reverse channel and/or data buffering (both of which are necessary for ARQ protocols) is not available, then FEC is a necessary alternative. Although many powerful error-correcting coding techniques have been known and used for other applications, their use in data communications via modems has found little

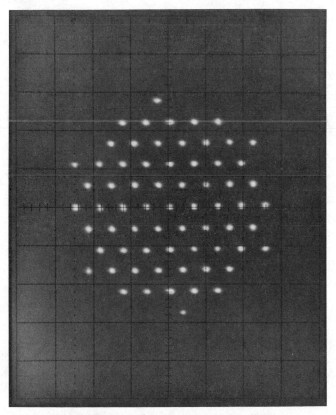

(C) Oscillogram of Codex SP 14.4 constellation.

for 2400-baud voice-grade modems.

Table 3-5. Logic for V.29 QAM Constellation

Q_2	Q_3	Q_4	Phase Change
0	0	1	0°
0	0	0	45°
0	1	0	90°
0	1	1	135°
1	1	1	180°
1	1	0	225°
1	0	0	270°
1	0	1	315°

Absolute Phase	Q_1	Relative Signal Element Amplitude
0°,90°,180°,270°	0	3
	1	5
45°,135°,225°,315°	0	$\sqrt{2}$
	1	$3\sqrt{2}$

Notes: Logic for quadbit assignment to signalling points in Fig. 3-26 (9600 bps).
(1) Fallback to 7200 bps uses constellation in Fig. 3-27 (Q_1 is set at 0).
(2) All modes at 2400 baud.

favor since the binary error-correcting codes, which decode after hard decisions, achieve their coding gain at the expense of increased bandwidth—a scarce commodity on voice-grade lines.

The objective of trellis-coded modulation (TCM) is to obtain the advan-

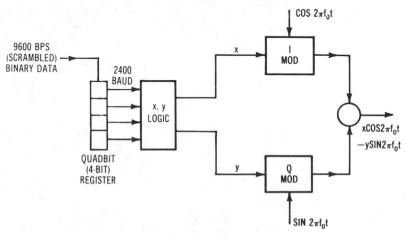

(A) QAM modulator.

Fig. 3-25. QAM Modulation and demodulation.

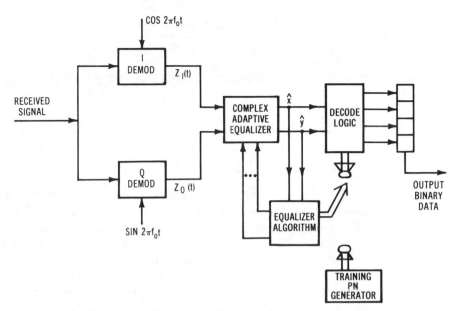

(B) QAM modulator including complex adaptive equalizer.

Fig. 3-25. (cont.)

tages of error-correcting coding without incurring the penalty of increased bandwidth. This can only be accomplished by combining the modulation and coding and then using soft-decision decoding.

In all coding for combatting errors, the patterns of symbols that are used to represent allowed messages are restricted to a subset of all possible pat-

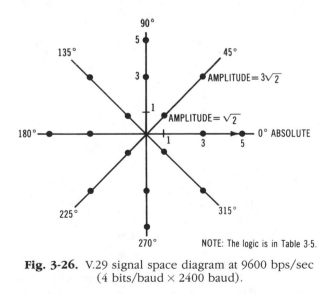

Fig. 3-26. V.29 signal space diagram at 9600 bps/sec
(4 bits/baud × 2400 baud).

Table 3-6. Logic for Dibits

Data Dibits		Quadbits				Phase Change
		Q_1	Q_2	Q_3	Q_4	
0	0	0	0	0	1	0°
0	1	0	0	1	0	90°
1	1	0	1	1	1	180°
1	0	0	1	0	0	270°

Fallback to 4800 bps (2400 × 2 bits/baud).

terns. Good codes are those that allow the use of the largest subset, such that the "distances" between any pair of allowed members is maintained large enough to ensure that impairments will not cause the message pattern, that was sent, to be confused with another legitimate pattern. For *traditional binary codes*, this distance measure is the so-called *Hamming distance*, which is the number of places any two codewords differ. For *modulation coding*, the appropriate distance is the so-called *Euclidean distance*, which is the energy in the arithmetic difference in the modulation waveforms representing the message patterns.

The idea of trellis-coded modulation is to generalize the use of QAM. Redundancy is added by using more signal points in the constellation than are needed for the same data rate in conventional QAM. The selection of which constellation point is chosen is determined by convolutionally encoding selected bits in the data stream. This introduces a dependency between successive signal symbols. Thus, only certain *patterns* or *sequences* or QAM signals are allowed. The allowed sequence of transitions can be modeled as a trellis structure. All valid sequences are defined by trellis.

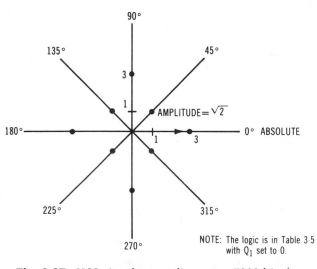

NOTE: The logic is in Table 3-5 with Q_1 set to 0.

Fig. 3-27. V.29 signal space diagram at 7200 bits/sec (3 bits/baud × 2400 baud).

Table 3-7. CCITT Synchronous Modems for the Voice-Grade Telephone Channel (National and International)

CITT Designation	Data Rates	Baud	Transmission Mode	Line Type	Modulation	Carrier Frequency (Hz)	Comments
V.22 bis	2400/1200	1200	HDX	Switched	DIFF PSK	1800 ±1	Most Common for PCs 212A compatible.
V.26	2400	1200	FDX	4-wire leased point-to-point and Multidrop	DIFF QPSK A or B[2]	1800 ±1	75-bps FSK reverse channel.
V.26 bis	2400/1200[1]	1200	HDX	2-wire switched network	DIFF QPSK	1800 ±1	Same as V.26; may require line conditioning and compromise equalizer.
			FDX	4-wire switched network	B		
V.27	4800	1600	HDX	2-wire leased	DIFF 8-PSK	1800 ⊥1	Same as V.26 bis with manually adjustable equalizer and scrambler.
			FDX	4-wire leased			
V.27 bis	4800/2400	1600/1200[1]	HDX	2-wire leased	DIFF 8-PSK	1800 ±1	Same as V.27 and use of automatic adaptive equalizer.
			FDX	4-wire leased	DIFF QPSK,A		
V.27 ter	4800/2400[1]	1600/1200	HDX	2-wire switched	DIFF 8-PSK	1800 ±1	Same as V.27 bis.
			FDX	4-wire switched	DIFF QPSK,A		
V.29	9600 (7200/ 4800/2400)[3]	2400	HDX	2-wire leased point-to-point	16-QAM	1700 ±1	More elaborate automatic adaptive equalizer data scrambler, line conditioning. Multiplexer option.
V.32	9600/4800	2400	HDX/ FDX	2-wire switched	TCM/QAM	1700 ±1	
V.33	14,400	2400	HDX	2-wire	TCM	1700 ±1	

Notes: 1. Switch to lower rate on poor international connections.
2. A and B refer to use 0°, ±90°, 180°, for alternative A; differential phases and ±45°, +135° for alternative B.
3. Optional fall-back rates.

When channel impairments cause the pattern to be altered to an invalid sequence of signal points, the decoder can search through the trellis using the Viterbi algorithm and select the one which is "closest" to that of the received signal. Errors due to noise, distortion, and intersymbol interference can be avoided to the extent that these combined impairments do not cause a given transmitted sequence to be closer to another valid sequence. *Channel Coding With Multilevel/Phase Signals* by Gottfried Ungerboeck[26] gives several methods of constructing the codes so that the Euclidean distances between QAM (and PSK) modulation sequences are optimally large.

The key idea in TCM is that the decoding is not based on a symbol-by-symbol demodulation but rather by the decoding of the entire sequences of symbols. This is possible to do efficiently only because of the trellis structure imposed by the convolutional encoding. The first use of TCM for voice-grade commercial modems were the Codex 2360 and 2660 modems introduced in 1984.

Conventional QAM as illustrated in Fig. 3-24 maps blocks of bits into a waveform represented by a constellation point. For example, in Fig. 3-24C, every 6-bit data block is mapped one-to-one into one of the 64 points shown on the oscillogram.

The Codex 2660 Modem uses an 8-state trellis (constraint length 3 convolutional code). The QAM constellation which will make up to TMC sequence is 128 points, as shown in Fig. 3-28. For every 6-bit sequence, two for the bit shown are convolutionally encoded in a rate 2/3 code so that seven total bits are derived from the six. These seven bits map the $2^7 = 128$ constellation points. The symbol rate is 2400 baud and the Viterbi algorithm is used for decoding. All operations are performed with custom VLSI chips and are controlled by a 68000 microprocessor. Transmission rates up to 16.8 kbps have been achieved with these modems on voice-grade lines with automatic fall-back to 14.4 kbps if the line degrades.

3.4.4 Data Scrambling

In synchronous modems, it is essential that phase tracking and symbol timing be established at call set-up and maintained during data transmission. In some earlier modems, the carrier phase acquisition is achieved with pilot tones, which are undesirable, since harmonics of these tones cause problems and the equalizer does not have an opportunity with a single tone to adapt to the entire frequency band of the channel. Furthermore, pilot tones take precious power and do not provide symbol timing. The solution to this problem is to scramble or randomize the data so that the power density of the signal is spread almost uniformly across the band. No harmonics that can cause problems are generated, the equalizer gets information necessary to adjust to the conditions of the channel across the entire band, and, even if the transmitter sends idle patterns, there always continues to exist in the signal enough information for symbol timing extraction. A self-synchronizing scrambler-descrambler of the type shown in Fig. 3-29 is now universally used for modems.

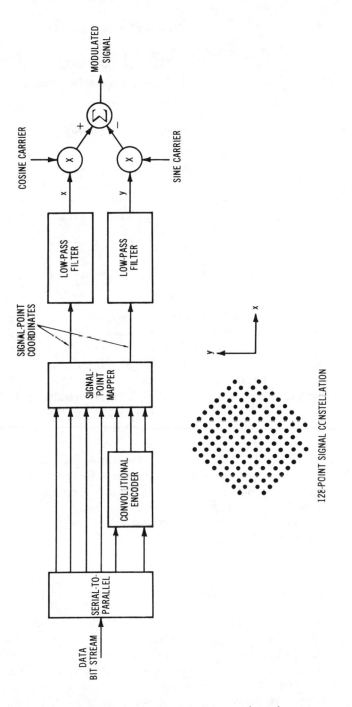

Fig. 3-28. 14.4 kbps trellis-coded modulation (TCM) transmitter.
(Courtesy Codex Corp., Division of Motorola, Inc.)

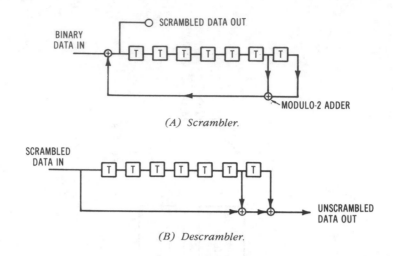

(A) Scrambler.

(B) Descrambler.

Fig. 3-29. Self-synchronizing scrambler-descrambler for CCITT V.27 modems.

The scrambler consists, in general, of an *n*-stage binary linear-feedback shift register with modulo-2 addition of selected taps for feedback. The description of which taps are fed back is specified by a polynomial whose coefficients are either 1 or 0, depending on whether the stage corresponding to the power of the indeterminate, x, is connected or not, respectively. The descrambler is a linear feed-forward shift register. The scrambling-descrambling process does not require block synchronization, hence the term self-synchronizing. The scrambler-descrambler does require bit timing for the shift registers. V.27 modems use a 7-stage register. V.29 modems use a 23-stage register, with the polynomial $1 + x^{-18} + x^{-23}$. The scrambler is also used to generate the training patterns for initial handshaking between modems. Details of specific recommended protocols for the scrambler-descrambler are given in *Data Transmission Over the Telephone Network*,[7] and an excellent theoretical treatment of the subject is to be found in *Timing Recovery and Scramblers in Data Transmission*, by R.D. Gitlin and J.H. Hayes.[15]

3.5 Special Model Features and Uses

A functional block diagram of a modem is shown in Fig. 3-30. Except for a few analog filter and power supply (PS) components, modern modems use digital signal processing for virtually all functional elements and, more often than not, the functions—in particular, transmit control (XMT) and receive control (RCV)—are performed by a programmed, if not user-programmable, set of microprocessors. It is, therefore, possible to incorporate a large number of special features; we will describe a few of the more prevalent ones.

One feature that is being introduced into the newer less-expensive modems is automatic dialing. In the past, automatic dialing for modems used

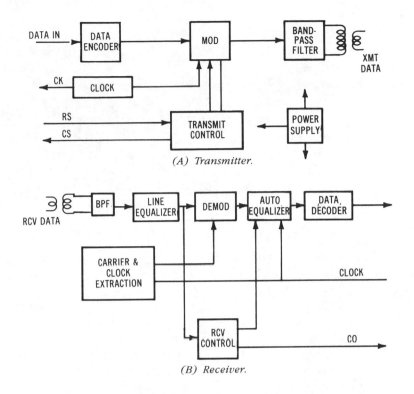

Fig. 3-30. Functional elements of a modem.

on the DDD network required the use of a separate and relatively expensive Automatic Call Unit (ACU), which is a stand-alone unit with its own interfaces to the modem and to the computer (see Figure 3-31). Autodial can be used for polling or as a dial-up back-up feature when a leased line goes bad. Some autodial modems have a repertoire of numbers, which can be programmed by the user through the terminal RS-232C interface.

Inverse multiplexing and multiport operation is another relatively recent innovation. Multiport operation (sometimes called split-stream) is actually a multiplexing operation at the data input side of the modem. This allows several different data streams, at the same or different rates, to be combined into one modem signal. An example is in the V.29 modems which operate at 9600 bps. It is possible to have an option whereby four 2400-bps independent data streams are combined to form 9600 bps. Alternatively, we can have a two 2400-bps and a one 4800-bps stream, etc. The quadbits which dictate the 16-ary QAM signal are chosen selectively from the independent data streams—a bit or two at a time, as the case may warrant. At the receiving end, the bits are selectively distributed to recover the independent data streams.

Inverse multiplexing actually is a modem support device that enables several voice-band modems to be used together with several lines for the purpose of transmitting a single stream of data at much higher rates than can be accommodated using a single line. For example, a 19.2 kbps data stream can be

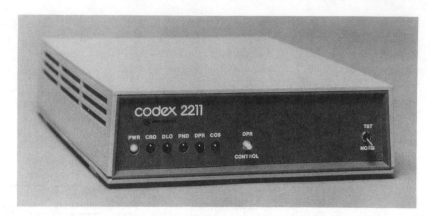

Fig. 3-31. An automatic call unit. *(Courtesy Codex Corp., Division of Motorola, Inc.)*

inverse multiplexed so that the odd bits occurring at 9.6 kbps are sent via a 9.6 kbps modem and a voice-grade line, while the even bits are sent via another 9.6 kbps modem and a second voice-grade line. This is illustrated in Fig. 3-32. A major reason for using an inverse multiplexer is that there is a gap in the available channels at data rates above 14.4 kbps.

In this area, voice-grade lines can be used with modems and a 56 kbps digital link on AT&T's DDS (or equivalent) but this is much more expensive than two voice lines and may not even be needed. Secondarily, inverse multiplexing affords a *fail-soft* back-up. If one line fails, the other can continue at reduced rates. A severe technical problem with inverse multiplexing is that the reconstruction of the bit stream from two or more lines, with widely different and varying propagation delays, requires elastic buffering and dynamic alignment at the bit steams without losing any bits. Considering that one path may be propagating over thousands of miles on terrestrial facilities, while the other may be routed via satellite, compensation for as much as 800-ms differential delay is not uncommon. An examples of an inverse multiplexer that

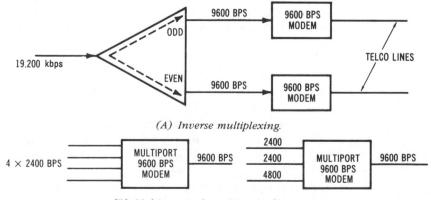

(A) Inverse multiplexing.

(B) Multiport modems. Two configurations.

Fig. 3-32. Inverse multiplexing and multiport modems.

operates at 19.2 kbps is the Codex biplexer. If the input data rate is less than 19.2 kbps, and one or both of the modems is multiport, the excess available capability may be filled through the extra modem ports.

As discussed earlier, many HDX modems provide a low-data-rate reverse channel which can be used for signalling and/or automatic repeat-request (ARQ) acknowledgements in link protocols. Some modems have the ability to alternate data and voice on a single line. Other options include synchronous-to-asynchronous conversion and elastic buffering, which permits the instantaneous input rate to be different from the output rate, controlled by an external clock.

Modems can be configured into networks other than polling arrangements. They are used to support time-division multiplexers (TDM) and statistical TDMs (STDM), which require that the synchronous modems be master-slaved.

Many commercial modems come equipped with a variety of diagnostic features and options that can monitor both the local and remote modem, as well as the line, by means of a remote digital loopback. This tests the modem-line combination and the analog loopback to make a fault isolation of the lines. Other options for diagnostics include an internal eye pattern generator, which can be used to check tolerances of phase jitter, timing inaccuracies, noise, line hits, etc. All modems have built-in and standardized handshaking protocols to establish the initial synchronization.

There are special modems that operate at frequencies well above the voice band to provide FDX data, as well as voice, on the metallic telephone wires within a building or a local-area campus. The reason this can be done is that the lines are unloaded, and the band-limiting filters are not applied by the telephone company until the wires reach the switch. An example of this is Adminet's Simultaneous Modem, which operates with FSK 9600-bps data at about 40 MHz in one direction and about 75 MHz in the other direction. This technique will operate also through an analog PBX so that it can be used to create an inexpensive voice/data local-area network. There are also *limited-distance modems* that will operate on metallic wire-pairs up to 20 miles at baseband.

Finally, there are *no-modems*, or *null modems*, and *modem eliminators*, which are nothing more than cable adapters for connecting terminals or personal computers together using the EIA RS-232C interface.

One of the largest current uses of modems is to provide inexpensive networking capability of stand-alone personal computers. For this purpose, modems are available as plug-in cards that fit into a vacant slot in a PC. The card interfaces with the computer bus and allows software driven operation of the modem. Such modems, together with the software are dubbed "intelligent modems." The most popular of these products is the Hayes Smartmodem™ which has become a de-facto standard. The software provides for a command set which can be used to program various functions such as going "off-hook," dialing a remote modem, setting parameters and maintaining a database of telephone numbers. All of this can be entered via the keyboard and controlled by the keyboard or a mouse. The computer screen may be used to observe the process and/or the modem could be programmed for unattended data transfer at a specified later time. Security features are also available as are error control protocols. These modems may operate in the asynchronous or synchronous mode up to 2400 bps over switched telephone lines. Various de-facto industry standards for flow control such as XON/XOFF, DTR/CTS, and RTS/CTS are provided. For asynchronous operation the error control is usually MNP™ (originally introduced by Microcom, Inc.) which works by automatically re-transmitting lost data when a garbled signal is detected.

The newest generation of modems have an architecture which is based on Programmable Digital Signal Processors (DSP). All of the filtering, modulation, demodulation, coding, and equalizer functions are performed in the DSP under the control of a DSP program residing in a read only memory (ROM). A separate general purpose microprocessor (μP) is used to support control functions, protocols and for communicating with external modem software such as Autodialing with an "AT" command set (such as Hayes) including extensions such as Autosynch™ (for 3270 support with asynchronous modems) and Auto-stream™ (for multisession synchronous operation). The basic architecture is shown in Figure 3-33.

The advantage of such an architecture is that it affords full flexibility for a modem to assume alternative formats. Thus the same device can function as a Bell 201A, a V.29, a V.21 (which is used for Group 3 facsimile), or a V.32 (full-duplex 9600 bps) modem or any other that might be advanced in the future. Error control may be added as an option even if several standards emerge (such as the change from MNP to V.42 or the new error control mode (ECM) which is included in the latest Group 3 facsimile standards T.30 and T.4. Even data compression methods of a V.32 modem can be programmed which can increase the "effective" rate to as much as 38.4 kbps. All this means that the basic modem can be easily upgraded by changing the contents of the ROMs.

3.6 Multiplexers

In the introduction of this chapter, we discussed the basic motivation for multiplexing which, as shown in Fig. 3-2, was to save line and modem costs by

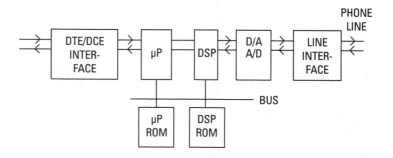

Fig. 3-33. DSP-based modem architecture.

sharing a common channel that usually had more capacity than a single source, such as a terminal, can deliver.

3.6.1 Types of Multiplexers (Voice and Data)

Multiplexing is used by the common carriers (AT&T, etc.) extensively internal to their network for voice. This type of trunk multiplexing should be distinguished from data multiplexing used by end users. We will briefly describe the two in the following sections.

3.6.2 Multiplexing by the Common Carriers

The idea of multiplexing has its origins from early radio and telephony communications where a transmission medium, such as a broadcast radio or tv band, is subdivided into "channels," with each occupying a distinct subband. Similarly, when a broadband coaxial cable or a microwave line-of-sight (or a satellite transponder) bandwidth is subdivided into distinct nonoverlapping channels, with each carrying a different original transmission, it is possible to separate the individual signals without interference from the others by proper filtering at the reception end. Indeed, this technique, called frequency-division multiplexing (FDM), has been, and continues to be, the most prevalent means for efficiently using wideband and expensive long-haul trunks, such as cable, microwave, and satellite systems, for analog voice transmission. Typically, the FDM system is built on a hierarchy of 4-kHz chunks of spectrum, each carrying one analog telephone voice channel. A typical arrangement is to stack twelve 4-kHz channels into a "group," then five groups into a "supergroup" (giving 60 voice circuits), and then 10 supergroups into a "mastergroup" (giving 600 voice circuits), etc., until the bandwidth is filled. When we use a long-distance voice-grade line, either for voice or for data (with a modem), the modem signal is more than likely located somewhere along the route assigned to one of those many 4-kHz frequency slots—somewhere in the FDM hierarchy.

Some of the newer trunking systems, especially within metropolitan areas, have changed to a digital time-division multiplexing (T-carrier) system which uses pulse-code modulation (PCM) to digitize each voice signal to 64 kbps. Again, digital TDM hierarchies exist in the network. The multiplexing hierarchy is organized (in North America) to collect 24- and 64-kbps channels into a 1.544 Mbps T1 carrier, then four T1 carriers into a 6.312-Mbps T2 carrier, with seven T2 carriers collected into a 44.736 Mbps T3 carrier. Then, six T3 carriers are collected into a 274.176-Mbps T4 carrier. The T3 and T4 carrier levels, containing 672 and 4032 independent 64-kbps channels, respectively, are currently used on microwave systems, coaxial cables, and fiber-optical (light-guide) cable systems in many networks designed primarily for voice communications. Similar systems (not compatible) are in use in Europe, Japan, and elsewhere.

3.6.3 Multiplexing by End Users

Although it is important to be aware of what the common carriers do internal to their networks, the principal focus of this book is addressed to the user of these networks and, more specifically, to the use of data communications.

End users now have many transmission "pipes" into which they may multiplex their sources in order to minimize their communications costs. They may use a traditional voice grade line which, with modern modems, can accommodate up to 19.2 kbps. Alternatively many Interexchange Carriers offer Digital Data Service which provides direct to end user access of subT1 digital access at 2.4K, 4.8K, 9.6K and 56K bits per second. More recently, common carriers offer full T1 digital service to end users. (An example is AT&T's Accumet 1.5 which provides 1.544 Mbps.)

The end users can then multiplex digital voice, data, and other traffic by purchasing a dedicated T1 nodal processor from vendors such as Timeplex, Strata Com, Newbridge, Northern Telecom, and others.

In using a voice-grade line, the signals may indeed be multiplexed and/or sampled and digitized, etc. As seen by the user, it is still a connection (albeit a complicated one) which has the characteristics of voice-grade facilities, as discussed earlier in Sections 3.3 and 3.4.

The earliest use of multiplexing for data transmission of voice-grade lines was in the use of FDM, with the data on each channel using binary FSK. An example of dividing the voice channel into FDM subchannels for various data rates is CCITT R.39, shown in Table 3-8. At 75 baud (equals 75 bps here because of *binary* FSK), the channel spacing needs to be 120 Hz to avoid interference. The tones at this rate are ±30 Hz from the center frequency which, for channel 1, say, is 420 Hz (420 + 30 = 470 Hz for MARK and 420 − 30 = 390 Hz for SPACE). At 75 bps, 24 channels can be accommodated in the voice band; at 150 bps, only 12 channels, and at 600 bps, only two channels will fit. Although CCITT R.39 has been used for quite some time, the U.S. military has a different (or incompatible) set of frequency assignments. These are shown in Table 3-9.

Table 3-8.   CCITT R.39 Operating Frequencies for FDM Multiplexing

Channel Number	75 Baud Chan. Spacing 120 Hz FSK ±30 Hz	150 Baud Chan. Spacing 240 Hz FSK ±60 Hz	600 Baud Chan. Spacing 1440 Hz FSK ±240 Hz
1	420	480	1080
2	540	720	2520
3	660	960	
4	780	1200	
5	900	1440	
6	1020	1680	
7	1140	1920	
8	1260	2160	
9	1380	2400	
10	1500	2640	
11	1620	2880	

Table 3-8. (cont.)

Channel Number	75 Baud Chan. Spacing 120 Hz FSK ±30 Hz	150 Baud Chan. Spacing 240 Hz FSK ±60 Hz	600 Baud Chan. Spacing 1440 Hz FSK ±240 Hz
12	1740	3120	
13	1860		
14	1980		
15	2100		
16	2220		
17	2340		
18	2460		
19	2580		
20	2700		
21	2820		
22	2940		
23	3060		
24	3180		
25	5300 ← Out-of-Band		

Table 3-9. MIL STD-188B Operating Frequencies for FDM

Channel Number	110 Baud Chan. Spacing 170 Hz FSK ±42.5 Hz	200 Baud Chan. Spacing 340 Hz FSK ±85 Hz
1	425	510
2	595	850
3	765	1190
4	935	1530
5	1105	1870
6	1275	2210
7	1445	2550
8	1615	2890
9	1785	
10	1955	
11	2125	
12	2295	
13	2465	
14	2635	
15	2805	
16	2975	
17	3145	
18	3315	

Although FDM is still occasionally used for data, it has been displaced by time-division multiplexing (TDM) and, more recently, by statistical time-division multiplexing (STDM). With the introduction of microcomputers and sophisticated resident software, this has turned the multiplexer into a very powerful and intelligent device that can do more than mere multiplexing. STDMs are now the most common types available. The distinction between the three types of multiplexing is shown in Fig. 3-34.

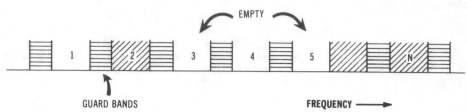

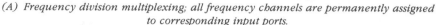

(A) Frequency division multiplexing; all frequency channels are permanently assigned to corresponding input ports.

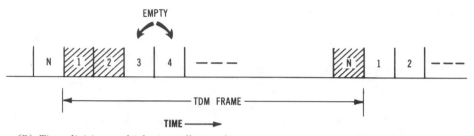

(B) Time division multiplexing; all time slots are permanently assigned to corresponding input ports.

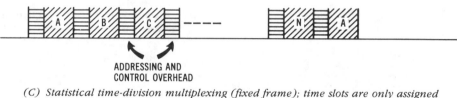

(C) Statistical time-division multiplexing (fixed frame); time slots are only assigned to active ports.

(D) Statistical time-division multiplexing (variable frame); the variable time slots are only assigned to active ports.

Fig. 3-34. Different types of data multiplexing.

FDMs do not require separate modems, since each channel essentially operates as a subvoice-grade FSK modem. TDMs assign N slots (repeated every TDM frame) among the various import ports on a fixed basis. For example, in using a 9600-bps modem, we might have 32 slots per frame, so that each slot can support an average of 9600/32 = 300 bps. For asynchronous terminals using 8-bit ASCII characters, plus two more for start and stop bits, this is equivalent to each time slot supporting 300 bits/second ÷ 10 bits/character = 30 characters/second. Other combinations are possible. "Dumb" asynchronous terminals usually receive asynchronous data at 10, 15, or 30 characters/second. Remember that, when using a manual keyboard-entry mode, even a fast typist can barely maintain 6 characters per second or about 75 words per minute. Thus, much of the time, any particular slot will just send idle characters; therefore, capacity and bandwidth are wasted.

FDM suffers from the same problem since channels are permanently assigned.* Although TDM is more efficient that FDM, in that it does not require guard bands and it operates directly in digital form, both are left behind by the advantages of STDM which takes advantage of the statistics of data transfer in several sophisticated ways. This permits a ten-fold increase in the efficiency of channel use, and in some cases, even more.

STDM does not make a fixed assignment of time slots so that any port which is idle does not receive a (full) slot. In order to identify which slots correspond to which data stream, it is necessary to append address and control symbols to each slot that is used. This "overhead" is usually small and is more than compensated for by the increased efficiency derived from not having to take up channel space with idle bits.

There are many versions of STDM. All require buffering of data (as does TDM). They can be classified as fixed-frame, as in Fig. 3-34C, or variable-frame, as in Fig. 3-34D, where the size of the slots and the frame are not fixed but depend on the data itself. STDMs also are built either for asynchronous data, synchronous data, or both.

TDMs and STDMs require a modem in order to interface with the voice line, but this may be built in. All modern STDMs have a least one and, usually, many microprocessors with programmed and programmable functions of great diversity available that are over and above the basic multiplexer functions. For this reason, they are referred to as "smart" or "intelligent" MUXs.

3.6.4 Intelligent Multiplexers

STDMs emerged about a decade ago and their features keep multiplying, but their *raison d'être* remains that of improving link utilization. Although all STDMs take advantage of the intermittent statistical characteristics of data traffic, there are other statistical characteristics, such as the nonuniform distribution of the frequency of character occurrence in natural language and in higher-level computer-language text, that can be used by data-compression techniques to further reduce wasted bandwidth utilization. Furthermore, there is additional *deterministic* excess baggage, such as start and stop bits in both asynchronous character transmission and in synchronous transmission, control symbols, filler characters for synchronization and certain flags, trailing blanks in card images, and waiting for acknowledgements in some protocols. All told, STDM can improve the transmission efficiency by a factor of about 10 for asynchronous data and by a factor of 2 to 6 for the various types of synchronous data transmission. The higher latter figure is for protocols, such as IBM's

---

*In the common-carrier network and in some satellite systems, this is not the case. Computer-controlled switching centers perform a *demand assignment* in order to take advantage of statistical traffic fluctuations.

Binary Synchronous Communication (BSC), which is character-oriented. The lower figures are for protocols, such as Synchronous Data Link Control (SDLC) or the equivalent ISO's High-Level Data Link Control (HDLC) which are bit-oriented.

For asynchronous data transmission, the major efficiency improvements (measured in the percentage of time saved by various techniques) break down approximately as follows (the actual values will vary with the application):

1. Stripping off start/stop bits and reinserting them at the other end..20%

2. Taking advantage of HDX operation (balanced) 50%

3. Duty factor of character at a time terminal data.....................200–800%

4. Data compression of English text..50%

If all techniques were fully used, they would result in about 1000% reduction in the time needed to transmit a given amount of *information* bits, or an improvement of about a factor of 10.

For synchronous data, items 1 and 3 cannot be used, and some protocols allow FDX operation, thereby removing item 2 also, so that only item 4 and the removal of redundant frame overhead is available. Hence the lower figures for synchronous data.

The techniques of items 1, 2, and 3 are almost self evident. Data compression requires some explanation. In any sequence of data representing a natural language, such as English, some letters and symbols occur much more frequently than others. For example, a *SPACE* occurs about 17% of the time, the lowercase letters *e*, *t*, *a*, *i*, and *r* collectively occur about 30% of the time, whereas the letters *J*, *Z*, and *W* occur *less* than 0.1% of the time. Therefore, why assign the same number of bits (7 plus 1 parity, in ASCII) to all, including the rarely used control characters? The better way is to assign a few bits to the most frequently occurring symbols, and the larger number of bits (if necessary) to those rare ones. That way, the *average* length will be small. In order to be able to uniquely decipher a string of these variable-length codewords without separators, the prefix of any codeword that represents a character, itself, cannot be a (shorter) codeword representing another character. Techniques for accomplishing this assignment, in an optimum way which reduces the *average* number of bits/characters to the minimum possible, have been well known. The codes are called *Huffman codes*, and their theory and construction is detailed in *Information Theory and Reliable Communications*, by R.G. Gallager.[14] Their use in statistical multiplexers was pioneered at Codex Corporation and is reported in articles by G.D. Forney, R.W. Stearns, and W.Y. Tao[12,13].

The use of variable-length bit representation of characters requires special handling of encoding and decoding, and the STDM becomes a variable frame type. Although simple tree search algorithms exist for Huffman coding, it is more convenient to use storage tables. The article by Forney and Tao[13] gives some clever ways of using such tables for decompression without having to use excessive storage. The price for increased throughput efficiency in an STDM is that all incoming data must be buffered. This translates into additional delay and possibly blocking (due to filled buffers) under peak-load conditions.

The rigorous analysis of delay due to queuing and blocking (probability of buffer overflow) is usually very complicated. The classical works on this subject are the articles "A Study of Asynchronous Time Division Multiplexing for Time Sharing Computer Systems," by W.W. Chu, "Demultiplexing Considerations for Time Sharing Computer Systems," by W. W. Chu, "Demultiplexing Considerations for Statistical Multiplexers," from *IEEE Transactions on Communications*, and "On the Analysis and Modeling of a Class of Computer Communications Systems," by W.W. Chu and A.G. Konheim (see references 5, 6, and 8), and some of this is summarized in *Computers Communication Network Design and Analysis* by Mischa Schwartz.[24] Also, fortunately, buffer overflow is not a significant problem in modern STDMs since ample storage is available and the results of theoretical work in the references corroborates that fact. The queuing delays should not be a significant factor in a well-designed multiplexer that is not overloaded.

Nevertheless, practical issues relating to intermultiplexer frame format design, such as overhead, play an important role in the delay performance of an STDM. Therefore, we present an elementary model of an STDM along with a heuristic analysis of its delay performance, which will permit a reasonably accurate quantitative evaluation. The model assumes that the data traffic from all the active sources is homogeneous (rare in practice) and that statistical equilibrium has been reached, which does not apply at startup or after abrupt traffic changes.

The elementary model of an STDM is shown in Fig. 3-35. In this model, the *average* arrivals from each of the statistically homogenous active terminals, to each of the buffers* shown, is λ bps. There are assumed to be **N** sources (terminals), of which **F** are active (filling F slots in the STDM frame).

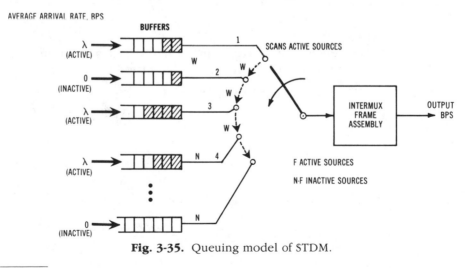

Fig. 3-35. Queuing model of STDM.

---

*Actually the buffers are polled. This improves efficiency.

The multiplexer commutator spends an average of **W** seconds* (walk time) for each of the N terminals, active or not. The multiplexer delivers **C** bps into the channel, which is its capacity.

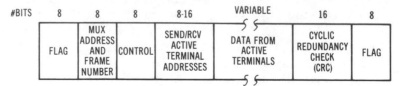

(A) Direct or indexed addressing.

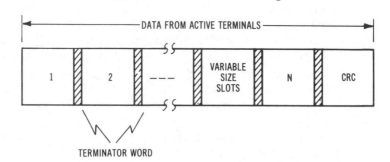

(B) Use of variable size slots and terminator works to reduce frame overhead.

Fig. 3-36. Intermultiplexer frame format for STDM.

In assembling the frame, the multiplexer executes a complete scanning cycle and the *average* time to complete this type is T_c, which is given by

$$T_c = \frac{Q_1}{\lambda} \text{ sec.} \tag{3-1}$$

where,

Q_1 equals the *average* number bits in each active buffer, since $Q_1 \times \lambda = T_c$, the time necessary to have accumulated Q_1 bits arriving at λ bps.

T_c may also be calculated by adding the average time to unload all F active buffers, which is $Q_1F \div C$, plus the total average walk time, Nw, to scan all N sources. Hence,

$$T_c = \frac{Q_1F}{C} + Nw \tag{3-2}$$

Equating Equations 3-1 and 3-2, we get

$$Q_1 = \frac{NW}{\dfrac{1}{\lambda} - \dfrac{F}{C}} \text{ bits}$$

*This represents the addressing and other overhead shown in Figs. 3-34C and 3-36.

or,

$$T_c = \frac{NwC}{C - L}$$
$$= \frac{OH}{C - L} \ seconds$$

(3-3)

where we have defined the total frame overhead in bits as OH =NwC and the offered load, **L**, of all the F active terminals as L = Fλ/C bps.

The total delay is the sum of the queuing delay given in Equation 3-3 plus the B/C to transmit a frame that contains a total of B bits at C bps, plus the processing delay, PD. Thus, we have for the STDM time delay, in seconds,*

$$TD = \frac{OH}{C - L} + \frac{B}{C} + PD$$

(3-4)

Typical delay curves representing Equation 3-4 are shown in Fig. 3-37, which is plotted for OH = 20 bits, B = 480 bits, and PD = 8 ms. For these parameters, use a C = 9600-bps channel and an *aggregate average* load of L = 9200 bps. The delay given by Equation 3-4 works out to 108 ms, as shown in the left-most curve of Fig. 3-35. Note that the overhead, OH, and the frame buffer size, B, are *not* independent of the load, L. Note also, that as L

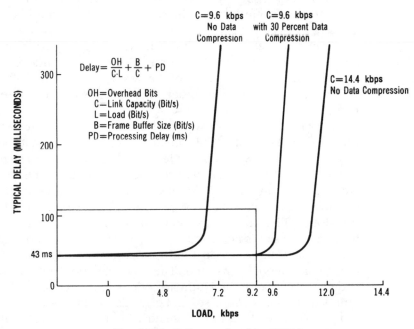

Fig. 3-37. Delay vs. load in STDM.

---

*This is the *average* time delay for *statistical equilibrium* and *homogeneous traffic*.

approaches the capacity, C, that the delay becomes very large. This simply reflects the usual queuing curve which indicates that if the aggregate arrival rate is very close to the net maximum service rate, the queue will begin to grow very fast. It is not possible to have a stable queue when L > C.

A very important consequence of Equation 3-4 is that overhead of *any kind* can have a drastic effect on delay and, as a consequence, for a specified allowable delay, on the maximum load (throughput) that the STDM can handle. This effect of overhead is illustrated in Fig. 3-37 by the middle curve which is drawn for C = 9600 bps, but data compression of 30% is used so that the *effective* capacity is $9600/(1 - 0.3) = 13.7$ kbps, and the delay drops to 43 ms, which is *greater* than a 30% reduction from no data compression. This nonlinear behavior is due to the first term in Equation 3-4. It would have required an actual capacity at 14.4 kbps to achieve the same 43-ms delay without data compression.

A major consideration which determines the frame overhead is the intermultiplexer frame form used by the STDM. Various manufacturers differ in the detailed design of the intermultiplexer frame. A common format is to use a structure very similar to that used by SDLC and HDLC level-two link protocol in standardized data networks. This is shown in Fig. 3-36, which contains opening and closing flags, multiplexer address (in networking), frame number (for ARQ error control), active terminal addresses, and cyclic redundancy checks (for error detection). The sum of these can amount to a substantial overhead (about 56–64 bits). The STDM delay for this figure of overhead, using the same offered load and capacity as above, would give a delay of about 288 to 328 ms.

Frame formats, such as that shown in Fig. 3-36A, can use either direct addressing to indicate which terminal is active, or indexed addressing which signifies the relative position of the next active terminal after the current one. Indexing saves overhead under high traffic since a smaller address field is needed.

A totally different format, which avoids explicit addresses or byte counts, is illustrated in Fig. 3-36B. This scheme, used by Codex in its 6000-series STDMs, formats the frame with variable-length Huffman-code characters and provides a slot for each of N (active as well as inactive) sources. If characters from a source are queued in an active buffer, then any number of them (Huffman coded) up to a maximum number can be placed into the slot reserved for that source. If the slot is filled to its maximum, then no terminator code word is used. If, however, the slot is not filled to its maximum, then a 2-bit terminator, which is part of the Huffman code (and therefore uniquely distinguishable from the other characters), is inserted. The inactive slots contain only the terminator code word. Because the Huffman code is uniquely decodable, this scheme requires no terminal addresses and gives data compression at the same time. The scheme is more efficient than standard frame formats at high loads.

The overwhelming majority of STDMs operate on asynchronous data. Only a few manufacturers offer STDMs that are designed to handle synchronous data, such as BSC, SDLC, and HDLC, which are used by "smart" terminals.

While the *average* aggregate data rate cannot exceed the capacity of the data link, it is possible for the aggregate *peak* rate delivered to an STDM to exceed capacity over short intervals, since the buffers will absorb the difference. The management of the buffers is an important task performed by the microprocessors in an STDM. Pooling of the total buffer space among all the data input ports affords more flexibility and efficiency than dedicated buffers and is usually preferred. Its drawback is that failure is catastrophic. A happy compromise is to have small groups of input ports share distinct buffer spaces. In practical statistical multiplexers, buffer size has little to do with delay and throughput. The buffer size need be no larger than that required to accommodate peaks in the aggregate traffic load.

STDMs use standard "GO BACK N ARQ" with a standard 16-bit CRC for frame-error detection, and N is variable (7 to 127) to allow the user to "fine-tune" for optimum throughput.

The top-of-the-line intelligent STDMs provide automatic terminal speed recognition, echoplexing, protocol intervention, protocol transparency, and detailed user-friendly (menu-driven) reports to the operator. These reports are presented on the front panel, and more elaborately, via the RS-232C (CCITT V.24/V.28) interface to a standard crt terminal. The reports include local and remote diagnostics, alarms, current status, message statistics, processor and buffer utilization, ARQ retransmission rates, and terminal and channel states. These STDMs have from tens to hundreds of data input ports which can accommodate data rates varying from 50 bps to 9.6 kbps, and from 1 to 6 trunk ports, each of which operate at up to 64 kbps (more usually, at 9.6, 14.4, and 19.2 kbps), with or without switching and routing capability.

Such intelligent STDMs require several microprocessors to handle all these functions, and careful consideration has to be given to the internal architecture of the device. There are probably as many architectures as there are designs and models. Examples of two alternative multiple microprocessor configurations are shown in Fig. 3-38. In both configurations, a high-speed head-end microprocessor controls centralized functions, such as routing, diagnostics, report generation, etc. One or several (up to 16) terminal processors (TP), each with about 32–64K memory for programs and buffers, are grouped so that each can handle all the functions associated with about 16 input data ports, such as automatic speed recognition, data compression, flow control, echoplexing, etc. If synchronous data capability is present, this is usually handled by a separate processor which strips off the data, handles the line protocol, etc. The network processor(s) (NP) formats the intermultiplex frames and handles the intermultiplex protocols.

The major difference between the architectures in Figs. 3-38A and 3-38B is that the latter has a network interface controller (NIC) that handles the composite terminal traffic and coordinates scheduling with the head-end so as to reduce contention among the terminal processors. There are tradeoffs in these and many other designs.

The photograph of a modern Intelligent STDM is shown in Fig. 3-39. This device, manufactured by Codex has a capacity of 32 asynchronous/synchro-

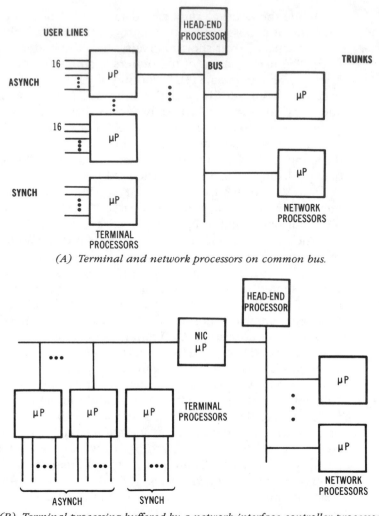

(A) Terminal and network processors on common bus.

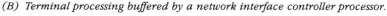

(B) Terminal processing buffered by a network interface controller processor.

Fig. 3-38. Multiprocessor architectures for intelligent STDM.

nous input channels, one trunk output port, and most of the intelligent features described above. Its high-end dimensions are approximately $8 \times 16 \times 10$ inches; it weighs about 25 pounds and consumes less than 200 watts.

3.7 Concentrators

The word *concentrator* simply refers to a device that can collect data traffic from M sources and transmit them through N facilities or trunks where M > N. Traditionally, concentrators were programmed and/or programmable devices

Fig. 3-39. An intelligent STDM. *(Courtesy Codex Corp., Division of Motorola, Inc.)*

that had store and forward as well as switching capabilities. With the development of intelligent programmable STDMs, it has become more difficult to distinguish them from traditional concentrators. Indeed, some intelligent STDMs are far more versatile than were the very expensive and bulky concentrators of only a short time ago.

Perhaps the principal distinguishing features of concentrators in the current data communication scene is that concentrators are usually called upon to handle Level 3 protocols in the ISO-OSI reference standard, such as CCITT X.25, as well as Level 2 (data link control) protocols. As such, the concentrator is more of a full-fledged network node which does switching, routing, flow control, load leveling, polling control, traffic monitoring, etc. A typical network configuration that shows the use of STDMs, concentrators, and front-end processors in a distributed computer-communication network is given in Fig. 3-40. On leased and dial back-up telephone channels, modems must be used (not shown) or they may be integral to the devices. For Dataphone Digital Service (DDS) lines operating a 2.4, 4.8, 9.6, or 56 kbps, a Data Service Unit (DSU) is required (not shown).

The Codex 6050 Distributed Communications Processor is an example of a top-of-the-line communications node. The architecture for this machine is shown in Fig. 3-41. The 6050 DCP provides distributed processing by localiz-

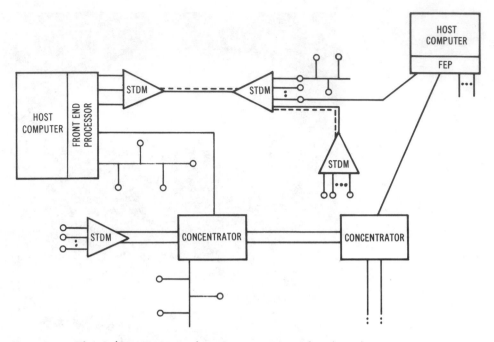

Fig. 3-40. STDMs and concentrators in a distributed computer-communications network.

ing processing functions. Network port functions, for example, ARQ retransmissions, node-to-node synchronization, etc., are processed by network port processors within the port nest. Terminal port functions, for example, autospeed character detection, bisync state machine, dial-connection handshake, adaptive data compression, etc., are handled by terminal port processors. Terminal port processors can support up to 16 async or bisync ports while HDLC terminal ports and network ports have a ratio of one port per processor. There are currently three versions available of the memory processor shown in Fig. 3-41: a 6800 with 64K memory, a 6809 with 64K memory, and a 6809 with 128K of memory (paged). The communication interface shown in the Port Nest of Fig. 3-41 can be one interface per processor for network ports, SDLC or high-performance bisync, or up to 16 interfaces per processor for asynchronous or high-performance bisync.

By removing these processing functions from the mainframe, the mainframe can devote its compute power to building frames and supporting network-routing algorithms, thus improving the character-handling performance by a factor of 3 to 4. Additionally, the number of ports supported is increased even though mainframe software is larger as the data buffering can be distributed.

Incoming characters are processed locally for appropriate functions and are buffered in a FIFO, which generates an interrupt to the mainframe. When the interrupt is serviced, multiple characters can be taken from the FIFO under a single interrupt (reducing the mainframe processing per character).

The mainframe builds network port frames according to a routing table

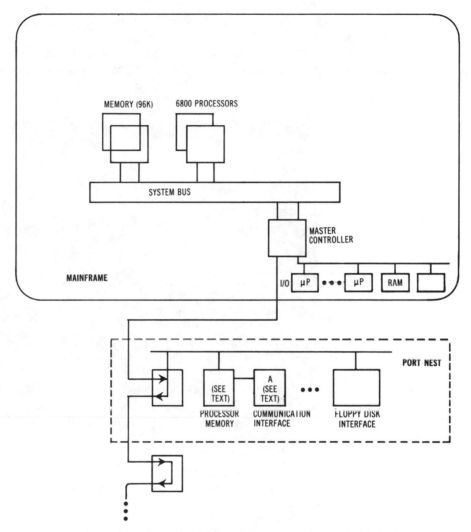

Fig. 3-41. The architecture of the Codex 6050 Distributed Communications Processor.

which is updated as required (if links go down or become congested). When the network port processor removes characters from its local FIFO, an interrupt is generated which allows the mainframe to provide characters to the network port. Data is only stored in the mainframe until the network port takes the characters.

Interprocessor communication is used to guarantee end-to-end data integrity and flow control. This interprocessor communication is accomplished by control packets (called address packets) which are routed through the network by any available path.

Dynamic routing is performed by considering that each new call requires a connection. Whenever a network link fails or becomes congested, calls are reestablished without data loss, provided terminal processor buffers are not exceeded.

The 6510 IXP supports CCITT X.25 for packet switching and can address up to 2500 virtual circuits in a network. It has a modular structure of both software and hardware so that additional features may be added as needed, or as they become available. The packaged system is shown in Fig. 3-42.

Fig. 3-42. The Codex 6740 Distributed Communications Processor.
(Courtesy Codex Corp., Division of Motorola, Inc.)

The delay analysis for concentrators is similar to that described above for STDMs. The architecture, software, and special characteristics of concentrators varies widely among manufacturers. The optimal cost-effective use of concentrators requires careful consideration to questions of network topology, traffic considerations, network management, and the constantly changing technology that is making it possible to do many of the concentrators' functions with smaller, cheaper, and sometimes more versatile devices, such as intelligent multiplexers.

3.8 The Present and the Future

The introduction of the personal computer and its proliferation has opened up a vast new market for modems since dial-up telephone facilities offer an immediate, inexpensive, and universal communications-access capability. For geographically dispersed small users, the telephone network is likely to continue to be the only feasible and economic means for arbitrary long-distance interconnectivity for decades to come. As a result, manufacturers have started to cater to this new market and some very inexpensive and standardized modems have emerged. However, the continuing need for modems for large users has not subsided. On the contrary, because of the universality of the telephone network, this channel continues to be the dominant means of data communications (even when leased facilities are warranted by economics) since most leased facilities are still mostly telephone channels. In addition, the read cost of long-distance dial-up connections is coming down.

There are several developments, however, which moderate the growth of voice-grade modems. First and foremost is the expanding availability of end-to-end digital networks, such as AT&T, MCI, and other similar networks. While these networks are not yet fully public switched, and they are far from universal, they do utilize the extensive T-carrier (Digital Communications) network by placing a 64-kbps digitized PCM voice channel which provides a 56-kbps digital channel directly to the user through a baseband Digital Service Unit (DSU). The 56 kbps is submultiplexed into either twenty 2400-bps, ten 4800-bps, or five 9600-bps data channels (any combination displacing just *one* voice channel). End-to-end digital transmission offers much better quality for data. As T-carrier proliferates into the long-haul trucking network on cables, microwave, lightguides, and satellites, and as the new digital switches displace analog switches, it is likely that a very fast circuit switched digital public network will develop. This network, although developed for digitized voice telephony, is also ideal for data as well as other services, such as graphics, facsimile, conference tv, etc. Indeed, there are already standards for such an Integrated Services Digital Network (ISDN), emanating from CCITT for protocols, user interfaces, and the use of the two-wire telephone-customer local loop that is to be used for simultaneous digitized voice and full-duplex 64-kbps digital connections to every current and future telephone outlet. Such a development, which will take several decades, would radically alter the need for modems.

Some telephone administrations have in the past tried to discourage data transmission on analog voice lines by charging a higher tariff for modem use than the use of the *same lines* for voice. There is some logic on this side since the signal properties of voice are such that speech interpolation, FDM loading plans, and other techniques which can be used to squeeze more voice signals into an analog channel cannot be used when modem signals occupy the channel. In addition, when modem signals are sampled and coded as if they were voice by a T-carrier channel bank, certain undesirable effects may become present and cause interference. In spite of these observations, the use of modems for data transmission on the public telephone network has a secure future for at least a decade or more.

There are other public networks. These are the so-called value-added networks (VAN), such as packet-switched networks (Telenet, Tymnet, Datapac, in

North America), but important and useful as they are, they are unlikely to become as universal as the telephone network in the foreseeable future.

With the public offering of T1 lines and the availability of T1 multiplexers and T1 Nodal processors, large organizations have created their own private digital networks which bypass the traditional telephone network not only for data base but also for voice and image transmission as well. The major use of these T1 networks however is for providing Wide Area Network (WAN) connecting to geographically dispersed Local Area Network (LAN). The terminals/workstations communicate locally to file servers, printers, and each other on a LAN such as Ethernet or a Token Ring. The LAN gains access to the T1 lines through a bridge or a router which provides ISO peer level 2 or level 3 connectivity respectively between the remote LAN systems.

Because of widespread economic, regulatory, and technological changes in WAN's, new ideas for internetworking have emerged. Among the most prominent is the notion of *Frame Relay* and *Fast Pocket Switching*. The former is described by CCITT I.122, "Framework for Additional Packet Mode Bearer Services" and ANSI T1S1/88-2242, "Frame Relay Bearer Services". The objective of both Frame Relay and Fast Packet is to provide *flexible* capacity to allow transmission facilities to be used efficiently without minimizing the overhead and slowness of X.25 networks.

Regardless of how digital networks emerge, intelligent multiplexers and other smart networking elements are bound to grow in influence and importance in data networks. Distributed networks to handle both voice and data will probably grow even faster than the breakneck speed they are growing at now. Greater sophistication will be required to efficiently multiplex both voice and data. (This is discussed in "An Analysis of a Voice/Data Integrated Multiplexer," by A.G. Konheim and R.L. Pickholtz.[19]) Additional demands will be made to interface with the emerging local-area networks (LANs), such as the Ethernet Contention bus, IBM's token ring systems, and PBX-based LANs.

Because the emphasis of the future is towards more distribution of the intelligent functions, greater reliability and fault tolerance will be required. Currently, a mean time between failure (MTBF) of communications equipment should be at about 100,000 hours. This would probably have to be quadrupled.

3.9 References

1. Balkovic, M.D., et al. "High Speed Voice Data Performance on the Switched Telecommunication Network," *Bell System Technical Journal*, Vol. 50, No. 4, April 1971.

2. Bell System Technical Reference, *Data Communications Using Voiceband Private Line Channels*, PUB41004, October 1973 and revisions.

3. Bingham, John A. *The Theory and Practice of Modem Design*, New York: Wiley-Interscience, 1988.

4. *CCITT Recommendations x.20.32*. Vol. VIII, "Data Communications, Networks and Interfaces," Red Book 1984, Blue Book 1990.

5. Chu, W.W. "A Study of Asynchronous Time Division Multiplexing for Time Sharing Computer Systems," *AFIPS Conference Proceedings*, Fall 1969.

6. Chu, W.W. and Alan G. Konheim. "On the Analysis of Modeling of a Class of Computer Communication Systems," *IEEE Transactions on Communications*, Vol. COM-20, No. 3, June 1972.

7. *Data Transmission Over the Telephone Network*, Yellow Book, Vol. VIII.I CCITT, Geneva, 1981.

8. "Demultiplexing Considerations for Statistical Multiplexers," *IEEE Transactions on Communications*, Vol. COM-20, No. 3, June 1982.

9. Douglas, Jack L. and W. Zubko. *More about Modems*. Available from Universal Data Systems Division of Motorola, Inc., Huntsville, AL, 1983.

10. Duffy, F.P. and T.W. Thatcher, Jr. "Analog Transmission Performance on the Switched Telephone Network," *Bell System Technical Journal*, Vol. 50, April 1971.

11. Feher, Kamilo. *Digital Communications*, Englewood Cliffs, NJ: Prentice Hall, 1981.

12. Forney, G.D. and Robert W. Stearns "Statistical Multiplexing Improves Link Utilization," *Data Communications*, July/August 1976.

13. Forney, G.D., and William Y. Tao. "Data Compression Increases Throughput," *Data Communications*, June 1976.

14. Gallager, R.G. *Information Theory and Reliable Communications*, New York: John Wiley, 1968.

15. Gitlin, R.D. and J.H. Hayes. "Timing Recovery and Scramblers in Data Transmission" *Bell System Technical Journal*, Vol. 54, No. 3, March 1975, pp. 569–593.

16. Glasgal, Ralph. *Techniques in Data Communications*, Norwood, MA: Artech House, 1983.

17. Held, Gilbert. *Data Communications Networking Devices*, 2nd ed., New York: John Wiley & Son, Inc., 1989

18. *IEEE Journal on Selected Areas in Communications (JSAC)*, Special Issue on bandwidth efficient modulation, Vol. 7, No. 6, August 1989.

19. Konheim, A.G. and R.L. Pickholtz. "An Analysis of a Voice/Data Integrated Multiplexer," *IEEE Transactions on Communications*, January 1984.

20. McNamara, John E. *Technical Aspects of Data Communication*, 2nd ed., Bedford, MA: Digital Equipment Corp., 1982.

21. Proakis, John G. *Digital Communications*, New York: McGraw-Hill, 1983.

22. Quereshi, Shahid. "Adaptive Equalization," *IEEE Communications Magazine*, March 1982, pp. 9–16.

23. Quereshi, Shahid V.M. and Hassan Ahmed. "A VLSI Chip Set for Digital Signal Processing in High Speed Voiceband Modems," *IEEE JSAC*, Vol. SAC-4, No. 1, January 1986.

24. Schwartz, Mischa.. *Computers Communication Network Design and Analysis*, Englewood Cliffs, NJ: Prentice-Hall, 1977.

25. Sudan, Lee K. and Edwin G. Brohm. "Not all Statistical Multiplexers Are Created Equal," *Data Communications*, May 1983.

26. Ungerboeck, Gottfried. "Channel Coding with Multilevel/Phase Signals," *IEEE Transactions on Information Theory*, January 1982.

27. Weinstein, Stephen S. "Echo Cancellation in the Telephone Network," *IEEE Communications Society Magazine*, January 1977.

Protocols

John D. McQuillan

Dr. John D. McQuillan is one of the foremost authorities in computer networks. He began his career at Bolt Beranek and Newman (BBN) with pioneering work on the ARPANET, the first packet switching network. He then founded a consulting department to conduct network studies for international airline and banking communication systems, and for major industrial and financial organizations in the U.S. and Europe.

In 1982 he formed his own consulting firm to apply his talents and experience in planning new computer communications systems. In his consulting practice, Dr. McQuillan assists vendor and user organizations in planning strategies and architectures, selecting high-performance low-cost systems, and adopting successful implementation tactics, both technological and organizational. He continues to apply his expertise in all phases of computer networking as a consultant, educator, and advisor.

Dr. McQuillan received his undergraduate and Ph.D. degrees in Applied Mathematics (Computer Science) from Harvard University. He has authored over 250 papers, reports, and presentations in the field of computer communications and office automation. He serves as either a columnist or advisor to several prominent business and technical publications. He is also active in conducting in-house courses, seminars, and executive briefings on high-technology developments.

4.1 Introduction

The word *protocol* has been borrowed from common usage to describe computer communications. In brief, the word means something similar in both instances. It describes conventional social behavior on the one hand and the orderly exchange of information between computing equipment on the other (Fig. 4-1). One common example of the social analogy is the college classroom. If all the students spoke simultaneously, as they felt the urge, the professor would struggle to make sense of the chaos and valuable information would be lost. For this reason, classroom protocol defines a process of raising hands in which students request that they be permitted to speak, resulting in the orderly exchange of data between several different people.

In computing, a protocol is necessary in order for two computers to create a path for exchanging information. The physical path may be some kind of

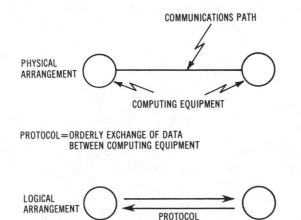

Fig. 4-1. What is a protocol?

analogy to a digital communications path containing the two devices. The protocol is merely the logical abstraction of the process which allows two different machines to share information. There are three fundamental functions that a protocol performs.

1. Establishing necessary conventions.
2. Establishing a standard communications path.
3. Establishing a standard data element.

It's in the establishment of this path that errors in the data stream may need to be detected. The control of traffic flow over the path may be simple or relatively complex, or it may be nonexistent. Finally, conventions are needed for starting and stopping data exchange over a path.

The protocol's final job is to establish standard data elements for use in communication over the path. In this way, the protocol creates a virtual data element to exchange between computing elements. For instance, two computers may wish to swap character streams. Sometimes they may need to deal in a simple data element, such as a letter or memo, while at other times, they deal in entire files. Or, systems may be constructed for exchanging a program or job between the two machines. Finally, in some applications, the element which needs to be transferred may be as complex as a graphic display.

To grasp the basic elements of a communications protocol, it's necessary to understand a few basic terms. The first is *handshaking*. Handshaking is the controlled two-way transfer of data across an interface. Two devices "shake hands" with each other via a sequence of interlocking steps. In doing this, one unit of information may be transferred (Fig. 4-2).

A second fundamental concept is the idea of standards, which can give users more flexibility in the selecting and interconnecting of equipment. Standardization will drastically reduce system-development time and maintenance while allowing for evolution as computing needs change.

For two computing elements to communicate, *conventions* must be established. The agreed upon protocol convention determines the nature of the data representation, the format and speed of the data representation over the communications path, and any sequence-of-control messages which are sent. (A control message may be the "hello" which initiates the connection, or any other supervisory or control step.) In other words, protocol conventions range from describing what a zero (0) and a one (1) look like to the control messages which "start" and "stop" data traffic.

The protocol can also build a standard communications path between computing devices. This entails translating the physical realities of the path between the two devices into a more useful *virtual communications path*. Ideally, this is a medium suited to both pieces of equipment. In establishing the virtual communications path, several items may need to be defined. For example, it may be necessary to have an addressing structure over the path which allows for communications with another device, or with several others. A terminal and its connected computer may need to address other computers

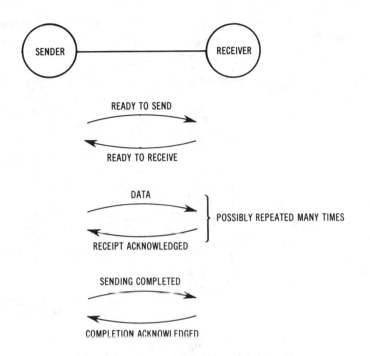

Fig. 4-2. Protocols use "handshaking."

or printers. It's here that a level of priority may be defined. Messages flowing over the path may need to be sequenced, or they may not.

Suppose you have four different kinds of information sources, such as mainframe computers, minicomputers, etc. Perhaps these four source devices need to exchange data with three different types of receivers (including terminals, graphics terminals, word processors, and personal computers). Unless there's a standard shared protocol, you will need 12 different protocols to permit all the possible connections. This is illustrated in Fig. 4-3. Such a system demands that each protocol must serve a special purpose.

The preferred solution for interconnecting equipment entails introducing a standard protocol which would require only 7 implementations (4 sources plus 3 receivers). This is shown in Fig. 4-4.

Finally there's a fundamental difference between protocols and interfaces. *Protocol* is the set of rules for communications between similar processes. *Interface* refers to a set of rules between dissimilar processes. It is also a physical connection between two devices or processes, while a protocol is a logic concept only. For example, there can be an interface between a host computer and packet-switching node. In turn, there can be a host-to-node protocol as well as host-to-host protocol. Fig. 4-5 illustrates this.

Protocols serve a diverse range of functions. It's necessary to discuss communications protocols in the larger context of networking. In computer networks, more than one protocol is usually required, each designed to provide a particular set of functions.

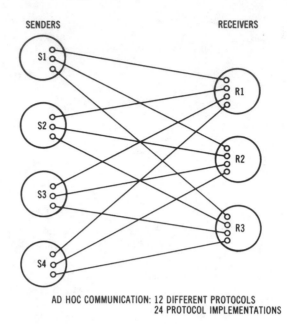

Fig. 4-3. Protocols without standards.

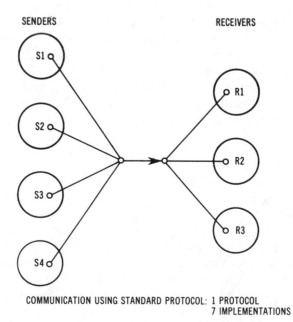

Fig. 4-4. A standard protocol.

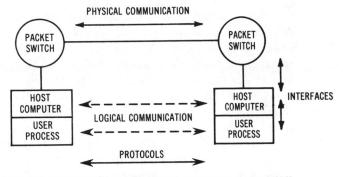

PROTOCOLS: RULES FOR COMMUNICATION BETWEEN *SIMILAR* PROCESSES
INTERFACES: RULES FOR COMMUNICATION BETWEEN *DISSIMILAR* PROCESSES

Fig. 4-5. Protocols and interfaces.

4.2 Choosing Subnetwork Protocols

A computer network is comprised of a *subnetwork* (the switching modes and the transmission facilities) and *subscriber* equipment. A typical list of subscriber equipment will include hosts, terminals, and various front-end processors. The subnetwork is the collection of transmission equipment, like multiplexers and switches, which permit data to travel over the network. The communications subnetwork must provide specified levels of performance while helping certain necessary network applications and functions. A successful subnetwork ensures effective resource sharing among the hosts, terminals, and other subscriber equipment. The subnetwork must be cost-effective.

4.2.1 General Issues in the Subnetwork

The subnetwork protocol design is the key to resource sharing among network devices. In subscriber equipment, processes within host computers communicate with other host processes or with processes in terminal handlers via computer protocols. By a similar method, the subnetwork transports data by means of low-level protocols, framing the heart of computer communications.

There is one primary philosophical choice which must be made in protocol design: whether the protocol should be *transparent* to the user or whether they should perform a *virtual communications* function. Although it exists, the transparent protocol cannot be seen by the user, thereby providing a service that the user doesn't control. The virtual protocol performs a tangible service, such as creating a virtual file. However, the virtual protocol is only a logical entity and has no physical existence.

Of course, it's impossible to answer the question "transparent or virtual" in a general manner. However, a protocol should be transparent wherever possible since this makes operation easier for the user. Subnetwork protocols should be virtual when higher-level protocols must be built on top of lower-level protocols. In these cases, the lower protocols must establish certain virtual communications. Over the past decade, a consensus has formed that virtual protocols are usually the best choice when designing complex systems.

Another choice of equal stature is between a single level of protocol versus several layers of protocol in a hierarchy. A one-level protocol has the advantage of being simple to implement. Most one-level protocols are application-dependent special-purpose protocols and they work best in that context. A multilayer protocol permits the separation of function, which is useful in designing a complex system. This lets the responsibility for resource management be segregated into different areas corresponding to different resources. More importantly, a multilevel protocol supports evolutionary changes in the network since each level of the protocol acts as a separate module. In general, multilevel protocols are most often recommended, particularly when special-purpose protocol levels can be substituted or used in parallel with the standard protocols. This enables the multiple levels to be completely general while retaining the advantages of single-level protocols for special functions.

There are several protocols within a subnetwork hierarchy. Typically, the subnetwork will use a node-to-node protocol for the basic transmission function between packet switches. An end-to-end protocol within the subnetwork deals with overall integrity of transmission. Protocols exist between subscribers as well as between subscribers and the network. There may be several protocol levels between subscribers, including the host-to-host level as well as applications protocols at higher levels. An applications protocol might control the format and content of electronic mail for example.

In an attempt to ensure system compatibility, there have been several international standards defined at these different protocol levels. In the terminology of the *Consultative Committee on International Telephony and Telegraphy* (CCITT), hosts and terminals are known as *data terminal equipment* (DTE). DTEs connect to multiplexers, switches, or modes which are called *data circuit terminating equipment* (DCE). CCITT notes four levels of protocol between DTE and other equipment. At Level 1 is the physical interface (or plug) between DTE and DCE. The currently defined standard for this interface includes the ever-present RS-232 electrical interface as well as X.21 and others.

Level 2 describes the link-control procedure, which will be explained in detail later. The prime example of Level 2 is the standard *high-level data link control* (HDLC). At Level 3, the network control protocol permits using an interface between a DTE and a DCE that is involved in packet-switching networks, like the one developed by national PTTs (Post, Telephone, and Telegraph authorities). The X.25 protocol is the International Standard at Level 3. The host-to-host protocol exists at Level 4 and is used to connect one DTE to another on what's called an end-to-end level. While such protocols are not yet standardized internationally, they will eventually be further defined.

When two protocols of different levels communicate, the lower-level protocol first accepts all data and control information from the higher-level protocol before performing a number of functions on it. Usually the lower-level protocol treats all the data and control information uniformly as data, adding its own envelope of control information. For instance, the host-to-host protocol will accept the application data from the user program and add on its own control information. As the information travels further, the link-control procedure will add on more information, and the network itself will contribute subnetwork control fields. It is in the format of messages flowing through a network that the concept of protocol hierarchy becomes clear. The format of transmitted messages shows the distinct layering of functions just as a nesting of parentheses defines the levels in a mathematical function.

4.2.2 Link-Control Procedures: Level 2

The core protocol for most networks is the *link-control procedure* since it's the most basic. The various link-control procedures in the world today share six primary functions.

1. Data transparency functions
2. Connection and disconnection
3. Failure recovery
4. Error control
5. Sequencing
6. Flow control

The most prominent link-control procedures are the HDLC (high-level data link control) protocol and IBM's SDLC (synchronous data link control) and BSC (binary synchronous communications) protocols. It is best to study the major functions of link control before examining the HDLC protocol as a specific example.

4.2.2.1 Data Transparency

Among the key functions of any link-control procedure is the provision for data transparency. Both data and control messages must travel the link. Certain techniques are necessary in order to distinguish data bits from control bits. Alternatively, the problem is how to tell where a data block begins and ends without restricting the block's contents. There are two widely utilized methods for achieving data transparency. The first, *byte stuffing*, is employed in the BSC protocol. The related method, which is used in the HDLC protocol, is *bit stuffing*. Protocols work by assigning a control meaning to certain data patterns. For example, the beginning of a block of data will be flagged with a pattern of ones (1s) and zeroes (0s). In byte stuffing, this design is comprised of a pair of characters; in bit stuffing, it's a series of 8 bits. Even though the patterns travel in a message, data transparency must be achieved. To ensure this, the sender's hardware interface adds special bytes or bits which the receiver's interface removes, preserving transparency of the original pattern of data. Whenever the control byte needs to flow as data, it's doubled; so where the receiver's interface recognizes two control bytes in a row, one of them is automatically removed. The bit-stuffing procedure works similarly (Fig. 4-6).

The Problem: How to tell where a data block begins and still be able to send any data pattern.

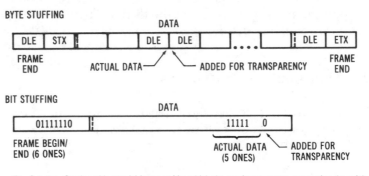

Fig. 4-6. Data transparency.

4.2.2.2 Connection and Disconnection

Any conversation that occurs in the link-control procedure must be established and terminated. When the connection is opened, the devices swapping information may also exchange various types of identification. Parameters of different kinds may also be set at this time. In addition, provisions are made for disconnecting and reconnecting in the event of an error. Such techniques guarantee that the Level 2 protocol can operate in the face of errors or total failure in the link itself and in the computer at each end.

4.2.2.3 Failure Recovery

The link-control procedure must be capable of recovering from failures of either the computer or the circuit. Usually this means that the link must allow its communications parameters to be explicitly reestablished after a failure. At a fundamental level, this means the computer equipment operating the link must continuously perform a test to see that the link is operating normally. If the link is judged inoperative by the test, both ends must take measures to recover. Both ends must recognize that the link is not working properly, even though, in physical terms, it may only be down in one direction. When both ends realize that the link is malfunctioning, they begin to monitor the circuit. When it's working correctly, they can both employ it by establishing a new virtual connection. These mechanisms must be fail-soft so that the link can continue functioning despite any errors in transmission of data or control information.

4.2.2.4 Error Control

In order to perform failure recovery and to achieve accurate communication under normal conditions, the link-control procedure must manage transmission errors. Error control can be handled by a variety of methods. The most practical approach demands an error-detection mechanism for each transmitted message, allowing for retransmission by the source if the receiver does not acknowledge a correct error-free reception. In this general class of procedures, the retransmission can be triggered either by a negative acknowledgement from the destination, when the message is not received, or by positive acknowledgements when messages arrive. A time-out mechanism in the source can also retransmit messages when positive acknowledgements are not received. Generally, positive acknowledgements are preferred since the negative approach is not sufficient (the negative acknowledgements can themselves be lost).

Errors can be detected by many methods, including *parity checking*, where a simple 1-bit indicator gives the parity or "sameness quality" of the data's binary sum. More complicated systems for discovering errors include *cyclic redundancy checksums*, a more comprehensive process that is capable of detecting large numbers of error bits. When a block contains errors, the destination device can ignore the block. After a certain amount of time, usually equal to the expected time to receive a positive acknowledgement, the source can retransmit the block. In general, the source identifies each of the blocks it is transmitting by some number. This number can be one of simple sequence which counts from zero to some fixed limit before recycling. The destination can detect missing blocks by this procedure. The numbering also lets the destination identify duplicate blocks. Any messages with numbers lower than the lowest expected number, or higher than the highest are automatically duplicates.

4.2.2.5 Sequencing

Sequencing traffic is not a primary function for the link-control procedure. Nevertheless, traffic sequencing is often used to ensure that traffic leaving a particular link is identically sequenced to traffic entering. In large packet-switching networks with many links, sequencing traffic in individual links is unnecessary and inefficient, since it can be sequenced at the final destination.

In centralized networks, the opposite decision is often made. Data blocks are typically ordered by assigning a sequence number to each block. This number is used in detecting missing and duplicate blocks. It also maintains status information to the sender and receiver. This adds to other error-control logic, a further argument for sequencing data blocks. The other argument is probably historical. Most link-control procedures were designed for early systems in which there was only one link between the central computer and the peripherals.

4.2.2.6 Flow Control

A sender's transmission rate is matched to the receiver's ability to accept traffic through the link-control procedure. One solution involves an explicit allocation of resources. This means the receiver explicitly tells the sender that it can accept traffic. A designated storage area is usually allocated for messages to be transmitted. The receiver can also notify the sender by specifying a supportable transmission rate. Preventing the receiver from becoming overloaded with traffic is the challenge. Any systems which deal with flow control by allocating the number of messages to the sender are essentially notifying the sender of the receiver's instantaneous reception rate. The concept of a window in which a limited number of messages can travel from source to destination is one way to approximate flow control.

Most flow-control systems are based on some type of feedback control. In the *feedback-control method*, the sender transmits messages until the receiver begins to cut the amount of allocated space. Many current link-control procedures have unsophisticated flow control. The feedback in these systems may consist of a simple on/off control, thus limiting the link's efficiency. Flow-control functions can also be performed by using error-control mechanisms, such as not sending positive acknowledgements. This increases the link's flexibility more than is possible with the simple on/off control. ARPANET, the Defense Department's international packet-switching network, has successfully used error-control messages to perform flow-control functions. A final type of flow control within link control involves the discarding of messages when they can't be accepted. This method relies on a higher-level protocol to retransmit the messages later.

4.3 An Example: CCITT X.25 Interface and Its Link Control Protocol

The X.25 communications standard is the interface approved by the CCITT plenary session in October 1976 and subsequently in 1980 and 1981. It defines the interconnection of DTE and DCE for terminals operating in the packet mode on public data networks. The X.25 standard gains particular importance with its widespread support. It is the accepted data communications protocol for carriers in the United States, the United Kingdom, France, Japan, Canada, and dozens of other countries. Virtually every computer manufacturer has announced support for the standard. For instance, IBM offers an X.25 network to its SNA network. The X.25 interface incorporates a link-control procedure as one of its lower-level protocols. The X.25 link control is the combination of several early standards.

4.3.1 X.25 Overview

The X.25 protocol defines several levels of interface. At the physical level, there is the electrical connection between the DCE and the DTE. This level uses the X.21 standard for full-duplex synchronous transmission. The X.21 standard is related to familiar American Standards like the RS-232 standard. The second level of X.25 clarifies the *link-access procedure* (LAP). The LAP manages the link between the DTE and DCE. In doing so, the X.25 standard uses a subset of HDLC. The X.25 borrows a particular group of parameter settings from HDLC for error control, flow control, and so on. The third level of the X.25 standard describes a packet-level procedure which controls virtual calls through a public data network. This permits the establishment of end-to-end virtual circuits analogous to voice telephone calls. Finally, the X.25 standard elucidates the function of the packet assembler/disassembler (PAD). This includes a procedure within the node for handling the virtual terminal concept. The LAP of the X.25 standard, which is a subset of HDLC, is worthy of close study because of commercial importance and since it exemplifies many of the concepts described above.

4.3.2 HDLC Basics

The protocol which underlies the X.25 standard is the *high-level data link control* (HDLC) procedure. HDLC is an internationally adopted standard that is similar to IBM's SDLC. The American National Standards Institute (ANSI) has adopted another closely related protocol: the Advanced Data Communications Control Procedure (ADCCP). HDLC is actually a family of link-control procedures defined by a number of modes and options. As originally defined, HDLC had two basic modes of operation.

1. *Normal Response Mode.* Designed for centralized systems in which a primary station polls the secondary.
2. *The Asynchronous Response Mode.* Designed for situations in which either station may transmit at any time.

HDLC is continuously developing to meet the changing needs of world-wide networks. Newer modes include a balanced mode of operation in which neither station is designated primary or secondary. The frame format in HDLC allows the transparent communication of data by a bit-stuffing procedure. An 8-bit address and 8 control bits are also used to control the information flow. A 16-bit checksum is appended to the end of each frame.

4.3.3 Second-Level X.25: Link-Access Procedure Data Transparency

The *link-access procedure* (LAP) for the X.25 standard guarantees data transparency for network users by using bit stuffing. Data messages or frames carry a flag byte with the value 01111110. Within the data message, the transmitting interface inserts a zero (0) after each five "1" bits. The receiving interface deletes the "zero" bits, which serve as markers. The LAP frame ends with a 16-bit cyclic redundancy checksum which the X.25 standard defines. This checksum is the error detector mentioned in an earlier section.

4.3.4 HDLC Transmission

The HDLC link-control procedure requires that the DTE and DCE maintain a number of variables for error control and flow control. The *send-state variable*, V(S), denotes the sequence number of the information frame in line to be transmitted. This variable can assume any value between zero (0) and seven (7). It is incremented by one with each information-frame transmission. Using Modulo-8 arithmetic, it cannot exceed N(R), the *receive-sequence number* of the last received frame, by more than the maximum number of outstanding frames (K). The *send-sequence number*, N(S), can only be carried in information frames. Before an information frame is transmitted, the value of N(S) is set to equal the number of the send-state variable.

The *received-state variable*, V(R), denotes the sequence number of the information frame that is about to be received. This value is between zero (0) and seven (7), being incremented by the receipt of each error-free in-sequence information frame with a send-sequence number, N(S), equal to the receive-state variable. The receive-sequence number, N(R), resides in all information and supervisory frames. It holds the sequence number of the next receive frame in line to be accepted. Before one of these frames is transmitted, the value of N(R) is matched to the current value of the receive-state variable.

The *Poll/Final bit* functions in both the command frames and response frames. The Poll bit may be set to one (1) by the sending interface when it wants a marked response from the responder. When the responder receives a command frame with the Poll bit set, it tries to respond with a frame in which the Final bit is set to one (1).

If the initiator has an information frame to send, it transmits the frame with an N(S), or send-sequence number, equal to the current send-state variable, V(S). It will also match its N(R), the receive-sequence number, to the current receiver-state's variable value, V(R). After the information frame leaves, the initiator will increment its send-state variable, $V(S)$, by one (1). If the send-state variable, $V(S)$, is equal to the last value of $N(R)$ plus the maximum number of outstanding frames (K), the initiator won't send any more information frames.

If the send-sequence number, $N(S)$, equals the receive-state variable, $V(R)$, the responder will accept the information field in this frame. It will then increment its receive-state variable, $V(R)$, by one (1). After doing this, if an information frame is ready for transmission, the responder may acknowledge the information frame received by setting its $N(R)$ in the control field of the next transmitted frame to equal the receive-state variable. If no information frame is awaiting transmission, the responder will transmit an RR (Receiver Ready) control message with the $N(R)$ equal to the $V(R)$, or receive-state variable.

Frames with checksum errors won't be accepted by the receiver. No action will be taken with such a frame. If the responder receives a frame with an incorrect send-sequence number, $N(S)$, it will discard the information content of the frame and transmit an REJ (Reject) response with the receive-sequence number, $N(R)$, set one higher than the $N(S)$ of the last correctly received information frame. The responder will then discard the information content of all frames until the expected frame is properly received. These set variables and procedures allow HDLC to dodge errors in transmission while tracking information frames and their sequence.

4.3.5 X.25 LAP Link Control and Connections

All the transmissions in the link are embedded in a frame with the following structure: first, an address byte; secondly, a control byte; and finally, some number of information bytes. The addressing structure of the X.25 standard is worth noting. All the commands to the DCE are given the same addresses as the responses from the DCE. This address differs from the one given for commands and responses traveling between the DCE and DTE. The control byte either contains a command or a response. In addition, it carries a sequence number where applicable. This is shown in Fig. 4-7.

There are three general types of commands in the link. An information-transfer format controls data transfers. The supervisory format supervises link-control functions like acknowledgements and flow control. An unnumbered format provides additional link-control functions.

An initiator requests set-up by transmitting a *set asynchronous response mode* (SARM) command to the responder. Upon receiving an SARM command, the responder replies with an *unnumbered acknowledge* (UA) response, setting its receive-state variable, $V(R)$, to zero (0). Receiving the UA response, the initiator sets its send-state variable, $V(S)$, to zero (0) in preparation for data exchange. Both ends of the link must prepare for a full-duplex line. After swapping SARM and UA commands, the initiator accepts and transmits information and supervisory frames. If no UA response is received, the initiator continues to retransmit SARM commands.

Internally, a frame has the structure:

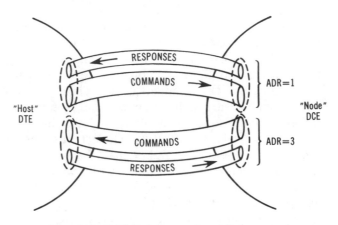

ADR=HDLC "Address" Byte
CTL=HDLC Control Byte
INF=Optional Information Bytes

Logically, the link is multiplexed into four flows:

Fig. 4-7. X.25 link access-level link control.

To reset the connection, the initiator transmits a SARM command and receives a UA response. The responder then sets its $V(R)$ to zero while the initiator sets its $V(S)$ to zero. These commands are retransmitted similarly to the connection initiation commands.

4.3.6 X.25 LAP Error Control and Flow Control

All information commands are numbered in sequence. The sequence number for HDLC is Modulo-8. The X.25 standard specifies a window of some width "K" in the sequence number space. K represents the number of frames which may be in transit between the sender and the receiver. K must be less than or equal to seven.

Three basic supervisory commands help the responder indicate error- and flow-control information to the sender. The *receiver-not-ready* (RNR) supervisory frame is the responder's busy signal, indicating its temporary inability to accept information. Information frames numbered up to and including $N(R) - 1$ are acknowledged. The status of these frames is indicated in later exchanges. When the busy state clears and information frames are receivable, a valid response is communicated. The *receiver-ready* (RR) supervisory frame lets the responder acknowledge information frames numbered up to and including $N(R) - 1$. The *reject*, REJ, supervisory frame requests retransmission of frames starting with number $N(R)$. All information frames numbered $N(R)$

— 1 and below are acknowledged. Frames awaiting transmission are sent after the transmission of previous frames that have been rejected. Only one REJ exception may be established for a single direction at any time (Fig. 4-8).

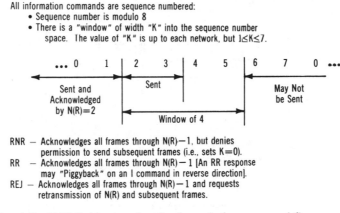

All information commands are sequence numbered:
- Sequence number is modulo 8
- There is a "window" of width "K" into the sequence number space. The value of "K" is up to each network, but 1≤K≤7.

RNR — Acknowledges all frames through N(R)−1, but denies permission to send subsequent frames (i.e., sets K=0).

RR — Acknowledges all frames through N(R)−1 [An RR response may "Piggyback" on an I command in reverse direction].

REJ — Acknowledges all frames through N(R)−1 and requests retransmission of N(R) and subsequent frames.

Fig. 4-8. X.25 link access-level acknowledgement and flow control.

4.3.7 X.25 LAP Formats

All of the LAP commands are encoded into a single 8-bit field. Information frames must carry both N(R) and N(S) values. The only other frames that carry sequence numbers are the supervisory responses which carry N(R). All information frames have a Poll or Final bit. The other bits in the 8-bit field distinguish various supervisory and unnumbered commands and responses. This is shown in Fig. 4-9.

4.4 Host-Level Protocols

In addition to lower-level protocols which connect DCEs to DTEs, there are the higher-level protocols residing beyond the subnet interfaces. These host-level protocols have several levels. At the lowest level, host-to-host protocol performs end-to-end interprocess communications (communications between processes on different computers). This may occur on different networks or within the same host. Even at this layer, desired types of network services might vary greatly. For example, the system may require multidestination, broadcast, or nonsequenced service. The predominant service might include low-delay or high-reliability point-to-point data transport.

It's best to begin studying host-level protocols by looking at basic principles; then work through a continuum of host-level protocols whose characteristics strongly depend on the type of interprocess communication desired, the network interface needed, and the services available to support the host level.

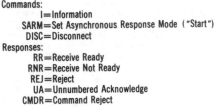

Format	Commands	Responses	Encoding							
			1	2	3	4	5	6	7	8
Information	I			N(R)		P		N(S)		0
Supervisory		RR		N(R)		F	0	0	0	1
		RNR		N(R)		F	0	1	0	1
		REJ		N(R)		F	1	0	0	1
Unnumbered	SARM		0	0	0	P	1	1	1	1
	DISC		0	1	0	P	0	0	1	1
		UA	0	1	1	F	0	0	1	1
		CMDR	1	0	0	F	0	1	1	1

Poll/Final ⟶

```
Commands:
        I=Information
     SARM=Set Asynchronous Response Mode ("Start")
     DISC=Disconnect
Responses:
       RR=Receive Ready
      RNR=Receive Not Ready
      REJ=Reject
       UA=Unnumbered Acknowledge
     CMDR=Command Reject
```

Fig. 4-9. X.25 link access-level control byte structure.

The area above the host level has cavalierly been labeled the *application level* or the *user level*. The terms are in deference to the boundless opportunities for standards, or the lack of standards, at the upper levels. The issues which arise in formulating standards for virtual terminals, file transfer, and electronic mail are complex but worth exploring in any study of host-level protocol.

4.4.1 Basic Principles 1: Abstract Models

There are three fundamental principles in network protocol design.

1. Layering.
2. Interfaces.
3. Symmetry.

Layering is the principle of separating protocol functions into different levels. Some of these levels are *side-by-side* and independent of each other. Some levels support others. For example, virtual terminal TELENET is supported by the host-to-host level in the ARPANET. The separation into layers potentially simplifies each layer and also allows networks to access services at different layers (Fig. 4-10). Yet, for layering to succeed, it must employ stable and well-defined *interfaces* between protocol layers. In this way, a layer can

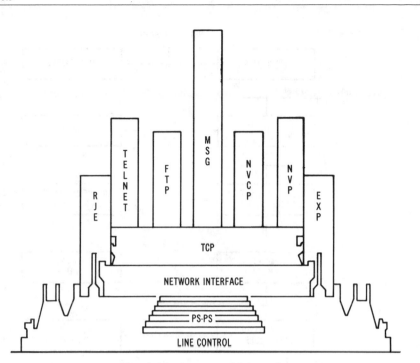

Fig. 4-10. A protocol hierarchy.

be changed without affecting the interface, so services are optimized in an evolutionary way without alteration of higher-level protocols. With layering, there is no need to lose services in transitions in technology (Fig. 4-11).

Symmetry in protocol design works in two ways. First, each layer has at least two or more ends. Drawing contours around protocol and processes at each layer should produce a model like a sliced onion. If the contours slip, there's a problem; perhaps one participating "end" is at the wrong layer of protocol. This is illustrated in Fig. 4-12.

The next aspect of symmetry is harder to characterize. For distributed systems in which no single site is in central control, it is essential that protocols work properly, even if all systems work concurrently but are essentially independent. In its simplest form, this aspect of symmetry appears in designs that don't depend on the master/slave relation.

A simple analogy for symmetry may be drawn by comparing the postal service with the public-switched telephones. With the mail system, two people can simultaneously send letters which cross in the mail without adversely affecting communication. However, two phone calls can collide during dialing making information exchange impossible until someone connects (Fig. 4-13).

The asymmetrical protocols (caller/called model) do not mix with symmetric ones if the asymmetrical one is trying to support the other. Peculiar ambiguities arise when these protocols are mixed.

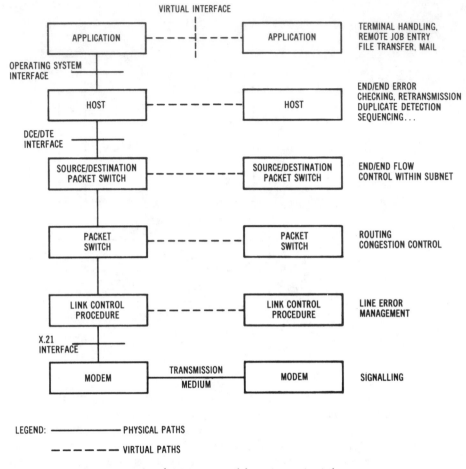

Fig. 4-11. Protocol layering principle.

4.4.2 Basic Principles 2: Protocol Objectives

It is difficult to grasp the notion that different protocol layers may independently contain common objectives. Flow control is an example of this. On the surface, this duplication appears wasteful. However, repeating objectives in different layers is sometimes essential to sharing or protecting resources fairly in the layers.

There are four major generic objectives. Most, but not necessarily all, of these objectives appear in some form in communication protocols.

1. Separation of control and data.
2. Synchronization.
3. Resource management.
4. Resource sharing.

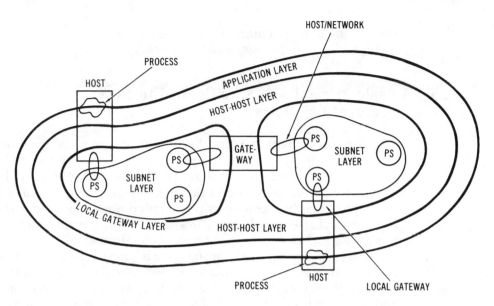

Fig. 4-12. Onionskin model of protocol layers.

Separation of control and data, or data transparency, is achieved in the HDLC protocol discussed earlier through bit-stuffing and a special frame character. In the X.21 standard, different electrical leads are used for signaling and for data. In other protocols, standard formats distinguish information from control data. Maintaining the state of each of the two or more ends of a protocol in close correlation is called *synchronization*. This notion is exhibited in sequencing or flow-control mechanisms.

Resource management appears as flow control if, for instance, the resource to be controlled is buffer space. *Resource sharing* typically presents

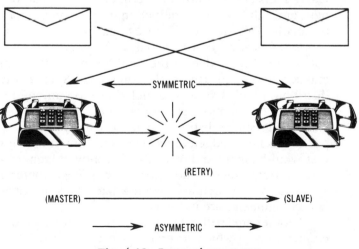

Fig. 4-13. Protocol symmetry.

itself in the form of multiplexing where a common address structure permits multiple access to the resources addressed.

4.4.3 Basic Principles 3: Specific Host-to-Host Protocol Objectives

The host level of protocol furnishes sufficient commonality of the process of port addressing and of the data format to allow communication between the processes. Given the variety of available operating systems and equipment architectures, successful networks must adopt common conventions. Pairwise agreement between hosts (bilateral conventions) fit this model. However, general resource-sharing demands the cost-effective decision to adhere to a single standard for host-to-host communication.

Commonality can also be maintained by translating one host protocol into another. In this case, the translator becomes the shared convention. This means different mechanisms share the translation rules that relate the objects and operands from one protocol to another. This strategy results in the same disadvantages as pair-wise convention agreements. Nevertheless, translation may be a practical solution for political or even technical reasons. For example, if the operating system cannot be modified, translation may be practical.

An example of this idea appears in the ARPANET, where a host-to-host protocol (TCP) is adjacent to the network voice protocol (NVP). The former supplies reliable point-to-point interprocess communication, while the latter carries compressed speech over a low-delay nonsequenced, nonguaranteed network-datagram service.

The design of reliably sequenced full-duplex point-to-point protocols is reasonably well-understood, even in the context of multiple networks. Multipoint services such as broadcasting to several processes, or conferencing, are less understandable now. Experiments with shared satellite channels, ring nets, and Ethernets have helped in the exploration of cooperative distributed protocols. One discovery proves that in a true broadcast system, where all processes hear all transmissions, distributed control protocols will naturally cooperate. This is due to their ability to run the same control or decision-making algorithms against the same data. Such a solution works to achieve distributed multiaccesss channel allocation among multiple ground stations that access a common satellite channel.

Broadcasting reliability is still in an early stage of development. The usual positive acknowledgement schemes become unwieldy when a single broadcast would stimulate thousands of acknowledgements. The only true broadcast protocols, such as those for packet-speech conferencing, are the real-time applications in which loss of a few packets is not catastrophic. Thus, data acknowledgements are not necessary.

Another area still explored less is the provision of synchronized real-time connections in which several connections (possible broadcast) drive multimedia input/output devices. Such devices might include a joystick or cursor-tracking facility which might be combined with a virtual graphics protocol using different interprocess connections. For such streams to be useful, they must be played in relatively close synchrony. This would enable a user to see the motions and images while hearing the speech in proper relation. Without synchronization, the display cursor might point to the wrong place on the screen while the speech would be delayed. A teleconference on such an unsynchronized facility would become telechaos.

Other services might include end-to-end encryption for privacy, or the choice of priority, reliability, and delay mechanisms. Delay mechanisms might be useful for the deadline scheduling of messages or packet transmission. Among the many tough issues facing protocol designers is whether to place a service in one layer or another in horizontally adjacent protocols. Theoretical guidance for these issues is improving to meet the growing demand for design expertise.

Integrated Voice/Data Networks

Richard S. Kagan

Richard S. Kagan is from Brooklyn, New York. He received his B.S.E. in Engineering Science (with honors) from the University of Michigan, Ann Arbor, MI, in 1980, and was awarded the Andrew A. Kucher Award for outstanding contributions to engineering research. In 1981, he received the M.S.E.E. degree from the University of California, Berkeley, CA.

Mr. Kagan joined Bell Laboratories in 1980, and worked on telecommunications power processing systems at the Energy Systems Engineering Laboratory in Whippany, N.J. In 1983, he joined ROLM Corporation in Santa Clara, CA, where he worked in the Technology and Advanced Development Department on projects involving high-speed data transmission, local area network architectures, and electromagnetic compatibility. Mr. Kagan is currently the European Director of Business Development for Echelon Corporation, the developers of LonWorks* Technology which is a system for developing Intelligent Distributed Control systems.

Mr. Kagan has authored technical articles on the subjects of bioengineering and electronic power processing, and has lectured on the subject of distributed processing. He is a member of the IEEE and Tau Beta Pi.

Chapter 5

5.1 Introduction

5.1.1 Integrated Voice/Data Networks

Electrical and electronic telephone systems have served the voice communications needs of business for over 100 years. Over the past 30 years, digital computer and communications technology has brought new features to business voice telephone systems. In addition, this same technology has enabled voice communications systems, termed "Integrated Voice/Data Communications Systems," to provide many of the features of local Area Networks (LANs) and Private Branch Exchange (PBX) telephone systems in a single, integrated system.

5.1.2 Local Area Networks

The ability to move data between systems in a fast, flexible, and economical manner is a requirement for an effective information network. Within the limited geographic area occupied by a business establishment, a *local area network*, or *LAN*, provides a common means for interconnecting and integrating heterogeneous elements using a shared communications system.

Local area networks represent a significant departure from the hierarchical communications architecture typified by the early mainframe computer systems. The structure of LANs reflects their principal functions of multiple connectivity and resource sharing: the communications resources of a LAN are shared among all devices attached to the network, and this, in turn, allows users to gain easy access to one another and share common resources.[3]

The LAN's ability to support a range of applications and equipment is achieved by strictly defining the low-level details of the information flow. A LAN always includes a specification of the following:

1. A *communications medium* over which data passes in going from one device to another.
2. *Network adapters* that provide devices with an interface to the communications medium.
3. A physical *topology* by which the medium is extended between adapters.
4. An *access protocol* carried out by the adapters to ensure an orderly and fair use of the medium.
5. A *logical format* for data transmissions on the medium.
6. An *electrical specification* of data encoding and transmission on the medium.

A distinction often drawn between integrated voice/data networks based on PBXs and broadband (or baseband) LANs is that, while LANs are distributed in structure, the PBX network is more centralized. Most broadband and baseband LANs extend a common communications medium throughout the local area to each end user, and spread the adapters out along the medium (Fig. 5-1). In contrast, the medium in most PBX LANs is short and concentrated. The adapters are located together in a central place, and the distances between user devices and the common communications medium are longer (Fig. 5-2).

While the impact of these architectural differences may not be immediately apparent, the PBX architecture is particularly well suited to the design of integrated voice and data networks. The goals addressed by a PBX based voice/data network are summarized as:

- *Accessibility*—Connection points to the network are ubiquitous and can be easily extended to any user location within an establishment.

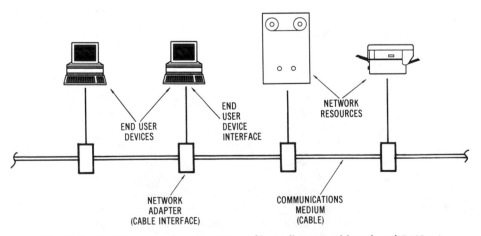

Fig. 5-1. Architecture characteristics of broadband and baseband LANs. A common communications medium, to which devices are attached via network adapters, is extended throughout the local environment.

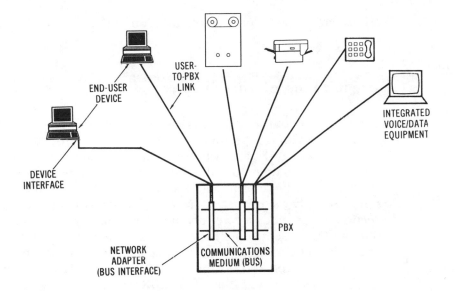

Fig. 5-2. PBX LAN architecture. The communications medium is short and devices connect over user links to co-located network adapters.

- *Capacity*—The network can supply each user with sufficient bandwidth to provide for satisfactory performance over a range of applications.

- *Reliability*—The network exhibits a low bit-error rate under normal operating conditions, is tolerant of failures in individual network elements, and provides a level of service consistent with its role as the primary controller of office communications.

- *Manageability*—The network offers a means for managing configuration and growth, and for controlling network access and traffic flow.

- *Maintainability*—Repairs, upgrades, expansions, and changes can be performed with minimal impact on the majority of network users.

- *Compatibility*—Standards and protocols may be supported to allow many types of equipment from different vendors to share the network.

- *Economy*—The network provides cost-effective connections for a wide range of user devices.

5.1.3 Limitations of Local Area Networks

Effective design and use of a LAN depends upon understanding its limitations as well as its capabilities. Most importantly, a local area network provides a *means* for communication. However, connection to a LAN does not *guarantee* communication. The ability to communicate is ultimately a property that resides within end-user devices and not in the network that connects them.

A local area network provides connections, but may not provide communications.

5.1.4 Organization of This Chapter

The remainder of this chapter is organized into two parts. The first part, consisting of Sections 5.2 through 5.7, presents background material for those unfamiliar with PBXs and with basic data communications concepts. Much of this material should help to illuminate the discussions that follow in the chapters that cover broadband and baseband LANs. Specifically, Section 5.2 presents an overview of the key problems addressed by local area networks. Section 5.3 provides a brief definition and history of the PBX. Sections 5.4 through 5.7 present some important concepts relating to the physical "nuts and bolts" of data communication, and includes discussions of bandwidth, switching, control, and reliability. With this material as background, Section 5.8 describes the application of the PBX voice/data networks to data communications problems. Section 5.9 concludes with a discussion of network administration in a PBX environment and summarizes how the PBX network addresses the objectives presented in this section.

5.2 Modern Data Communications and Requirements

5.2.1 Data Communications vs. Voice Communications

5.2.1.1 Voice Communications: Regulations, Standardization, and Simplicity

Most people are only vaguely aware of the enormous size and complexity of the U.S. public-switched telephone network, which connects over 170 million users.[4] It is usually taken for granted that nearly anyone can successfully make a telephone call, and that placing a call from one phone proceeds in much the same manner as from any other phone, regardless of the phone's location or its manufacturer. It is instructive to view modern data-communications systems in light of the familiar public voice-communications network. The switched network's appearance of uniformity and general ease of use make it an excellent model for any hypothetical data network.

There are two main reasons why the public telephone network is so easy to use. The first is that the interface to the network has been rigidly standardized. The standards encompass the telephone equipment, the wiring, the numbering scheme, and the feedback provided to users during call progress, such as dial, busy, and ringing tones. Second, the internal operation of the network is transparent to the user. Once the dialing sequence has been completed, the network is responsible for routing the call and maintaining the connection without further user involvement.

The strict standardization of the voice network evolved principally because the network was regulated by the government and dominated by its major supplier, the Bell System. Even with the deregulation of customer-premises terminal equipment and long-distance service, the existing industry standards remain and ensure that any equipment designed accordingly will operate properly on the network. This is a benefit both for communications equipment suppliers and the end users.

5.2.1.2 Data Communications: Competition, Diversity, and Complexity

In contrast with the public switched-telephone network, local data-communications products have evolved in an environment dominated by competition and diversity.[24] Nearly every major computer vendor has defined a proprietary data-communications standard that is largely incompatible with those of other vendors.[8] The same manufacturer's standards may even vary from one product line to another.[18] The differences in standards impact every aspect of data communications, including wiring, transmission formats, data rates, connection set-up procedures, addressing and routing schemes, and even the binary codes used to represent basic units of information, such as alphanumeric characters.[6,7] Unlike the common analog telephone, the notion of a "universal data terminal," that can be simply plugged into any arbitrary port, is still in the realm of science fiction.

5.2.2 Connections, Virtual Connections, and Communication

The distinction that was made in the introduction between connections and communications is an important one. *Communication* is the exchange of meaningful information between two or more parties. Communication is supported by one or more connections, which are paths for data exchange. To the communicating entities, a *connection* appears to be a physical path dedicated solely to their use. However, not all connections are supported by a distinct physical path. For example, a single pair of wires can be used to support a number of simultaneous virtual connections, which share the common physical connection. *Logical connections*, as virtual connections are sometimes called, are also used for data exchange among processes executed within a common computer. To the software processes, these internal logical connections may be indistinguishable from connections to remote devices over hardware links.

While a connection is required for communication, it does not guarantee that communication can occur. Consider a telephone conversation. Although it may be relatively simple for a caller in the United States to establish a connection with a telephone in Japan, the possibilities for communication are quite limited if the calling party does not speak Japanese and if the called party speaks no English.

5.2.3 The ISO OSI: A Model for Data Networks

The concept of communication, as a "high-level" function, supported by a connection, which is a "lower-level" function, is appropriate for data communications as well as voice conversations. A multilevel hierarchical view of data networks can greatly simplify their design by enabling designers to focus on a manageable set of well-defined, and clearly related problems.

Several standard organizations, most notably the International Standards Organization (ISO), have developed logical models for communications in distributed data networks composed of heterogeneous equipment.[21] The ISO reference model for Open Systems Interconnection (OSI)[23] has been widely publicized and it serves as a common basis for the comparison of network architectures.[13] The model is composed of 7 layers and is depicted in Fig. 5-3.

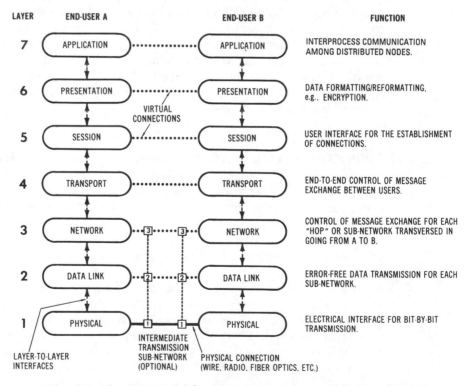

Fig. 5-3. The ISO model for Open Systems Interconnection (ISO). Information passes physically only at layer 1. Higher layers appear to be connected to corresponding layers across the network by virtual or logical connections.

A primary goal of the ISO model is to decompose data communications functions into manageable pieces with well-defined interfaces. The model is analogous to the U.S. Constitution, which defines the overall structures, functions, and relationships among the government's branches, but stops short of defining specific laws that implement the structure. Similarly, the ISO OSI defines the layers and their interactions, but does not define specific protocols used to implement the functions within each layer.

Each layer of the model defines a peer process which communicates with the corresponding peer process at the other end of the connection. The only physical connections exists at layer 1; layers 2 through 7 communicate with their peers over virtual connections established in software. Although layers 2 through 7 exchange information with their neighbors above and below through layer-to-layer interfaces, each layer "sees" only the virtual connection to its distant peer. Only layer 1 exchanges data directly with its peer.

By defining only the functions of layers and their interfaces, the architects of the reference model have attempted to define a structure that allows the particular protocols that implement a layer to change without a need to change other layers as well. As a result, when the implementation of a layer changes to reflect changes in technology, the integrity of all other layers is preserved. Any two processes that use compatible sets of protocols at each level are able to communicate.

The function of each layer in the OSI model, which is given in Fig. 5-3, can be better understood using a telephone call example. The application served by the telephone network might be a sales call and, thus, a voice-quality circuit is selected to serve this application. The actual communication, while supported by the network, takes place in the minds of those engaged in the communication (i.e., the end devices). The communicants are only concerned with the way in which information is presented to them; as sounds, in a language that both understand.[23] The caller establishes a session by dialing a network address (called the party's telephone number) and listening for the called party to answer.[25] The caller is not concerned with how the network manages to locate and ring the called party's phone, or with how his information gets from his mouth piece to the distant party's earpiece, provided that transmission is error free. Moreover, intervening local and long-distance subnetworks, which may use satellite, microwave, fiber optic, or copper-wire links, do not care about the content of the information carried, provided that the physical connections that comprise each data link are compatible at each end.

5.2.4 Basic Communications Problems

5.2.4.1 Early Compatibility

Prior to the development of inexpensive semiconductor and disk memories, processors and their memories were centrally located. The *data terminal equipment*, or *DTEs*, used for input and output were unintelligent devices, with no more capability than that required to change received signals into visible characters and keystrokes into transmitted signals. As a mainframe computer system represented a huge investment in both capital and man-hours of programming, users of one manufacturer's equipment were unlikely to purchase another vendor's equipment unless the equipment was directly compatible with the existing system. Computer manufacturers saw little need to conform with the architectures of their competitors, and developed proprietary protocols for input/output between DTEs, processors, and peripherals, sometimes introducing a new standard with each new product.

As a rule, users were expected to go wherever the DTEs were located, which was usually within the vicinity of the computer room. Terminals near the computer were connected using direct hard-wired links which offered low-error transmissions at fairly high speeds using synchronous transmission. (Synchronous transmission will be described later.) Users at remote locations were serviced using facilities leased from the public telephone network.

While analog public telephone circuits are more than adequate for voice service, they offer limited data-carrying capacity, and they exhibit nearly 10,000 times the error rate that is experienced on hardwired links. In addition, the cost of leased telephone circuits, at several dollars per mile per month, can be significant.

The situation changed a great deal, however, with the introduction of minicomputers. These systems were designed with flexible architectures to serve a broad range of applications. More importantly, as a minicomputer represented perhaps a tenth of the investment required for a large mainframe, it came within the reach of smaller units within the corporate hierarchy and could be tailored to the needs of a smaller user community. As these systems were deployed in increasing numbers, software applications were written to serve a wider range of functions. As a result, more users demanded access to the computer. Users also became less willing to go to the computer; instead, they demanded access to computing from their desks. They were accommodated by manufacturers who produced cost-effective asynchronous terminals that used less-complicated protocols than their synchronous counterparts. Minicomputer manufacturers also began to provide software to support the terminals made by other vendors, in order to allow users a wider range of choice.

The asynchronous terminal interface that has become standard is designed to support terminals located near the host. The standard, which is labeled RS-232C by the Electronic Industry Association (EIA), and V.24 by the International Telegraph and Telephone Consultive Committee (CCITT), supports transmission at rates up to 19,200 bits per second (19.2 kbps), up to a distance of 50 feet between the DTE and the host. Remote terminals are supported by an intervening data circuit between the host and DTE, using a class of devices known as *data circuit terminating equipment*, or *DCE*s, as shown in Fig. 5-4. Installations that used an analog PBX to support the voice telephone network within an establishment used this existing distribution system for data, using DCEs that were known as *mo*dulators-*dem*odulators, or

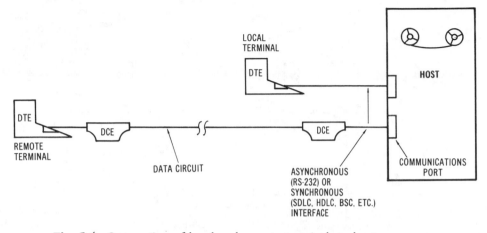

Fig. 5-4. Connection of local and remote terminals to host processors.

modems. Modems condition the data signal for transmission through voice channels, although the data rate is usually limited to below 9600 bps by the limited data capacity (or bandwidth) of the voice channel, as explained later in Section 5.4.

The maximum data rate of 19.2 kbps available through an RS-232C interface is more than adequate for character-oriented applications accessed by low-function asynchronous terminals. At that rate, a 24-line by 80-character display can be updated in less than 1 second. However, this rate is a severe bottleneck for an interprocessor communication that involves transfers of large files with several million bits. The high-speed ports of many computer systems can supply data at rates up to 50 megabits/second (Mbps). File transfers, although at much lower speeds, are also required for personal computers and other desktop equipment with resident processing and storage. Higher data rates are also useful for terminals that support high-resolution graphics. These applications require a faster and more flexible interface, with communications software that can manage the transactions.

5.2.4.2 A Hypothetical Data Network

Many organizations, in the process of evolving from a mainframe to a more distributed environment, created data networks similar to that depicted in Fig. 5-5. The limitations of this "network" point out a number of problems addressed by local area networks.[19] These are detailed below.

Fig. 5-5 actually depicts two isolated networks: the minicomputer system and the mainframe computer system. The personal computers, shown as stand-alone devices, are not a part of either network. Mainframe users cannot access applications on the minicomputers, because the proprietary synchronous transmission protocols used by their terminals are not supported by the minicomputer communications ports or protocols.

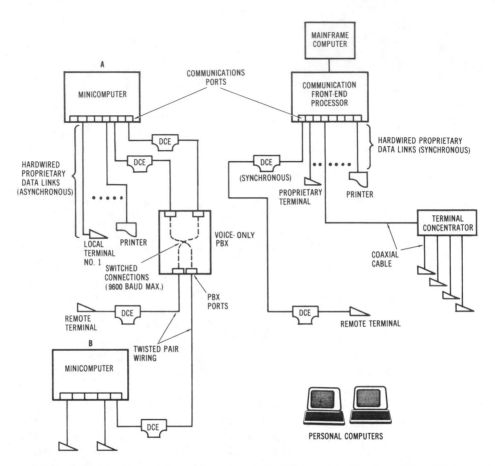

Fig. 5-5. A representative data network that is supported by an analog PBX.

Remote synchronous terminals cannot be connected to the mainframe using the analog PBX, because their synchronous DCEs operate at a rate that exceeds the bandwidth of an analog, voice-only circuit. The synchronous terminals also use expensive wiring, which must be run to a new location each time a user is added or moves to a new office. Unused cable runs are usually abandoned, filling cable raceways and walls.

Although minicomputer users cannot access the mainframe system, they can access a program on a minicomputer to which they are not directly attached. However, to do so entails an inefficient use of resources. For example, to access a program on Computer B from Terminal No.1 requires 3 computer ports, 2 DCEs, and a PBX voice circuit. It also requires Computer A to act as a communications front-end for Computer B. The bandwidth limitation imposed by the analog PBX circuit also limits the bandwidth of their connection to 2400 bps using a common low-cost modem. Interprocessor communication is also limited by the PBX circuits. In addition, Terminal No. 1 may only be used occasionally, but it ties up a computer port continuously.

The PBX voice connections are not used efficiently and the call set-up is cumbersome. These connections are established just like voice circuits, by dialing the extension of the host's DCE, which answers with a carrier tone. Setting the terminal characteristics to match the DCE characteristics proceeds by trial and error. In addition, the voice circuits remain connected until either the user or host disconnects, although data flows in short blocks during only a fraction of the connection time. As most voice PBXs provide for fewer connections than are needed to support all users simultaneously, this inefficient use of voice connections competes for a scarce resource.

In Section 5.8, we will present a PBX-based network that can interconnect and integrate the system shown in Fig. 5-5 to provide a more functional network.

5.3 The PBX

5.3.1 A Brief History

The *Private Branch Exchange*, or *PBX*, has been in existence in one form or another for about 100 years. The PBX belongs to a class of systems known in the telephone industry as *customer premises equipment*, or *CPE*. The early PBXs were systems installed in an organization's building with the sole purpose of switching telephone calls between parties located both within and outside the facility. Fig. 5-6 illustrates a telephone central switching office serving a large representative business establishment and it illustrates the motivation for developing the PBX.

In a typical business environment, only one-sixth of the voice stations are in use during the busiest hour, and only two-thirds of these are connected to outside parties.[9] Without the PBX, a dedicated pair of wires would be required

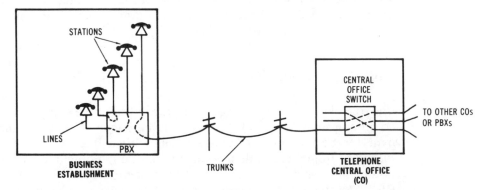

Fig. 5-6. The PBX reduces the cabling required between an establishment and the central office. It also reduces the load on the central office switch. Lines connect user stations to the PBX; trunks connect the PBX to the central office switch.

between each station in the user's building and telephone central office. The equipment in the central office would switch all of the business's traffic, including the internal calls. Several operators would also be needed in the telephone central office for receiving incoming calls (to the business's main number) and for routing the calls to the desired extensions.

The PBX is used because it reduces the cabling burden between the central office and the business establishment, and it reduces the cost of external lines for the business. Assuming typical telephone traffic statistics, it is possible to extend only one connection, or trunk, between the central office and the business's PBX for every five to six stations in the establishment. The telephone company's savings in copper wire alone is substantial for large installations that are located far from the central office. In addition, a PBX gives a business office greater control over the features and costs of its communications system.

PBX technology has evolved much more rapidly over the past 20 years than during any other period in its history as a result of developments in the marketplace, in technology, and especially in the regulatory environment. Specifically, the deregulation of customer premises equipment has brought a new element to the design, manufacture, and sales of PBX systems—competition. Prior to 1968, the telephone operating companies, led by the Bell System were the sole U.S. suppliers of PBXs. In that year, the Federal Communications Commission (FCC) issued its landmark Carterfone decision. The FCC ruled that the Bell System had to provide connections to non-Bell equipment, as long as the equipment met Bell's technical standards and did not damage the public network. This ruling opened the previously closed PBX industry, which continues to attract entries from both new and established companies.

The effect of competition in the PBX industry has been magnified, because increased user demands have come at a time when new technology is available to meet them. As data traffic in the office has risen, PBXs have been judged increasingly on their ability to carry data as well as voice traffic. At the same time, the low power requirements of VLSI silicon circuits, coupled with their high density and speed, have made digital technology the basis for essentially all modern PBX systems.

5.3.2 Defining the PBX

The role of the PBX has changed as its capabilities have expanded beyond voice communications. Many PBX vendors have generated unique names and acronyms for their equipment, in order to differentiate their products from the older PBXs and from those of their competitors. Examples include the PABX (Private Automatic Branch Exchange), the EAX (Electronic Automatic Exchange), the CBX (Computerized Business Exchange), the DBX (Digital Branch Exchange), etc. For purposes of simplicity, it is best to group all of these products under the PBX umbrella and define a "generic PBX" as follows:

"A PBX is a system which, in response to dynamic demand, establishes communications paths between the devices terminated on its input/output ports by receiving, processing, and transmitting electrical signals. Devices connected to a PBX include voice-communications terminals (telephones), data terminals, integrated voice/data workstations, computers and computer peripherals, gateways to public and private voice or data networks, and other PBXs. PBXs are most commonly installed on the premises of the customers they serve."

5.3.3 PBX Architecture and Evolution

A PBX consists of a *switching system, interfaces* to the switching system, and a *control mechanism*. A block diagram of a typical PBX system is shown in Fig. 5-7. While each functional block is shown as a distinct subsystem, the switching, interface, and control functions are less segregated in some systems, as described in subsequent sections.

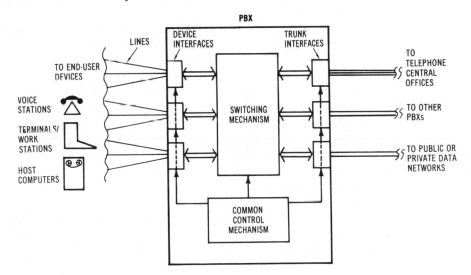

Fig. 5-7. A typical PBX architecture.

In the earliest PBXs, the switching system consisted of a switchboard; the control mechanism was a human operator. These were later followed by entirely electromechanical PBXs based on step-by-step switches and metallic crosspoints.

In 1963, the Bell System placed the first PBX controlled by a computer into service.[14] The 101 EES (Electronic Switching System) utilized a stored computer program to supervise a time-division-multiplexed semiconductor switching system. The stored-program control added great flexibility, while the semiconductors allowed for a great reduction in the size of the switching systems. These systems also needed far less maintenance than their electro-mechanical counterparts. The 101 ESS switched discrete samples of the analog signals, which were taken at regular intervals, using a technique known as pulse amplitude modulation, or PAM. After switching, the samples were sent through a filter to recover the original analog signal.

The first PBX to switch signals in digital form was produced in 1971 by Digital Telephone, Inc. In the early digital systems, the analog signals that were presented to the interfaces by voice lines were first converted into binary digital signals, which were then presented to the switching network. The analog-to-digital (A/D) and digital-to-analog (D/A) conversions were performed by devices known as *coder-decoders* (or codecs) located on or near the interfaces. The technique used to encode speech signals digitally in the Digital Telephone PBX is known as *delta modulation*, in which the difference between the two successive speech samples is translated into a binary number. As discussed later in Section 5.4, the encoding scheme that has become a recognized standard world wide is known as *pulse code modulation*, or *PCM*. The first digital PBX to use PCM encoding was introduced in 1975 by the ROLM Corporation.

Although the majority of the traffic handled by early digital systems consisted of analog voice conversations, trends in semiconductor technology had already made it possible to design all-digital switches that were cost competitive with analog switching techniques.

Transmission between the user station and the PBX has yielded to digital technology. Large-scale integration has made possible such devices as low-power single-chip codecs, which can perform A/D and D/A conversion within the telephone set, and which eliminate the need for codecs at the PBX interfaces. Digital transmission also offers greater immunity to noise and signal degradation than analog transmission. In addition, digital techniques for interleaving two or more distinct bit streams are used to provide integrated voice/data links.

The PBX continues to evolve in response to both voice and data requirements. Private voice networks are increasingly attractive to large organizations. In addition, data switching features enable a PBX to bridge between other LANs and to serve as a LAN in its own right.

5.4 The Physical Layer: Bandwidth, Media, and Topology

This section covers some of the key physical aspects of data communication. The intent is to provide basic definitions of the terms most often used to define LAN architectures and interfaces, such as the data rate (or bandwidth), the wiring used for data transmission (or media), and the structure described by the LAN wiring (or physical topology). A few basic engineering concepts that are related to data communication will aid in an understanding of how LANs operate at the physical level.

5.4.1 Analog and Digital Signals

In the previous section, we indicated that PBXs were first used to switch analog voice traffic. The principal feature of analog signals, for our purposes, is that they are continuous. This means that the signals can take on all possible values between the lowest signal level and the highest, as shown in Fig. 5-8A.

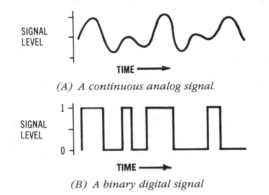

(A) A continuous analog signal.

(B) A binary digital signal

Fig. 5-8. Analog and digital signals.

Binary digital signals have only one of two possible values, corresponding to the *bi*nary dig*its* (or *bits*) 0 and 1, shown in Fig. 5-8B. Digital signals can be used to encode any desired entity, such as the number 3.57 or the letter W. They can also be used to encode analog speech signals. Analog signals are encoded by taking groups of bits together to represent binary numbers. These bit groups correspond to the value of the analog signal at a given instant. For example, using all the combinations for 8 bits, it is possible to represent 256 analog values. The analog value encoded by a binary number is discrete; it encodes only a single, predetermined analog value. The specific values represented by a set of binary numbers can be assigned according to any desired scale, with either fixed steps between successive values (which yields a linear scale) or variable steps (which yields a nonlinear scale).

5.4.1.1 Analog Speech Bandwidth

Analog telephones convert the variations in sound pressure made by the human voice into corresponding variations in an analog electrical signal. The number of periodic variations that occur each second defines the frequency of the signal. This frequency is expressed in hertz (Hz), or cycles per second. A speech signal may be represented as the summation of a number of pure tones that occur simultaneously. The difference between the maximum frequency and the minimum frequency present in the signal is called the analog signal bandwidth. Human voice signals contain significant energy at frequencies from 100 Hz to 5000 Hz. However, analog telephone circuits limit the highest frequency to about 3500 Hz, and the lowest to 300 Hz, resulting in an analog signal bandwidth of about 3200 Hz. This bandwidth is sufficient for the transmission of highly intelligible and recognizable speech. The bandwidth limitation is purposefully imposed by the telephone and the PBX circuits, and not by the intervening wiring. The bandwidth limitation imposed by telephone wires is a complicated function of several properties of the wire, of which length is perhaps the most important. This is further discussed in Section 5.4.6.1.

5.4.1.2 Digital Speech Bandwidth

Analog speech is represented in digital format through the processes of *sampling* and *analog-to-digital conversion*. The continuous analog waveform is sampled at regular intervals in time and the analog values are then converted into binary numbers. One encoding technique, illustrated in Fig. 5-9, is known as pulse code modulation, or PCM.

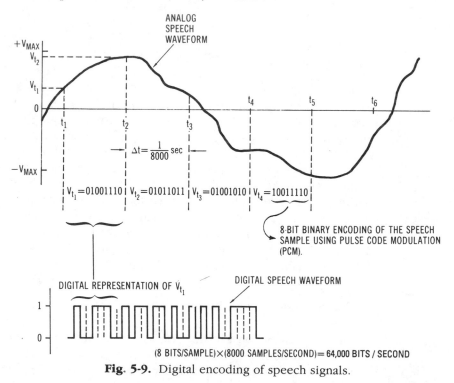

Fig. 5-9. Digital encoding of speech signals.

By sampling a signal of limited bandwidth at twice its highest frequency, which for speech is taken as twice 4000 Hz (or 8000 times per second), it is possible to reproduce the speech signal perfectly. However, the process of assigning a discrete binary number to each sample introduces an error known as *quantization error*. This unavoidable error is the difference between the actual value of the analog sample and the nearest value encoded by one of the binary numbers. The average quantization error is a measure of the trade-off between using a scale with more bits per sample (which yields smaller steps) versus using a coarser scale that requires fewer bits. The standard scale used in North America is an 8-bit nonlinear scale known as *u-law 255*. The required bit rate, or digital bandwidth, for a PCM-encoded speech signal using u-law 255 is then:

$$8 \text{ bits} \times 8000 \text{ samples/second} = 64,000 \text{ bits/second} = 64 \text{ kbps}$$

PCM encoding according to u-255 is standard throughout the United States; European countries use a different coding algorithm known as *A-law*.

5.4.1.3 Bits per Second and Baud

Data transmission rates expressed in bits/second are unambiguous and indicate the rate of data transfer exactly. The *baud* rate, however, refers to the rate of symbol transitions impressed onto a transmission line. As there are a number of ways to represent a bit (or a series of bits) as transitions on a transmission path, there is only a loose correlation between the bit rate as expressed in bits per second and the symbol rate as expressed in baud. Some encoding schemes, such as Manchester encoding, require two bauds per bit. Other schemes, such as Nonreturn to Zero or NRZ encoding, use a single baud per bit. However, some schemes encode more than one bit with each baud, and, thus, the baud rate of a data stream may be higher or lower than the bit rate. As a result, the bandwidth required to transmit at a given data rate is a function of the encoding scheme used. However, the signalling rate rarely differs from the bit rate by more than a factor of 2 or 4 when wireline transmission is used.

5.4.2 Logical Representation of Information in Digital Systems

There are several standards in use for representing basic character-oriented and print-control information in digital systems. The two most widely used standards are the *American Standard Code for Information Interchange (ASCII)* and the *Extended Binary-Coded-Decimal Interchange Code (EBCDIC)*. EBCDIC is a *de facto* industry standard used in a wide range of IBM and IBM-compatible equipment. ASCII is the character set recognized by many asynchronous terminals. A program written for use with ASCII-encoded data cannot interpret EBCDIC-encoded data without first converting from one code to another. This is complicated by the fact that some EBCDIC codes have no direct ASCII counterparts, and vice versa.[11] This type of code conversion is one of the functions performed by the presentation layer (layer 6) of the ISO OSI model.

5.4.3 Serial and Parallel Transmission

Within data-processing equipment, groups of bits are operated upon as single entities. The most common grouping is that of 8 bits, which is called a *byte*. The transmission of an entire byte between two machines can be accomplished in a single operation using 8 transmission paths, one for each bit. This method, known as parallel transmission, is common between computers and high-speed peripherals that are located close to one another. However, over longer distances, the expense of running a transmission path for each bit becomes excessive. Using serial transmission, a single transmission path is used, and the bits are sent one at a time. The serially transmitted bits are temporarily stored and reassembled into bytes in the receiving equipment before they are processed.

5.4.4 Synchronous and Asynchronous Transmission

Asynchronous data transmission is commonly used for data rates below 19.2 kbps. It is the scheme used in the vast majority of ASCII terminals used today. In asynchronous transmission, the internal timing references, or *clocks*, of the transmitter and the receiver run independently. The transmitter initiates a transmission by sending out a *start bit* that tells the receiver to get ready, and it then causes transitions to occur at fixed time intervals, according to the bit rate for which it is programmed and the bit pattern being transmitted. The receiver, after noting the start bit, samples the incoming bit stream at fixed time intervals, according to the rate for which it has been programmed. As long as the transmitter and receiver are programmed at the same bit rate, the receiver interprets the incoming stream properly. Following the start bit, the transmitter usually sends a single byte, and then sends one or more *stop bits*, indicating the end of transmission. Since only a handful of bits are sent at a time, the receiver can resynchronize its clock at the beginning of each transmission and, thus, the clock doesn't need the accuracy that would be required to remain synchronized for a long, continuous series of bits. To aid in the detection of transmission errors, a *parity bit* can be appended to the end of each byte. The parity bit is selected to make the total number of "1" bits an even or odd number, depending on whether even or odd parity checking is selected. Parity checking can detect single bit errors, which is usually sufficient, given the smaller number of bits sent for each character.

Synchronous transmission is used for long uninterrupted bit streams and is particularly useful for high-speed transmissions. In synchronous transmission, the clock information is encoded along with the data and the receiver uses the incoming bit stream itself to adjust its internal clock rate (which allows the data to be recovered). This is one reason for the use of Manchester-type code, which provides two transitions per bit. By doing so, it is possible to send long uninterrupted strings of bits without stopping to resynchronize. Other synchronous standards group the bits logically into frames and embed an easily detected pattern into the bits that mark the frame boundaries. A receiver can scan the incoming stream for this pattern in order to become synchronized.

Frame synchronization is used in T carrier systems, which were originally designed for transmitting digitally encoded voice streams. The *T1-D3* standard, developed by the Bell System and used in North America, specifies how 24 PCM-encoded, 64-kbps voice channels are multiplexed into a single 1.544 Mbps stream. (A similar standard used outside of North America is defined by the CCITT at 2.048 Mbps and carries 32 PCM channels.) Each frame contains an 8-bit sample from each of the 24 voice channels, plus one framing bit used for synchronization, which alternates in a 101010 . . . pattern. The 193-bit frames repeat 8000 times each second, yielding the 1.544 Mbps T1 rate. Standard rates for continuous synchronous data transmission range from 1.2 kbps to the T1 rate, although the telephone network employs systems that use the "T4" rate of 274.176 Mbps. T1-type transmission is finding increasing use for data transmission between PBXs and their hosts, as will be discussed later.[26]

Synchronous transmission is also used for transmitting finite blocks of data, in which the beginning of the data stream, or *preamble*, is used for synchronization. Committee 802 of the Institute of Electrical and Electronic Engineers (IEEE), with responsibility for the development of standards for local area networks, has defined standard rates of 1, 4, 5, 10, and 20 Mbps for synchronous transmissions. Errors in block synchronous transmissions are checked by appending an error-detecting code, such as a *block-check character (BCC)*, or *cyclic redundancy code (CRC)* to the end of the transmission. The use of several error-detecting bits allows the detection of multiple bit errors, which are likely to be missed by simple parity checks.

5.4.5 Simplex, Half-Duplex, and Full-Duplex Transmission

Simplex transmission refers to one-way data exchanges. This, of course, requires only a single pair of wires. *Duplex transmission* refers to two-way data exchanges between two parties. In *half-duplex transmission*, signals are sent in only one direction at a time. In *full-duplex transmission*, signals are sent in both directions simultaneously.

Both half- and full-duplex transmission can be accommodated using one or two pairs of wire. As shown in Fig. 5-10A, *half-duplex, four-wire operation* dedicates a transmitter and receiver to each pair of wires, only one of which is used at any given time. The two parties utilize a protocol to "turn the line around," in which they trade roles as talker and listener. If both parties are free to transmit at the same time, the same four-wire operation becomes full-duplex.

A single two-pair wire can be used for transmission in both directions, either alternately (half-duplex) or simultaneously (full-duplex). For *two-wire full-duplex transmission*, the expense incurred for the elimination of the second pair of wires is a circuit at each end of the link known as a *hybrid*, which performs the two-wire to four-wire conversion (see Fig. 5-10B). Analog hybrid circuits have been in use for many years for two-wire full-duplex voice

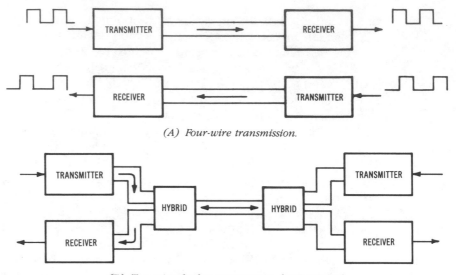

(A) Four-wire transmission.

(B) Two-wire duplex transmission (with hybrids).

Fig. 5-10. Duplex transmission.

transmissions, and are used with standard analog telephones. Hybrids can also be used for full-duplex two-wire digital transmissions at high frequencies (e.g., 256 kbps), allowing full-duplex voice and data service on one pair of wires.

5.4.6 Wiring: Media and Topology

Wiring technology and media specifications are central to any LAN implementation. Most buildings are wired for voice service and essentially all PBX installations utilize a *star* wiring topology, which is also known as "home-run" wiring. Each voice/data station is supported by dedicated wires that run from the user's terminal (i.e., telephone) to the PBX. The number of pairs of wire required for each user depends upon the services provided to his terminal and the type of transmission used. Most building locations are usually wired uniformly with the same number of wire pairs. Most PBX vendors require their customers to install two to four pairs of wire between the PBX and each end-user location.

The most common PBX wiring plans specify 24-gauge, unshielded, twisted pairs of insulated solid-copper wire. Wire of this type is sometimes referred to as UTP. The advantages of UTP include a wide range of inexpensive tools and accessories available for cable distribution, termination, and testing. These advantages are familiar to a large number of trained telephone technicians. UTP is also less expensive relative to most other types of cabling. In large quantities, a cable that contains three twisted pairs for indoor use costs $0.075/meter. A single coaxial cable costs from 4 to 5 times this amount.

Star wiring simplifies moves and changes, when compared with *ring* or

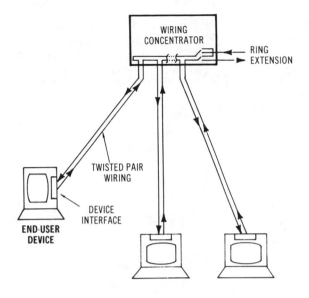

Fig. 5-11. Star wiring topologies can support ring, bus, and point-to-point networks. IBM recommends the star configuration depicted here for wiring devices into a baseband token-passing ring.

bus-oriented wiring plans. In its submissions to the IEEE 802 committee, IBM recommends a star wiring approach for a ring network, as shown in Fig. 5-11, based upon the improved service characteristics of centralized wiring concentration.[1] Star wired installations require a minimum of effort to relocate a user, since only one connection is affected. Star wiring also provides a central point for testing and troubleshooting.

5.4.6.1 Bandwidth Limitations of UTP

The *bandwidth* of any transmission line is a function of its length, because the transmitted signal is attenuated through various loss mechanisms as it propagates along the medium. Losses are a function of the transmitted frequency and usually increase rapidly above some limiting frequency. Several factors affect the data rate that a pair of wires can support, and thus it may be misleading to speak of the bandwidth of a UTP in a general sense. The performance of a communications link is constrained by several factors, including the transmitter and receiver characteristics and the environment in which the cable is found. The signals on the wire must be strong enough to be received with a low probability of bit errors, and yet must not be strong enough to cause interference in neighboring systems through cross coupling or by radiating energy into the environment. While the determination of an acceptable error rate is left to the discretion of system designers, interference limits are imposed by FCC and other regulations.

One of the best examples of the bandwidth that is available with UTP wiring is the performance of the T1 digital link.[12] This link supports reliable noninterfering full-duplex digital transmission at a rate of 1.544 Mbps for distances up to 2000 feet, using two pairs of UTP. For shorter distances, even higher data rates are possible on UTP. The relationship of bandwidth to distance for UTP is shown in Fig. 5-12, based on the specifications of some available data communications system.

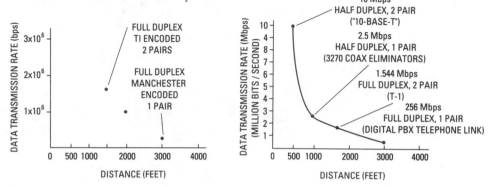

Fig. 5-12. Data rate vs. distance characteristics of 24-gauge interior telephone wiring as indicated by currently available commercial communications equipment.

5.5 Switching Concepts and Systems

5.5.1 Bandwidth as a Resource

Bandwidth is the basic commodity provided by any communications network. The switching function makes bandwidth available to most devices so that they may exchange information. Determining the time, place, and quantity of the bandwidth allocation is the responsibility of the control mechanism, which will be discussed in the next section. In this section, we examine some of the basic means by which bandwidth may be provided and partitioned in order to switch data among users.

5.5.1.1 Circuit Switching and Packet Switching

Circuit switching and *packet switching* are two basic techniques for allocating bandwidth. A number of generalizations may be made concerning the characteristics of these two techniques in terms of common implementations.

Circuit switching, most often associated with voice traffic, is often controlled by a centralized, hierarchical control mechanism with global knowledge of the network's configuration. On the other hand, packet switching is (often reflexively) associated with data traffic, and this lends itself to distributed control mechanisms in which most network nodes require very little information about the network configuration in order to get data from source to destination. These generalizations reflect the nature of circuit and packet switching in their most common implementations. However, the hardware used for circuit switching can support packet switching services, and packet switching hardware can support circuit-like connections. In many applications, the features of both circuit and packet switching systems can be combined to realize the best solution.

A *circuit* may be defined as "a route between certain limits or boundaries." In communications, circuit switching usually refers to the establishment of a connection in which the data path is fixed in time and space. Moreover, the path remains fixed until the circuit is disconnected.

To establish a circuit-switched connection, it is first necessary to find an available data path, seize it, and dedicate it to the exclusive use of the communicants. As a result of this circuit set-up overhead, circuit switching is most efficient for connections that carry a large amount of data relative to the data that must be exchanged during set up. Once the connection is in place, little or no processing is required to maintain it. However, the bandwidth and other resources allocated to a circuit are "owned" by the communicants until the connection is terminated. The circuit thus represents an efficient use of resources only to the extent that the allocated bandwidth is utilized. Circuit switching is naturally suited to voice conversations, which tend to be long lived (about two minutes on the average) relative to the set-up time required (about 0.1–0.5 seconds). Further, data flow occurs during a relatively large percentage of the connection time in most voice conversations.

Packet switching is an allocation technique that utilizes bandwidth only when there is data to be transmitted. The efficient use of bandwidth comes at the expense of an increased processing and data content overhead that is incurred with the transmission of each packet. As shown in Fig. 5-13, packets are formed by adding information to the beginning and end of each group of user data. The packet *header* identifies the source of the data and its destination, and it can also identify the nature of the data, as well as providing billing and accounting information. The *trailer* contains error checking information, such as a CRC, which is used to determine whether the packet has been corrupted in transmission. Packet switching is a form of message switching in which the length of each transmission is limited to the maximum packet size. Long messages are broken up into a number of packets which are reassembled into the original messages on the receiving end.

Packet switching is most efficient in transaction-oriented environments, in which occasional bursts of data are exchanged only during the small fraction of the time that processes are logically connected, or "in session" with one another. This is especially true when the amount of data sent in each packet is large relative to the packet overhead.

An example of such an environment is an airline reservations system. Communications costs for agents at remote locations, connected logically with a central flight reservations data base, can be weighted to reflect the

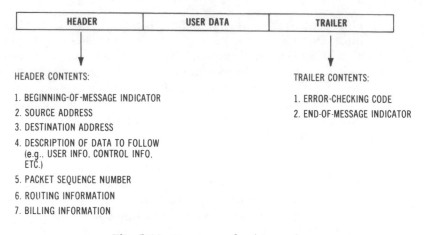

Fig. 5-13. Structure of a data packet.

actual amount of data transmitted, rather than just the total connection time. Packet switching also lends itself to situations in which users switch rapidly and often between a number of applications, or are in communication with multiple applications simultaneously.

5.5.1.2 Access and Transmission Delay

Several concerns, in addition to efficiency, usually determine the suitability of packet or circuit switching to a given application. A major concern is the delay experienced between the time a device is ready to transmit data and the time the data is received at the destination. The total delay is a combination of the *access delay* and the *transmission delay*.

Transmission delay is the time required to send a message once transmission has started. For a message of a given length, transmission delay varies more or less directly with the distance between communicants and inversely with the bit rate. This applies to both packet and circuit switching.

Access delay is the time that a device which is ready to send data must wait before transmitting. In circuit switching, the bandwidth allocated to a connection is immediately and continuously available to the users following the initial circuit set-up delay. In packet switching, an access delay is incurred before the transmission of each packet if the system bandwidth is in use, or if other users waiting to send data have a higher access priority. Some packet-oriented networks, most notably those based on a token-passing scheme, offer a deterministic "maximum possible" delay that can be incurred by any single user; this will depend upon the number of users on the network and the distances between them. In other schemes, such as the CSMA/CD access method used by Ethernet, the maximum delay is probabilistic. Although the probability of incurring a long delay may be minimized by properly restricting the number of users, it is theoretically possible for the delay to increase without bound.

Protocols established at layers 3 and 4 in the OSI model can be used to provide virtual connections, which behave much like circuits, in and between packet switching networks.[5] Conversely, fast circuit switching, which is a means for improving bandwidth utilization in circuit-switched systems, requires a circuit set-up procedure whose delay is just a small fraction of the 0.1–0.5 seconds common with voice-switching systems. Both of these control methods will be discussed in greater detail in Section 5.6.

5.5.2 Space-Division Switching and Time-Division Switching

5.5.2.1 Analog Space-Division Switching

Prior to the advent of electronic switching, the early manual and electromechanical PBXs utilized space-division switching networks. These systems established connections between the switching network's ports by providing a unique dedicated physical path for each conversation. A single-source port and a single-destination port occupied a full-duplex physical path for the duration of the call. The physical path in manual and electromechanical space-switching networks carried continuous analog signals.

5.5.2.2 Blocking and Nonblocking Switches

Space switches are arranged with some number of inputs, N, and some number of outputs, M. In order for a single-space switching network to provide simultaneous connections between each input and any available output, a total of $N \times M$ switching elements are required. Thus, to simultaneously connect 100 users to any of 100 devices would require 10,000 bidirectional switching elements. However, the nature of voice telephone traffic is such that the probability of every user needing service simultaneously is extremely small. For this reason, most voice PBXs provided for fewer paths than required to support simultaneous connections between every line and any other line or trunk. Should all switch paths become filled, all subsequent calls are blocked until a path becomes free. A completely nonblocking system is one that can provide any possible combination of line-to-line or line-to-trunk connections, involving all lines and trunks, simultaneously. Such systems are usually unnecessary for voice service and are only cost effective in extreme cases.

A standard measure of voice-switching service is expressed by the probability that a user will be blocked from service as a function of the *number of lines* connected to the system and the *average traffic* presented to the system by each line. The total traffic is expressed as the product of the number of calls in progress times the average duration of each call (in seconds) during a 1-hour period. Each simultaneous call that a system can handle is equivalent to 1 call $\times$ 3600 seconds (per hour), or 3600 *call-seconds*. This is written as 36 *ccs* (hundred call-seconds). In a typical business environment, 90% of all lines offer less than 6 ccs of traffic during the busiest hour. For a switching system with 1800 ccs capacity, the system is nonblocking for 100 users, since the system can support 50 two-way connections at 36 ccs traffic. If the same 1800-ccs system is used to serve 400 lines, at an average of 6 ccs per line, the probability that a user will be blocked during a call attempt is less than 0.0007, which is once in about 1400 call attempts.

5.5.2.3 Digital Switching and Data Buses

A *data bus* is a high-bandwidth data path that is shared among a number of devices. In PBX networks, the voice stations, data terminating equipment (DTEs), or personal computer/workstations (PCs) gain access to the data bus through bus interfaces, which provide one or more device ports, as shown in Fig. 5-14. Most digital PBXs employ one or more data buses to concentrate data prior to switching.

Switching takes place in a switching network attached to the bus, or it can take place on the bus itself. Such centralized buses are often referred to as short buses. Short buses can use relatively inexpensive components and can use parallel transmission to support very high bandwidths.

Communication between the user device and the data bus is supported by a link extended between PBX port and the device. While the data bus operates

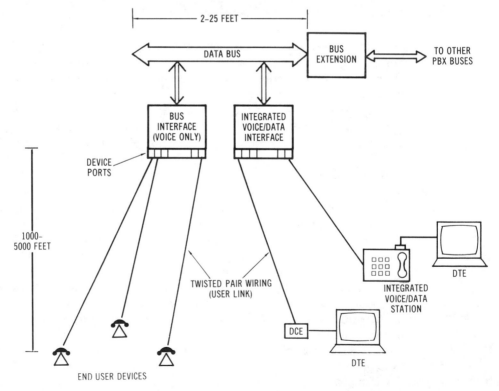

Fig. 5-14. Short-bus PBX architecture.

at a very high rate in order to support many users, the bandwidth of an individual link to a telephone, DTE, or personal computers can be much lower. Different links operating at different rates can be tailored to support a range of device types, at a cost that is appropriate for each.

Long, distributed buses carry the full bus bandwidth to each user device as shown in Fig. 5-15. This type of bus is most commonly associated with baseband and broadband local area networks. Long buses usually employ serial data transmission over a single cable to reduce wiring costs. However, the requirements of high-speed and long transmission distances tend to increase the cost of transmitter/receivers (called transceivers), and necessitate the use of more-costly, high-bandwidth cabling. Since the shared medium is distributed to the locations of workstations, a transceiver and workstation interface are usually dedicated to a single device. As a result, the cost of connecting to a long bus can be greater than the cost of connecting to a short bus. The benefit of the long bus is that the full bus bandwidth can be made available to each user for short times, although this is also possible with short buses, as will be shown later.

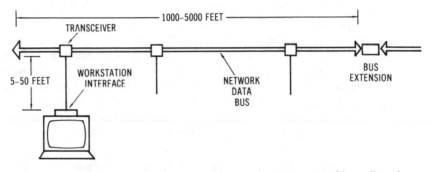

Fig. 5-15. Long-bus architecture that is characteristic of broadband and baseband LANs.

5.5.2.4 Time-Division Multiplexed Switching

Time-Division multiplexed (TDM) switching is a means of allocating bus bandwidth and can be used to accomplish a switching function. As an example, consider a 64-kbps, PCM-encoded voice signal that is obtained by taking 8000 8-bit-samples-per-second of speech. Using a parallel bus with 8 transmission paths, this voice signal can be transmitted from a source to a destination by transmitting an 8-bit sample over the bus 8000 times per second, which corresponds to a bus rate of 8000 bus cycles per second. If the bus rate is doubled to 16000 bus cycles per second, an additional connection between another destination and source can be accommodated by alternating the user of the bus between the first connection and the second. The bus may be thought of as providing a frame, which repeats 8000 times each second, consisting of two consecutive *time slots*. By allowing the first source and destination to exchange data during time-slot number 1 and the second pair to exchange data during time-slot number 2, the two connections are multiplexed onto the common bus.

The bandwidth available in each time slot is the product of the number of bits transferred and the repetition rate.[23] Generalizing from this simple case, it may be seen that the total bandwidth of the time-multiplexed bus is the product of the number of time slots in one frame, the frame repetition rate, and the number of bits exchanged in each time slot. Thus, an 8-bit parallel bus that provides 8000 frames per second, each frame containing 500 time slots (500 t-s), provides an aggregate bus bandwidth of:

$$8 \text{ bits/t-s} \times 8000 \text{ frames/second} \times 500 \text{ t-s/frame} = 32 \text{ Mbps}$$

The bus cycle rate is the product of the number of time slots and the frame repetition rate which, in this example, is 500×8000, or 4 million cycles per second. Such a rate is well within the capabilities of the commonly available semiconductor components. Some buses use 32 or more transmission paths and have bus rates over 15 MHz.

The bandwidth of a TDM bus can be parceled out in a variety of ways. For switching voice, it is convenient to allocate bandwidth in 64-kbps segments, which carry one direction of a PCM-encoded voice conversation. Control of the switching is straightforward if the bandwidth available in one time slot is an integer multiple of 64 kbps, because managing conversations becomes equivalent to managing time slots. If the time slot bandwidth is exactly 64 kbps, the maximum number of simultaneous connections that can be supported is equal to one half the number of time slots supplied on the bus.

TDM can be applied to analog as well as digital signals; it is the technique in effect any time that the use of a common channel is alternated periodically among different connections.[24] The first application of TDM was in the Bell System's 101 PBX. Here, TDM was used to switch analog voice signals which were not digitized. Discrete analog samples of speech signals were switched at regular intervals, using a technique called pulse amplitude modulation, or PAM. The initial 101 ESS utilized two PAM buses, each of which provided a 25-time-slot frame that repeated 12,500 times per second. Bell's Dimension PBX, introduced in 1975, also utilized a PAM bus. The original Dimension bus provided a 64-time-slot frame with a 16-kHz repetition rate.[14]

5.5.2.5 Time-Multiplexed Space Division and Multistage Switching

Commonly available semiconductor switches operate over one million times faster than their electromechanical counterparts. The speed of these devices makes possible space switches that may be multiplexed in time and shared among a number of simultaneous connections. In *time-multiplexed space-division (TMSD)* switching, an array of space switches is instructed to set up a new set of connections between its inputs and outputs during each time slot. A nonblocking space switch with 10 inputs, 10 outputs, and 100 switching elements can handle 10 unique connections per time slot. Used in a system that provides a frame with 500 time slots, this TMSD switch can provide the equivalent of 5000 connections, by providing a unique set of 10 connections during each of the 500 time slots. Such a network is referred to as a *time-multiplexed switch*, or *TMS*.

A TMS provides for more connections than the physical number of inputs by multiplexing the use of its physical connection paths in time. In order to fully utilize this capability, the inputs and outputs of the TMS must be connected to a different set of users during each time slot, using another switching stage.

Large, high-capacity PBXs often employ multistage switching architectures. The architectures of these systems are described using shorthand notation that shows the type of switching utilized at each stage, by indicating a T, for time division, or S, for space division. The bandwidth of the innermost stages is usually the greatest. In the shorthand method, a system using a space-division network, such as a TMS, to interconnect a number of TDM-switched buses, would be called a time-space-time, or TST, network.

5.6 PBX Control Mechanisms

The PBX control mechanism is responsible for coordinating the actions of the switching network, the device interfaces, and any additional network resources, such as internetwork gateways, in conjunction with other PBXs and public or private networks. The control mechanism accepts inputs from peripheral devices through their interfaces and translates these inputs into actions that provide system services. These services include basic end-user services, enhanced end-user services, and system administration functions, as listed in Table 5-1.

Basic end-use services and most system administration functions are usually provided by the control mechanism itself, while enhanced services usually involve the participation of additional devices such as application processors and peripheral input/output equipment. Access to system administration is usually provided through an administrator's console via a maintenance and administration port. Administration is covered in greater detail in Section 5.9.

5.6.1 Common Control Architectures

A principal difference between broadband LANs and PBX networks is the degree to which control resources are shared. Control is completely distributed in broadband and baseband LANs, in that each network interface is equipped with the control necessary to access the common medium. As the number of devices contending for the medium increases, the average bandwidth available to each

Table 5-1.   System Services Coordinated by the PBX Common Control

Basic End-User Services	Enhanced End-User Services	System Administration Functions
Circuit-switched voice connections	Interactive data-call set-up Pocket-switched and high-speed circuit-switched connections, voice messaging	Moves, adds, and changes, call detail reporting
Circuit-switched data connections	Protocol conversion	Diagnostics, error reporting, and fault isolation
Call processing features; e.g., hold, transfer, forward, camp-on, seed dialing, etc.	Electronic mail	Traffic monitoring and logging
Resource sharing (trunk queuing, port queuing, modem pooling, etc.)		Service restriction (class-of-service)
Resource Management (least-cost routing, etc.) routing, etc.) Call	Integrated voice/data services	

user declines. However, the control function required of an individual user's adapter is the same, regardless of the total number of users on the network.

In PBX networks, both communications bandwidth and control resources are shared by a number of devices. As a result, the processing load on the PBX control mechanism increases with the number of users on the network. PBXs are designed to cope with an increasing number of users in several ways. At one extreme a single master processor and switching network, capable of handling the maximum complement of users, is used independently of the number of devices attached. However, the costs associated with this powerful processor are a penalty for the smaller systems. This penalty is particularly significant in PBX systems, which must be cost effective over a wide range of customer sizes.

In order to meet the requirements of large systems and remain cost effective for smaller customers, control functions can be distributed. Large PBX systems are usually partitioned into a number of nodes with each node supporting a portion of the user community. Within each node, the control functions may be partitioned into "higher" and "lower" functions, which are handled by processors distributed throughout the node.

5.6.1.1 Single and Multinode Systems

Centralized switching systems can use a single switching node through which all devices are connected and switched. Distributed systems utilize multiple nodes, each of which terminates a portion of the user population. Distributed systems may be physically centralized, with all of the equipment located in a single room, or they may be spread throughout a building or campus.

The traditional method of nodal interconnection uses a hierarchical switching structure. In this case, end nodes connect directly to end users, and they usually switch traffic between their own users internally (Fig. 5-16A). Internode traffic is routed up the switching hierarchy to a tandem node which switches internode traffic.

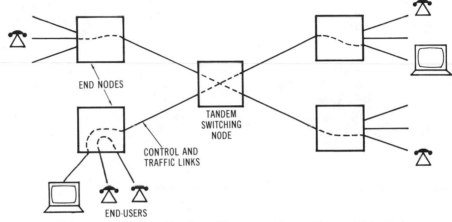

(A) Hierarchical multinode architecture with a tandem switching hub

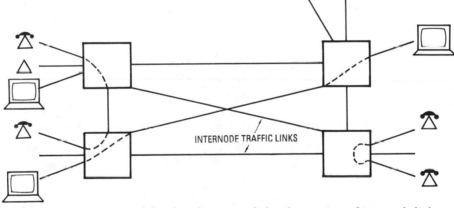

(B) Fully interconnected distributed system with 4 nodes requiring 6 internode links.

Fig. 5-16. Interconnection of nodes in multinode PBX LANs.

Some PBXs utilize a fully distributed architecture as shown in Fig. 5-16B. In this case, each node is a complete stand-alone entity, at an equal level in the hierarchy with all other nodes. Distributed nodes may be fully or partially interconnected. Full interconnection, which requires a point-to-point link between each node and every other node, requires $N(N-1)/2$ internode links for a system with N nodes. Partial interconnection, which provides less than the full number of point-to-point links between nodes, is feasible when the amount and distribution of internode traffic can be well characterized in advance. Nodes that exchange a large amount of traffic are connected directly to one another, while the traffic between nodes that exchange a modest amount of data is routed through intermediate nodes. Full interconnection becomes expensive and complex for systems with many nodes, due to the large number of internode links and the associated costs. For this reason, internode tandem switches are often used to interconnect large numbers of nodes.

5.6.2 Stored Program Control

The early, electronically controlled PBXs executed a control algorithm implemented in hardwired logic. Changes to the control structure and the addition of new features required a change in circuitry. Modern PBXs operate under the direction of software that resides in the common control memory. The control program is executed by one or more central processing units in each PBX node. The block diagram of a PBX node is shown in Fig. 5-17.

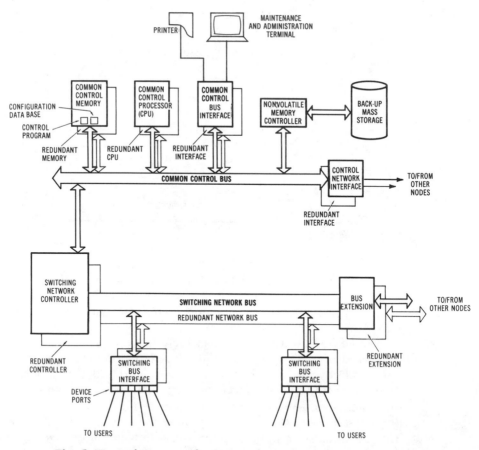

Fig. 5-17. Architecture of a PBX node. Redundancy in most critical elements is usually available as an option.

5.6.2.1 Control Functions

Control functions may be partitioned into asynchronous *event-driven* tasks and synchronous *time-driven* tasks. The event-driven tasks are those associated with processing service requests from user devices and peripherals. Devices signal a need for service by changing state, such as going from on hook to off hook, or by entering control commands. Time-driven tasks are those that are initiated repetitively by some part of the control structure itself. For example, system administration tasks, such as diagnostics, are run periodically to provide and up-to-date picture of the system status.

5.6.2.2 Intra-Node Connections

The architecture shown in Fig. 5-17 depicts a centralized control structure with a TDM switching bus. Circuits are established through a coordination of the bus interfaces and the switching bus, under the direction of the CPU. The control algorithm executed by the CPU is stored in the Common Control Memory, which also contains the configuration data that records the location, or bus address, of each user device on each bus interface on the switching network. Configuration data is fairly static and changes only when users are added, moved, deleted, or require a new class of service.

The *switching-network controller* orchestrates the transactions on the switching network using data in the *connection table*, which changes dynamically. The connection table stores the addresses of the devices that exchange data during each TDM bus time slot.

5.6.2.3 A Data-Call Example

A user at a remote DTE wishes to establish a connection with a host computer. By pressing the request-for-service key on his DCE, the user sends a signal to the PBX data bus interface indicating the desire to call a data resource. The bus interface may then interrupt the CPU or wait to be polled before responding, at which time the address of the device requesting service will be passed to the CPU. In this example, the information passes between the CPU and the bus interface via the switching network, although a separate message-passing bus could be used instead. Using the configuration data base, the CPU can determine that the address of the device requesting service corresponds to a data interface. Data-call software is then used to establish the connection.

Assuming that the connection table is not filled to capacity, an idle time slot is reserved for use by the DTE. Using this time slot, the CPU sends a message over the switching bus to the *bus interface*. The message is forwarded to the DTE and appears on the terminal screen. In response to the message, which may be a menu of services that the user may access, the user types the command **Call**, followed by the name, or number, or the desired resource. The user command is forwarded to the CPU, which again uses the configuration data to translate a named resource, such as **Production** for the factory floor computer, into a *bus address*. The bus address identifies the specific interface circuit to which the **Production** host is connected. If the host is connected to the PBX through several ports, each may be scanned in turn, and, if all are in use, the CPU will send a corresponding message to the user. At this point, the user may then queue and wait for a host port to become free, as discussed in more detail in Section 5.8.

If a port to the **Production** computer is available, the CPU reserves the port for the user, marks it as busy, and places the bus address of the free port into a connection table location corresponding to an idle time slot. The CPU then instructs the PBX interface to signal the host's DCE to indicate an incoming call. During this time, the CPU may also inform the user via the terminal screen that it is **Calling Production**.

When the host responds by sending a "ready" signal to the PBX interface via its DCE, the interface sends a message to the CPU. The CPU then binds the connection between the user and the host. The connection table allows only the host's interface to receive data transmitted by the user's interface during the user's time slot. Likewise, data transmitted by the host's interface, during its assigned time slot, will be received only by the user's interface. Once the connection is bound, the call will remain in progress without further action on the part of the CPU. During each bus frame, the switching network will cycle through the connection table, and data will flow between one source device and one destination device assigned to each time slot. Since each bus interface buffers the flow of data between the user and the switching bus, a range of data rates can be supported, up to the full time slot bandwidth.

To end the connection, one of the participating devices issues a disconnect command to its corresponding interface. When the disconnect request is forwarded to the CPU, the time slots that were in use are freed and the bus interface ports are marked as idle. The resources are then available for reuse by other devices.

5.6.2.4 Distribution of Function Within Nodes

The processing load on the central processor can be reduced by assigning the responsibility for repetitive "low-level" tasks to the bus interfaces. Interfaces can scan for busy and idle lines, collect and process commands, and perform periodic diagnostic tests on each line. Functionality can extend between devices terminated on the same interface.

The distributed architecture of a switching node may be extended to the point where all call processing is handled by the bus interfaces themselves. The interfaces exchange messages directly with one another to establish connections, instead of relying on a central processor to control the state of the system. With the advent of powerful, inexpensive single-chip microprocessors, such PBX architectures are increasingly cost effective. These architectures provide for modular growth and do not require the overhead cost of a powerful central processor. This modularity comes at the expense of an increase in complexity that is associated with the control required at each interface.

5.6.2.5 Packet Switching on PBX Networks

With the addition of the appropriate control intelligence, the architecture shown in Fig. 5-17 can implement a broadcast-type, short-bus, packet-switching service. If groups of bus interfaces are configured to recognize a common bus address, the switching network of Fig. 5-17 becomes a *broadcast bus* and a number of interfaces can simultaneously receive the data sent by one user. The bandwidth of the broadcast bus can be varied by varying the number of time slots used for the broadcast mode. The technique of dedicating a group of time slots to the same connection, known as *supermultiplexing*, is also used for establishing high bandwidth circuit-switched connections. In most broadcast bus transactions, data are transmitted in packets, and the header appended to each packet addresses it to a single destination. Thus, one function, in addition to supermultiplexing and a broadcast capability, is required for PBX bus packet switching: either the bus interfaces or their attached devices must have additional intelligence in order to recognize the destination addresses in the packet headers. This is necessary to route packets to their proper destination. Access to bandwidth in short-bus LANs is controlled according to a protocol common to all interfaces. The user-link protocol used between the bus interface and the user workstation is, in general, not the same as the bus protocol used on the high-speed bus. Different link protocols, supported by different bus interfaces, can be tailored to accommodate a range of user devices. As such, each bus interface performs a protocol conversion function, and translates between the bus protocol and the user-link protocol. Bus access can be controlled centrally by the CPU or the network controller, or the bus interfaces themselves may arbitrate requests to transmit.

Using a technique known as *fast circuit switching*, the central controller interacts with the bus interfaces to establish point-to-point connection between the source and destination devices. Circuits must be set up quickly in order to minimize access delay and limit the amount of data that must be buffered in each interface. Fast circuit switching places a sizable processing load on the central controller. As a result, it is more effective to move control down to the device interfaces or the network controller. With a facility for broadcast transmission or fast circuit switching, a PBX network can support packet-switched and circuit-switched connections on a common switching bus.

The packet-switching bus of a short-bus LAN can be distinct from the circuit-switching bus. The near-negligible transmission delay offered by a centralized bus allows the design of access schemes with excellent throughput characteristics for a wide range of loads.[17] These centralized LANs can be integrated with circuit-switching PBXs to support networks that route different types of traffic over the most suitable path.[2]

5.7 Reliability

As the central controller of voice and data communications, the performance of a PBX network greatly affects the performance of the community it serves. In the intensive environment of today's communications, disruptions in service are more than mere inconveniences; they fundamentally impair the function of an organization. Recognizing this responsibility, PBX systems are designed to provide continuous dependable service.

5.7.1 Three Measures of Network Performance

Three effective measures of a communications system's performance are the system's *reliability*, *availability*, and *serviceability*. These are defined as follows:

1. *Reliability*—The probability that a system component will not fail. This is often expressed as the mean time between failures, or MTBF.

2. *Availability*—The probability that the system's services will be available at any given time, upon demand. At the user level, this is often expressed as the line availability, or the probability that an individual user requesting service will receive it.

3. *Serviceability*—The ease with which a system can be repaired in the event of failure. This is often expressed as the mean time to repair, or MTTR.

5.7.2 Voice and Data Availability

From the user's standpoint, line availability is perhaps the best single measure of system performance. While reliability and serviceability may affect maintenance costs, the end user may be shielded from the service impacts of failures through proper system design. However, most users who have had any experience with computers maintain a double standard when assessing the performance of voice services and data services. Through long association with the public network and its generally excellent service, residents of the United States came to expect a level of voice service that is unavailable in most other countries. In many countries, after lifting a handset, there may be a delay of several seconds before receiving dial tone. In the United States, most users will hang up after only a second or two and will assume that the telephone is out of order if no dial tone is present. But when it comes to data service, people are accustomed to the fact that computers fail relatively frequently when compared with telephone systems.

It should be clear that a digital PBX is itself a computer and, thus, can employ a number of processors to distribute the computing load. The hardware components used in PBXs are largely indistinguishable from those used in other computing machines, and they fail according to the same rules. The PBX, however, is expected to provide an extremely high level of availability. While there may be steps that a designer can take to increase component-level reliability, PBX systems employ three tactics to provide high availability: *modularity*, *redundancy*, and *self-diagnostics*.

5.7.3 Hardware Techniques: Modularity and Redundancy

We have already mentioned modularity as a design criterion for a PBX network from the standpoint of maintaining a relatively level cost per line over a wide range of customer sizes. A natural outgrowth of this building-block approach is that individual blocks can be designed with a high level of functional independence. A failure in one block does not propagate to adjacent blocks. The partitioning of networks into independent nodes is an application of modularity at the system level. In this case, the impact of a failure in any given node depends upon the position of the node within an overall hierarchy. Failures in independently controlled, fully interconnected nodes affect service only to the users on the failed node. In hierarchical systems, failure of a tandem node affects traffic between all nodes connected to the tandem.

For example, bus interfaces are usually designed to service from 1 to 16 users. With proper design, the failure of a critical component on any one interface affects only those users connected to it. This modularity may be exploited in the configuration of the network to control failure groups. For instance, in assigning host-computer ports to PBX interfaces, a common practice is to spread the computer ports of one host over a number of device interface circuit cards, such that the failure of any one interface card will not be sufficient to cut off all access to the host.

At higher levels in the functional hierarchy, subsystems tend to be shared by a larger numbers of users. The central processor in a hierarchically controlled switching node is shared by all users and, thus, the failure of the processor affects all users on the node. In this case, the availability of a user line is limited by the availability of the processor. An alternative to modularization, which distributes the processing down to the interface level, is redundancy.

Redundancy eliminates single points of overall system failure. Central components, such as the common control, the switching network, and the power system, can be fully duplicated, such that the failure of one central element does not compromise line availability. Some systems offer redundancy down to the bus interface level.

The impact of the failure of a duplicated subsystem depends on the state of the back-up system at the time of failure and on the time required to switch the back-up system on-line. The smoothest transition occurs if the back-up system is operated in a *hot standby* mode. For example, the memory of a hot standby processor is constantly updated by the on-line processor, so that the dynamic portion of the standby memory reflects the most current state of the system. If the on-line processor fails, the standby can be switched in place without pausing to update its memory. In this type of operation, most PBXs will retain all connections that had been established before the time of the failure. Only those calls that were in the process of being set up will be lost. Without such a feature, the standby processor would be faced with a sudden barrage of call attempts when it came on-line as users attempted to reestablish their connections. Under these conditions, it could take only minutes for the system to return to normal operation.

5.7.4 Self Diagnostics

The design of a duplicated system poses some interesting problems. For example, how does the system determine that a component has failed and what mechanisms can be trusted to take a failed unit of out service and activate the standby? In the case of the power system, the answer is conceptually simple: When one power supply fails to deliver power, another supply on a common bus can pick up the load automatically. But more complex systems, such as processors and switching networks, can fail in more subtle ways. These systems must be designed with continuous internal and external monitoring features that detect and correct errors early on, before they become serious. These monitoring functions, referred to as self diagnostics, depend on a coordinated effort between hardware and software and are applicable to nonduplicated and duplicated system components alike.

Returning to the question regarding duplicated active systems, there are several methods that may be used to switch between duplicate sets of hardware. A common method is the use of a "watchdog timer." The timer, which is a simple and therefore reliable device, is periodically reset by a healthy processor in the normal course of operation. Should the processor fail through either a component failure or a system error, the timer will exceed a critical threshold and force the failing processor into the standby mode while placing the back-up processor on-line. Additionally, the processor itself can be designed to continuously check memory circuits, down to the bit level, to determine if a particular memory device is failing.

Nonduplicated hardware, such as bus interfaces and port circuits, may be periodically checked in a number of ways. Loop back is a common means of testing transmission-path integrity through the PBX, the building wiring, and the user device interface. The PBX can initiate an internal path test by establishing a connection between the desired port circuit and a test generator that resides on the switching bus. The output of the port circuit, which would normally connect to the user's line, is looped back internally to the switching bus. The test generator produces a predefined pattern, which is analyzed by the processor for correctness. Similarly, the transmission path through the building wiring and a DCE may be tested by sending a signal which causes the DCE to go into *loop-back* mode. Again, the common test generator is used to send a known signal through the PBX port to the DCE, where it is turned around and sent back to the PBX for inspection. Such tests are often run at night or whenever there is little traffic on the network. In many cases, imminent faults may be detected and corrected before a user notices a degradation in service. The loop-back test is one example of the benefits of central network control and the use of shared-network resources for fault detection and correction.

5.7.5 Error Logging and Remote Diagnostics

When an error is detected, a PBX may take a number of actions, depending on the severity of the problem. In the case of a failed processor or switching network element, the switch over to the redundant standby may be accompanied by a number of error-reporting actions. In most cases, failure of a critical system element causes the on-line processor to light a visible alarm indicator on the PBX cabinet and send an audible and/or visible alarm indication to the operator's console. By arrangement with the PBX manufacturer's service organization, the alarm may also be reported to a nearby service center over public telephone facilities. In order to facilitate troubleshooting and repair, the system may also maintain an error log in its memory, which can be examined by a system administrator or service technician. The log records details of the fault using an error code and can include information to reflect the state of system at, and just prior to, the occurrence of the error. Such information is used to determine the causes of an error and is especially useful for isolating the sources of intermittent problems.

The centralized control afforded by a PBX network provides a convenient point for network access by remote service personnel. The PBX maintenance port can be connected to a modem and accessed by a remote terminal over the public telephone network. A service technician can inspect the error log and other service statistics and instruct the PBX to run specific tests or display the contents of its memory. In all cases, minor actions such as these should not affect the service provided to users of the network.

5.8 Applications of the PBX in Data Communications

In this section, we present the application of a digital PBX to the data-communications problems outlined in previous sections.

5.8.1 Using the PBX to Connect Terminals to Hosts

With appropriate PBX control software and using mostly circuit-switched connections, the digital PBX provides an efficient means for distributing host ports to terminals and also provides network management features to aid in controlling communications costs.

5.8.1.1 Asynchronous and Synchronous Terminal Interfaces

As shown in Fig. 5-18, there are two basic methods for connecting an asynchronous terminal with a digital PBX. The first, used by the terminal in the upper left corner of Fig. 5-18, uses a physical data path distinct from the voice path.

The link connects a PBX data interface circuit with a small desktop DCE that provides an RS-232C interface for the terminal. Using one or two pairs of UTP, these devices usually support circuit-switched data connections at asynchronous rates up to 19.2 kbps for distances of about one mile. The digital links between a PBX manufacturer's bus interfaces and DCEs are usually designed according to proprietary protocols. However, all vendors' links are designed to preserve the features of the standard protocols they support.

The remaining terminals in Fig. 5-18 are connected to the PBX through integrated voice/data stations. These stations connect to integrated voice/data

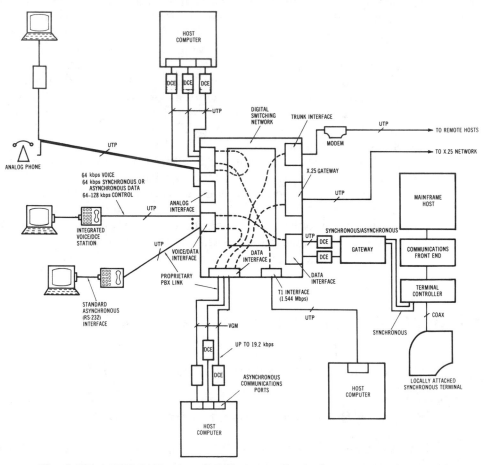

Fig. 5-18. A PBX LAN using digital circuit-switched connections to provide terminals and hosts with access to each other and to remote hosts, a packet network, and a mainframe computer.

interfaces in the PBX. The link to the PBX consists of voice, data, and control-bit streams multiplexed into a single, synchronous stream. Common implementations include a 64-kbps voice channel, one or more 64-kbps data channels, and an 8- to 64-kbps control channel that carries command and control information between the station and the interface. Data connections are usually supported using an optional data module that is added to the basic digital phone. The module provides an RS-232C terminal interface and provides buffering between the terminal and the data channel which is extracted from the multiplexed link. Data modules usually allow the user to select from among a number of asynchronous data rates up to 19.2 kbps, and some provide an option to select synchronous rates from 1.2 to 57.6 kbps. Synchronous devices that require special protocols or higher-speed transmission require more complex interfaces; they will be covered later in this section.

5.8.1.2 Interfacing the PBX to Local Host Computers

Individual asynchronous and low-speed synchronous computer ports are connected to a PBX with DCE, or data module, that are similar, if not identical, to those used with terminals. Data modules can usually be configured to behave as either DTE or DCE. This type of connection requires a dedicated data module and a corresponding interface in the PBX for each computer port. Using a dedicated data module offers flexibility in assigning PBX ports to host ports, but requires racks of these devices and a fair amount of wiring to the computer room for large installations. As a result, computer and PBX manufacturers have developed a standard for a link that handles several terminals with a single interface.

The specification for the multiplexed *Computer-to-PBX Interface*, or *CPI*, was developed jointly by Digital Equipment Corporation and Northern Telecom Inc., who have licensed the specification to other computer and PBX manufacturers.[10] The physical layer of CPI is based on T1 transmission at a rate of 1.544 Mbps, full duplex. The link provides 24 channels, each of which can support one asynchronous connection at up to 19.2 kbps, or one synchronous connection at up to 56 kbps.

PBXs can use techniques internal to the switching system to achieve efficiencies in the usage of the available bandwidth. One such technique, known as *submultiplexing*, is used to pack a number of low-speed data connections into what would normally be used for a single voice connection. For example, the 64-kbps bandwidth of a voice connection can be used to switch twelve, simultaneous, 4800-bps data connections.

5.8.2 Data-Call Processing Software

In the introduction, we said that a data network should be as easy to use as the voice telephone network. However, this does not mean that data calls should be handled in exactly the same way as telephone calls. Indeed, the nature of terminal-to-host and interworkstation communications offers unique requirements, particularly with respect to session initiation. Data-call processing software provides a session-layer interface that improves human-machine interaction and also aids network management and resource sharing.

5.8.2.1 Port Contention and Queuing

It is not always possible or cost effective for a computer installation to provide as many computer ports as there are terminal users. If terminal users are in contention for a limited number of computer ports, a user can be blocked from accessing a host, even when connections through the PBX are available. One function of PBX data-call processing software is to arbitrate contention for computer ports. For example, blocked callers can be placed into a queue on a first-come first-served, or prioritized basis. As ports are released, the queue can be updated and the PBX can send messages to the user's terminal indicating his position in the queue. When the caller reaches the head of the queue and a port becomes free, the PBX can reinitiate the data call. In the meantime, the caller is free to attend to other business.

The use of queues for controlling resource access provides useful data for network management. Queue statistics, such as average and maximum number of queued callers, the typical time spent in the queue, and the number of calls completed or abandoned, provide an indication of resource utilization. Queuing can be used for a number of resources in addition to computer ports, as will be seen in subsequent sections.

5.8.2.2 The Human Interface

Anyone who has spent a few hours trying to access an unforgiving host will agree that computer access via dial-up facilities can be extremely frustrating. A common reason for experiencing difficulties when attempting to establish a terminal-to-host connection is a mismatch between the terminal's telecommunications characteristics and those of the computer port. For example, if a DCE that is set at 1200 bps is to access a 9600-bps computer port, or if even parity is enforced at one end of the connection and odd parity is selected at the other, communication will be impossible. Callers who are either unaware of these details or are unable to determine the status of the host, and who are not prevented from calling incompatible devices by the call-processing software, must usually resort to trial and error, perhaps aided by some appropriate vituperations.

Another function of PBX software is to shield users from the numerous details involved in host access, using an interactive data-call setup from the terminal keyboard. A user requesting service is put into session with the PBX software, which supports a high-level interface for establishing a connection with the desired resource. One feature described in Section 5.6 is the use of names or acronyms for network resources. For example, the corporate computer can be known as MIS, the warehouse computer as INVENTORY, etc. With such names, users are far less likely to "dial the wrong number." More importantly, names are easier to remember than numbers and are far less harrowing to trainees and casual users.

Data-call processing functions can permit a user to interactively examine and modify his DCE and PBX port parameters, and then store and retrieve sets of these parameters for use with different hosts. More advanced software can be used to make the details of the host access completely transparent to users.

5.8.3 Connecting Users and Remote Hosts

Occasionally, it may be undesirable or infeasible to support a direct, hard-wired connection between a PBX and the host computer. This is most often the case when the host is physically distant from the user's site and is beyond the transmitting range of DCEs, or when it lies on the far side of a right-of-way that may not be crossed by the PBX wiring. The PBX provides access to remote facilities using public, private, or leased transmission services.

5.8.3.1 Analog Transmission Facilities

A common means of remote host access is via public switched or private, leased-line telephone facilities. The majority of the facilities available today are designed for analog telephone transmission; therefore, modems are used to interface a PBX port to the telephone trunk. For data rates greater than that which can be supported by the standard analog voice bandwidth (i.e., 2400–4800 baud), special telephone lines are required, at a substantially increased cost.

5.8.3.2 Modem Pooling

Modem pooling, depicted in Fig. 5-19, provides a means for controlled access to modems, using software techniques similar to those employed for computer port access. Users request connection to the modem pool in order to access remote hosts. Queuing services and queue statistics can be provided for controlling and managing the modem pool. Modem pooling is used with originate-only, answer-only, and originate/answer modems that both initiate and receive outside calls. For outgoing calls, most PBXs provide least-cost routing software that selects the most economical facility over which to place the call. Trunk management software can also provide trunk-queuing features.

5.8.3.3 Remote Access Over Digital Transmission Facilities

Examination of Fig. 5-19 reveals that in using an analog modem pool with a digital PBX, the data stream undergoes several A/D and D/A conversions.

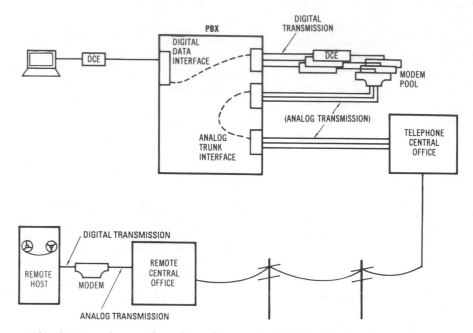

Fig. 5-19. A cluster of modems (or modem pool) forms a shared resource for accessing remote digital facilities. Modem pools can be configured for both outgoing and incoming data calls.

Indeed, the interface between any analog device (such as an analog telephone) and a digital switching system requires A/D and D/A conversions. As a result, it generally costs less to connect digital devices to digital switches, because the digital interfaces do not require A/D and D/A conversion hardware. For the same reason, it is also more cost effective to interconnect digital switches using a digital transmission facility.

Digital transmission facilities, of which the T-carrier systems are the most widely used, are used extensively for interswitch communication in the public telephone network. A number of PBX manufacturers have adapted the T1 standard to support voice and data transmission between distributed parts of their systems.

5.8.4 Protocol Conversion and Internetwork Communication

For the purpose of interconnecting low-function terminals and their hosts, the PBX functions as a transparent data-transport service. Data leave a device according to some format and protocol and are reproduced at the far end-device's interface according to the original format and protocol. The PBX connection supports the physical-level (layer 1) and datalink-level (layer 2) protocols used by end devices. Once the connection is established, the PBX appears like a direct hard-wired link, independent of the means used internally to complete the connection.

The transparent data-transport service of a PBX supports a number of logically independent subnetworks that share the common transport facility. Each subnetwork is comprised of the devices that use compatible protocols. The subnetworks can include a group of minicomputers and their associated terminals, a mainframe computer and its peripheral devices, or a group of identical word-processing stations. Communications between users in different subnetworks is facilitated through the use of *internetwork gateways*. In a PBX network, the gateway can be an add-on device or an integral part of the PBX itself.

A gateway can be integrated into a PBX in a number of ways. In practice, hardware and software within the PBX, or an external device, are usually dedicated to the protocol conversion function. The PBX acts as an "intelligent patch-panel" and interposes protocol conversion equipment between communicants on different networks.

5.8.4.1 Gateways to Public Data Networks

One application of a gateway is for connecting asynchronous and synchronous terminals and hosts with *public data networks*, or *PDNs*. Many of these networks, such as TYMNET and TELENET, offer an interface based upon a set of CCITT protocols known collectively as X.25. The X.25 specification addresses OSI layers 1 through 3, and specifies an RS-232C physical interface, a synchronous data link at rates from 1.2 to 56 kbps, and a packet layer for breaking up user messages into smaller transmission units. Although packet networks usually make their services available over dial-up telephone facilities using synchronous modems, the X.25 interface is less expensive for all but casual users, since charges are weighted more heavily by data traffic than by connection time.

A host or personal computer equipped with a synchronous communications interface and the software required to execute the X.25 protocols can connect directly to the RS-232C interface provided by the PDN. However, the purpose of an X.25 gateway is to allow asynchronous hosts, personal computers, and low-function terminals to access the PDN resources. An X.25 gateway, as an integral part of a PBX LAN, enables any user to access the PDN by establishing a switched-data connection with the gateway.

The gateway performs a *packet assembly/disassembly*, or *PAD* function by assembling segments of asynchronous data into X.25-formatted packets in one direction, and by stripping the headers and trailers from packets before retransmission to asynchronous devices in the other direction. A PBX X.25 gateway also performs an address translation function between the user's PBX extension and his X.25 address. The use of a shared gateway is a cost-effective means for providing low-function terminals, computers, and personal workstations with access to the growing number of transmission and information services. Note that the X.25 standard provides no more than a packet delivery service: X.25-formatted data presented to the network by the sender is reproduced without errors in X.25 format at the destination. Higher-level protocols are required to provide end-to-end control of applications, such as file transfers.

5.8.5 Integrated Voice/Data Services

5.8.5.1 Integrated Voice/Data Terminals

Integrated voice/data terminals (ITs) combine a data terminal with a digital telephone into a single unit. The block diagram of such a unit is depicted in Fig. 5-20. Initially, these units were proprietary devices specific to a given PBX manufacturer. They communicate with the PBX over proprietary voice/data links. Fully integrated links multiplex the voice, data, and control-bit streams onto a common set of wires. The digital telephone requires 64 kbps (full duplex) for the digitized voice circuit. The data connection is typically a 16-kbps to 128-kbps link which may be circuit- or packet-switched within the PBX. The control link can require from 8 kbps to 64 kbps of bandwidth and is used to send commands and status information between the IT and PBX.

Commands from the PBX cause the IT's microprocessor to activate the ringer and flash indicator lights of the telephone, while the IT's status (such as on-hook, off-hook, request for service, request for disconnect, etc.) is constantly reported to the IT interface in the PBX. With additional IT memory and utility software, the IT can provide services, such as an electronic directory with autodialing, personal calendar, message-display service, etc. The IT also

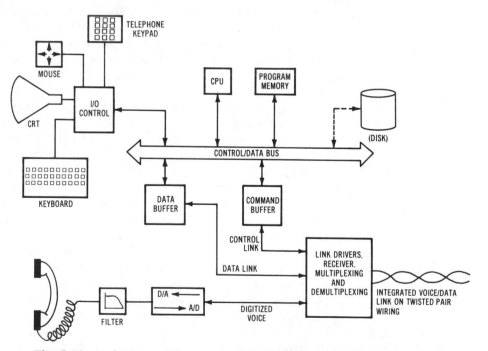

Fig. 5-20. Architecture of an integrated voice/data terminal. Note that with the addition of a suitable operating system, the same architecture supports a diskless personal computer workstation. A mass-storage disk and disk operating system can also fit within the IT architecture.

permits the user to store a number of DCE configurations, and allows the user to automatically reconfigure the IT's internal DCE with a given host's parameter set, using a simple high-level command.

5.8.5.2 Applications Processors

Integrated services are often controlled by dedicated *application processors*, or *APs*, operating in conjunction with the PBX control processor. APs can perform protocol conversion, text processing, image processing, voice compression and storage, file storage, and data-base management. In an integrated system, APs are closely coupled with the PBX common control processor(s), and have access to the system configuration memory. The close coupling between the APs and the PBX common control is the key to functional integration. This is illustrated in Fig. 5-21 using the example of a *voice-messaging system (VMS)*.

Integrated *voice-messaging systems* interface to the PBX common-control processor, which can signal the VMS if a user's phone is busy or does not

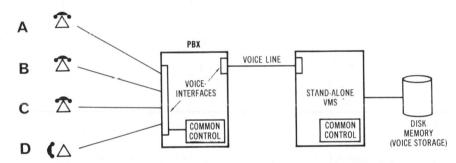

(A) Nonintegrated VMS. When user A calls user D and receives a busy signal, he must hang up and dial user D's voice mailbox extension on the VMS.

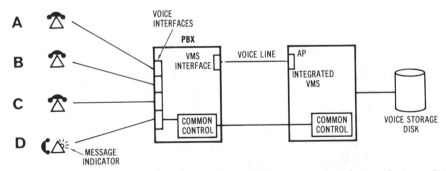

(B) Integrated VMS. When user A calls user D, the PBX common control notes that user D is busy, sends a message to the VMS, and connects user A to the voice mailbox of user D. The VMS sends a message to the PBX to signal user D's message waiting.

Fig. 5-21. Integrated and nonintegrated voice-messaging systems (VMS).

answer after a prescribed number of rings. When this occurs, the system automatically connects the caller with the messaging system, which answers the user's phone with a standard or personalized response and instructs the caller to leave a message. Provided that the user's telephone or IT has a message-waiting indicator, the system provides the user with a visual indication when messages have been received. Such systems can also permit messages to be annotated and forwarded to other users, and can allow users to reply to a message from another system user without calling the sender. This type of enhanced functionality is made possible by the physical integration of hardware and software components.

5.8.5.3 ISDN Interfaces

As mentioned earlier, the original ITs available from PBX manufacturers were proprietary devices that communicated with the PBX using proprietary, multiplexed voice/data link formats. More recently, the emerging standards for integrated voice/data services in the public switched telephone network are impacting PBX and IT architectures. Specifically, standards enduring in support of the Integrated Services Digital Network, or ISDN,[25] make possible standard ITs that can be used with a variety of PBXs.

One of the many standards defined under ISDN includes definition of integrated voice/data link formats. The standards include definition of services at several layers of the OSI model, including the physical, link, and session layers.

The ISDN link layer protocols are usually based on a format known as "$N \times B + D$," where N is the number of circuit-switched channels at a "B" bit/second data rate, and D is a channel for control information and packet switched data. A common format for ISDN terminals (telephones and Its) is $2B + D$, where B is 64 kbps for circuit-switched voice and data, and D is a 16 kbps control/data channel, for a total link rate of $2 \times 64 + 16 = 144$ kbps. At the physical layer, the ISDN "U" interface defines a $2B + D$ link that operates over a single twisted pair for distance over 3 miles.

5.8.6 A Summary of PBX LAN Characteristics

There are many ways to apply a given PBX technology to data communications, and there are as many different PBX architectures as there are PBX manufacturers. As we've seen, PBXs can support packet switching and they employ centralized or distributed switching networks, using hierarchical or distributed control. However, the following features are common to all PBX-based networks.

 1. Except for a relatively small number of systems that carry only data traffic, PBXs provide voice communications. Because voice traffic is

handled most easily using circuit-switched connections, most PBX designs provide efficient circuit switching.

2. Each PBX manufacturer specifies a wiring plan that extends two, three, or four pairs of wire from the PBX to each user location in the installation. Since end-user data devices, such as terminals or personal computers, are usually co-located with telephones, a common PBX wiring plan can be used to support much of the data in addition to all of the voice-traffic requirements. The UTP wiring already installed in many buildings can carry data at rates up to 1 Mbps for distances up to 2000 feet, and can support even higher data rate (10 Mbps) for shorter distances.

3. The control memory of a PBX and the associated disk or tape back-up system stores the configuration of the entire system in a central place. This configuration data base can be manipulated using software utilities supplied with the system. As a result, the voice and data facilities of the network can be managed in a coordinated way. Moves, adds, and changes can be configured centrally, and often remotely, over ordinary public telephone facilities.

4. Traffic flow through the PBX is monitored and analyzed in order to tune system performance and optimize resource utilization. Network-monitoring features can be provided with the system software.

5. Critical components, such as processors and power supplies, can be duplicated in order to provide the desired level of system availability. The PBX system can derive power from battery- or engine alternator-based, uninterruptible, power systems. As a result, life-line functions, such as basic voice service, which are completely powered from the PBX, are maintained during power outages.

6. The centralized control that can be exercised with a PBX system aids error detection, trouble reporting, fault diagnosis, and troubleshooting.

7. The PBX LAN allows the system administrator to configure different users for different levels of service according to their needs and the availability of resources.

8. The network can be serviced by the same personnel responsible for the voice network.

9. PBX networks have demonstrated the ability to evolve into functionally integrated voice/data networks.

5.9 System Administration

Communication networks, like the organization they serve, are dynamic. People move, new user devices are developed, system requirements change, and networks must evolve and grow. Communications network administration is an increasingly visible function in many organizations, as managers come to realize that the success of their business depends on the quality of their communications. Perhaps the most important benefit of a PBX network is the extent and ease with which the network may be managed, measured, controlled, and configured using shared resources.

5.9.1 System Administration Functions

System administration is an iterative process in which the parameters change with each iteration. At the time of its initial installation, the network is configured to provide services to users in accordance with their individual needs. The system administrator establishes a numbering (or addressing) plan and distributes a network directory so that users can gain access to network resources and to other users. Over time, users change locations or job functions and system resources are added or replaced. At the same time, users provide feedback on system performance, while monthly bills for services and maintenance reflect the costs of operating the network. The system administrator must digest these inputs, determine necessary actions, modify the network accordingly, and reflect these modifications in documentation. When this is done, the process starts all over again.

The result of improper system administration is severe—a costly system that delivers poor performance. In order to aid the system administrator, PBX networks may offer the following services:

1. Software-based reconfiguration to accommodate moves, adds, and changes.
2. Directory data-base management.
3. Restricted access to selected services and resources.
4. Traffic statistics, analysis, and queue logs.

5.9.2 Configuration and Service Restrictions

The configuration data in the PBX is a map that associates with each PBX port the type of device terminated on the port and the services that are available to the user. The initial configuration, which is permanently stored on disk or magnetic tape, is usually generated by the PBX manufacturer based on the customer's specifications. In addition to specifying the ports bus address and the device characteristics, the configuration assigns to each device a class of service. The service class includes the access priority and services allowed for the user. For example, particular DCE service classes may be prevented from accessing restricted host computers.

When an employee moves, acquires new equipment, or changes job function and requires access to new resources, the system administrator reflects these changes in the configuration data base. PBXs provide the system administrator with access to configuration management software, using either a specialized maintenance and administration terminal or a general-purpose terminal. The software provides a high-level interface for manipulating the configuration data base. The administrator controls the network, centrally, using this facility. Additionally, the PBX vendor's service personnel can access the configuration data base from a remote terminal over public telephone facilities by establishing a connection with the PBX maintenance port through a modem.

5.9.3 Directory Data-Base Management

PBX system software may include facilities for manipulating and documenting the directory data base. In order to reduce the number of directory updates, software reconfigurability allows users to retain their extension numbers when they move within the area served by a related group of PBX nodes.

Integrated PBX networks require an addressing scheme for voice and data ports. The most common scheme assigns an extension number to each voice or data port on those nodes accessed by a common prefix. The prefix is assigned by the telephone central office that serves the network. Within a corporate network, users can often access remote extensions using abbreviated codes assigned by the network administrator.

5.9.4 Network Monitoring

Queue logs, call reports, and traffic statistics are useful for assessing network effectiveness and for planning network growth. Queue logs provide a measure of resource utilization. These logs can be used to assess the need for additional computer ports, modems, or interswitch trunks. Call reports facilitate cost allocation among user groups and aid in tracking down abuse of system resources. Traffic statistics show the organization's communications patterns, which may be correlated with user complaints of slow response or poor service. The system administrator can use these reports to reconfigure the network and distribute the communications load. This maximizes resource sharing and avoids unnecessary or premature additions of equipment.

5.9.5 Conclusion

This chapter began by stating the goals of a PBX network. We have shown that the PBX provides:

- *Accessibility* by specifying a uniform wiring plan throughout an establishment.
- *Capacity* by providing a flexible high-bandwidth switching bus.

- *Reliability* by employing redundancy for critical elements, continuous self diagnostics, and partitioning to control failure groups.

- *Manageability* by providing several classes of service, service restrictions, centralized software reconfiguration, traffic statistics, call reports, and queue logs.

- *Maintainability* by employing modular design to allow graceful expansions, upgrades, and servicing.

- *Compatibility* by establishing and supporting standard interfaces between PBXs and office automation products, providing protocol-transparent wire-like services, and supporting gateways and protocol conversion.

- *Economy* by providing a range of cost-effective interfaces covering the needs of low-function and high-function devices, and allowing user networks to evolve as new devices are developed.

5.10 References

1. Abramson, Paul and Franc E. Noel. *Local Area Network Media Selection for Ring Topologies*, Research Triangle Park, NC: IBM Corporation, July 27, 1982.

2. Acampora, A.S., et. al. "Performance of a Centralized-Bus Local Area Network," *Proceedings of Localnet 1983*, Pinner, U.K., New York: On-line Publications Ltd., September, 1983.

3. Beauchamp, K. G. *Computer Communications*, 2nd ed., New York: Chapman and Hall, 1990.

4. Bellamy, John. *Digital Telephony*, 2nd ed., New York: John Wiley & Sons, 1991.

5. Bhargava, Amit. *Integrated Broadband Networks*, Norwood, MA: Artech House, 1991.

6. Black, Uyless. *Computer Networks: Protocols, Standards, and Interfaces*, Englewood Cliffs, NJ: Prentice-Hall, 1987.

7. ———. *The V Series recommendations: Protocols for Data Communications Over the Telephone Network*, New York: McGraw-Hill Book Company, 1991.

8. Briere, Daniel D. *Long Distance, Services (A Buyer's Guide)*, Norwood, MA: Artech House, 1990.

9. Electronic Industry Association, "EIA Standards Project SP-1474-Private Branch Exchange (PBX) Switching for Voiceband Applications," Issue 1, December, 1981.

10. Ellis, Robert L. *Designing Data Networks*, Englewood Cliffs, NJ: Prentice-Hall, 1986.

11. Haykin, Simon. *Digital Communications*, New York: John Wiley & Sons, 1988.

12. Held, Gilbert. *Digital Networking and T-Carrier Multiplexing*, New York: John Wilcy & Sons, 1990.

13. Helgert, Herman J. *Integrated Services Digital Networks; Architecture, Protocols, Standards*, Reading, MA: Addison Wesley Publishing Co., 1991.

14. Joel, Amos E., et. al. *A History of Engineering and Science in the Bell System—Switching Technology (1925–1975)*, Whippany, NJ: Bell Telephone Laboratories, Inc., 1982, pp. 494–528.

15. Katsuyama, T., et. al. "Handwritten Message Switching via an Integrated EPBX," *Proceedings of Localnet 1983*, Pinner, U.K., New York: Online Publications Ltd.

16. Langford, G.J. "Local Area Network User Needs," *Proceedings of Localnet 1983*, Pinner, U.K., New York: Online Publications Ltd.

17. Lidinsky, W.P. "LANs, Internetworking, and Public Networks," Australia, December 14–16, 1982.

18. Markley, Richard W. *Data Communications and Interoperability*, Englewood Cliffs, NJ: Prentice-Hall, 1990.

19. Muller, Nathan J., and Robert P. Davidson. *LANs to WANs, Network Management in the 1990's*, Norwood, MA: Artech House, 1990.

20. Obenzinger, Mark, M. *The Personal Computer Market: A Profile for Growth*, New York: Lehman Brothers Kuhn Loeb Research, January, 1983.

21. Rose, Marshall T. *The Open Book, A Perspective on OSI*, Englewood Cliffs, NJ: Prentice-Hall, 1990.

22. Sager, Ira. "CPU-to-PBX Interface Standard . . . ," *Electronic News*, July 18, 1983.

23. Tanenbaum, Andrew S. *Computer Networks*, 2nd ed. Englewood Cliffs, NJ: Prentice-Hall, 1989.

24. Turin, William. *Performance Analysis of Digital Transmission Systems*, Whippany, NJ: Bell Telephone Laboratories, Inc., 1990.

25. Verma, K., et. al. *ISDN Systems: Architecture, Technology, and Application*, Englewood Cliffs, NJ: Prentice-Hall, 1990.

26. Vignault, Walter L. *Worldwide Telecommunications Guide for the Business Manager*, New York: John Wiley & Sons, 1987.

Baseband Local Area Networks

David Potter

**David Potter** is a member of the technical staff at Thinking Machines Corporation. He was a co-founder and Vice President of Interlan, Inc., a leading manufacturer of local area network systems and components. Prior to the founding of Interlan in 1981, Mr. Potter held several technical and management positions with Digital Equipment Corp. The last such position was as manager of local network hardware development, in which he participated in the development of the DEC-Intel-Xerox Ethernet specification. He has also been a design engineer for General Radio Company, now GENRAD, and an officer in the US Army.

Mr. Potter holds B.S.E.E. and M.S.E.E degrees from Northeastern University. He is a member of ACM and of the IEEE and its Computer and Communications Societies. He was one of the original members of the IEEE 802 Local Area Network Standards Committee.

6.1 Introduction

The local area network (LAN) is today an integral part of most large and many smaller computer installations. This widespread adoption of the network as a key element of computer systems occurred in the decade of the 1980s. The initial publication of the Ethernet local area network specification occurred in 1980. This was the first example of a multicompany, open specification for communication that extended beyond simple physical signalling. Since that time, national and international standards for local network protocols have been written and adopted. Equipment is now offered for sale that can provide network access for virtually every computer suitable for business and scientific use. Electronic mail, shared file systems, and libraries of application programs are now routine among workstations and computers.

In this chapter we will examine the common forms of baseband local area network, starting with a definition of the meaning of the term.

6.1.1 Networks

In the usage we give it here, a network is a set of independent computing entities (such as workstations, minicomputers, standalone printers, etc.) that are equipped to communicate with each other. The concept of independence is important. While one can argue that there are networks of terminals connected in some fashion to a central computer, the issues of concern in the field of local networks do not pivot on such master-slave networks, and the technical advances in local network were made in the service of improving peer-to-peer communications.

6.1.2 Local Area Networks

What is a "local area network"? By definition, it is "local," which means a limited physical extent. In the case of the local network standards that have been created by industry and professional groups, there is also a concept that the *local* network can be implemented so as to be assured of a very high data-transmission rate and a very low error rate. Those assumptions mean that certain forms of communications protocols can be used profitably in local networks that would not be appropriate in wide-area networks. These protocols, which will be discussed later, have the virtue of simplicity. This, in turn, means that they can be implemented in the form of VLSI chips at a reasonable cost. The availability of such chips, which is now a reality, makes the local network interface a readily implemented cost-effective part of the equipment needed for office and professional work enhancement. The local network is a part of today's work environment, and it promises to remain a key part of it for years to come.

There are several ways to create a local area network. One way of classifying local area networks is by the cable or other means used to carry messages from one station to another. The technique that we will examine in this chapter is based on the physical distribution technique called "baseband." The meaning of "baseband" is simply that one and only one signal can utilize the distribution medium at a single instant. This is in contrast to "broadband" techniques that, like the television channels in a cable television system, allow several signals to occupy the same distribution medium simultaneously through the use of frequency division multiplexing.

The baseband network allocates the use of the shared resource (the distribution medium) through time sharing, or time-division multiplexing. The rules under which the various using stations are allocated use of the medium fall into several broad classifications. These classifications have become another way of classifying local networks.

We speak of a CSMA/CD network, or Ethernet, when we mean a network in which use of medium is acquired through a contention mechanism, while a Token network implies that the right of access is explicitly passed from one station to the next in some order or sequence. Other networks are based on one station polling the others for their need to access the medium. Also, there are those networks that utilize fixed timing relations among all the stations on the network to send their traffic in a strict sequence.

The applications for local networks are diverse. The automated office and factory are concepts that depend on a local network as the linking element for individual workstations or factory process points. The laboratory can be automated around a local network, and the applications in military communications and command and control situations are numerous. For example, the fire-control system on a naval vessel involves many different sensors, computers, and control devices that are intimately linked. Such a system could utilize a local network to effect the same or better communication while substantially reducing the cost and weight of the cabling required. Office workers, to cite another example, find that the electronic mail capability of a local network is a significant help in communications without the normal "telephone tag."

The use of personal computers in the office has led to the development of local area networking designs that are intended to link together lower-cost equipment, and to designs that provide significant capability to support personal computers and more powerful equipment as well. Factory automation has created demand for networks that satisfy the needs of that environment. The coming years promise to be the era of the personal computer and the era of the local area network!

Standards have been written and adopted for various forms of local area networks, reflecting office applications, factory requirements, and even metropolitan networking.

6.2 History of the Local Network

The local area network had its genesis in several different places and by several groups. The idea did not come forth suddenly in a flash of insight, but evolved, and is evolving still, in response to a set of needs.

The minicomputer made computing inexpensive. The result was a growth of laboratory and development uses and, later, more uses in the general time-sharing and business areas, in which a number of separate computing devices served the needs of a more or less closely allied set of people. The need to share data among different computers led to the development of easily used storage devices that used portable media, such as tape and removable disks. The flexibility of being able to process a task on one machine and then move it to another to be used by someone else, or being able to develop a program on one machine and then run it on a bigger faster machine, was recognized as a significant advantage to the owners of the equipment. Over time, a community of users grew up, especially in the universities, who shared common interests and desired the advantages of shared programs and data bases, but who were widely scattered. Links to the computers over telephone lines were common, both for short distances and for very long distances.

The telephone links proved superior to sending tape by mail, both in terms of speed and reliability. The Department of Defense, through its Advanced Research Projects Agency, initiated over the telephone network a system of permanent links among a network of research computer centers throughout the world. These circuits utilized packet switching. This network became the ARPANET, which for many years was an important communications link among computer scientists. Most long-haul network connections were carried through some part of the telephone system in ARPANET, as well as through commercial and private corporate networks.

In the absence of other techniques, many local networks were implemented using local telephone wiring and techniques. Both switched-circuit and packet-network protocols were used, the latter often drawn from the ARPANET work. A number of researchers investigated the use of other data-distribution techniques from the local connections in order to improve the available transmission rate, eliminate telephone line charges, or both. One such effort, undertaken at the University of Hawaii, linked users with the computer over uhf radio, using an early contention protocol in what was called ALOHANET. It is discussed in "ALOHA Packet Broadcasting—a Retrospect," by R. Binder, et al.[2] A more complete description of the ALOHANET protocol is given later in this chapter.

The ALOHANET was the first local network implemented with packet broadcast techniques over radio. The bulk of the local networks that have been investigated in the research community and brought to the marketplace by manufacturers are based on the use of some sort of guided-wave medium—coaxial cable, twisted-pair cable, optical fibers, or a combination of these.

The interest in local networks usually came about in a particular research community in support of some other goal, usually that of giving researchers, and sometimes students, access to computer facilities in a cost-effective or timely way. The advances in the local network art that are most prominent today came about in such a fashion and, in at least one instance, from a deliberate attempt to investigate local networks for their own merit.

The Ethernet was a result of an ARPA investigation undertaken at the Xerox Palo Alto Research Center. (See "Ethernet: Distributed Packet Switching for Local Computer Networks," by R. Metcalf and D. Boggs.[9]) This network design was one of the few that was actually built in more than a limited laboratory environment. Xerox Corp. integrated the Ethernet into their research offices as a production tool for everyday use. They later expanded its use into most of their facilities for use in conjunction with an in-house-designed professional work station. In 1979, Digital Equipment Corp. and Intel Corp. joined with Xerox's System Development Division to extend and upgrade the original Ethernet design. They completed the revision in September of 1980 and made the specification public to encourage widespread use in the industry. (More details are given in *The Ethernet: Data Link and Physical Layers.*[4])

The Ethernet specification that came from this three-company collaboration later formed the basis for one element of the IEEE 802 Local Area Network Standard. There has been widespread use of the specification and an implementation of half a dozen VLSI protocol controller chips for the protocol. Ethernet and its derivative IEEE 802.3 standard seem destined to serve the needs of industry and commerce for a long time to come.

Ethernet was not the only approach to networking in the local area. M.V. Wilkes at Cambridge University and D.J. Farber at the University of Delaware have described local networks based on a ring topology in their articles, "The Cambridge Digital Communication Ring"[11] and "A Ring Network."[5] The basis for the ring topology network will be discussed in a later part of this chapter. The IEEE 802 Standard for local area networks includes a ring topology specification, as well as a CSMA/CD and a token-passing bus definition. The IEEE 802.5 Token Ring Standard is a descendent of the networks described by Wilkes and Farber, but has been designed for compatibility with the other

IEEE 802 networks at its interface to higher layers. This compatibility of interface means that higher-level and application software need not be concerned with the method of data transmission or the details of how a channel is shared among several using stations since it sees a consistent, and methodology-independent, interface.

There have been numerous other networks that have been derived in research laboratories, described in the technical literature, and never implemented. There are others that have been implemented and used for everyday communication, albeit in a restricted domain. Prominent among the latter are the early Spidernet of Bell Labs[6] and its replacement, DATAKIT.[7] Several computer firms have implemented local networks for their equipment:

1. Prime Computer has a token ring, *Ringnet.*

2. HP/Apollo Computer has a token ring, *Domain.*

3. Digital Equipment Corp. has a CSMA/CD bus, *Ethernet.*

4. IBM has a token ring network based upon IEEE 802 standards.

6.3 Classification of Baseband Local Area Networks

Two general attributes are used to classify local area networks—baseband or broadband distribution techniques. In baseband networks, we can identify general classifications relating to both topology and access method.

The topologies that local area networks have adopted include:

1. *Bus Network.* This is a topology in which all stations are connected in parallel to a single pair of wires, coax, or optical fiber (Fig. 6-1A). An example, probably the best-known local network, is the Ethernet.

2. *Ring Network.* This topology is literally a ring of stations that are connected, one to the next, with the last station connected back to the first (Fig. 6-1B). Both Prime Computer's Ringnet and the Cambridge Ring are examples that have seen widespread implementation.

3. *Star Network.* This topology has all stations connected to an active central hub that provides switching and access rights to the periphery stations (Fig. 6-1C). An example is a telephone exchange, either public or private, that switches terminal lines to host computers.

4. *Mesh Network.* This topology (Fig. 6-1D) is still used in local area networks, even though it is derived from the topology of wide-area networks. The connections among stations are point-to-point, usually with not all stations connected to all other stations. The intermediate stations must serve as routing nodes for traffic that is destined for stations not in the immediate communication.

The topology of a network is not the only discriminant. The next most widely used difference is the *access method*—the rules that determine the

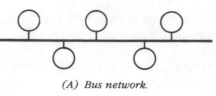

(A) Bus network.

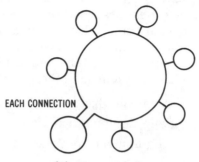

EACH CONNECTION

(B) Ring network.

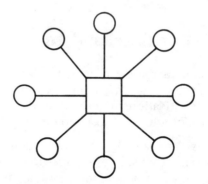

(C) Star network.

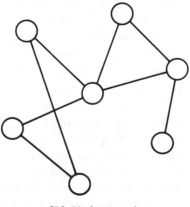

(D) Mesh network.

Fig. 6-1. Topologies of local area networks.

order in which stations are allowed to use the shared-communication channel. In general, Mesh topology networks do not have a shared-communications channel, so they need not be considered in the following. The others all have some common link that must be allocated in some way among all the stations that use it. The goals of an access method include:

1. *Efficiency.* The rules must not require an inordinate amount of the communication channel bandwidth or the processing power of the host station to implement.

2. *Robustness.* The methods used to allocate the shared resource must be capable of recovery from error conditions, either in the transmission or in the ordering of control or data packets. Ideally, the recovery mechanisms will involve no more than the stations that were involved in the communication when the error occurred.

3. *Nonblocking behavior.* Access rules should ensure that every station on the local area network can utilize some portion of the resource; i.e., have some net traffic throughput, even under conditions of very heavy load on the network.

Some networks are designed for "fairness," where no station can have more of the net capability of the network than any other station. Other networks are based on a "priority of access" that allows classes of stations to have access to relatively more of the bandwidth of the channel than other classes. Note that priority access implies that some stations may have transient blocking under heavy load.

The implementation of various networks include as examples several of each of the previously listed topologies and access methods:

1. *Ethernet (IEEE 802.3).* A CSMA/CD network defined for a bus topology. The CSMA/CD protocol is implemented by having each station on the bus network monitor the network for another station's transmission and, then, refraining from sending its own transmission until it hears no other station. There is a small probability that two stations will attempt to transmit during the time that it takes the signal from one station to reach the other, and they are required to cease transmitting if that occurs, wait a random amount of time, and try again.

2. *Token Bus (IEEE 802.4).* An explicit access protocol defined for a bus topology. The token bus access method is implemented by establishing a sequence of stations and having the right to transmit (the "token") passed explicitly from one station to the next, in sequence, until it returns to the initial station, and so on. Each station may send one or more messages during the time that it holds the token, and it then sends a message that is the token to the next station.

3. *Token Ring (IEEE 802.5).* An explicit access protocol defined for a ring topology. The token ring access method is implemented by having a small control packet, or "token," circulate around a physical sequence

of point-to-point connections between stations that receive and retransmit it, usually with a 1-bit delay. (Note the difference in meaning of the term "token" when used in the context of a bus.) The station having a message to send will receive the token packet, alter it to be a "connector," and append its message to the connector. When the message packet has been circulated around to the sending station again, that station must restore the connector to being a token again. The next station in the ring that has a message to send may then use the restored token to send its message.

4. *Star (PBX or CBX)*. A form of topology that usually provides an active hub with the responsibility for establishing a connection between a requesting station and another station or stations. The familiar PBX, or automatic switch, is the most prevalent. Here, access is provided through point-to-point wiring to a line-card unit in a central switch. The switch grants access (signaled through the dial tone in most implementations) and accepts a request for a connection that is signalled by a sequence of numbers designating the station to be connected to. If the target station has a free circuit to the switch unit, the connection will be made and maintained until broken by the station that requested it to begin with, or by some supervisory or priority action from another station. The star topology has also been defined in IEEE 802 standards for both CSMA/CD (802.3) and for Token Ring (802.5) since it is suitable for large installations in which having equipment in wiring closets is desirable.

5. *Mesh (point-to-point with intermediate routing)*. A topology that has widespread use in wide-area networks, such as the ARPANET and CSNET, and in private data networks that employ packet switching. Mesh topology has had use in local area networks since it is so easy to implement with wide-area network components and is supported as a network capability in the offerings of many of the major vendors of data-processing equipment. The mesh topology employs point-to-point connections among the stations in the network without requiring either full connectivity (each station connected to every other) or single connection among stations. The stations have the requirement to receive, interpret routing information, and retransmit every message that is not addressed to them. This allows them to utilize alternative paths if such exists in the mesh of connections between the sender and the ultimate destination, but it requires significant expenditure of data-processing resources in those stations that are on the path of heavy message traffic.

Other classifications are possible but will not be attempted here. The implementation of local area networks is still in an early stage, with a rapid growth of both utilization and technology likely. The appearance of standards, principally the IEEE 802 Local Area Network Standard, will help to focus the development of LAN products into the classifications discussed here, so the industry will mostly apply its energy in product development and refinement, rather than in the development of new and different topologies and more exotic access methods.

6.4 Distribution Techniques

There are two general approaches to signal distribution in local area networks—electrical cables and optical fibers. There are some networks implemented that use radio, infrared light, or carrier-current signals on power wiring, but such systems are not widely used and will not be discussed further here. It should be emphasized that the local area network is uniquely distinguished from the wide-area network in the availability of low-loss, low error-rate, and high data-rate communication distribution techniques. Many of the design decisions made in implementing the protocols for communication in a local network are based upon the low-error rate and high data-rate characteristics of the physical channel.

6.4.1 Cable Techniques

The most common technique for physical connection of the stations in a local area network is using cables. These cables are usually either coaxial or twisted pair. The difference is in the physical construction of the cable:

- Coaxial cable has two signal conductors, one of which is completely surrounded by the other and separated from it by a layer of insulator (Fig. 6-2A). This form of cable has widespread use in radio communication and data signal wiring.
- Twisted pair is a pair of wires that are laid side by side and then twisted around each other in a regular way (Fig. 6-2B). The cable may be shielded as well, especially if the circuit that will use it is balanced in respect to the shield reference.

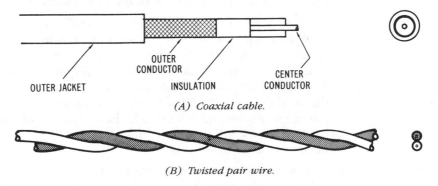

(A) Coaxial cable.

(B) Twisted pair wire.

Fig. 6-2. Cabling.

The trade-off between coaxial cable and twisted-pair wiring involves several variables, some of which may be discretionary for a specific application and some of which will not.

1. *Cost.* In general, coaxial cable is more expensive by a factor of two or three than twisted pair, and more expensive by a smaller factor than shielded twisted pair. There are both material costs and installation costs to be considered. For practical purposes, the installation cost of either coax or twisted pair will be the same. The cost of terminating the cable at each host station must be included, and will vary widely according to the method and type of cable selected. The net cost of the installation will include:

   (A) Material: X meters at $M/meter.

   (B) Installation: X meters at $I/meter.

   (C) Termination: H stations at $T/stations.

      The total cost will be Cost = X(M + I) + HT.

      There are also techniques that use ac-distribution wiring for interconnecting stations, but they suffer from extremely low data-rate restrictions. They will not be discussed further.

2. *Data Rate.* The difference between coax and twisted pair is nowhere more apparent than the data rate that they support. Coaxial cable is manifestly suitable for signal bandwidths up to several hundred megahertz, which implies data rates up to numbers in the order of a hundred megabits per second. For comparable distances to be spanned, twisted pair will typically be suitable for data rates at least an order of magnitude less. If the data rate of choice is 1-megabit per second, then either coax or twisted pair will suffice at distances out to several hundred meters. The IEEE 802.3 10BaseT standard defines the use of unshielded twisted pair at 10 Mbps. The standard defines the use of signal processing techniques to allow this high a data rate, and distances are restricted to 100 meters. The use of active hub equipment is mandatory. Above 10 Mbps, the use of coax or optical fiber is required.

3. *Compatibility with a Range of Equipment.* The local network field is by now sufficiently mature that a number of well-designed networking systems have been made commercially available. There are many vendors who include a local network connection as part of their product. The availability of standardized connection methods and cables will dictate the choice of cable type in many instances. Users with an eye on future expansion and a need to include a variety of station equipment in the network will install a standard form of cable rather than face the necessity of replacing it later.

4. *Electromagnetic Compatibility.* The electromagnetic environment and existence of statutory limits on limits of radiation from electronic

equipment have to be considered when choosing a cabling system. In general, the coexistence capability of cables and intense electromagnetic fields is greatest for coax and shielded twisted pair and less for ordinary twisted pair. This balances the relative cost advantage that twisted pair has, since there may be installations that could utilize it except for the presence of strong rf fields that can cause interference and disrupt communication. A specialist in the field of electromagnetic compatibility should be consulted if there is doubt about the environment that a network will be in. There is also the possibility that radiation from equipment and cables may cause harmful interference with other equipment, especially radio communications or navigation equipment. In such cases, it would be the responsibility of the owner of the equipment to eliminate the interference. The use of cables with a higher ability to contain the radiating fields is one approach to preventing such problems.

5. *Security.* Cables that employ copper conductors can easily be breached by listening equipment. Such considerations may not be a part of every installation but, if they are, then the use of cable of any sort may be undesirable. Or, the portions of the installation that can be provided with full-time physical security can be implemented with copper wire and the rest with alternative techniques, such as fiber optics. The key point is that connection to a copper wire, either coax or twisted pair, is rapidly and easily accomplished by any professional in the espionage field. The use of any wire at all may make it necessary to have additional costs associated with it in order to provide conduit, guards, and special techniques (such as multiple cables that are randomly used for parts of messages and the design and security of the systems themselves). Parenthetically, it is best to remember that no system can ever be perfectly secure. It is only possible to raise the cost of penetration to deter some attempts. Even fiber-optic lines can be tapped without detection.

6.4.2 Optical Fiber Techniques

The use of "wires of glass" has begun to assume economic importance over the last decade, although cost factors continue to restrict the use of fiber optics to applications where there is a special need that they fulfill uniquely. This cost penalty, like that imposed upon broadband systems due to the cost of the rf modems and head-end equipment, is due to the necessity of changing from one mechanism for signaling (electricity) to another (light) and back. The optical fiber distribution system can exhibit a net cost advantage over cable when certain requirements are included in the budget and fairly evaluated (Fig. 6-3). Factors such as the following may indicate that fiber optics is the appropriate medium for signal distribution.

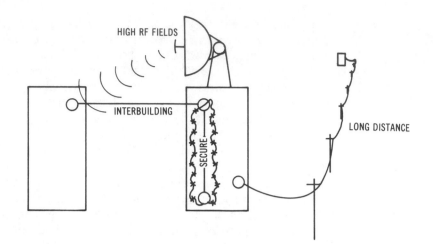

Fig. 6-3. Fiber-optic applications.

1. *Extreme Electromagnetic Environments.* When signal cables must penetrate areas of very high electromagnetic fields, the use of optical fibers is indicated. (Fields that are greater than 2–5 volts/meter represent extreme environments for most electronic equipment. Fields of this intensity can occur in the near field of a commercial broadcast transmitter, either radio or television, and in the beam of a high-power radar, or in close proximity to a high-energy discharge, such as the arc which results from the switching of a high-current power line that powers a heavy motor or machine.) Care in selection or design of the interface equipment is necessary since the optical-to-electrical converter must operate with very small signal amplitudes and may be the most susceptible element of the system to the electromagnetic fields. Similarly, the computer or other equipment that utilizes the optical fibers for communication may prove more susceptible to the fields than the communication cables would have been, so care in selection, design, and installation is needed for the communicating equipment as well as the communications cabling.

2. *Interbuilding Links.* Due to the very high differences in potential that may exist between two buildings during a lightning storm (it isn't necessary for one of them to be struck by lightning for such potentials to exist), any data cable that carries signals from one to the other could be damaged or contribute to damage of connected equipment. While there are methods for protecting against equipment damage from all except a direct hit by a lightning stroke, these methods must be factored into the cost of any interbuilding installation of local network cabling. The optical fiber, since it is not an electrical conductor, has complete immunity to damage from lightning-induced potentials. Its use as an interbuilding link is recommended.

3. *High Security or Electromagnetic Security Applications.* The use of optical fiber in signal wiring prevents the emanation of potentially compromising radiation. Applications where such considerations apply can utilize fiber optics, in concert with appropriate measures to both control emanations from host station equipment and to provide physical security to the fiber runs, to completely eliminate the danger of having a leakage from any electrical conductor that will compromise sensitive information. In this area, fiber optics is unsurpassed.

4. *Very Long-Distance Runs at High Data Rates.* Because optical fiber possesses an extremely low loss per unit length and because it can carry very high data rates over long distances (up to kilometers), local area network installations can utilize them to carry signals over long distances without the need to store and retransmit information. This results in less delays and less cost for interface equipment. This is an area where the cost model for the network must be worked out with care. The cost for the electrical-to-optical converter needed at each end of the link, and for the fibers used to connect them, must be compared to the cost for an equivalent link based on other transmission means. One such equivalent means would be a store-and-forward "router" that would communicate with an equivalent "router" at a distant network segment. The cost of the "routers" and the electrical connection between them would be compared to the equivalent optical system to determine cost benefits.

As the local network evolves, the day when Ethernet or a slow token ring will no longer satisfy the needs of an organization is visible to network planners. Accordingly, it is common practice to extend networks using optical fiber components when the cost of installation is significant. This tactic anticipates the need for higher data rate networks in the future and provides transmission medium that can support them.

6.4.3 Applications in Different Network Topologies

One thing that the standards for local networks specify is the type of cable and applications limits for it. This both reduces the freedom of the user or the network designer to specify cable type and use, and it saves the same user or designer from the consequences of an improper or incomplete design. Some of the network topologies lend themselves to mixing types of cable, others do not. Ring networks, for example, can mix cables since each station's connection to the next is unique to that pair. There is no need to be compatible with the rest of the connections. An Ethernet would not have that freedom since all stations are connected to the same cable. Table 6-1 shows the cables and connectors specified in the IEEE 802 standard.

Table 6-1. Cable Types and Applications

Network	Topology	Cable	Connectors
IEEE 802.3 10Base5 10Base2	Bus	50-Ω Coax	Type N
1Base5 10BaseT	Bus	Unshielded twisted pair	Not specified
IEEE 802.4	Bus	75-Ω Coax	Type F and CATV
IEEE 802.5	Ring	Shielded twisted pair	Unique

6.4.4 IEEE 802.3 (Ethernet) Cables

Two cables are specified for the IEEE 802.3 (Ethernet) standard. The shared communication path is a coaxial cable, of 50-ohm characteristic impedance, with a solid center conductor and four layers of shielding. Both PVC and PTFE versions are specified, with the latter for those applications where fire codes or good engineering practices would require a cable that does not create toxic fumes in a fire.

The cable has the properties described in Table 6-2. Using this cable, a full-sized IEEE 802.3 network can span a 2.5-km circle. It will be composed of 500-meter (maximum) segments with repeaters to either extend the distance or branch out to a new segment to create a tree configuration.

Table 6-2. Characteristics of IEEE 802.3 Cable

Characteristic	Property
Center conductor diameter	0.0855 ± 0.00005 inch
Inner shield diameter	0.242 inch minimum
Outer shield diameter	0.319 inch minimum
Outer shield coverage	90% minimum tinned copper
Outer jacket diameter	0.405 ± 0.007 inch polyvinyl chloride or 0.375 ± 0.010 inch fluoropolymer
Bend radius	10 inches nominal
Characteristic impedance	50 ± 2-Ω average, ± 3-Ω periodic, variations <2 meter period
Attenuation	17 dB/km at 10 MHz
Velocity of propagation	0.77 times speed of light in a vacuum

The connection between the station and the coax in the IEEE 802.3 network is made through a medium-access unit (MAU), or transceiver. The MAU is an active device. It contains transmitting and receiving circuits to couple the station onto the coax and a circuit to detect collisions. Between the transceiver and the station equipment is a twisted-pair cable with separate signal pairs for the transmitted signal, the received signal, the collision presence signal, and power for the transceiver. The connector for the twisted-pair cable is a standard 15-pin, D-subminiature termination.

Connectors and cables for the IEEE 802.4 Token Bus standard are not specified other than by reference to industry practice in the cable television area. Configuration of an IEEE 802.4 network is assumed to be based upon an existing or uniquely designed cable system, either baseband or broadband, and it is not specified in the standard.

Configuration of an IEEE 802.5 Token Ring network is based on a high-impedance twisted-pair cable and a specific IBM design for a connector. Distances and signal levels are specified or implied by the standard. The level of detail in the IEEE 802.5 standard is not such that independent implementations are guaranteed to be compatible.

6.5 Access Protocols

Access protocols are the rules under which the shared medium (the wire or other switching means) is shared by the stations in the local network. Local networks differ from long-haul or wide-area networks (WAN) in having a shared wire or switch for which stations must compete. For this reason, local networks are usually classified by *access method* as well as by topology.

The types of access method that are in actual use in commercial products today include:

1. Carrier-sense multiple access with collision detection (CSMA/CD).
2. Token passing on a bus.
3. Token passing on a ring.
4. Time-division multiple access.
5. Polling.

Each of these access methods deserves an explanation. In the interests of space, the descriptions given will be limited to explaining the operation of the protocols, but not exhaustively defining all the special cases and error-handling procedures. The literature of networking has had numerous contributions for analyzing the microscopic behavior of most of the access methods and the numerous variations of them. Reference to the bibliography will give the reader material for more detailed exploration.

6.5.1 Carrier-Sense Multiple Access with Collision Detection (CSMA/CD)

The CSMA/CD access method is used on baseband or broadband bus systems. The basic protocol is that a station with a message to send must monitor the bus to see if any other station is sending. If another station is sending, the second station must wait, or "defer," until the sending station has finished. Then, it may send its message. If no station was sending at the time that it first listened, the station may send its message immediately. The term "carrier sense" indicates this "listening-before-transmitting" behavior.

If two stations (or more) have messages to send at the same time and they are separated by significant distances on the bus, each may begin transmitting at roughly the same time without being aware of the other station(s). The signals from each station will superimpose on the bus and be garbled beyond the decoding ability of the receiving station. This is termed a "collision." The protocol requires a transmitting station to monitor the bus while sending each of its messages and to detect such "collisions." When a collision has been detected, each of the sending stations must cease transmitting, wait a random length of time, and then try again. The randomly chosen time interval gives a reasonable probability that one station will begin transmitting long enough before the others that the slower station(s) will detect the bus signal and defer. The station that wins the retransmission contest is said to have "acquired" the bus.

A short definition of CSMA/CD in a computer-like language would be:

```
IF MESSAGE_READY=TRUE THEN          ;if a message is ready
  WHILE BUS_BUSY=TRUE               ;check the bus for other
    DEFER                           ;traffic
  END WHILE
  WHILE MESSAGE_BUFFER_FULL=TRUE  ;send the message
  OUTPUT MESSAGE_BUFFER
  IF COLLISION=TRUE THEN            ;if a collision occurs
   WAIT RANDOM_TIME                 ;stop for a random time
  END IF                           ;then begin again
  END WHILE
END IF
```

The algorithm for generating the random number is a prime determinant of the behavior of the protocol. Various methods for choosing numbers have been explored. One method is based on knowing the maximum number of stations on the network and choosing a random number such that the probability of transmitting after a collision is inversely proportional to that number.

$$p = 1/(\text{number of stations})$$

where,

p is the retransmission probability, $0 < p < 1$.

The actual use of the random number is as follows:

1. The sending station, upon detecting a collision, will stop sending and choose a random number from a previously generated list.

2. The number will be an integer whose range is between zero (0) and

the maximum allowed. In the case under discussion the maximum value is the same as the number of stations using the network.

3. The sending station will wait a number of "time slots" equal to the number chosen. For example, on a 100-station network, the random numbers will all lie between 0 and 100. If the number chosen is 22, the sending station will wait 22 "time slots" before transmitting a second time. The station with which the collision occurred will have also chosen a random number from the same range, 0 to 100, and will wait the number of "time slots." The duration of a "time slot" must be chosen as to be the time required for a signal from a station at one extreme of the bus to propagate to the other extreme, and return, and be detected. This is called the "round trip" time. In our example, the second station may have chosen the number 54, meaning that it will wait 54 "time slots" before retransmitting. The first station will transmit after only 22 time slots, however, and will "acquire" the bus when it does. The second station will reset its timer and will transmit when it detects the end of transmission of the first station.

The efficiency of this protocol is constrained by two things:

1. It is necessary to choose, and program each station with, the worst-case retransmission probability possible to ensure that multiple station collisions are resolved. The delay times chosen by colliding stations will be, on the average, equal to half the number of allowed stations times the round-trip time.

2. Studies have shown that message traffic on local networks tends to be "bursty." There are long periods in which very little traffic is present. During these periods, choosing a small number for the retransmission delay period would result in less delay time in resolving the collision, but by always using a small number, problems could occur when many stations have messages to send.

The retransmission algorithm of Ethernet[9] was designed to overcome these constraints. It is called "Binary Exponential Backoff." This means that the interval from which the random number for retransmission is chosen is not the number of stations on the network, but is a variable based upon the amount of traffic. The algorithm is stated as follows:

1. On the first collision, the stations chose a random number that is either 0 or 1, and wait either 0 or 1 round-trip times before trying again.

2. If a second collision occurs, the interval is doubled and the random number is chosen from the set 0, 1, 2, 3.

3. On each successive collision for the same message attempt, the random number is chosen from an interval that is double that of the previous attempt's interval until either one station successfully acquires the bus or some arbitrary number of attempts is made and the protocol gives up.

This method has the virtue of giving the least delay for lightly loaded networks and of rapidly adapting to the extremely infrequent occasions when a lot of stations have traffic to send. It is the basis for the original Ethernet design and is now standardized by the IEEE 802.3 CSMA/CD local network standard (IEEE 802.3). There has been much discussion in the literature about the probabilistic nature of the time required to acquire the bus, most of which has ignored the fact that any shared medium will exhibit probabilistic access time due to the statistical nature of error conditions and the number of stations and their traffic which affects operation.

The facts are that CSMA/CD has a different probability distribution of access time than the other access protocols, but they are all probabilistic.

It is also true that, in any general-purpose application where there are numerous software processes involved in the creation and management of the communication channels which utilize the local network bus or other topology, the delays in acquiring the bus are not significant in determining the overall delay from end to end between user processes. The local network is unique in having more capability in its physical channel than can be utilized by most of the connected stations, so its limitations will seldom be discernible.

6.5.2 Token Ring Passing on a Bus

Another method of determining the right to transmit messages on the shared bus is to explicitly identify the station that may send traffic, and then transfer that right in some order to all the other stations. The message that informs the next station in the sequence that the *right to transmit* has just been received is called a "token." An arbitrarily large number of stations may share a common bus by passing the token around. Each station will be allowed to "hold the token" for a fixed length of time so that no station may monopolize the network. The *minimum* length of time that a station will hold the token is just that length of time that is required to retransmit it to the next station in the sequence, which it *must do* if it has no message to send.

In the same computer-like language, a token-passing access protocol looks like this:

```
WHILE TOKEN=TRUE AND TOKEN_HOLD_TIMEOUT=FALSE
  WHILE MESSAGE_BUFFER_FULL=TRUE
    OUTPUT MESSAGE                    ;send message
  END WHILE
  OUTPUT TOKEN                        ;pass token to next
END WHILE                            station in sequence
```

The apparent simplicity of the algorithm is deceiving. Because each station in the sequence must properly receive, utilize, and pass on the token, any error that occurs can destroy the logical progress of the token. Stations must be equipped to detect and recover from certain errors, such as:

1. Loss of the token when a station that should receive it does not do so due to a transmission error, the lack of a receive buffer, or the cessation of operation of either the station that holds the token or the station that would receive it next.

2. Duplication of the token due to the improper operation of any of the stations in the sequence.

3. Monopolization of the token by any of the stations in the sequence due to a malfunction of their token-holding timer and the presence of a process that supplies a large number of messages for transmission (such as a large file transfer).

Each of these errors, and others, can be managed with the proper implementation of the network interface. The IEEE 802.4 Token Bus Standard has specific rules for recovering from any number of error conditions so that a network implemented under the 802.4 specifications should be as reliable as any other.

6.5.3 Token Ring Networks

When ring topology networks are implemented, a variety of access methods are available. Several of these have been examined in literature and are available in commercial products. The most prevalent method is the so-called "token ring" protocol. This method uses a short message that circulates around the ring to indicate that the ring is available for traffic from any station. A station that has a message to send must copy each message that goes by until it receives this "token" message. It must then convert the "token" to a "connector" message and append its own message immediately after. The connector message differs from the token message in only one bit, so that converting from one message to the other is readily accomplished by inverting that single bit as the message is being retransmitted in the required 1-bit delay that each station provides.

The station that "seized the token" must convert the connector back to a token when the message returns to it, after having circulated completely around the ring. Each station around the ring must receive the message and decide, based upon the destination address in the message, whether the message is intended for it. The station that is the intended destination may mark the message, in a field position near the end of the message, as having been properly received. The transmitting station may then pass on to the next message in its transmit queue.

The right to send another message immediately after the first may be provided in the protocol (up to maximum length of time for each station). This time interval is intended to prevent any station from holding the token, or monopolizing the network, for excessive periods and, if properly implemented, will serve to overcome some types of faults in the interface circuits.

The token ring access protocol can be described in a computer-like language as follows:

```
WHILE MESSAGE_BUFFER_FULL=TRUE
   INPUT MESSAGE                    ;read passing traffic
      IF MESSAGE=TOKEN THEN
         CONVERT TOKEN TO CONNECTOR ;special operation to
      END IF                        change token to connector
   OUTPUT MESSAGE
END WHILE
OUTPUT TOKEN                        ;send token message
```

The apparent simplicity of this protocol is misleading because of the requirement that each station in the ring properly repeat the message. If any station malfunctions, the message will not return to the sending station, and may not be received by the intended destination. A well-designed implementation of this protocol will provide for recovery from the faults that the ring may experience and will provide acceptable reliable operation. Providing the additional states and other mechanisms needed for proper operation and error recovery will add considerably to the implementation complexity, but not to the degree that token ring protocols cannot be economically implemented.

The IEEE 802 Standard includes a token ring specification, IEEE 802.5. This specification provides:

1. *Token Access*. The token is a 3-octet field that circulates around the ring until a station with a message to send converts it to a connector by inverting one bit.

2. *Priority Message Access*. The token must be marked as having one of four priorities. Only messages that have associated priorities at the level of the token, or higher, may be sent using that token. Messages at a lower level of priority must wait for a lower-priority token.

3. *Timers for Access Time and Loss of Token*. The first timer is used to limit the length of time that a station may transmit successive messages without sending a token. The second timer is a supervisory timer that is used to recreate the token, in case the station that should have sent it failed to do so.

The IEEE 802.5 Standard is based upon laboratory development work, chiefly by the IBM research center in Zurich, Switzerland, and upon industrial and research experience with ring protocols since the mid 1970s.

6.5.4 Time-Division Multiple Access (TDMA)

There has been at least one commercial local network product based upon an access protocol in which each station in sequence is assigned a time slot in which to transmit. The slots are synchronized by a master station that broadcasts a short timing message, following which each station counts time intervals until its interval arrives. The station may then send any messages it has accumulated since its last opportunity occurred. If it does not transmit, the interval goes unused. Stations may join the sequence by requesting access during the interval following the synchronizing message. The master station assigns the next interval number and the requesting station waits until its assigned interval arrives.

The stations must implement a common counting interval. The interval must allow for network round-trip times, clock variations, and for the longest message that a station is allowed to transmit. The waiting time that a station must endure between one transmission interval and the next is determined by the length of the interval and the next is determined by the length of the interval and the number of stations with assigned access rights. Priorities may be implemented by having the master station send a priority level in the synchronization message which tells the stations that only those stations with a message or station priority higher than that designated in the message may participate in the next sequence of transmissions.

TDMA is not the most efficient protocol for local networks with a high variability in the number of stations needing access at any time since each station must wait the maximum length of time for each access. It is well suited to communication over satellite links, for example, where end-to-end delays are large and the need to maximize channel utilization will lead to long message queues in the sending stations.

In a computer-like language, the access protocol of TDMA is:

```
VARIABLE_INTERVAL_NUMBER:INTEGER        ;assigned interval
WHILE INTERVAL_NUMBER<0                  ;valid interval number
  INPUT MESSAGE                          ;watch net traffic
  IF MESSAGE=SYNCH_MESSAGE THEN
    INTERVAL=0
    WHILE INTERVAL<INTERVAL_NUMBER
    CALL INTERVAL_TIMER                  ;times each interval
    INTERVAL=INTERVAL+1                  ;increments interval
    END WHILE
  END IF
  IF MESSAGE_BUFFER_FULL=TRUE            ;if a message is queued
    OUTPUT MESSAGE                       ;send it
  END IF
END WHILE
```

The somewhat more complex definition of TDMA access allows a more robust access scenario. It is not necessary for each station to participate properly in each sequence of transmissions. Stations may disappear without affecting other stations, although stations that malfunction in calculating the interval will cause problems for others. The loss of the master station will cause the entire network to cease operation until another master station is created. Proper design will provide for alternative masters that are activated when a synchronizing message does not appear within a specified interval, and it will provide mechanisms to minimize the likelihood that interval calculations are made improperly.

6.5.5 Polling Access

One of the simplest forms of control for network access is that of having a master station poll each of the other stations in the network. This consists of the master station sending a message to each station in turn, with the message being an interrogation of the state of the slave station's message buffer. If the slave has a message to send, it sends it to the master station. The master station then sends the message to the intended destination, or keeps it if the message is for itself. The master station then polls the next station in sequence to determine if there is a message waiting there.

This protocol has the advantage that very simple implementations are possible in the slave stations. This makes polling access attractive for simple networks in which machine tools, security stations, temperature sensors, or similar things with limited functionality are to be controlled by a central computer. It is less suitable for peer-to-peer communication among data processors, work stations, and computer-controlled industrial-process equipment due to its dependence upon a vulnerable central station and the delays associated with sending each message twice.

With proper design, the polling protocol can be made relatively robust and performance can be improved to make it acceptable for a variety of applications. This protocol has been used extensively in process and industrial-control applications. A computer-like language description of the slave part of the protocol would look like the following:

```
WHILE ACTIVE_STATUS=TRUE
   INPUT MESSAGE                        ;read traffic
   IF MESSAGE=POLL_MESSAGE THEN         ;when polled by master
     WHILE MESSAGE_BUFFER_FULL=TRUE     ;send any message that
       OUTPUT MESSAGE                   ;is in the queue
     END WHILE
   END IF
END WHILE
```

The master station has a more complex sequence since it must have a list of stations to interrogate and must perform retransmissions.

None of the preceding examples are full implementations of the respective protocols. None include the necessary error-handling or network fault-recovery procedures that comprise large parts of the real implementations of network software.

6.6 Performance

Local area networks are fundamentally different from wide-area networks in that they can be implemented at a reasonable cost, with a physical channel that has both a very high data-rate capability and a very low error rate. For this reason, most local area networks are constrained in performance by higher-level protocol operation and by competition within the equipment that is connected to the network, for resources such as memory and CPU time. As new technologies evolve, this may change.

To understand network performance, and the related communication resources available to the network user, it is necessary to examine various contributing aspects of the topic:

1. *Data Rate.* In general, data rate and performance are correlated. It is not true, though, that increasing the data rate will necessarily yield a similar increase in net performance.

2. *Loading.* The number of stations competing for use of the shared resources of the network influences the performance.

3. *Access Method.* This aspect of performance is important under conditions of very heavy network traffic.

4. *Topology.* Certain topologies perform better than others.

5. *Error Rate.* A key determinant of performance is error rate. The recovery mechanisms for most errors can be significant in influencing performance.

6. *Procedural Protocols.* The protocols used to send and receive messages between communicating entities, above the level of the simple data-link protocols, can have a profound effect upon end-to-end performance.

6.6.1 What Is "Performance"?

The generality called "performance" is used to sell everything from cars to professional athletes. So it is also with local networks. Let us be specific about the properties we include in the term.

1. The net data rate between communicating processes. These processes are usually understood to be end-user processes with no network overhead included.

2. The delay in data transmission between communicating processes.

3. The time required to determine an error condition and recover from it when that error condition prevents communication.

4. The time required to establish a communication link between communicating processes.

6.6.2 Data Rate Influence on Performance

The net data rate that a network can support is determined in part by the access method and the number of stations competing for use of the physical channel, but the major influence is the data rate of the transmitted packets. It is clear that a 10-Mbps data-rate network can sustain more net data transfer per unit time than a 1-Mbps data-rate network. What does not follow is that a single station can utilize the network at either data rate to the full extent of its capacity. The data rate of the transmitted packets is an attribute of the physical channel, not necessarily a service that is available to users. Bruce Watson studied the net throughput of two different local networks and found that a factor of 10 difference in the data rate resulted in no discernible difference in throughput between two stations. The networks both had high data rates, one being 4 Mbps and the other 50 Mbps. The action of network software in the stations was such that the physical channel data rate had no effect on the net data-transfer time between stations. This was reported in "Performance Comparison of Hyperchannel and Ethernet Local Area networks" in 1980.[10]

The basic premise of the local network is that the physical channel can be implemented to offer a data rate that is much greater than any station can possibly make use of. Networks that run at 10 Mbps do so in order to make the time required for any station to send a message as short as possible. This allows many stations to utilize the shared channel. The lower data-rate networks, such as are popular for personal computers, have traded off the ability to share the channel among many stations to achieve a lower cost. Their inclusion in a large network would require a store-and-forward service for each packet through what is called a *router* or *gateway*. (A router serves to transmit packets from one network segment to another based on the address of the packet. It can filter packets from one network onto another that has a higher data rate but, otherwise, with the same protocols. A gateway provides a routing function but it also translates one set of communications protocols into another set to allow stations on dissimilar networks to communicate.)

The primary effect of data rate on the performance of the network is to determine the extent and number of connected stations that may share the same channel. Net throughput is, at least in today's networks, determined by the processing required to execute higher-level protocol software, contend for memory resources, and execute context switching among the processes that are competing within the station.

6.6.3 Loading: How Many Stations Are Trying to Use the Channel?

The most direct influence on performance, as perceived by an individual user, is the number of other stations that are actively competing for use of the shared resource at the same time. The resource may be the channel over which all messages must pass or it may be a network utility, such as a dedicated station that acts to store and retrieve files. Any shared resource has a limit on its capability to serve multiple users and, when that limit is reached, it may either block further use or offer a lower level of service to all.

The effects of loading on throughput of a network has been studied for various access methods and data rates. (See the papers described in References 9, 10, and 11.) The studies have all emphasized abstraction and the microscopic behavior of specific elements of networks rather than what throughput actually is when available on a network that is composed of several hierarchical protocols operating on real equipment. The studies have value to network theoreticians, but are apt to be misleading to those whose background and requirements are other than theoretical.

To understand the effect of loading on the performance of a network, consider that a network has one or more shared resources: the physical channel and one or more shared servers. Any of the shared resources represent limitations in performance that may be perceived by network users. The data-transmission rate from one station to another is a good place to look for an example.

In a network, the net data-transmission rate available to a user's process is just a fraction of the physical channel's available data rate, and that is the channel data rate divided by the number of users that are active at a particular time. This says nothing about the effects of access method, protocol overhead, or other factors that reduce the number. It says that in a shared resource, each station gets an equal share and no more.

The curve of throughput versus number of users in shown in Fig. 6-4. The limitations imposed by the station in moving data out of memory, protocol processing time, and other factors is represented by the horizontal lines intersecting the hyperbola. The limits in station throughput capability vary according to the station's equipment and what else beside communication is being accom-

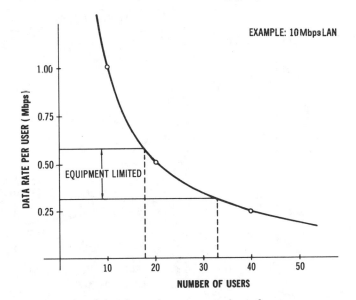

Fig. 6-4. Throughput vs. number of users.

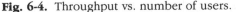

plished in it. In a local area network, it is likely that the physical channel is capable of more data throughput than the stations connected to it can sustain. This means that, as long as the number of users is below that position corresponding to the point on the curve where the equipment limits determine the throughput, the user will not perceive any difference in throughput as the number of other users varies. The curve of Fig. 6-5 illustrates what an individual station will have as theoretical data throughput as the number of users increases. The actual curve will depend heavily upon specific details of each network.

In real networks, the data rate available to individual stations is not the same as the theoretical hyperbola for a large number of users. Access methods differ, but all have a certain penalty to impose upon networks with large populations. Errors in transmission require time and network resources to correct, and these tend to increase in networks that are large and have many users. The true data throughput curve tends to depart from the hyperbola for very large numbers of users, and much of the controversy among advocates of different networks involves the degree to which this departure exists. Fig. 6-6 shows the effect of large numbers of users.

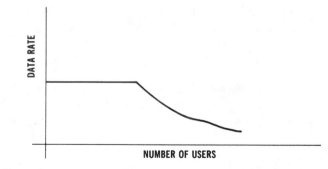

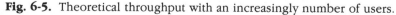

Fig. 6-5. Theoretical throughput with an increasingly number of users.

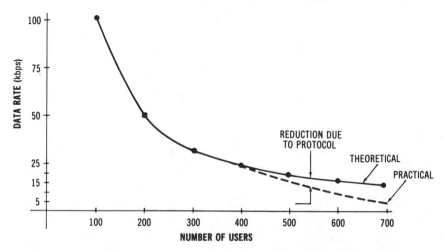

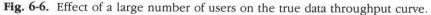

Fig. 6-6. Effect of a large number of users on the true data throughput curve.

In trying to decide which network to use, it is easy to be overwhelmed by the conflicting claims of advocates of one technique or another. In fact, any network will impose limitations upon the user community as that community gets large enough. The proper approach to providing a useful network for a large community is to understand the needs of the community and design the installation accordingly. For example, in a typical business, the network is used to provide electronic mail, file and data-base sharing, and document distribution. The amount of traffic that crosses departmental boundaries is significantly less than that which is transmitted intradepartment. Such departments can be isolated from the rest of the network with a routing station which passes on any message that is intended for a station outside the department (see Fig. 6-7). Such an approach will have the effect of reducing the number of users on the department network to just those who actually have messages for the department. In terms of Figs. 6-4 and 6-5, the number of users has been reduced and each user has more of the resources of the network available.

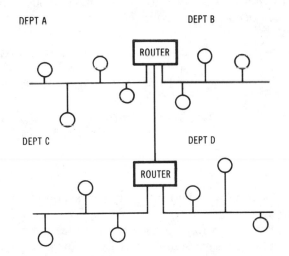

Fig. 6-7. Using routing stations to isolate departments.

An analysis of delay times in sending and receiving messages will reveal a situation very similar to that of throughput. There are message delays in the station and in the network. Up to a certain point, the network delays are insignificant when compared to the station delays, and users are unaffected by the amount of usage of the network. Beyond that point, delay may become significant as usage increases.

In the early development of the network standards, much attention was paid to the analysis of mathematical models of network behavior, and vast conclusions were drawn based on them. Since the latter half of the 1980s, with the number of networks in everyday use grown tremendously, there has been less attention given to the properties of the abstract models. The evolution of diskless workstations and networks based on a client-server model have shown that the server is the resource that becomes congested long before the network does.

6.6.4 Error Conditions: Cause and Effect

When errors occur, a well-designed network protocol recovers from them. That recovery will take time and will require the use of resources in the network and in the stations that are communicating. Different protocols use different amounts of resources.

The most fundamental error that a local network can experience is a bad bit in a message. The error rates of local network are orders of magnitude less than the error rates of long-haul networks, but the data rates are greater. The probability of a bad bit occurring within a specific time is worth considering. For example, the bit error rate of an Ethernet is one in ten to the minus ninth. If the network is 30% utilized, about 3,000,000 bits per second are transmitted. Errors occur, on the average:

$$
\begin{aligned}
\text{Errors/sec} &= \text{bits/sec} \times \text{error/bit} \\
&= 3 \times 10^6 \times 10^{-9} \text{ error/sec} \\
&= 3 \times 10^{-3} \text{ error/sec}
\end{aligned}
$$

$$
\begin{aligned}
\text{Time between error} &= 1 \div \text{errors/sec} \\
&= 1 \div 3 \times 10^{-3} \\
&= 0.333 \times 10^{-3} \text{ sec} \\
&= 333 \text{ sec}
\end{aligned}
$$

That's about one bad bit every 333 seconds, or roughly one error every 5.5 minutes.

Error rates for most good local area networks are similar. In fact, many installations have significantly better error rates. Obviously, the overhead involved in error handling is not going to be significant if only line errors are to be considered.

There are other sources of errors, and by that, we mean circumstances wherein a message fails to reach its destination. Some of these causes are:

1. Lack of resources at the destination. The most likely cause of a lost message is not having a buffer available in the receiving station. Buffers are the parts of memory that are shared dynamically by all the software processes that are running on the computer. Since there is only a finite amount of memory in any computer, it is necessary to allocate the part used for temporary storage of messages to several processes on a time-shared basis. The occasion arises on heavily used systems when a message will arrive during an interval in which there are no buffers available to store it. Different systems react in different ways to such an event but, in almost all, the message will be discarded. The IEEE 802.5

standard provides a means where the loss of a message due to the lack of a receiving buffer is to be signaled to the originating station. In most general-purpose communication protocols for higher-level functions, there are mechanisms to avoid such a situation and provisions to recover from lost messages.

2. Failure of one or more components of the network.

3. Transient conditions that alter the network and cause lost messages. The token-passing protocols are sensitive to a loss of stations in the sequence and to the time required to reestablish normal operation.

4. Very high-noise ambients caused by electrical or radio equipment. These circumstances typically occur only in heavy industry and are dealt with by means of special physical channel equipment.

The effect of any of the preceding error causes is situation development. In general, any persistent problem will make interactive use of the network difficult, so terminal users will have trouble. Other uses will continue with a lower level of performance as the network resources are used to recover from errors. It is important in any network to have an adequate means of identifying and correcting the cause of errors when they occur. Network monitors help a network manager detect fault conditions. The network management processes in each station should be set to notify the person responsible when error rates exceed certain limits or when a persistent fault condition exists.

6.7 Local Area Network Standards

The standards activity in local networks has been intense since 1980. The leading activity in the field has been under the sponsorship of the Institute of Electrical and Electronic Engineers (IEEE) Computer Society. This effort has been organized as IEEE Project 802, with the charter to create a standard for the local area network.

The resulting document actually specifies several incompatible standards for local area networks. In view of firmly entrenched opinions and the committed efforts of several VLSI vendors, it was recognized by the committee that no single approach to defining a network would gain full acceptance by the user community. Rather than create a standard that would compete with a significant body of alternate practice which was not compatible in any sense with the standard, the IEEE 802 committee chose to standardize three of the leading approaches to access-control and physical-cabling topology. They also, and most significantly, provided a common sublayer of protocol that provided the interface to higher levels of communications services. That means that any access method at all can be used, provided it is one of the standard three; the application tasks and communication services that utilize it need not be concerned with which access method it is. The relationship of the different access methods and link control sublayers is shown in Fig. 6-8.

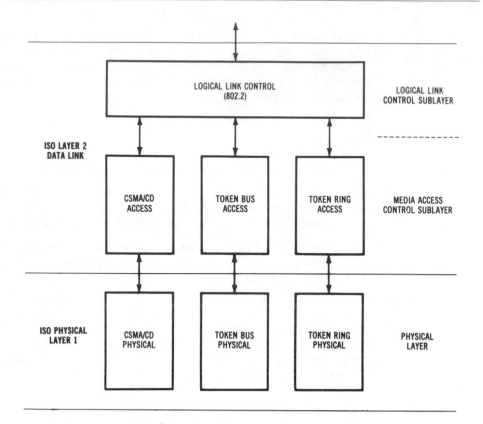

Fig. 6-8. IEEE 802 LAN reference model.

6.7.1 Logical Link Control

The logical link-control sublayer provides a common interface to higher-level protocols and communication service providers. The service that it provides to the higher level consists of:

- *A Connectionless Service.* This means that there is no explicit acknowledgment of message receipt or definition of a "connection" between communicating stations.

- *A Connection-Oriented Service.* This means that there is a "connection" established between communicating stations. The connection requires a specific action (messages) to begin, manage, and terminate it. The logical link-control sublayer must provide such actions if the access sublayer does not. None of the IEEE 802 access sublayers do.

This defines the services that are provided, not how they are provided (which is not specified) or the manner in which a specific service is requested. Those details are more complex than it is possible to detail here. The documents themselves are available from the IEEE Computer Society. Refer to Section 6.9.2, item 2, for the address.

6.7.2 Media Access Sublayers

In order to provide either of these services to higher layers, the Logical Link Control sublayer may utilize any of several subordinate layers. The task of the subordinate sublayers is to provide a particular form of "media access." That means that each access-control protocol, either CSMA/CD, Token Passing on a Bus, or Token Passing on a Ring, has its own definition in a unique sublayer.

Each media-access sublayer interfaces to a different physical layer. The interfaces between the media-access sublayers and their respective physical layers are unique to the particular media-access method—CSMA/CD, Token Bus, or Token Ring.

6.7.3 Physical Layer Definitions

The physical layer definitions provide:

1. *802.3 standard*: Several techniques, including both coax and twisted pair at several data rates:
   - 50-ohm coax, 10 Mbps signalling rate, bus topology.
   - Unshielded twisted pair, 1 Mbps signalling rate, bus topology.
   - Unshielded twisted pair, 10 Mbps signalling, active hub topology.
2. *802.4 standard*: A Token Bus physical layer that provides three different cable schemes:
   - 75-ohm coax, 1 Mbps signaling rate.
   - 75-ohm coax, 5 or 10 Mbps.
   - Broadband cable television system, 1, 5, or 10 Mbps.
3. *802.5 standard*: A Token Ring physical layer using shielded twisted-pair cable at 1 or 4 Mbps.

Table 6-5 gives a detailed comparison of the different media-access and physical approaches.

6.7.4 International Standards

The IEEE 802 standards were adopted and are now the basis for ANSI American National Standards IEEE85a-d. The ANSI documents are virtually identical to the IEEE standards.

The International Organization for Standardization (ISO) has adopted the IEEE/ANSI standards as ISO8802.

Table 6-5. Media-Access/Physical Approaches

Characteristic	802.3 CSMA/CD	802.4 Token Bus	802.5 Token Ring
Access protocol	CSMA/CD	Token passing	Token ring
Address size	16 or 48 bits	16 or 48 bits	16 or 48 bits
Network size	2800 meters maximum diameter	7600 meters, 1 Mbps based on attenuation for other frequencies	Not specified
Maximum station	1024	Not specified	Not specified
Minimum packet	56 or 64 octets	9 or 17 octets	3 octets
Maximum packet	1518 octets	8191 octets	Not specified
Data signalling rate	10 Mbps,	1, 5, 10 Mbps	1, 16 Mbps
Type of cable	50-ohm coax, twisted pair	75-ohm coax	150-ohm twisted pair

6.7.5 Other Networks

The adoption of standards and subsequent availability of communications equipment based on them has reduced the number of nonstandard networks in use to vanishingly small numbers. There are some, such as Apple Computer's AppleTalk®, that are in widespread use for low-end desk top machines. Above that level, the IEEE standards dominate.

6.8 FDDI

The Fiber Distributed Data Interconnect (FDDI) is the popular name for a standard produced by ANSI accredited standards committee X3T9.5. It specifies a high-speed network, based partly on the IEEE 802 standard, that is suitable for back-bone or high-speed interconnection networks. We include it here since it is a form of local network.

6.8.1 Overview of FDDI

FDDI is a token ring, similar in some respects to the IEEE 802.5 standard. It differs in its data rate, 100 Mbps, which is far higher than the original 4 Mbps or new 16 Mbps of the IEEE 802.5 standard. The organization of the FDDI standard is as follows:

> Logical Link Control IEEE 802.2
>> Layer Management
>>> Medium Access Control
>>> Physical Protocol
>>> Physical Medium Dependent

The Medium Access Control (MAC) sublayer is intended to interface to an IEEE 802.2 Logical Link Control sublayer, and to be equivalent in terms of the services provided to other 802 MAC sublayers. The user would not perceive any difference in service; software that works on Ethernet/802.3 will continue to work on FDDI. Since the base data rate is 100 Mbps, performance should be substantially better.

The Physical Protocol sublayer defines the data encoding and decoding. The higher data rate of FDDI prompted its developers to specify a different data encoding scheme than any of the 802 Physical sublayers use. In FDDI, every 4-bit pattern is encoded as a 5-bit pattern chosen for certain characteristics that improve the physical transmission. For instance, there is no pattern that transmits more than 3 consecutive zeros. That facilitates the use of phase-lock circuity to synchronize the receiving station clock with the sending station clock and prevents errors due to timing differences between the two. At 100 Mbps it takes care in circuit design to implement the FDDI interface.

The Physical Medium Dependent sublayer specifies the physical implementation of the transmission system between elements of the ring. The implementation specified is a fiber optic link. The optical fiber is 62.5/125 micrometers (μm), that is the inner diameter is 62.5 and the outer diameter of the cladding is 125 micrometers. There are alternatives specified at 50/125, 85/125, and 100/140 micrometers. The light source is specified to operate at a wavelength of 1300 nanometers, which places it in the infrared part of the spectrum. The system is a multimode transmission, representing a compromise between distance and cost that is well suited to the local network or high speed backbone. FDDI links may be up to 2000 meters long between nodes, and the whole system may be up to 200 kilometers around.

6.8.2 Applications of FDDI

FDDI interfaces are more expensive than lower data rate interfaces. This will probably be true for some time, although standardization will lead to competition and bring down prices. The data rate of FDDI is more than most individual users need, so the best place to use FDDI is as a high data rate backbone network linking subnetworks. It is also ideal to hook together naturally high data rate devices (graphics displays and their processors, file servers in a shared file environment) for which a low data rate communications service degrades performance.

6.9 References

6.9.1 References Cited in the Text

1. Arthurs, E., and B.W. Stuck, "A Theoretical Performance Analysis of Polling and Carrier Sense Collision Detection Communication Systems," a document submitted as a working paper to IEEE 802 Local Network Standards Committee, 1982.

2. Binder, R., F. Abramson, F. Kuo, A. Okinaka, and D Wax. Aloha Packet Broadcasting—a Retrospect. *AFIPS Conference Proceedings*, Vol. 44, 1975 NCC, Montvale, NJ: AFIPS Press, 1975.

3. Clark, David. D., Kenneth T. Pogran, and David P. Reed. "An Introduction to Local Area Networks," *Proceedings of the IEEE*, November 1978, pp. 1497–1517.

4. Digital Equipment Corp., Intel Corp., and Xerox Corp. *The Ethernet: Data Link and Physical Layers*, September 1980 (No longer available).

5. Farber, D.J. "A Ring Network," *Datamation*, Vol. 21, No. 2, February 1975, pp. 51–53.

6. Fraser, A.G. "Spider—An Experimental Data Communications System," *Conference Record, International Conference on Communications*, 1974, pp. 21F1–21F10.

7. ———. "DATAKIT—A Modular Network for Synchronous and Asynchronous Traffic," *Conference Record, International Conference on Communications*, 1979, pp. 20.1.1–20.1.3.

8. "Local-area Subnetworks: a Performance Comparison," *Proceedings of IFIP 6.4 International Workshop on Local Area Networks*, pp. 157–180.

9. Metcalf, R. and D. Boggs. "Ethernet: Distributed Packet Switching for Local Computer Networks." *Communications of the ACM*, July 1976, pp. 395–404.

10. Watson, Bruce. "Performance comparison of Hyperchannel and Ethernet local area networks," *Presentation to IEEE 802 Committee on Local Area Network Standards*, Scottsdale, AZ, 1980.

11. Wilkes, M.V., and D.J. Wheeler. "The Cambridge Digital Communication Ring," *Proceedings of the Local Area Communications Network Symposium*, May 1979, pp. 47–61.

6.9.2 General References for Background Study

1. Clark, David D., Kenneth T. Pogran, and David P. Reed. "An Introduction to Local Area Networks," *Proceedings of the IEEE*, November 1978, pp. 1497–1517.

2. IEEE Standards for Local Area Networks

   802.1-Higher Level Interface

   802.2-Logical Link Control

   802.3-CSMA/CD

   802.4-Token Bus

   802.5-Token Ring
   Available through the IEEE Computer Society Publications Office, PO Box 80452, Worldway Postal Center, Los Angeles, CA 90080.

3. *Introduction to Local Area Networks*, Maynard, MA: Digital Equipment Corporation, published under order number EB-22714-18, 1982.

4. Stallings, William. *Local Networks*, New York: Macmillan Publishing Co., 1990.

5. ———. *Handbook of Computer-Communications Standards, Vol. 2, Local Area Network Standards*, Carmel, IN: Sams, A Division of Macmillan Computer Publishing, 1990.

6. Tanenbaum, Andrew S., *Computer Networks*, Englewood Cliffs, NJ: Prentice-Hall, Inc., 1981.

Broadband Local Area Networks

John K. Summers

John K. Summers is the Technical Director of the Information Systems and Technology Division of The Mitre Corporation in McLean, Virginia. For 6 years he was responsible for research on applications projects involving local area networks. In particular, he directed projects that were among the first to use the DoD standard levels 3 and 4 network protocols, TCP/IP, in a local area network.

In his current position, Mr. Summers is responsible for the development and operation of information systems for corporate and client use.

7.1 Introduction

This chapter discusses broadband local area networks. The primary emphasis is on broadband local area networks that are implemented on a coaxial cable where analog service such as off-the-air TV can be intermingled with the digital communications of an organization. Technology today supports 10–16 megabit transmission over both unshielded twisted copper pairs or shielded twisted copper pairs over limited distances (e.g., 100 meters). Fiber optic cables can support the transmission of gigabits of information over kilometers without repeaters. These systems could be called broadband also.

The methods of implementing local area networks are not mutually exclusive. Organizations can and do use combinations of media to wire the same offices. Today there is an emphasis on "client server" architectures where some functionality is at the local personal computer or workstation and remote "servers" are used for other functions. These architectures can require high bandwidth between the client and the server. Twisted copper pairs or optical fibers are sometimes used as well as coaxial cable into the same office or work area. The coaxial cable allows multiple analog channels such as TV to be distributed as well as the digital signals which can be on the same cable or on other media. However, the special emphasis of this chapter is to contrast broadband coaxial networks and PABX networks. The special considerations include the advantages of being able to use the same physical medium for many different communications paths as well as system control. In addition, a section on privacy and security is also included.

7.2 Definitions

A local area network (LAN) is usually defined as a communications system to interconnect heterogeneous computers, terminals, workstations, and office machines in a geographically bounded area for the purposes of resource and data sharing. The distinction between a local area network and a metropolitan area network is vague, but we usually think of a local area network as encompassing a building (or buildings) or a campus, while a metropolitan area network covers a city and its environs. Both of these terms are contrasted with the term "long-haul network" which is used to refer to a communication system spanning long distances—a state, a nation, or multiple nations.

In the 1980s the most important distinctions between the types of networks rested on the communication speed involved. However, optical fiber is being used for long haul networks today, and these fibers are capable of carrying gigabits of information. Whereas in the past it was not economical for the telephone companies to offer services in the megabit range, such offerings are now available at affordable costs. Speed of transmission is no longer a distinguishing characteristic between LANs and long-haul networks.

7.3 Resource and Data Sharing

Local area networks are used for resource and data sharing. A user at one resource (terminal workstation, or computer) can have access to all of the resources on the LAN. Through "bridges" and gateways the users can have access to interconnected LANs or long-haul networks. What the user is able to do at the destination is dependent upon the compatibility of the communication protocols.

7.3.1 Resource Sharing

Resource sharing has two important benefits. The first major advantage is that a user need have only one terminal or workstation to access all of the computers on the network. The computers may all be made by different manufacturers and are referred to as heterogeneous computers. A LAN user doesn't have to switch from the terminal of manufacturer A to the terminal of manufacturer B to access their respective machines. This may run counter to the marketing strategies of the individual computer manufacturers, but market pressure is forcing conformance. It also elevates in importance the issues of electrical and protocol standards that cross manufacturers' lines. The second major advantage of the resource sharing is that the cost of wiring a terminal to the computer(s) is paid only one time. It is not necessary to run an individual wire from each terminal to each computer. All are, in fact, connected to a common pathway.

7.3.2 Data Sharing

An easy illustration of data sharing is to look at a document production cycle using computers for word processing. User A, sitting at his terminal or workstation using local or centralized word processing, composes a document for publication. Upon completion of the draft, the document is sent over the LAN to his boss for review. His boss makes changes and suggestions and sends the document back to the originator. The changes are incorporated and the document is sent over the LAN to the print shop for publication. Other examples of data sharing include the coordination of schedules and activities by project personnel scattered throughout several buildings. Each individual can access a master copy of the schedule and can always stay up to date on project changes. Another widely used example occurs in the "client server" architectures. A centralized capability (the server) provides a service such as database access to many different workstations (the clients). This permits many users to have access to a common service such as a database. The higher cost of the database server is shared by many users. In addition, one common up-to-date database is available to all.

Data sharing allows information to be shared by spatially separated people in less time. It permits compression of time and space.

7.4 Corporate Communication Systems

The requirements for a LAN can be looked at from several viewpoints:

1. What are the requirements for terminal-to-computer, workstation-to-computer, and computer-to-computer information transfer?

2. What are the information transfer requirements in the organization; e.g., terminal-to-computer, computer-to-computer, closed-circuit TV, fire detection, door alarms, telephones, etc.?

The first viewpoint considers digital data transfer. The second viewpoint takes a broad view of the analog and digital communications requirements of the organization. This broad view is particularly relevant in an area where more and more communications are going digital and where the application of the concepts of office automation are requiring that more and more bandwidth be available in each office. Whether it is more economical to transmit a signal in analog or digital form changes as the technology changes from year to year. The advent of low-cost optical fiber with a capacity of hundreds of megabits to gigabits of information makes it feasible to carry information such as closed-circuit TV that was not economical in the past. However, the cost of analog to digital and digital to analog converters must be factored in as a part of the total cost of system installation. The cost tradeoffs are dependent upon the cost of the technology available at the time of the tradeoff.

A local area network that tries to satisfy the larger organizational requirements will, of necessity, be a broadband local area network. A broadband local area network means that the media has high bandwidth; that is, it can carry many channels of information simultaneously. Coaxial cable with a total available bandwidth of 400 megahertz is a medium frequently used, although fiber-optic cable is being used more and more. A baseband local area network, on the other hand, carries only one digital channel of information. The broadband cable network can carry many types of digital and analog information.

- Computer-to-computer communications.
- Terminal-to-computer communications.
- Off-the-air television.
- Closed-circuit TV for door and hallway security.
- Telephone circuits.
- Intrusion-detection sensor signals.
- Fire alarms.
- Process control and status monitoring signals.

Planning for the installation of a local area network must take into account both the short- and the long-term benefits to be gained. The benefits must be weighed against the relative short-and long-term costs.

A major difference between baseband and broadband nets is the media used. Baseband nets use twisted, fiber, or coaxial cable as the media while the broadband nets typically use coaxial cable. Broadband cable nets are more expensive to install as the media costs are higher, and each station requires a modulator-demodulator(modem) to put a signal on a given frequency and to take it off that frequency. However, one of the major costs of a local area network is the actual labor involved in installing the media. This does not vary much from one type of system to another. Further, the labor costs tend to dominate the actual cost of the media itself. However, the installation costs are nominal or nonexistent if one is going to use an already installed PABX system.

7.5 Advantages of a Broadband System

"Civilization is made possible by communication in its various forms" (see *The Wired Society* by James Martin[6]). This quote can be amended to say, "The strength and responsiveness of a corporation is built upon the flexibility of its communication systems." A futurist's dream of an office of the future would include extensive communications systems (Fig.7-1). Two-way video teleconferencing (both local and global), access to libraries and information data banks, text and graphic facsimile, communicating office machines, management information terminals, and integral text and graphic document production facilities will all be features of the future office.

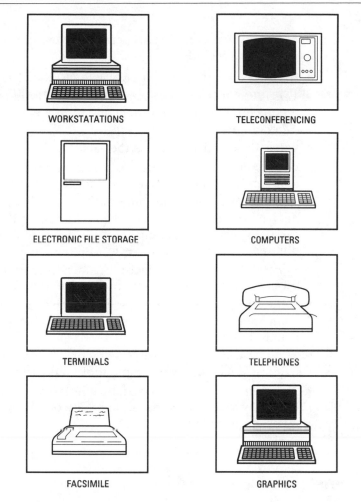

WORKSTATATIONS

TELECONFERENCING

ELECTRONIC FILE STORAGE

COMPUTERS

TERMINALS

TELEPHONES

FACSIMILE

GRAPHICS

Fig. 7-1. Elements in the automated office.

It is very difficult to predict when technology and costs will come together to make these capabilities commonplace. However, if we look backward at the rate of growth , and if we expect it to continue at the same pace in the future, we must plan for the introduction of these capabilities. The installation of a broadband communications backbone involves relatively low costs and may be considered as a hedge against future requirements. It is very difficult to predict the future communications requirements of an organization. How many of us, ten years ago, could have predicted the prevalence of personal computers and workstations in each office? History tells us that we have almost never had too much communications bandwidth available. Communication requirements are the same as most other requirements. They are a combination of a technology push and a user pull. Technology tells us what can be done and what it costs, and people tell us what they need to better and more efficiently get their jobs done and what they are willing to pay.

A broadband coaxial cable LAN permits the use of many capabilities today, and its advantages include:

- High speed with a low bit error rate (BER of 10^8 to 10^{11}).
- *Versatility.* It is not necessary to predict all future requirements. Current technology allows us to economically put coaxial cable outlets in every office.
- Voice, data, and TV can use the same medium.
- *Geographic Independence.* Coax systems are inherently broadcast systems, and gateways permit access to external systems.
- *Multiple Channels.* The same media can carry multiple digital channels. As the capacity of one channel is exceeded, additional stations can be placed on other channels. Bridges are used so that devices on different channels can converse with one another.
- *Control Flexibility.* The decision on whether to use centralized or distributed control mechanisms can be different for each channel.
- *CATV Components.* The CATV industry has developed highly reliable components for its subscribers. Coaxial cable systems can ride on a mature industry.
- *Maintenance.* Coaxial cable components are simple and are easily fixed by personnel with simple tools and easily learned skills.
- *Noise Immunity.* Since coaxial cable is shielded, it has better noise immunity than twisted pairs. Immunity of 80 dB from a noisy environment can be achieved.

7.6 Modems

Digital communications systems are binary systems which are inherently direct-current (dc) systems. When a dc system is introduced directly on the media, it is a baseband system and uses the available bandwidth of the media since, typically, there is no attempt to limit bandwidth. Only one communications channel is possible on a baseband system. However, many signals may be multiplexed on this one channel. On broadband systems, a carrier signal is modulated with a digital information signal at the transmitter; at the receiver, the signal is demodulated to recover the original signal. The modulation and demodulation process is the origin of the term *modem*. This digital signal can be placed on a carrier anywhere in the frequency spectrum of the media. The amplitude, frequency, or phase of the carrier can be modulated to carry the signal (Fig.7-2). In amplitude modulation (am), the strength of the signal is used to represent a 0 and a 1, respectively. In frequency modulation (fm), two or more closely adjacent frequencies are used (shift). In phase modulation (pm), the phase of the carrier sine wave is shifted abruptly to indicate the 1s and 0s.

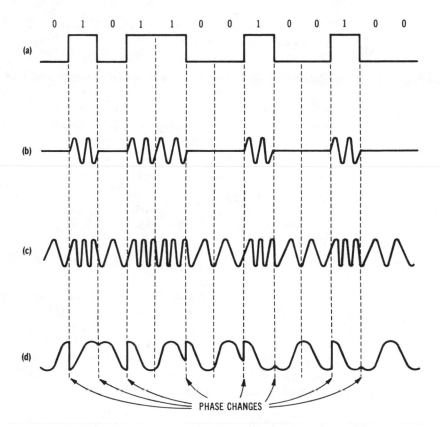

Fig. 7-2. Modulation of the carrier with (a) a binary signal, (b) amplitude modulation, (c) frequency modulation, and (d) phase modulation. *(Redrawn from Reference 10)*

Each digital user of a broadband coaxial network has a modem, a feature that is not needed in a baseband network, but which does make a bandwidth of 400 megahertz available to the network designer.

Modems come in two varieties for local area networks: fixed-frequency modems and frequency-agile modems. The fixed-frequency modem operates at only one frequency so that only users operating at the same frequency can directly communicate with one another. Communications between two stations on different frequencies must take place through a device that is using both frequencies and acts as a message switch. This device can be designed to do only the one job. In this case, it is called a bridge. Or, it can be a computer operating on both frequencies.

Users connected to the LAN via a frequency-agile modem can communicate on any one of a number of channels. Under computer control (either local or remote), the modem can be switched from one frequency to another. A frequency-agile modem has many operational advantages:

- *Expandability.* With enough stations added, all channels, regardless of speed, will sooner or later run out of capacity. The ability to use many channels is a hedge against future requirements.

- *Privacy.* By controlling the frequencies at which individual stations are able to operate, users with sensitive data can be assigned to limited access channels. This can be done by either limiting the frequencies that can be tuned by a station or by controlling the station tuning from a central point.

- *Access Control.* A given frequency can be used for "logins" and for authenticating the rights of a particular user to access the network or to access a particular host. A user will "login" to a central point and indicate which host or which facility he wishes to use. After his access rights are affirmed, the modem of the user will be switched by the central control point to the frequency of the desired host or facility. The frequency-agile modem, in this case, acts as one layer of a privacy/security protection mechanism.

The use of a central switch and frequency-agile modems on a LAN brings with it some of the problems of a star configuration. The central switch becomes the single point of failure for connection setups. Reliability and redundancy design considerations now come into play. Frequency-agile modems use microprocessors to perform the switching functions. The cost of a frequency-agile modem is higher than the cost of a fixed-frequency modem. This adds to the connection cost of each station on the network.

7.7 Physical Plant

Broadband networks are inherently broadcast networks. A signal which is generated by one station is seen by all other stations on the network unless some action is taken to block the signal. Furthermore, the topology of a broadband network must be a tree network (Fig.7-3). There cannot be more than one path between two stations or signal interference would occur due to a multipath transmission. The tree network consists of a distribution system and a headend. The distribution system is composed of cables, amplifiers, taps, splitters, etc. The cable is one-way distribution system. An amplifier boosts the signals going in one direction and attenuates signals going in the other direction. All stations send signals on an inbound path to the headend where they are turned around and sent out on an outbound path. Thus, Station A, who wishes to communicate with Station B, who is downstream (with respect to the headend), must send a message to the headend where it is turned around and sent to Station B.

The inbound path and the outbound path can be on the same cable or on two physically separate cables. If the two paths are on the same cable, the paths are separated in frequency to avoid interference. If amplifiers are used,

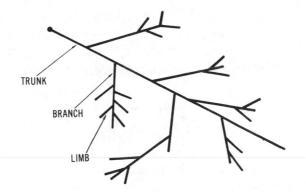

Fig. 7-3. A tree network.

there are two—an upstream and a downstream amplifier. Two types of frequency splits are used, "midsplit" and "subsplit." In a *midsplit* system, half of the frequencies are used for the inbound path and half for the outbound path. In a *subsplit* system, some frequencies (e.g., from 5 to 30 MHz) are used for inbound signals, and the remainder of the frequencies (to 400 MHz) are used for the outbound direction. Subsplit systems are the easiest to retrofit on existing one-way CATV systems. In midsplit systems, using a 400-MHz cable, only 200 MHz is available for use.

A frequency converter is used in single-cable systems to move the incoming signals to the proper outbound frequency. The advantage of single-cable systems is that the material and installation costs are cheaper. Also, in some cases, it may be possible to convert an existing cable system to a LAN.

In two-cable systems, one cable is used for transmitting and one for receiving. Each station is connected to both cables. Material costs for installation are higher than single-cable systems, but twice as much capacity is available. It also has the advantage that one cable can be optimized for error-free transmission, and the other cable can be optimized for error-free reception. Overall, this gives the system greater noise immunity.

The CATV industry was born in 1949 when the first community antenna was installed. As the industry grew and matured, heavy emphasis was placed on the development of low-cost highly reliable components. When a cable system is servicing thousands of homes in a community, service calls must be minimized. Many broadband LANs use the highly reliable components developed by the CATV industry. The cable amplifiers, taps splitters, etc., can be bought off-the-shelf. The cable used is high-quality low-loss cable. The signal loss in a cable is a function of resistance (cable quality), temperature, and frequency.

"Within the CATV industry, it is accepted practice to specify cable loss in dB of attenuation at the highest operational frequency. Most systems use 300 MHz as the highest operational frequency but, at times, 400 MHz is used if the system requires additional bandpass for the distribution of additional signals in the forward direction. This establishes a common reference and ensures industry-wide verbal and written consistency in specifying cable length. A typical cable specification is as follows: 1.63 dB of loss per 100 feet at 300 MHz measured at 68 °F." (See page 15 of Edward Cooper's article, Reference 2.)

Additional signal loss in a system is caused by compressions of the cable, by taps for each station, and by splitters. The total length of the backbone cable is determined by the number of amplifiers that are used. A signal amplifier is installed when the highest system frequency has been attenuated by 20 dB. Many amplifiers can be placed in tandem to develop a system that is many miles in length. As an illustration of this, the following is taken from a system specification.

- Maximum distance of 50 miles.
- 14 Mbps of total bandwidth.
- 32,000 devices.
- Either switched or virtual calls on permanent virtual circuits.
- 56 kbps dedicated service.
- 20 channels for general applications.
- Individual device speeds up to 19.2 kbps for switched lines and 56 kbps for dedicated lines.

The only active elements in a coaxial cable distribution system are the amplifiers. The taps and splitters are passive elements. A *tap* is used to bring the signal to an individual station. A tap is a resistor network designed so that all terminals receive the same level signal. This is important because it permits a terminal to be attached anywhere in the network without adjustment to account for the received signal level. If a tap is close to an amplifier, it receives a higher level signal than one further away. The tap attenuates the signal so that the level leaving the tap is constant regardless of geography. A *splitter* does what its name implies. It divides the signal into two paths. It is the component that permits branches off the main trunk of the tree.

When high reliability is critical, amplifiers are installed in pairs so that a second amplifier can take over when and if the first fails. When a capability for remote testing of the amplifiers is added, it is possible to design an extremely reliable network.

7.8 Frequency Allocation

A television channel requires a 6-MHz bandwidth on both the inbound channel and the outbound channel. Because of the CATV heritage and component availability, and because of the desire to carry commercial and closed-circuit TV, bandwidth allocation on the LAN is usually done in increments of 6 MHz. The first frequencies to be assigned are for devices that cannot be easily purchased at customer-selectable frequencies. The digital channels require variable amounts of bandwidth, depending on the method of signalling and transmission speed. Requirements range from 300 kHz to 20 MHz. A frequency allocation plan must consider present requirements, FCC regulations, and future requirements.

7.9 Topologies

A fundamental design principle of a LAN is that any station must be able to send a message to any other station. Modifications to this principle may be made for purposes of privacy or security but, in general, the principle holds. In theory, all nodes could have wires connecting them directly to all other nodes. This would not only be costly for the initial installation, but adding and subtracting nodes to and from the network becomes extremely complex and costly. LANs provide a shared communication medium for the interconnection of stations. It is desirable that each station not need the logic and the computational load necessary to make routing decisions. Local area network designers work with simple structured topologies like the star, ring, and bus (Fig.7-4). These simple topologies permit uniform and effective network control strategies. These topologies and their attendant control strategies will be discussed next. As the discussion proceeds, it should be noted that there is a difference between a physical and a logical topology. For example, a logical ring control structure can be implemented on a physical bus structure.

7.9.1 Star Topology

In a star network (Fig.7-4A), all stations are connected to a central node. All message routing decisions are made in the central node. All other nodes in the network can be simple. This type of topology is frequently used to connect terminals to large systems. Since there is one connection from the central node to each of the other nodes, the amount of cable to be installed can be larger. There are cases where the hallway leading to the computer room had to be lowered due to the amount of cable in the ceiling. The central node represents a single point of failure which must be analyzed for each application. The entire network is down if the central node is down.

7.9.2 Ring Topology

In a ring topology (Fig.7-4B), each node is connected to two other nodes. They are arranged so that the entire collection of nodes forms a circle. Messages travel around the circle from node to node. Each node must be able to recognize its own address and must be able to retransmit messages to the next

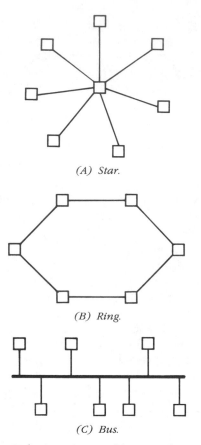

(A) Star.

(B) Ring.

(C) Bus.

Fig. 7-4. Star, ring, and bus topologies.

node. Control mechanisms in a ring network are needed to determine who is allowed to send a message and, also, to impose a fairness doctrine so that all stations have an equal opportunity to send messages.

The fairness doctrine is an important issue in network design. If it is not done properly, it may be possible for one station to dominate the medium and not leave transmission time for other stations. *Token passing* is a commonly used method. When a node receives a special token and the node has a message to send, the node keeps the token and sends the message. When the message is sent, the token is passed to the next node. The token can be a special control wire or it can be a special message or pattern of bits in the data. This approach implements a fairness doctrine and is an example of a distributed control strategy.

An alternative control scheme is to transmit around the ring a sequence of message slots. A slot is a series of bits large enough to hold a message. When an empty slot comes to a node that has a message to send, the message is inserted and the slot is marked full. In this scheme, the generation of the empty slots is a centralized function, while the decision as to when to send a message is decentralized. Also the fairness doctrine is not enforced as well as with other approaches because the probability of finding an empty slot changes as the nodal distance from the empty slot generator increases.

A break in the ring configuration, such as the failure of a repeater, will cause the network to fail. Ring networks are designed so they automatically go into a bypass or a reconfiguration mode when a component failure is detected. Provision is made for the regeneration of the control token if it should be lost during failure. These considerations increase the complexity of the individual node.

7.9.3 Bus Topology

In a bus topology (Fig.7-4C), all nodes are connected to a common communication medium. A transmitted message is heard by all nodes. Each node must recognize messages that are intended for it and accept those messages while rejecting all others. In contrast to star and ring topologies, messages are not received and retransmitted by intermediate nodes. The delay and overhead associated with retransmission are not present. Since each node is passive, failure of a single node will not affect the bus or the other nodes as long as it presents a high impedance to the network and does not fail with the transmitter on.

The strategies that are used for control on a ring network can also be used on a bus network; i.e., token passing and empty slot filling. A commonly used strategy for a bus network is the contention strategy. When a node has a message to transmit, it listens to see if the channel is available. If the channel is available, the node begins to transmit. If the channel is not available, the node waits until it is available and then transmits. The node then listens on the downstream channel. If the received message matches the transmitted message, then the transmission was completed error free. If the received message does not match the transmitted message, perhaps two transmitters were trying to send simultaneously. In any case, when a received message is garbled, the station waits a random amount of time and then transmits the same message again. This contention algorithm is known as *Listen While Talk-Carrier Sense, Multiple Access* (LWT-CSMA). It permits a good use of the available channel capacity. Under the right conditions, as much as 85% of the channel capacity can be used.

It should be noted that any of the control strategies (centralized, token, or contention) can be used with any of the topologies (star, ring, or bus).

7.10 Privacy and Security

The interconnection of the individual with local and global sources of data and information provides a rich environment for increasing the span of control and the productivity of the individual, but it is not desirable for all individuals to have access to all data. The issue of unrestricted data flow across national borders is a very difficult policy issue. If a nation spends millions of dollars on research in new weapons, it is clearly not in its best interest to indiscriminately share the data with everyone. On a more personal level, an individual's bank accounts, salary, and budgets are private and personal and should not be available for unintentional sharing. A corporation's budget and its research and marketing plans are privileged information and should be available only to designated members of the corporation. However, much of this information resides on computers which are used for many other purposes. What is to prevent an electronic mail user of a host computer from accessing the corporate salary information which may reside on the same machine. The traditional methods of computer security are to use a system of passwords to get on the computer and to add an additional layer of protection (passwords or a list of authorized users) to allow access to specific files of data or even records within a file.

When computers are placed on a network, whether local or global, the number of potential privacy or security violations is magnified enormously. The issue of permission to use the resources arises. For example, the electric company distributes power on a nationwide basis. Everyone who interconnects with the power grid must have permission to do so and must have a meter installed so that he pays for the resource used.

7.10.1 Value-Added Networks

Public packet-switched networks are operated worldwide. Once access to the network is obtained, communications messages are sent in milliseconds around the world. These networks are commonly called value-added networks (VANs) as they provide services above and beyond that provided by telephone companies. Some examples of additional services include addressing, routing, code conversions, mail, etc. Security is important to these networks to be sure that all subscribers pay for the service rendered.

7.10.2 Privacy and Security Issues

Privacy and security for terminals and computers linked together on local and global networks is a very complex issue. Among the issues which must be addressed are:

- *Network Access Control.* Does this user have permission to use the network? Are the administrative controls in place so that he will be billed for the network services used? If he is a hard-wire user, is his terminal properly identified? If he is a dial-up user, is his password valid?
- *Host Access Control.* In the general case, the host is owned by someone other than the owner of the network. Will the network pass on the network access password so that the user does not have to provide a

second password, or are a second "logon" and a second password necessary? What if the user accesses a second host computer during a session—will he be required to provide yet a third password?

- *Process Access Control.* Once access to a host computer has been gained, are all users allowed to run all programs? Is the user restricted by user ID? What about communities of users who need common program and data access?
- *Data Access Control.* How is the distinction between public data and private data made? Is private data controlled down to the file level, to the record level, or to the data field level?

The answers to the issues listed are closely interrelated. The number of security points that a user must pass through will be reflected in the complexity of the procedures that he must use. If all of the security checks are designed independently, the user will face an inordinately complex set of procedures. Furthermore, the system-wide security and privacy procedures must be examined as a whole before assurance can be gained that the overall privacy and security safeguards are in place.

7.11 DoD Computer Security Center

Because of national security requirements, the Department of Defense has taken the lead in examining the issues of computer privacy and security. The DoD Computer Security Center was formed in 1981 to encourage the widespread availability of trusted computer systems for use by those who process classified or other sensitive information. One of the first efforts was to define levels of security requirements and criteria for evaluating ADP systems. As stated in the preface of DoD 5200.28-STD 1985,

> "The criteria provides a basis for the evaluation of effectiveness of security controls built into automatic data processing products. The criteria were developed with three objectives in mind: (a) to provide guidance to manufacturers as to what to build into their new, widely available commercial products in order to satisfy trust requirements for sensitive applications as a standard for DoD evaluation thereof; (b) to provide users with a yardstick with which to assess the degree of trust that can be placed in computer systems for the secure processing of classified or other sensitive information; and (c) to provide a basis for specifying security requirements in acquisition specifications."

The criteria are divided into four divisions and seven classes:

Computer Security Evaluation Criteria

DIVISION D: Minimal Protection

DIVISION C: Discretionary Protection
    Class (C1): Discretionary Security Protection
    Class (C2): Controlled Access Protection

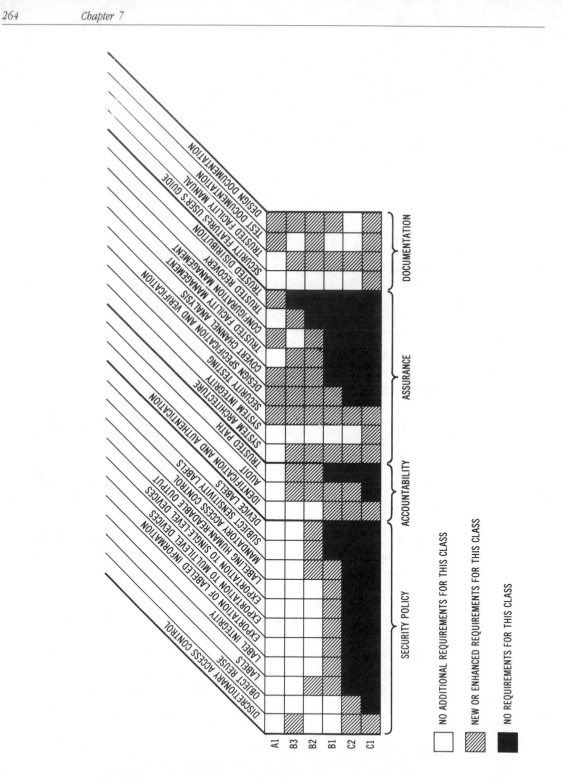

Fig. 7-5. Summary chart of the Trusted Computer System evaluation criteria.

DIVISION B: Mandatory Protection
    Class (B1): Labeled Security Protection
    Class (B2): Structured Protection
    Class (B3): Security Domains
DIVISION A: Verified Protection
    Class (A1): Verified Design
    Beyond Class (A1)

The specific requirements for each division and class are tabulated and illustrated in Fig. 7-5. While these criteria were directed at DoD, they have applicability to ADP industry as a whole. The DoD Computer Security Center has a program to carry out a commercial product-security evaluation.

7.12 Network Privacy and Security

The existence of DoD Computer Security Center criteria is a giant step forward in formalizing privacy and security controls. These criteria address only host systems and do not address the larger question of embedding a host system in a local or global network. Networks add a tremendous complexity to the question of privacy and security. If a system uses resources in a network which are accredited at different levels of privacy and security, what should we consider the overall privacy and security level of the network? Must the whole system be accredited at the lowest level of any of the components?

The DoD Computer Security Center has published the "Trusted Network Interpretation of the Trusted Computer System Evaluation Criteria" to provide criteria for integrating, operating, and maintaining trusted computer networks. The document identifies the minimum security protection required in different network environments such that network certifiers, integrators, and accreditors can determine what protection mechanisms and assurances are required.

Privacy and security consideration are difficult in a single computer. LANs and global networks make the problem even more difficult. Privacy and security will continue to be a major area of research for networks in the future.

7.13 References

1. Christie, Bruce. *Face to File Communication, A Psychological Approach to Information Systems*, New York: John Wiley & Sons Ltd., 1981.

2. Cooper, Edward. "CATV/Broadband Overview for Data and Telecommunications Managers," TR-81052 (November 1981), SYTEK Incorporated, © October 1981.

3. "Department of Defense Trusted Computer System Evaluation Criteria." DoD 5200.28-STD, 1985.

4. *IEEE Transactions on Communications*, Volume COM-28, No.4, published by IEEE Communications Society, April 1980.

5. *Introduction to Local Area Networks*, Digital Equipment Corporation, 1982.

6. Martin, James. *The Wired Society*, Englewood Cliffs, NJ: Prentice-Hall, Inc., 1978.

7. Mason, William F., et al. "Urban Cable Systems Summary," The MITRE Corporation Washington Operations, Westgate Research Park, McLean, VA, M72-57, May 1972.

8. McNamara, John E. *Technical Aspects of Data Communication*, Digital Equipment Corporation, 1977.

9. National Computer Security Center, Trusted Network Interpretation of the Trusted Computer System Evaluation Criteria, Version1, NCSC-TG-005, July 1987.

10. Tannenbaum, Andrew S. *Computer Networks*, Englewood Cliffs, NJ: Prentice-Hall, Inc., 1981.

Computer and Communications Security

Stephen T. Walker and William C. Barker

Stephen T. Walker is the founder and president of Trusted Information Systems, Inc., a privately owned small business specializing in consulting on the development and management of information systems, computer networks, computer security, telecommunications, and related fields to the government and industry. He is a Member of the Defense Science Board Task Force on Defense Data Network and of the Foreign Applied Sciences Assessment Center Panel on Computer Science.

As Director of Information Systems for the Office of the Secretary of Defense, Mr. Walker was responsible for the WWMCCS Information and Defense Communications Systems, including the Defense Data and Switching Networks. For his efforts in this area, and for initiating the major restructuring of the DoD data communications architecture, Mr. Walker received the Secretary of Defense Meritorious Civilian Service Medal.

Mr. Walker has a Bachelors Degree in Electrical Engineering from Northeastern University and a Masters Degree in Electrical Engineering from the University of Maryland. He has programming experience on a wide range of computer systems.

William C. Barker is the Principal Communications Security Analyst for Trusted Information Systems, Inc. Mr. Barker has 25 years of experience in the information security field. He served twelve years in cryptographic government service, followed by eight years managing development of cryptographic equipment in private industry. For the past five years, Mr. Barker has conducted research into the integration of trusted systems and cryptographic technologies in network security applications. Mr. Barker is a government-certified communications security professional and is former Vice President of PE Systems, a cryptographic equipment development company. He has served in Joint service, NATO, ANSI, and IEEE working groups on the design and implementation of secure networks. Mr. Barker is currently Director of Independent Research and Development for Trusted Information Systems and is active in development of trusted and cryptographically protected workstations for office and network environments. He is also assisting the Department of Defense in implementing a new automated information security policy for its contractor community and in a national level effort to achieve a government-wide industrial security policy. Mr. Barker earned a B.A. from Pan American University in 1964 and an M.B.A. from the Johns Hopkins University in 1970. He has served on the faculty of the National Cryptographic School and has conducted continuing education instruction at the University of Maryland.

8.1 The Nature of the Problem

The problem of protecting sensitive information while in transit and/or storage has troubled humanity since the beginning of recorded time. Much of the focus of this problem has been on the in-transit aspect as techniques for hiding or scrambling information evolved over the years. Large organizations were formed by governments and private groups in an attempt to protect their own sensitive information while trying to gain that of their adversaries.

As communications techniques improved, the opportunities to intercept vital information improved and the need for more and better protection mechanisms grew. With the advent of electronic communications, this cycle accelerated rapidly. Telegraph systems were marvels of instant communications but the wires that were strung out over open country were highly vulnerable to tapping or to physical destruction. The advent of radio communications opened vast new worlds for communication and for intercept. One could now talk with another person across hundreds and thousands of miles without any physical linkage. One could also intercept the communications of others in widely separated areas from the safety and comfort of one's own protected areas. As the capabilities to communicate improved, the need to protect those communications grew.

Throughout most of the evolution of these communications capabilities, the problem of protecting sensitive information "in storage" was principally a problem of ensuring that the people who have access to the information could be trusted to protect it. History is full of cases where people entrusted with such information failed to fulfill the expectations of their leaders or employers. The traditional means of protecting sensitive information entrusted to humans is to make it clear that the human can and will be held accountable for any loss or compromise of the information. This accountability ranges from losing one's job to criminal prosecution. The fact that humans can be held accountable for their actions (or lack thereof) in protecting information has been a key element in the evolution of security measures. The advent of sophisticated new communications and storage technologies, which could compromise information without human accountability, has seriously complicated the provision of protection mechanisms.

Just as with the advent of improved communications techniques, the coming of computers, with their vastly improved capabilities for processing and storing information, has brought with it new ways to achieve compromises of that information. The old techniques of bribery or infiltration continued to be available but, just as the use of radio enables one to intercept remote communications from one's own home ground, computers offer new opportunities to steal information from relatively safe sanctuaries.

This chapter is intended to provide an overview of the types of vulnerabilities that are inherent in modern computer and communications systems and describe some of the measures presently available for countering these vulnerabilities. The topics to be covered will include the various communications security techniques that are available for protecting in-transit information and the computer security techniques that protect information while it is in storage or being processed. The description will also include consideration of the traditional physical, administrative, procedural, and personnel security measures, and how they relate to the new technologies. Throughout the discussion, it will deal with the ever present need to balance the range of possible security protection measures against the threat to the information being protected.

The basic security question is one of determining the relative risk of losing information in a particular situation. Is the benefit of using a particular capability (be it the telegraph, radio, or a computer communications network) worth the risk of losing the sensitive information being entrusted to it? This question must be asked continuously during the design, implementation, and use of a capability. There exists for every situation a "benefit/risk" equation that must be properly balanced. If it is determined that a new technology must be used to store, process, or transmit sensitive information, then a balance of security measures must be found to ensure that the risk of losing the information does not outweigh the benefit of using the new capability. At the same time, care must be taken to ensure that the security measures do not so constrain or restrict the capability as to render it useless.

Of course, no single security measure by itself is adequate to protect valuable property. Security must be provided by a number of individual measures acting in concert to provide a total protection environment. Protecting one's home while on vacation involves a combination of measures that range from locking the doors and windows, making arrangements for newspapers and mail to be picked up, putting lights on a timer so it appears someone is home, and having the neighbors check the property every so often. Banks get protection from physical devices that require time to defeat, in combination with roving guards who are to detect any attempts to penetrate the physical devices.

Similarly, the protection of sensitive information requires a combination of many measures acting together. The determination of the risk portion of the equation, therefore, must consist of an examination of the completeness and effectiveness of the measures being employed.

Protection of military or diplomatic secrets requires the best available protection measures. The protection of a company's highly sensitive future product plans and strategies should receive similar treatment. Corporate financial, personnel, logistic, and research information deserves protection from disclosure to competitors. But what is the appropriate balance between benefit and risk for such information?

In the past, the problem of protecting sensitive corporate information was largely an issue of providing appropriate physical and personnel security measures. Only the people who had to know the information were entrusted with it and physical protection measures were taken to isolate the data from all others. In these cases, the risk to the information was reduced to the problem of trusting the individuals who handled it. The advanced planning of the company was done by a select staff element who were isolated from the rest of the company and had their own locked storage facilities and special-handling procedures. Only corporate management and that staff were allowed access to the information.

The advent of computers and communications systems has provided both powerful new capabilities and serious challenges in these areas. It is now possible to automate many of the previously laborious procedures of the office and, thus, provide much greater levels of productivity. Word-processing and electronic-mail systems are revolutionizing the office. But, by entrusting highly sensitive information to a computer or communications system, the benefit/risk equation has been seriously tipped. In the case of routine administrative work, the automated system is clearly superior and the risk of information compromise is so small that such capabilities are eagerly sought. Whole networks of word-processing systems are installed that have the ability to forward electronic mail throughout the company—greatly improving communications and overall productivity.

In the case of the more sensitive corporate plans, the benefits are still there but the risk aspect is now so sufficiently high that special protection measures must be taken. These measures frequently resort to simply keeping the most sensitive systems isolated from the rest of the routine administrative systems. While this provides protection to the sensitive information and keeps the risk side of the equation in reasonable condition, it results frequently in a serious loss of capabilities, with a negative impact on the benefit side of the equation. Within these limits, one will find the routine administrative aspects of an organization fully automated and functioning at peak performance while the vital planning, financial, and product development aspects of an organization continues to use procedures that are essentially manual, with all the burdensome overhead and inefficiencies. This is not a healthy situation for a growing organization.

8.2 Threats to Computer/Communication Systems

As indicated previously, there is a wide range of threats to computer/communication systems. As the benefit/risk equation dictates, a thorough understanding of these threats is needed before the overall risk environment and the required countermeasures can be determined. Fig. 8-1 is the now famous Computer Network Vulnerabilities chart from the Defense Science Board Task Force on Computer Security headed by Dr. Willis Ware in 1970. This chart depicts the full range of vulnerabilities one encounters in using a computer/communication system. These vulnerabilities range from the traditional human user/operator/programmer/maintenance man problem through communications threats, such as wiretap, crosstalk, and radiation, to threats associated with the computers, such as access control, hardware and software failures, and file protection.

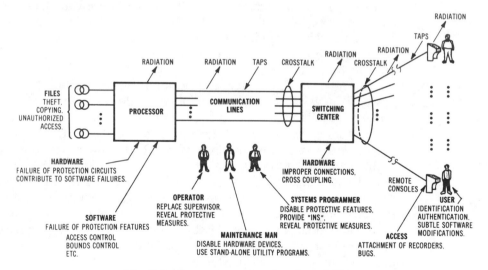

Fig. 8-1. Computer network vulnerabilities.

Every situation involving computers and communications networks includes some mix of these vulnerabilities. In a particular case, some of them may be of far greater concern than others. The following sections will describe the important characteristics of each vulnerability.

8.2.1 Physical Security Vulnerabilities

The vulnerabilities that are contained in this class include the full range of common-sense measures for protection of a computer facility from physical disasters, such as fires or floods. Also included are the protection measures one would normally take to protect any valuable physical resource, such as locking doors and windows, checking an individual's authorization to access an area, and similar measures. The physical security measures apply not only to the computer equipment itself and to its terminals but to all removable items, such as printouts, magnetic tapes, disc packs, etc. The area containing the computer equipment, including the remote terminals, must be protected to a level that is commensurate with the sensitivity of the information contained in the system. This protection must be continuous even when the equipment is not operating.

Many of these measures are simple common-sense steps that are dictated by prudent operation. Classic cases of improper physical security measures abound, such as locating the computer center below the cafeteria (resulting in a flood), or above the boiler, or in the main pathway to the parking lot. Lack of maintaining a reasonable physical-access control to either the computer center or to a remote terminal is a classic way that sensitive information is lost. It is important to note here that many of the other security measures that are to be discussed later are of little or no value if reasonable physical-access security measures are not put into operation.

8.2.2 Personal Vulnerabilities

As described earlier, one of the principle threats to the protection of sensitive information has always been the individuals who are trusted to properly handle the information. This vulnerability is as real in a computer/communications environment as anywhere else and, frequently, is seriously complicated because of the number of additional people who must be added to the "trusted" list. Whereas before, only the principals involved in the development of the sensitive information and those involved as messengers needed to be trusted, now whole sets of computer operators, programmers, and maintenance personnel are (or can be) exposed to the information and, therefore, have to be trusted. Various measures, which will be discussed later, can significantly lessen potential vulnerability with respect to these latter individuals. However, the vulnerability of information compromise by those charged with generating or receiving it will always remain. The military has the capability to conduct background investigations to determine the degree to which it should trust individuals. While such measures are beyond the scope of most commercial organizations, it is prudent, depending on the sensitivity of the information being processed, to conduct complete reference and credit checks on all personnel involved.

8.2.3 Procedural Vulnerabilities

In addition to physical and personnel vulnerabilities, it is necessary to have a reasonable and complete set of procedures for the operation of a computer or communications system in order to maintain the protection of sensitive information. Among the more obvious requirements in this group are such routine items as enforcing the changing of user passwords on a regular basis. Failure to utilize reasonable procedures in this area has led to many of the well-publicized computer hacker successes documented in recent times. Failure to enforce procedures for the routine checking of the physical security and the access-control measures has led to many breeches of system integrity.

8.2.4 Communications Vulnerabilities

Communications systems have always been subject to some of the most serious vulnerabilities in the protection of sensitive information. As indicated in Fig. 8-1, the ability of an adversary to tap into a communications channel, be it a wire, microwave, or satellite channel, is ever present. Once information leaves the physical environment in which it is generated or stored, it is subject to hostile analysis that is limited only by the level of effort that an adversary is willing to apply to it. If the information is of limited or perishable value, then measures that provide only limited protection may be sufficient. If, however, the information is highly valuable and/or retains its value for a long period of time, then the best protection measures available may be justified.

Information transmitted over a communications system is subject to a number of specific vulnerabilities. *Passive wiretapping* is the interception of messages that is usually without detection. The objective of passive wiretaps is usually to obtain the content of a message *but*, depending upon what protection mechanisms are in place, it can also be used for traffic-flow analysis or the determination of who is communicating with whom. *Active wiretapping* is the deliberate modification of the message stream. The objective may be to make arbitrary changes to the contents of a message, to inject false messages or replays of previous messages, or to delete messages. Active tampering may also be used to impersonate an authorized user or to deny service through jamming.

Included within the scope of communications-security vulnerabilities is the compromise of information by the emanation of electromagnetic radiation. It is possible in many cases to detect electromagnetic leakage from a terminal, printer, or other electronic device and thus recover the information that is being presented on the device—frequently from a remote location some distance from the device; for example, in a parking lot or adjacent office complex. This vulnerability is of particular importance to the military and a discipline, referred to as TEMPEST, has evolved over the past decade to deal with it. The physical effects of the problem are similar to the interference caused by some electronic devices, such as home computers, to local television reception. FCC regulations covering electromagnetic radiation of such equipment have helped many people to understand the nature of the problem and has to some degree reduced its impact.

8.2.5 Computer System Vulnerabilities

The vulnerabilities discussed so far are external to the computer system and are designed to protect sensitive information from disclosure to external threats. Very large computer communications systems, containing highly sensitive information, have operated for years with consideration for protection given almost exclusively to these external threats. For many organizations, these threats represent their major concern and they are satisfied with providing protection solely against them. The military have operated computer systems in this manner for years in what is called "system high" operation. The name comes from the concept that all personnel who have access to the system are cleared to see any of the information contained on the system; hence, the clearance of all users of the system is as high as that of any information in the system. The premise behind this operation is that regardless of what failures might occur in the hardware or software of the system, no sensitive information will be compromised since everyone on the system is cleared for access to all the data anyway.

System high operation is reasonable, if restrictive, when computers are operated in isolated centers serving local users all with the same immediate operational needs. But, as computers began to be linked to each other over major communications networks and as users at multiple sites could access information on each other's computers, the problems associated with clearing all personnel (on all systems in the network) to have access to all information on all the computers became very difficult. The need to be able to trust the operators of the computer system, with respect to controlling access to information on the computer, has become very important.

The nature of traditional physical and administrative security vulnerabilities, encountered in the operation of computers filled with sensitive information, is well understood. Only users trusted to the sensitivity level of the information processed on the computer complex are allowed access to the system. With the advent of trusted computer systems which allow the simultaneous use of computers by personnel with different sensitive information-handling requirements, an additional set of security vulnerabilities came into play. Table 8-1 illustrates one view of this new vulnerability spectrum as a series of concerns. Each of these concerns was not considered serious in previous systems because there was no need or opportunity to rely on the integrity of the computer hardware or software.

The first category is the *security policy* which the system must enforce in order to assure that users access only authorized data. This policy consists of the rules which the computer will enforce governing the interactions between system users. There are many different policies possible, ranging from allowing no one access to anyone else's information to full access to all data on the system. The Department of Defense security policy (Fig. 8-2) consists of a lattice relationship in which there are classification levels, typically Unclassified through Top Secret, and compartments (or categories) which are often

Table 8-1. Operating System Security Vulnerabilities

Category	Function	Vulnerability Resolution	Relative Security Risk
Software (Installation Independent)			
Security Policy	Establish security relationship between all system users, resources (e.g., DoD Security Policy).	Review	Moderate
System Specification	Establish policy relationship for each system module (e.g., Parnas I/O assertions).	For each module, establish security assertions which govern activity.	High
High-Order Language (HOL) Implementation	Transform System Specification provisions for each module into HOL (e.g., Fortran, Pascal, C).	Manual or interactive validation that HOL obeys system specifications.	High
Machine-language implementation	Transform HOL implementation into binary codes which are executed by hardware.	Compiler testing	Moderate
Hardware (Installation Dependent)			
Hardware Instruction Modules	Perform machine instruction (e.g., ADD instruction).	Testing, redundant checks of security-relevant hardware.	Low-except for security-related hardware.
Circuit Electronics	Perform basic logic functions which comprise instructions (e.g., AND, OR functions).	Maintenance testing	Low
Device Physics	Perform basic electromagnetic functions which comprise basic logic function (e.g., electron interaction).	Maintenance Testing	Very Low

mutually exclusive groupings. With this policy, a partial ordering relationship is established in which users with higher-personnel security clearance levels can have access to information at lower-sensitivity levels provided that the user also has a "need to know" the information. The vulnerability concern associated with the security policy is in ensuring that the policy properly meets the total organizational sensitive information-handling requirements.

The second general concern is at the system specifications level. At this level, the function of each module within the system and its interface to other modules is described in detail. Depending upon the exact approach employed, the system specification level may involve multiple abstract descriptions. The vulnerability here is to be able to assure that each level of the specification correctly enforces the policy previously established.

The next vulnerability is at the high-level language implementation level. This category constitutes the actual module implementation represented in a high-order language. This vulnerability involves the assurance that the code actually obeys the specifications. Below this level, on the list of vulnerabilities, is the concern that the machine-code implementation which actually runs

COMPARTMENT

LEVEL	A	B	Q	•••	
TOP SECRET					
SECRET					
CONFIDENTIAL					
UNCLASSIFIED					

MANDATORY CONTROLS:

TOP SECRET > SECRET > CONFIDENTIAL > UNCLASSIFIED

DISCRETIONARY CONTROLS:

"NEED TO KNOW" APPLIES TO ALL ELEMENTS ABOVE UNCLASSIFIED.

Fig. 8-2. Department of Defense security policy model.

on the hardware correctly represents the high-order language (HOL) version. This concern is primarily focused on whether the compiler faithfully implements the HOL version in machine code.

Next down the scale is the concern that the hardware modules which implement the basic machine instructions perform accurately the functions they represent. Does the ADD instruction perform an ADD operation correctly and nothing else? The last concerns on Table 8-1 include the functions of the individual integrated circuits that make up the hardware and the device physics that define the functioning of these circuits. The concern here is with whether these elements work as expected.

As can be seen by analyzing this vulnerability spectrum, some of the areas of concern are more serious than others. Relatively little concern is given to circuit electronics and device physics since there is considerable confidence that these elements will perform correctly. There is a concern with the hardware modules, though, in general, most nonsecurity-relevant hardware failures do not pose a vulnerability to the security of the system and will be detected during normal operations of the machine. Those hardware functions that are security relevant can be subjected to frequent software testing to ensure (to a high degree) that they are functioning properly. The mapping between HOL and machine-code implementation is a serious concern. The compiler could perform improper transformations which would violate the integrity of the system. This mapping may, in the future, be checked by verification of the compiler, but this process will not be available for a long time. Today, we must rely on rigorous testing of the compiler.

The selection of the security policy, which the system must support, requires detailed analysis of the application requirements but is not a particularly complex process and can be readily comprehended so that the level of concern is not too high for this category.

The system specification and HOL implementation are the two areas that are of greatest concern both because of the complex nature of these processes and because of the direct negative impact that an error in either has on the integrity of the system. Considerable research has been done to perfect both the design specification process and the methods for assuring its correct HOL implementation. Much of this research has involved the development of languages and methodologies for achieving a complete and correct implementation.

As stated earlier, this vulnerability spectrum constitutes a set of conditions in which the failure of any element may compromise the integrity of the entire system. In the high-integrity systems being implemented today, the highest-risk vulnerability areas are receiving the most attention. Consistent with the philosophy of having security measures in depth, it will be necessary to maintain strict physical and administrative security measures to protect those lower-risk vulnerabilities that cannot or have not yet been eliminated by trusted hardware/software measures. This will result in the continued need to have trusted operation and maintenance personnel and to periodically execute security-checking programs to detect hardware failures.

8.3 Computer Security

Much has been learned about methods of assuring the integrity of information that is processed on computers since the emergence of operating systems in the early 1960s. Early efforts were primarily concerned with improvements in the effective use of the larger computer centers that were then being established. Information protection was not a major concern since these centers were operated as large isolated data banks. There were many significant hardware and software advances in support of the new operating system demands. Some of these changes were beneficial to the interests of information protection but since protection was not an essential goal at that time, the measures were not applied consistently and significant protection flaws existed in all commercial operating systems.

In the late 1960s, spurred by activities such as the Defense Science Board study, efforts were initiated to determine how vulnerable computer systems were to penetration. The record of success of the "Tiger Team" system-penetration efforts, in penetrating all commercial systems that were attempted, led to the perception that the integrity of computer systems hardware and software could not be relied upon to protect information from disclosure to other users of the same computer system.

By the early 1970s, we had long lists of the ways that penetrators used to break into systems. Tools were developed to aid in the systematic detection of critical system flaws. Some were relatively simplistic, relying on the sophistication of the user to discover the flaw; others organized the search into a set of generic conditions which, when present, often indicated an integrity flaw. Automated algorithms were developed to search for these generic conditions, freeing the penetrator from tedious code searches and allowing the detailed analysis of specific potential flaws. These techniques have continued to be developed and have reached considerable sophistication. In addition to their value in searching for flaws in existing software, these algorithms are useful as indicators of conditions to avoid in writing new software if one wishes to avoid the flaws which penetrators most often exploit.

These penetration aids are, however, of limited value in producing computer systems that can be trusted to guarantee separation among users at different sensitivity levels. For, even if these techniques do not indicate the presence of any flaws, it is not possible to prove a positive condition (that a system can be trusted) by the absence of negative indicators (known flaws). There will always be that one remaining flaw that has not yet been discovered.

In early 1970s, the Air Force/Electronic Systems Division (ESD) conducted in-depth analyses of the requirements for trusted computer systems. The concepts which emerged from their efforts are today the basis for most major trusted computer system developments. The basic concept is a Reference Monitor or Security Kernel which mediates the access of all active system elements (people or programs running on behalf of people), referred to as *subjects*, and to all systems containing information (files, tapes, etc.), referred to as *objects*. All of the security-relevant decision-making functions within a conventional operating system are collected into a small, primitive, but complete, operating system that is referred to as the Security Kernel. The three essential characteristics of this module are that it be: (1) complete (i.e., that all accesses of all subjects to all objects be checked by the kernel), (2) isolated (i.e., that the code that comprises the kernel be protected from modification or interference by any other software within the system, and (3) correct (i.e., that it perform the function for which it was intended and no other function).

8.3.1 Trusted Computer Systems

The term "trusted computer system" is used to denote computer systems that have sufficient hardware and software integrity measures to allow their use in simultaneously processing information at several levels of sensitivity. The term refers to the internal capabilities of an operating system and its application software to isolate a user's data from other authorized users of the system. The intent is to allow controlled sharing of information where access to each element of sensitive information is controlled at all times.

A trusted computer system is assumed to be operated in a physically protected environment where threats from external attack are at a minimum. There are measures which a trusted system can take to protect against external attack but it cannot prevent the physical removal of resources or the modification of the hardware or the substitution of new software from defeating its protection measures. The principal thrust of a trusted computer system is to authenticate users (either local or remote) and ensure that they are granted access to the information on the system for which they are authorized but prevented from accessing information for which they do not have authorization.

8.3.2 Reference Monitor Concept

Various research efforts beginning in the early 1970s began to explore ways to improve the protection measures in computer systems. At first these efforts tried to determine the seriousness of the problem by attempting to penetrate existing operating systems. Virtually every system penetration that was attempted was successful. A long list of the various flaws in existing systems was compiled. Many systems were subject to multiple penetrations approaches. The attempts to patch flaws uncovered by the penetration frequently resulted in the introduction of other, sometimes more serious, flaws which were exploited in follow-on penetration efforts.

In an attempt to define at least a conceptual approach to a system which would not be susceptible to these penetration efforts, the concept of a *Reference Monitor* was identified. According to this approach, every element of a system is considered to be either a subject or an object. *Subjects* are the active elements of a system that are principally represented by processes running on behalf of a specific user. *Objects* are the elements of the system that contain information, such as files and programs. All objects are assumed to have some degree of sensitivity, ranging from highly restricted (for example, available to only a single user) to being generally available to any one on the system. Subjects have access privileges that represent the degree of trust which has been given to the person on whose behalf they are operating. The Reference Monitor (Fig. 8-3) is that portion of the operating system that checks the access privileges of a subject against the sensitivity levels associated with an object to determine if that subject has the right to obtain access to an object.

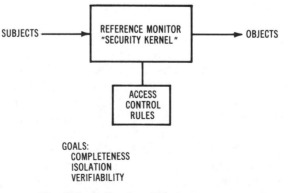

Fig. 8-3. Reference Monitor concept.

Whenever a process (subject) attempts to access a program or file (object), the Reference Monitor is invoked to check that the appropriate access privileges are present. For the Reference Monitor concept to work, these checks must be invoked for every access of a subject to an object. If there is a means to bypass the checks (as there is when a separate subsystem operates in parallel with RACF and bypasses its access checks), then the entire protection system can be defeated. The Reference Monitor uses some form of access-control data base to determine which subjects have access to what objects. The various ways of accomplishing this will be described shortly. In order to ensure the completeness of these access checks, it is necessary to organize them into a small subset of the overall operating system. Because this "security kernel" is responsible for enforcing all access checks in the system, the hardware and software which are involved in its functioning define the trusted portion of the system (referred to later as the Trusted Computing Base).

The kernel must be protected from modification by the other nontrusted portions of the system. This is normally done by running the kernel in the most privileged mode of the hardware and forcing all nontrusted portions to operated in less-privileged states. Thus, whenever an application program tries to access an object, its attempt to execute a privileged instruction will be "trapped" to the kernel for the appropriate access-control checks to be made. Since the kernel is the only software that can run in the privileged state, it is not possible for any nontrusted software to modify the kernel, so the isolation of the kernel is maintained.

The last principle which must be applied to the Reference Monitor concept is that it must be shown to correctly perform its intended functions and do nothing else. It must be demonstrated that the kernel correctly performs the access-control checks as defined by the access-control policy. It must also be shown that the kernel does not perform any other security-related functions not intended by the access-control policy. This aspect of the Reference Monitor concept has been the most difficult to achieve since it is very hard to develop proofs that complex software systems work correctly. The state-of-the-art in program verification presently allows for formal specification of various high-level abstractions of the design of a system but does not as yet extend down to the actual code that implements the kernel.

8.3.3 Access-Control Rules

The Reference Monitor concept provides a means of checking the access privileges of a subject to an object before such access is granted. A critical aspect of this (or any other approach to a trusted system) is the definition of what the access-control rules are. There are many ways to approach this problem. The simplest initial approach might be to associate, with the subject, a list of all objects that it is allowed to access. In this approach, the Reference Monitor need only check if the object being sought by a subject is on its access list and deny access if it is not. An equivalent approach associates a list of the subjects that are allowed to access it with each object. Both these approaches are fine for relatively small systems where either the number of subjects or objects is restricted. But, in a large system with many users and objects, the mechanisms for maintaining these lists become very cumbersome.

In these cases, it is necessary to define a more general access-control policy which the system must enforce. The security policy model in use within the government for protection of classified information is a very useful model for this purpose. Fig. 8-2 illustrates the structure of this model. The model is a partially ordered lattice or matrix consisting of several (usually four or more) rows that are ordered; that is, the higher the row the greater the sensitivity of the information. If one is "cleared" to access a particular level, access to those levels below in the matrix is then also granted. In the government model, these rows correspond to the *levels of classification*, ranging from Top Secret to Unclassified. The columns in the lattice represent what are called *compartments*, which are additional degrees of sensitivity associated with a particular classification level. Unlike the classification levels, the compartments are not comparable. Membership in one compartment says nothing about one's access privileges to another compartment.

In the government policy model, this matrix is termed the mandatory portion of the policy since the definition of what constitutes a particular level or compartment is defined by legislation or Executive Order. There is an additional aspect of the policy which is referred to as a discretionary access control. Within each level and compartment, the individual who controls an object must determine if other users have a "need to know" the information. The "need to know" determination is made at the discretion of the owner of the data and is therefore referred to as the discretionary aspect of the security policy.

This overall policy model has been employed by the government for many years and has served as a very useful way of categorizing sensitive information into major groupings; thus, it eliminates the need for elaborate lists of who has access to what information. Similar policies are in effect in commercial organizations although, in many cases, the emphasis of the policy may be shifted somewhat. In the government case, the most important element of the policy is the classification level (Top Secret through Unclassified).

In commercial organizations, the equivalent of the compartment is a *project* and this frequently is the dominant element of the policy. There are levels of sensitive information ranging from *Company Registered* or *Company Private Restricted* to *Unrestricted* (Fig. 8-4). But, in many commercial organizations, information is associated with specific projects first and then with the level of sensitivity within that project. The "need to know" principal applies in virtually all commercial policies.

The significance of this discussion of policy models is emphasized as one contemplates developing a computer system to handle the sensitive information-handling applications for a wide range of different users. The system must provide the user with a reasonably general means of specifying what portions of his data are sensitive and which users should be allowed access to what data. The lattice model described above and illustrated in Fig. 8-4 gives

PROJECT

LEVEL	A	B	Q	...	
COMPANY RESTRICTED CONFIDENTIAL					
COMPANY CONFIDENTIAL					
COMPANY PRIVATE					
UNRESTRICTED					

MANDATORY POLICY:

COMPANY RESTRICTED > COMPANY CONFIDENTIAL > COMPANY PRIVATE > UNRESTRICTED

CONFIDENTIAL DISCRETIONARY POLICY:
NEED TO KNOW APPLIES TO ALL LEVELS AND PROJECTS.

Fig. 8-4. Model of a commercial organization security policy.

the most general capability which the user can tailor to his particular needs. For example, if the user only deals in specific projects with no separation of sensitivity levels, then the matrix can be reduced to a single row with as many columns as there are projects. If, on the other hand, the user only deals with a hierarchy of levels of sensitive information, then the matrix reduces to a single column with as many rows as there are levels. If the user only has a "need to know" sensitivity, then matrix reduces to a single element with the discretionary controls enforced.

Having this kind of generalized structured policy model enforced by the computer system is valuable because each user can tailor the access matrix to his own needs without modifying the basic system. Regardless of the policy structure that the user has as he begins to use the system, he can modify it, adding additional rows or columns as needed without requiring any modification to the fundamental elements of the system. Of course, the user must have some form of sensitive-information control policy in order to make any use of such a system, but failure to identify the relative sensitivities of information is a classic management problem which must be solved outside of any automated information-handling system.

8.3.4 Trusted Computer System Evaluation Criteria

The previous discussion covered the essential features of a trusted computer system. The notion of an access-control mechanism operating in the most privileged state of a computer, checking the access rights of users to data in the system in accordance with a well-defined security policy, is fundamental to a trusted system. The degree to which this mechanism can be shown to properly enforce the security policy establishes the degree of trust that can be placed in the system. But few of today's systems employ such techniques to any significant degree. Furthermore, few vendors are likely to start new system developments to build such systems unless they can establish an evolutionary path starting with their present products. What is needed is a means of measuring the technical integrity of an existing product and projecting what improvements can be made to it at what cost. Also needed is someone to do the measuring in an objective and unbiased manner.

With the establishment of the Department of Defense Computer Security Evaluation Center at the National Security Agency in 1981, a very large step in both directions was taken. Following several draft versions which received extensive review by industry and government, the Center has recently published a document entitled "Trusted Computer System Evaluation Criteria" which describes in detail a structure of technical capabilities that cover the spectrum of trusted systems. There are four major classes of systems with seven overall levels (Table 8-2). These criteria include descriptions of the policy enforcement provisions, the mechanisms required to implement those provisions, and the degree of assurance that the mechanisms will work at each level in the spectrum. The levels run from Class D, which provides minimal protection (Class D systems essentially don't meet any of the criteria of higher-level classes), through Class C, which provides discretionary access controls, to Class B, which enforces labeling of objects against a mandatory type of security policy and on to Class A, which includes design-level formal proofs that the Trusted Computing Base properly enforces the required security policy provisions.

Table 8-2. Summary of Evaluation Criteria Classes

Class	Protection Required	Definition
Class D	Minimal	This class is reserved for those systems that have been evaluated by their failure to meet the requirements of a higher evaluation class.
Class C1	Discretionary Security	The Trusted Computing Base (TCB) of a Class C1 system nominally satisfies the discretionary security requirements by providing separation of users and data. It incorporates some form of credible controls capable of enforcing access limitations on an individual basis; i.e., ostensibly suitable for allowing users to be able to protect project or private information and to keep other users from accidentally reading or destroying their data. The Class C1 environment is expected to be one of cooperating users who are processing data at the same level(s) of sensitivity.
Class C2	Controlled Access	Systems in this class enforce a more finely grained discretionary access control than C1 systems, making the users individually accountable for their actions through "login" procedures, auditing of security-relevant events, and resource isolation.

Table 8-2. (cont.)

Class	Protection Required	Definition
Class B1	Labeled Security	Class B1 systems require all the features required for Class C2. In addition, an informal statement of the security policy model, data labeling, and mandatory access control over named subjects and objects must be present. The capability must exist for accurately labeling exported information. Any flaws identified by testing must be removed.
Class B2	Structured	In Class B2 systems, the TCB is based on a clearly defined and documented formal security policy model which requires that the discretionary and mandatory access-control enforcement found in Class B1 systems be extended to all subjects and objects in the ADP system. In addition, covert channels are addressed. The TCB must be carefully structured into protection-critical and nonprotection-critical elements. The TCB interference is well defined and the TCB design and implementation enable it to be subjected to a more thorough testing and a more complete review. Authentication is provided in the form of support for the system administrator and operator functions, and stringent configuration management controls are imposed. The system is relatively resistant to penetration.
Class B3	Security Domains	The Class B3 TCB must satisfy the Reference Monitor requirements that it mediate all accesses of subject to objects, that it be tamperproof, and is small enough to be subjected to analysis and tests. To this end, the TCB is structured to exclude code not essential to security policy enforcement, with significant system engineering directed, during both TCB design and implementation, toward minimizing its complexity. A security administrator is supported, audit mechanisms are expanded to signal security-relevant events, and system recovery procedures are required. The system is highly resistant to penetration.
Class A1	Verified Design	Systems in Class A1 are functionally equivalent to those in Class B3 in that no additional architectural features or policy requirements are added. The distinguishing feature of systems in this class is that analysis is derived from formal design specification and verification techniques and, thus, gives a resulting high degree of assurance that the TCB is correctly implemented. This assurance is developmental in nature, starting with a formal model of the security policy and a formal top-level specification (FTLS) of the design. In keeping with the extensive design and development analysis of the TCB that is required of systems in Class A1, more stringent configuration management is required and procedures must be established for securely distributing the system to sites. A system security administrator is supported.

1. Summarized from the DoD Trusted Computer System Evaluation Criteria.
2. The classes of systems recognized under the Trusted Computer System Evaluation Criteria are given here. They are presented in the order of increasing desirability *from* a computer-security point of view.

The essential concept of the evaluation criteria is that there are observable technical features of systems which can make them useful in certain sensitive information-handling environments even though they do not contain all of the features which might be desired in the best of all situations. This concept is in contrast to the situation one normally finds in the communications security world. In that case, once information leaves the confines of its protected environment, it must be assumed that an adversary will be able to intercept and record the information and will apply whatever analysis techniques are warranted by the sensitivity of the information. If the information is truly sensitive, then only the best possible encryption techniques will be sufficient, but those may not be enough against a particularly persistent adversary.

The trusted computer system has much more room for intermediate environments. In the situation in which all users are trusted to have access to any information on the system (the so-called dedicated mode in the Department of Defense), there is no need to rely on the integrity of the hardware and software of the system at all. In environments where everyone on the system is trusted but fairly strong "need to know" requirements exist (a situation which arises quite frequently in both the government and the private sector), systems of the C Class should provide adequate protection. In environments where users are all trusted to some degree but some highly sensitive information may also be processed (in the DoD, this is represented by a system running with both Top Secret and Secret users simultaneously), the B Class of systems is required. When a truly sensitive environment is encountered where a broad range of trusted users are involved and very sensitive data is processed, the A Class of systems must be used.

8.3.5 Application of Trusted Computer System Evaluation Criteria Systems

Shortly after the introduction of the Trusted Computer System Evaluation Criteria (TCSEC), there was growing need for guidance on where systems with particular levels of trust could be utilized. With publication of the *Computer Security Requirements, Guidance for Applying the Department of Defense Trusted Computer System Evaluation Criteria in Specific Environments* (Yellow Book), it was possible, at least for national security related systems involving classified information to determine suitable levels of trust for given applications.[4] Table 8-3 from the Yellow Book illustrates this process.[4] It is necessary to determine the highest level of sensitive information that will exist on a given system and the lowest level of cleared individual who will have access to the system. By looking at this matrix, one can determine the level of TCSEC trust required for that system. For example, if the highest level of sensitive information on a system is Top Secret and the lowest level cleared individual who will have access to the system has a Secret clearance, then a B2 level of trust is required.

By examining this matrix, one can determine that B1 and that C2 and below systems can only be used in system high dedicated mode applications where all persons who access to the system have the same clearance as the information contained in the system. B1 systems are useful where people who have access to the system either have the necessary clearances or easily can be

Table 8-3. DoDCSC Security Index Matrix for Open System Environments*

Minimum Clearance or Authorization of System Users[†]	Maximum Sensitivity of Data						
	U	N	C	S	TS	1C	MC
U	C1	B1	B2	B3	*	*	*
N	C1	C2	B2	B2	A1	*	*
C	C1	C2	C2	B1	B3	A1	*
S	C1	C2	C2	C2	B2	B3	A1
TS (BI)	C1	C2	C2	C2	C2	B2	B3
TS (SBI)	C1	C2	C2	C2	C2	B1	B2
1 COMP	C1	C2	C2	C2	C2	C2[‡]	B1[§]
M COMP	C1	C2	C2	C2	C2	C2[‡]	C2[§]

* Environments defined in the C1 and C2 areas are for systems operating in system high mode. No minimum level of trust exists for those operating in dedicated mode. Categories are ignored in the matrix, except for the inclusion of compartments at the TS level.

[†] U = Uncleared or Unclassified
N = Not cleared but authorized to sensitive information
C = Confidential
S = Secret
TS(BI) = Top Secret (Background Investigation)
TS(SBI) = Top Secret (Special Background Investigation)
1 COMP = Top Secret, one compartment
M COMP = Top Secret, multiple compartments

[‡] It is assumed that all users are authorized access to all compartments on the system. If users are not authorized for all compartments, then a class B1 system or higher is required.

[§] Where there are more than two compartments, at least a class B2 system is required.

granted the necessary clearances such as in intelligence systems where all individuals have at least a Top Secret clearance.

In order to operate in a true multilevel secure environment where more than one level of classified material is being handled, it is necessary to have a B2 or better system. The previous example of a Top Secret system with Secret cleared users at the B2 level is illustrative. As one gets broader risk ranges (the range between the highest level of sensitive information and the lowest level of clearance of individuals), the level of trust must increase. It should be noted that there are many combinations of broad risk ranges for which no level of trust is currently sufficient.

Other methods for determining the level of trust required for specific architectures have been examined by Landwehr and Lubbes.[9] These approaches combine factors concerning the type of communications and the programming capabilities afforded a user in a given architecture as well as the simple risk range approach described above.

The foregoing discussion was intended for use in systems employing national security related classified material. As noted in the section on access control rules, similar lattice models of hierarchical sensitivity levels and projects exist within civilian government and commercial applications and a similar environmental guideline mapping the levels of trust to requirements can be performed. Various attempts to do this have met with only limited success to date. But, with the growing availability of trusted systems at higher levels, a need for such environmental guidance for civilian government and commercial applications will continue to grow.

8.3.6 Evaluated Products List

With the publication of the Trusted Computer System Evaluation Criteria, the National Computer Security Center began evaluation of industry developed systems at various levels of trust. As of the publication date of this book, Table 8-4 indicates the availability of products at different levels of trust. At this time, the Trusted XENIX* operating system is the only system commercially available that meets the B2 or higher level of trust. Previously, the Multics and SCOMP systems, both Honeywell products, met the respectively B2 and A1 levels of trust, but those products are no longer available. There are several products that meet the B1 level of trust and are useful in limited environments, as pointed out in the environmental guideline section, and there are a growing number of systems that meet the C2 level of trust.

Table 8-4.   Available Products on the NCSC EPL

Level	Product	Supplier
B2	Trusted XENIX	TIS
B1	System V/MLS	AT&T
	Compartmented Mode Workstation Plus	Secureware
C2	VMS 4.3	DEC
	RACF/MVS	IBM
	RACF/VM	IBM
	ACF2/MVS	IBM
	ACF2/VM	IBM
	Top Secret/MVS	IBM
	A Series MCP AS	Burroughs
	UNIX UTX	Gould
	AOS/VS	ROLM/Data General
	SVS/OS	Wang
	PRIMOS	Prime
	MPE/VE	Hewlett-Packard

*XENIX is a trademark of Microsoft Corporation.

8.3.7 Interpretations of the Trusted Computer System Evaluation Criteria

When the Trusted Computer System Evaluation Criteria was being written in the early 1980s, the focus was on operating systems performing time-sharing functions such as the Multics system. The principles of the Trusted Computer System Evaluation Criteria, as described earlier, are true for a wide range of sensitive information handling applications but the specifics of the TCSEC, in addition to describing these principles, contain many details that are relevant primarily to monolithic operating systems.

When one wished to evaluate a packet switch or a database management system or a limited functionality system such as a virtual machine monitor, one frequently had difficulty with the specific details as enumerated in the TCSEC. Almost as quickly as it was published, efforts began to prepare interpretations of the TCSEC for specific systems. The first of these were specific Department of Defense developed application systems such as the BLACKER, an end-to-end encryption system, and the InterService/Agency AMPE system.

In 1985, an effort was begun to prepare an interpretation of the Trusted Computer System Evaluation Criteria for network systems. The focus was based on the fact that a packet switch or a communications front end frequently do not have users who log on in the same sense that they do to a time-sharing operating system. Yet, they handle sensitive information against the same or similar security policies as might be enforced by a more general purpose system. In 1987, the Trusted Network Interpretation (TNI) of the Trusted Computer System Evaluation Criteria was published.[12] It identified four protection sensitive areas which could be arranged in different combinations within specific network components: Mandatory Access Control (MAC), Discretionary Access Control (DAC), Identification and Authentication, and Audit. These components were identified as M, D, I, and A, respectively. A system which enforced mandatory access control but did not enforce discretionary access control and which employed identification and authentication and audit is a MIA system. A system which employed all four areas is a MDIA system. There have been a number of evaluations of various products against the TNI. Most notably, the Verdix Local Area Network is a MDIA system that meets a B2 level of the Trusted Network Interpretation.

In the same sense that networking systems while satisfying the principles of the TCSEC often do not always satisfy all of the TCSEC requirements, database management systems and other sophisticated transaction oriented application systems also frequently do fit the TCSEC mold. There have been efforts underway since 1987 to attempt to identify a Trusted Database Interpretation (TDI) or trusted application interpretation of the Trusted Computer System Evaluation Criteria. Various drafts of this document have been reviewed through the community and the difficulty and complexity of handling such sophisticated evaluations have become obvious.[11] It is anticipated that sometime in 1991, a version of the TDI will be published in a draft/final form.

Other major architectures have been considered for interpretation. Most notably, the concept of a virtual machine monitor in which an executive system, not a full blown operating system, runs on the hardware of the system and produces what appear to be a series of virtual machines on one hardware base allowing the use of multiple operating systems simultaneously on a single hardware. If one could guarantee the separation between these virtual machines, one could operate Top Secret, Secret, and Unclassified virtual machines simultaneously.

Virtual machine monitors have been of interest in the computer science community since the mid-1960s. The VM 370 system is the most well known example in the IBM world. Many manufacturers have considered building such systems and many products have been introduced over the years. In 1989, Trusted Information Systems, at the request of IBM and Amdahl, began preparation of a Trusted Virtual Machine Interpretation (TVI) of the Trusted Computer System Evaluation Criteria. This interpretation acknowledges that virtual machine systems perform mandatory access control, namely the separation of different security levels on virtual machines, while allowing the operating system on each virtual machine to handle discretionary access control. The difficulty with evaluating a VMM that does not perform discretionary access control directly against the TCSEC is that it would not pass the C2 level of trust. It is anticipated that sometime in 1991, a Trusted Virtual Machine Interpretation will be published thus allowing a broad class of highly useful architectures to be employed on major computer systems used throughout both the national security and commercial communities.

8.3.8 Confidentiality, Integrity, and Availability

As understanding of the nature of the computer security problem grew, it became apparent that the focus of the Trusted Computer System Evaluation Criteria was on access control and confidentiality insuring that only people authorized to access information were allowed access. Debates began to grow in the technical community over other needs such as integrity and availability. Integrity has to do with the quality of data within a system. Within the definition of systems by the TCSEC, a certain level of integrity of system control information is required so that the identity and access privileges of individual users can be reliably applied. Within communications systems, integrity deals with the quality of data within a communications channel being maintained from the point of origin to the point of exit. Within database management systems, integrity of data often deals with the issue of who's allowed to modify information. In many cases, large numbers of users can access and read information but only a limited number of people are authorized to modify it thus maintaining a high degree of integrity. The many definitions of integrity have made it difficult to define criteria for their implementation and evaluation.

Availability is a concept concerned with the reliability of a computer system. Availability requirements are often quoted as system will be "up"

99.9XX% of the time. A converse of availability is frequently termed as a security issue called "denial of service." Many applications are more concerned about availability or the lack of ability to deny service than confidentiality or integrity.

Confidentiality, integrity, and availability are all important to the overall security of a system. The difficulty in applying integrity and availability of service is the breadth of the factors which influence their effectiveness. In the case of confidentiality as described earlier in this chapter, a system will have users and processes operating on behalf of users who have specific access privileges and who are seeking to access information at particular sensitivity levels. The system is required to mediate the access of users and processes operating on their behalf to the sensitive information within the system, using some well defined access control security policy. The reference monitor concept is a specific formulation intended to ensure the proper mediation of access by subjects to objects.

In the case of integrity, and even more so, availability, it is difficult to identify a means to insure the effective implementation of measures such as are employed in enforcing confidentiality. Much unwarranted criticism has been leveled at the Trusted Computer System Evaluation Criteria over the years for its failure to adequately encompass integrity and availability. But when one realizes that to build a system that can be measured by its effectiveness in dealing with specific requirements, the lack of specificity implied in the definitions of integrity and availability make them far more difficult to deal with than confidentiality. Perhaps in the future, research will yield the same degree of understanding of methods for achieving integrity and availability as have existed for the past 15 years in confidentiality, but few such methods appear on the horizon at this time.

8.3.9 Information Technology Security Evaluation Criteria

When the Trusted Computer System Evaluation Criteria emerged in 1983, it grew to become the definitive criteria for the evaluation of trusted systems, but many communities attempted to evolve their own requirements, some slightly, some radically different. Most countries in the western world experimented with various extensions and revisions to their own criteria for evaluating trusted systems. In Europe, the Germans and the British evolved specific criteria and other countries were following suit when the Commission on the European Community began an effort to "harmonize" the European Criteria. In 1990, the first draft of an Information Technology Security Evaluation Criteria (ITSEC) emerged as a unified criteria for the evaluation of trusted systems.[8] The ITSEC grew from much experience with the U.S. TCSEC and attempted to extend these original concepts into the new areas of integrity, availability, and cryptography.

The 1990 version of the Information Technology Security Evaluation Criteria separated security features and assurance levels that are bundled in the

TCSEC. Under these criteria, one could achieve a wide range of security features with a single level of assurance. This makes it easier to handle such differences as the features required for a packet switch, an operating system, or a database management system while requiring the same level of correctness and effectiveness of the security measures. In a sense, this unbundling is trying to accomplish the same goals which the various interpretations of the TCSEC (the TNI, TDI, and TVI) are trying to obtain. It is not yet clear which approach will be more successful.

In addition to five feature levels, the Information Technology Security Evaluation Criteria also identifies the correctness of the features and a concept of effectiveness of the application of the features within a system. Thus, according to the ITSEC, an F5/E5 system maps approximately to a Trusted Computer System Evaluation Criteria B3 level of trust. Figure 8-5 from the ITSEC gives its approximation of the correspondence between the two criteria.

```
ITSEC              TCSEC
E0       ----->    D
F1, E2   ----->    C1
F2, E2   ----->    C2
F3, E3   ----->    B1
F4, E4   ----->    B2
F5, E5   ----->    B3
F5, E6   ----->    A1
```

Fig. 8-5. Approximate correspondence between ITSEC
and TCSEC levels of trust.

In addition to the F1–F5 security feature levels, the Information Technology Security Evaluation Criteria identified five additional functionality classes. F6 is for systems with high integrity requirements for data and programs. F7 is for systems which require high levels of availability in complete systems or in special functions. The F8 functionality class deals with systems requiring the safeguard data integrity during data exchange. Functionality class F9 is intended for systems with high demands for confidentiality of data during data exchange, for example, cryptographic devices. Functionality class F10 is intended for networks with high demands of confidentiality and integrity to be exchanged.

These five additional functionality classes are identified but do not have any range of security functionality or effectiveness applied to them and thus are not particularly useful at least as identified in the 1990 version of the Information Technology Security Evaluation Criteria.

The ITSEC introduces notions of both development and evaluation process, placing heavier emphasis on an understanding of the development process than normally applied by Trusted Computer System Evaluation Criteria evaluations.

Figure 8-6 from the Information Technology Security Evaluation Criteria illustrates the process that one must go through in establishing the character-

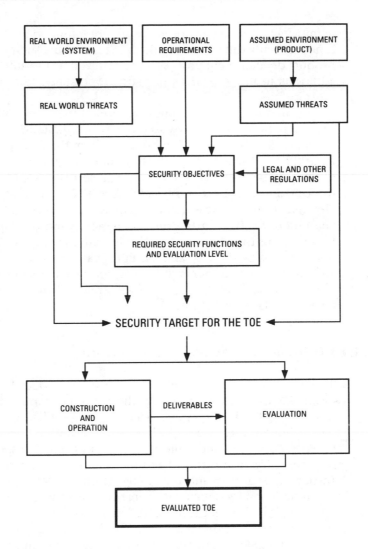

Fig. 8-6. Development of the evaluation process.

istics of the "Target Of Evaluation" (TOE) as envisioned by an ITSEC evaluation. Whether one is envisioning the evaluation of a specific system, such as a command and control system or a product intended for general purpose use, one must enumerate the threats the system is intended to overcome and develop a set of security objectives and required security functions and effectiveness levels. These combine to establish the security target for the Target Of Evaluation. Then the process of construction and operation of the system combined with the results of the evaluation need to be evaluated.

There are a number of identifiable differences between the Information Technology Security Evaluation Criteria and Trusted Computer System Evaluation Criteria. Work has begun on attempting to understand the differences, many of which are semantic and were not intended by the ITSEC authors to be fundamentally different from the TCSEC. Others such as the emphasis on the product development process were believed by the authors to be fundamental additions to the TCSEC and as such represent additional requirements that must be met.

As mentioned before, a new version of the Information Technology Security Evaluation Criteria is expected to be available in 1991 correcting some of the misunderstandings that have arisen from the early draft. It has been speculated that perhaps the best way to understand the similarities and differences of these two criteria is by conducting a series of simultaneous evaluations in the U.S. and Europe against their respective criteria of similar products. The Defense Advanced Research Projects Agency's Trusted Mach system under development by Trusted Information Systems and the Open Software Foundation is at this time being submitted for simultaneous evaluation at the U.S. B3 level of trust by the U.S. and the European F5/E5 level of trust by the British and German governments. It is expected that a great deal of understanding of the commonality of these criteria will emerge from projects such as the simultaneous TMach evaluations.

8.3.10 Information Security Foundation

The National Security Agency has over the past decade evolved a process for evaluating trusted systems against the Trusted Computer System Evaluation Criteria. In 1987, the Computer Security Act (Public Law 100-235) was passed which limited the responsibilities of the National Security Agency to the national security classified information and assigned responsibility for unclassified sensitive information handling within the government to the National Institute of Standards and Technology (formerly National Bureau of Standards).

It has been recognized for sometime that there is an additional major constituency which is not represented in any of the above, specifically, the commercial world. While some commercial users have made limited use of the results of TCSEC evaluations, the growing needs and specific interests of the commercial world must be represented by an organization which is beyond the role currently being performed by NSA and NIST.

In a report that has been termed the finest summary of the computer security problem in twenty years, the National Research Council report *Computers at Risk* published in December 1990, identified a series of measures that should be taken to further the availability of computer security systems in the commercial as well as government sectors.[3] Two specific recommendations of this report of relevance here are the development of Generally Accepted System Security Practices (GSSP) and the formation of an Information Security Foundation (ISF) separate from the evaluation activities at NSA and NIST but able to work in conjunction with them.

This report and its specific findings is receiving critical review within the community at the time this book is being written, and various activities are underway to explore the development of Generally Accepted System Security Practices and Information Security Foundation capabilities. It is envisioned that the Trusted Computer System Evaluation Criteria will form the early basis for the Generally Accepted System Security Practices as they apply to trusted systems but that the later document must be far more inclusive of all of the measures including physical, procedural, administrative, as well as technical trusted system and cryptographic techniques needed to provide accepted security practice.

The Information Security Foundation is currently being envisioned as a nonprofit, nongovernmental organization which will establish the Generally Accepted System Security Practices and the standards for evaluation of various products against them while enabling specific organizations in the commercial world to perform actual evaluations. In this manner, the ISF will be able to facilitate the establishment of evaluation procedures without requiring the massive investment in effort and personnel to establish a specific organization to perform evaluations.

The evolution of ideas such as the Generally Accepted System Security Practices and the Information Security Foundation in conjunction with the rapidly evolving Trusted Computer System Evaluation Criteria, their interpretations, and the European Information Technology Security Evaluation Criteria illustrate the technical response to a growing concern for the protection of sensitive information within computer systems. The acceleration of understanding of techniques and the complexity of the vulnerabilities of information systems is expected to continue well through the 1990s.

8.4 Communications Security

The evolution of techniques for hiding and/or scrambling information while it is in transit have been described in detail in such books as *The Codebreakers* by David Kahn. Included among these techniques are various forms of secret writing and other esoteric approaches. When communications over electronic media are involved, these techniques are confined almost exclusively to the use of encryption in any of several forms. This section will introduce a set of definitions of encryption-related technology (as defined by Dorothy Denning in her book, *Cryptography and Data Security*) followed by an analysis of the major techniques for communications security available today.[6]

Cryptography is the science and study of secret writing. A *cipher* is a secret method of writing whereby *plaintext* (or *cleartext*) is transformed into unintelligible *ciphertext*. The process is called *encipherment* or *encryption*; the reverse process is called *decipherment* or *decryption*. Both processes are controlled by a *cryptographic key*.

Figure 8-7 depicts the process by which a cipher system works. The encryption algorithm E operates on the plaintext X using the key K to produce ciphertext Y.

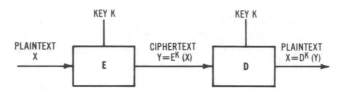

Fig. 8-7. General encryption/decryption process.

When the key has a length of M bits, the cipher algorithm can produce 2^M different enciphering functions. In most cipher systems, the algorithms for encryption (E) and decryption (D) are known, and the security of the system is obtained by keeping the key (or keys) secret. In general, it is not practical for an adversary to try all possible key combinations to break out the plaintext. But if there is a great deal of redundancy in the plaintext, or if the adversary knows several corresponding plaintext and ciphertext blocks, the task of recovering the key may be greatly reduced. In addition to carefully selecting the encryption and decryption algorithms to ensure that the output does not repeat or *loop*, it is necessary to make the key length large enough so as to make it impractical to try every key. The key length required to provide reasonable security is partially dependent on the encryption algorithm employed. Key lengths of up to 100 bits are considered sufficient for the foreseeable future for some algorithms, others need key lengths in excess of 600 bits, and others are unsafe regardless of key length.

There are three main classes of cipher systems: transposition, substitution, and combinations of the two called *product ciphers. Transposition ciphers* (also called permutations) alter the normal pattern of the characters in the original plaintext according to a specific procedure. Typical procedures include message reversal, geometric patterns, route transposition, and columnar transposition. *Substitution ciphers* replace characters in the plaintext with other characters. Examples include reciprocal, Caesar, monoalphabetic substitution, polyalphabetic substitution, and digraphic substitution. A *reciprocal* cipher is a substitution cipher which reverses the alphabet with Z replacing A and Y replacing B. A *Caesar cipher* involves shifting the alphabet some number of positions. A *monoalphabetic substitution cipher* is one which uses a single cipher alphabet for substitution. *Polyalphabetic substitution ciphers* use multiple substitution alphabets wherein the first plaintext character uses a substitution from one alphabet, the second character employs a second alphabet, and so on. A *digraphic substitution cipher* breaks the plaintext into pairs of letters and each pair is replaced by a substitution pair.

Block ciphers divide the plaintext into blocks, usually of a fixed size. Each block is operated on independently. Block ciphers are simple substitution ciphers where, given a common key, a particular plaintext block will always be transformed into the same ciphertext block. Block ciphers are simple substitution ciphers where a particular block will always be transformed into the same ciphertext block. Block ciphers must have very large alphabets in order to protect against character-frequency analysis. No plaintext character should ever appear directly in the ciphertext. A change of only one character in either the plaintext or the key should result in changes to approximately 50% of the ciphertext characters. In a *stream cipher*, every incoming plaintext character is encrypted into an output character in a manner that is dependent upon the internal state of the device. Thus, subsequent occurrences of the same plaintext character will usually produce a different ciphertext character. In a *synchronous stream cipher*, the output is dependent upon the particular input and its position in the stream, not on the characters before or after it. If a character is altered in transmission, only one character is incorrectly decrypted. Loss of a character will result in loss of synchronization and all characters following will be incorrectly decrypted. Self-synchronizing stream systems, also called ciphertext autokey, employ limited feedback of the output ciphertext in determining the encryption process. An error or lost character in such a system causes a fixed number of errors in the deciphered text after which the correct plaintext is again produced.

8.4.1 Data Encryption Standard Algorithm

Until recently, encryption techniques and systems were the domain of governments and amateur theoreticians. The devices for carrying out the transformations were expensive and, except for a few very simplistic ones, were generally unavailable to the public. That situation changed dramatically in the early 1970s with a renewed interest in the security of communications systems outside the government. This renewal was highlighted by the publication, in 1977, of Federal Information Processing Standards (FIPS) Publication 46 which specified the Data Encryption Standard (DES) algorithm as a Federal Standard by NIST. The DES is intended for use by the Federal government for all nonclassified but sensitive data communications. It is also intended for use by commercial organizations for protecting sensitive information. For the first time in history, a high-quality algorithm with acknowledged cryptographic strength was generally available.

The DES algorithm operates on 64-bit blocks of plaintext (or ciphertext), requires a 64-bit key, and produces 64-bit blocks of ciphertext (or plaintext). Of the 64-bit key, only 56 bits are used in the encipherment process; the remaining 8 bits establish off parity for each 8-bit byte of the key. The number of different keys available is 2^{56}. Since the encryption algorithm is known, the security of the system is totally dependent on the secrecy of the key.

The process of encryption consists of an initial permutation of the 64-bit block of plaintext followed by 16 separate rounds of encipherment, with each consisting of a product cipher or the combination of a transposition and a substitution function, and, finally, another permutation step which is the inverse of the initial permutation. Decryption takes place in the same manner except that the order of the 16 rounds of product cipher is reversed.

The Data Encryption Standard is basically a block cipher algorithm, The simplest method of operation is referred to as the electronic codebook mode, as related to the old manual codebook systems. Each bit of ciphertext output is a direct function of each bit of plaintext input and the key. A change of as little as one bit in the input or key will result in changes to approximately 50% of the ciphertext. Although extensive, this change propagation is limited to the block in which the change occurred and the decryption of other blocks is unaffected.

The DES may also be used as a key stream generator for a stream cipher. In the cipher feedback mode, the plaintext is combined with a matching number of key stream bits generated by the DES block cipher. The transmitted ciphertext is also fed into a shift register that forms the input to the DES encrypto. In this mode, cryptographic synchrony can be achieved if the sender and receiver use the same key and if both shift registers contain the same bit patterns. If an error occurs in the ciphertext stream, a portion of the decrypted plaintext will be incorrect but after 64 bits of error-free ciphertext are received, the decryption process will automatically resynchronize with the encryption process. To achieve initial synchrony, 64 bits of "fill" (to be ignored by the receiving end) are entered into the encryptor and transmitted.

8.4.2 Link Encryption

Encryption techniques as applied to communications systems are most commonly encountered in a form called *link encryption*, in which a pair of encryption devices is placed at either end of a communications link (Fig. 8-8). Once in synchronized operation, these devices scramble the information flowing across the link so that most passive and active wiretapping devices are thwarted.

The essential ingredient in synchronizing these link encryption devices is to have the same cryptographic key available at both sites. The key becomes the crucial portion of the system which provides the protection. If the key is lost or compromised, then an adversary could easily use it to decrypt the communications which had been previously intercepted over the line. It therefore becomes important not only to protect the key but also to establish a separate trusted means for passing new keys to both ends of the link.

Techniques for the proper application of DES and similar algorithms for link encryption have been described widely, and several commercial versions of DES suitable for use in link encryption modes are now available.

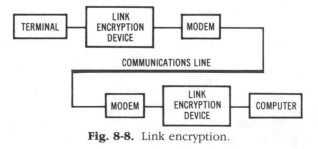

Fig. 8-8. Link encryption.

8.4.3 End-to-End Encryption

Another major application of encryption in communications systems is called *End-to-End Encryption* (E^3). Link encryption provides protection on a link by link basis. In a communications system where message switches (either packet switching or store and forward switches) are employed, link encryption provides no protection against loss or compromise of the information within the switch itself where the information must be decrypted and re-encrypted. Here again, the large numbers of personnel involved in the design, operation, and maintenance of the communications system have to be trusted to protect the information which may pass through the system.

Frequently though, one has no control over the communications path that is used, as in the case of a public switched network. In these cases, the operators of the network frequently are bonded in order to have at least a minimum protection against the improper use of information which they might encounter on the network. But this is not very convincing when one's vital planning or financial information is involved. Some more convincing form of protection is needed.

In its simplest form, E^3 is depicted in Fig. 8-9. The difference between E^3 and link encryption is that the information being sent from the terminal to the computer is encrypted before it enters the communications network and remains scrambled until after it has left the network. With this approach, there is no need for particular concern for the operators of the communication system since they do not have direct access to any of the information in the network. When E^3 is employed, the operators of the communications network are prevented from getting access to the contents of messages, but there is no way to prevent them from obtaining traffic-flow information.

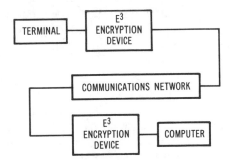

Fig. 8-9. E^3 encryption.

There remains the possibility, even when E^3 is used, that an operator of the network or anyone capable of intercepting signals on the communications links of the network could obtain information about which devices were in communication over the net since the address information by which the network determines the destination of a message must be in the clear. This process is referred to as traffic-flow analysis. If the fact that a pair of users are communicating is of any significance (as it frequently is in military situations and may be in certain financial environments), then additional measures beyond E^3 are required. Link encryption in conjunction with E^3 provides protection against traffic-flow threats by external wiretapping or radio intercept.

8.4.4 Key Distribution

Both the link encryption and the E^3 techniques require some form of trusted distribution mechanism for the delivery of the keying material to the encryption devices. Since the key being used for encryption is the essential aspect providing the security of the system, it is important that the key be changed with some frequency to preserve that security. Military systems usually employ key changes once every 24 hours. Commercial systems may require more or less frequent changes depending upon the sensitivity of the information being protected. Most encryption systems employ manual key changing procedures in which, at the appointed time, a human removes or overlays the old key (e.g., by pulling out a card or similar device) and inserts a new key. These techniques are acceptable in many situations but they are labor intensive, difficult to synchronize closely, and, because they involve human handling of the keying material, they represent a serious security vulnerability. The bigger the network that is commonly keyed, the more humans there are that have to handle the keying material, and the greater the risk of compromise.

This concern, coupled with the highly reliable transmission mechanisms offered by modern packet-switched communications networks, offers the possibility of automating the distribution of keying material to the remote users of the network. Such a capability offers not only protection against human compromise of keying material, but also effects a much more rapid distribution of the keys and a much more effective synchronization of the key change. In addition, if remote key distribution is employed, it is possible to consider having a separate key for each logical communication connection across the network.

Such a per-connection key-distribution mechanism is shown in Fig. 8-10. In this diagram, it is assumed that computer A wants to communicate with computer B. Each computer has its own E^3 device between itself and the network. Computer A will send a message to its E^3 device indicating that it has data for computer B. The E^3 device, sensing that no logical connection exists with computer B, will forward a request to the third major box in the diagram, the Access Checker and Key Distribution Center. The access checker will determine if computer A is authorized to communicate with computer B and, if so, will then request that the key distribution center issue a new key to be sent to both participants. This *session* key will be sent to each E^3 device in an encrypted form using a unique device key so that even if it is misrouted by the network, it will not be usable by anyone else. Once the session key is received by both parties, communications can be established in the normal manner.

When the session is complete, the session key is discarded and will not be used again.

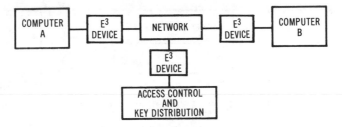

Fig. 8-10. Remote key distribution.

This form of key management represents one of the best methods of achieving communications security. It allows control of communications at the logical link level with up to the minute access control and even the possibility of breaking an existing link, if the access checker should determine that the link is no longer desirable. In addition to this highly responsive performance, the problems of manual rekeying of encryption devices are almost completely eliminated (some initial key fill is necessary). Variations of this approach are possible, such as using the access checker and key distribution center to issue periodic keys good for several hours or days rather than on a per-connection basis. Various organizations are working on commercial versions of this kind of encryption protection but it is not generally available yet.

8.4.5 Public Key Encryption

Link encryption and E^3 techniques that employ conventional algorithms for which key variables must be kept secret provide very useful capabilities and are the basis of most cryptographic applications. However, the new interest in encryption techniques that was sparked in the early and mid 1970s has led to public discussion of a whole range of additional encryption techniques and uses. Public key encryption techniques were first discussed by Diffie and Hellman in 1976 and by Merkle in 1978.[7] In both techniques, each user of the system had two keys, one of which was generally known to the public, E_A, and one which was private, D_A. The private transformation is related to the public one but it cannot be computationally determined from it. Two users could communicate knowing only each other's public keys.

This technique could be used to send either secret messages, or messages whose originator could be authenticated, or both. To send a secret message M, from point A to point B (see Fig. 8-11), sender A obtains receiver B's public key E_B, encrypts the message as

$$C = E_B(M)$$

and transmits the ciphertext C to receiver B. The private transformation of receiver B is the inverse of E_B, so receiver B can decipher text C and obtain the original message M.

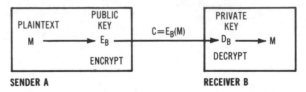

Fig. 8-11. Public key encryption for message secrecy.

To send a message whose originator is to be authenticated (see Fig. 8-12), sender A would apply its private transformation, D_A, to M producing

$$X = D_A(M)$$

and then transmit it to point B. Receiver B would then obtain sender A's public key, E_A, and use it to decrypt X,

$$E_A(X) = M$$

Receiver B could use sender A's public key to authenticate that the message did originate with sender A.

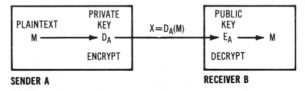

Fig. 8-12. Public key encryption for sender authentication.

Secrecy cannot be obtained with the message authentication process since any user can obtain E_A and compute X. To send a signed secret message, a combination of the above approaches is used; first applying the authentication function and, then, the secrecy function. Upon decryption, first the secrecy transform is applied and then the authentication transform.

Secrecy requires that the deciphering algorithm, D_A, be the inverse of E_A. Message authentication requires that E_A be the inverse of D_A. The only known public key cryptosystem that is widely accepted as meeting both these requirements is the *Rivest-Shamir-Adleman* or *RSA* scheme. There are a number of other public key cryptosystems that have been generally accepted as being safe for either secrecy or signatures but not for both.

Like almost all other ciphers, the security provided by public key systems is dependent upon the computational complexity of breaking them. Since these new cipher systems are based on rather simple and elegant mathematical properties, new mathematical knowledge could weaken them much more quickly than in the case of traditional cipher systems which depend on a more arbitrary complexity. The RSA process, for example, relies on the difficulty of factoring a very large prime number for its security. It was initially thought that an 80-digit prime would be sufficient for many years because of the difficulty of factoring such a large number. However, efforts at Sandia Laboratories have shown that primes of up to 69 digits can be factored in less than 33 hours using a Cray computer. More recent research in Israel suggest that exponents of less than 512 bits may be vulnerable to factoring. New breakthroughs in this field, both in establishing new algorithms and in the means to break them, can be expected to come rapidly in the next few years.

8.4.6 User-to-User Security

During the past decade, government, business, and academia have become increasingly reliant on computer networks for timely, reliable, accurate, and *secure* dissemination of critical information to support decision making processes. Electronic mail is beginning to replace traditional message traffic and paper mail for routine delivery of correspondence. Large-scale file transfer protocols are now employed to distribute operational data bases, distribute research and development processes, and forward raw data to processing centers. Some of the electronic transactions are protected between central communications centers and some between host processors. However, few transactions are protected from source user process to destination user process.[14]

Network security requirements include protection of network traffic from disclosure to unauthorized persons, detection of unauthorized modification of network traffic, and detection of attempts by unauthorized persons or processes to masquerade as legitimate network participants. Both cryptographic processes and trusted systems environments are necessary to satisfy network security requirements. Cryptographic processes provide encryption, message integrity encoding, and digital signature. Trusted systems protection enforces system security policies and controls access by users to system information and resources.

As indicated in Section 8.4.3, *end-to-end* security measures provide uniform protection for each message from its source to its destination. This is different from *Link* security which protects message traffic independently for each communications link.

Steve Kent and Victor Voydock, in a June 1983 *Computing Surveys* article, pointed out that end-to-end security permits an individual user or host to employ cryptography without affecting other users or hosts.[13] Thus, end-to-end techniques permit the cost of security to be more fairly apportioned and permit operational activities having modest cryptographic protection requirements from being forced to share in the cost of satisfying the more exotic requirements of others (e.g., the military intelligence community). Also, end-to-end security can be employed, not just in packet-switched networks, but in packet-broadcast networks where link-oriented measures are often infeasible. Note that link-oriented security measures can be implemented so that they are almost completely invisible to network users, while end-to-end security protocols usually extend beyond the communications subnet. This requires a greater degree of standardization in the protocols employed by end-to-end users. Fortunately, technical, economical, and political reasons are forcing protocol standardization; so standardization requirements are not a serious impediment to the adoption of end-to-end security measures in an open-system environment.

Traditional link encryption requires dedicated network facilities with physically secured switching centers. In these protected switches, all traffic has to be decrypted in order to reveal routing and addressing information, then re-encrypted for transmission over the next network link. In most cases, such protected switches are not able to properly provide partitioning of information requiring disparate distribution limitations. The result is that any data segregation capability in end-user systems is negated by most switches. The user community can ill-afford dedicated networks necessary to meet its network segregation requirements. The costs of maintaining and operating switching centers with personnel authorized access to all classes of information being communicated over the network, and the risk of compromise resulting from decryption of all information at these centers are prohibitive. Users need security techniques that are capable of providing cleartext header information to networks while protecting classified information being transferred via the networks. Further, information handling restrictions in force in many facilities (e.g., military combat operations centers with direct intelligence support) also require protection of some information from some users or workstations within their facilities. This is another example of the long-standing security axiom that information should be protected as close to the end user as possible (i.e., user-to-user protection rather than host-to-host protection).

Terminal-to-terminal and host-to-host forms of E^3 provide host-to-host protection. Protection is provided against eavesdropping on communications links, but no mechanisms are provided to prevent anyone who can connect to a processor from accessing any and all information within the processor. Though it is possible to isolate sets of local network nodes from other nodes through use of unique key variables for those user sets, no real privacy from other system users is provided within hosts or local networks.

While it is possible to employ trusted operating systems in hosts and computer workstations that connect to the network security devices, the lines connecting the workstations to the network security devices are protected only by physical and procedural measures. Most network security systems fail to provide mechanisms that reliably identify to a destination either the user or (in multilevel systems) the security level at which he is operating. One means for improving this situation is to provide encryption at a layer closer to the user. Application of network security services at the network layer would permit use of a trusted system's mandatory and discretionary access control features to associate protection mechanisms with user identity and security level. Association of key variables or public key certificates with users permits provision of privacy as well as security on a *user-to-user* "per connection" basis.

Many network security mechanisms are too slow to meet current and emerging user requirements for networking. Cryptographic mechanisms having sufficient throughput are available, but merging the cryptographic functions with network level protocol functions often results in insufficient *system* throughput. Associating cryptographic functions with the applications layer alleviates this problem. Faster cryptographic implementations such as memory-to-memory transfer can be used at the applications level, and the network protocol software is freed from the burden of cryptographic functions. The result is that classified networks can operate at data rates similar to those of unprotected networks. Voydock and Kent noted that, in cases in which protocol data units (PDUs) always arrive in order with no duplicates and no losses (e.g., most protocols above layer 4), the PDUs do not need to be independently encrypted and decrypted. Instead, the entire sequence of PDUs moving in one direction can be enciphered as a single stream. Encryption above the transport level is particularly advantageous in the case of common self-synchronizing cryptographic modes. For example, when PDUs are independently encrypted in the cipher feedback mode, a different initialization vector (IV) must be used for each PDU. These IVs must be unique for the life of an encryption key. Since a different IV must be used for each PDU, that IV must be transmitted along with the PDU.

8.4.7 Evolutionary Issues

One of the major problems associated with applying cryptography to networks is interfacing relatively static cryptographic systems to highly dynamic network systems. These systems and their protocols evolve rapidly. When cryptography is applied at or below the network layer, the cryptographic system must provide extensive protocol functionality. It takes five to ten years for the Department of Defense to evaluate and field a cryptographic design. Implementation of changes to cryptographic designs generally requires extensive and time-consuming security evaluation. The state of the art in networking is, on the other hand, changing rapidly. It has been observed that at the current rate of evolution of network systems, cryptographic systems' implementations of network interfaces will never catch up to the versions being employed by the network community. So long as cryptography is employed at or below the transport level, this observation remains valid. If, however, cryptography is applied at higher layers (e.g., the applications layer), then changes to network interface and protocols requirements will not impact the cryptographic interface. So long as new operating systems are backward compatible, the network can accommodate cryptographic key management requirements, and the cryptography has adequate throughput, a relatively static COMSEC design may meet the requirements of several generations of network evolution.

Applications layer cryptography offers real user-to-user network security, with the added advantages of avoiding cryptographic throughput reductions based on network interfaces and increasing the applicability of individual cryptographic designs to a variety of rapidly evolving network environments. Also, association of a transaction with its originator permits both recipients and administrators to know on behalf of whom network transactions occur. Special problems are, however, associated with encryption at the higher layers.

One typical form of cryptography at the higher layers is to route plaintext data from a computer to a cryptographic device, then route the ciphertext output of the cryptographic device back into the computer. Unless a trusted operating system is employed to control the flow of information to and from the cryptographic device, there is no assurance that unencrypted classified information will not be routed to the network together with or instead of the encrypted version of classified information. To be useful in cryptographic applications, trusted systems must provide mandatory access controls for separating information of different classification levels and must have been evaluated as providing adequate assurance for the range of classification levels involved. Such systems are designed and accredited to support input/output channels at different classification levels and to control access to or dissemination of information based on security officer-specified classification hierarchy, security officer-specified compartmentation, and/or user-specified restrictions. One problem that must be solved in trusted systems control of cryptography stems from the very strength of the separation mechanisms. The trusted system is designed to prevent the flow of information from a higher classification domain to a lower classification domain. Users specify the classification level at which they will operate a computer. They must take some prespecified authorized action in order to operate at a different classification level. The purpose of encryption is to provide a downgrade function so that classified information may be safely exchanged as though it were unclassified. So, plaintext classified information is sent from one computer process to a cryptographic process and is returned as cipher text at a lower classification level. Some trusted mechanisms need to be implemented and evaluated that permit users to

1. Interact with lower/unclassified network services.
2. Invoke encryption of information at a higher classification than one's login level.
3. Transfer the unclassified encrypted version of this information over a network.

Ironically, trusted cryptographic control mechanisms may be more easily implemented for high-bandwidth functions such as file transfers than for interactive low-bandwidth functions such as remote login and conversational mode data exchanges. For example, in the case of file transfers, a user who is logged in at an unclassified security level can pass the name of a file to be encrypted and transmitted to a classified process, then invoke the process without violating a system security policy that prohibits information from being written from a higher classification level to a lower level.

The alternative strategy of permitting a user to operate at some classified level and pass plaintext address and control information to the network inherently provides channels by which classified information might be caused to bypass the cryptography in violation of the system security policy. If this alternative strategy must be invoked for interactive communications, then means for detecting and controlling security violations must be developed.

In the case of over-the-air rekeying of cryptographic variables, some key information can be expected to pass through the computer. Implementation of true user-to-user security requires a capability for users to control the dissemination of key variables employed to protect their information (e.g., automatic invocation of two-party keying relationships). Trust engineering for cryptographic control systems can be simplified by insuring that only encrypted versions of the key variables are accessed by noncryptographic processes. Manually distributed certificates or keys can be used to initialize the cryptographic devices' key exchange mechanisms.

8.4.8 Privacy Enhanced Mail

Low assurance user-to-user cryptographic applications are widely available in the private sector. However, most applications offer inadequate protection to both key variables and the integrity of the cryptography.[1] Also, automated key variable management for user-to-user applications is generally not adequately supported. The financial community's ANSI X9.9, 9.17, and 9.23 cryptographic standards support automated key management, but fail to bind key variables to user identities. The Internet Activities Board has released a set of RFCs establishing standards for privacy-enhanced electronic mail exchanges that does bind keys to X.509 *distinguished names* in cryptographically signed certificates. The intent of the distinguished name is to unambiguously identify an individual. The RFCs specify implementations for encryption, message integrity encoding, and digital signature. Developed in accordance with the RFCs, Trusted Information Systems' (TIS's) Privacy-Enhanced Mail (PEM) prototype system is in *beta* testing at several Government and Contractor installations. TIS is also porting this PEM System to a Trusted XENIX operating system rated at the B2 level of the National Computer Security Center's Trusted Computer System Evaluation Criteria. B2 is the minimum level approved for separating classified information from unclassified information. A Trusted Mail (TMail) process controls security services through a local key manager (LKM). (See Fig. 8-13.) Certificates are obtained from a Cryptographic Administration Unit (CAU). The Trusted XENIX identification and authentication process completes the association of cryptographic protection with individual users by binding certificates to identities.

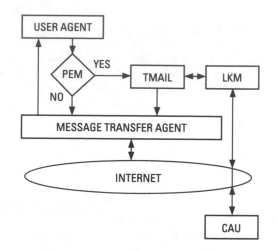

Fig. 8-13. TMail functionality.

Given a user-to-user cryptographic implementation such as PEM, it is now possible to maintain communications security across a heterogeneous and untrusted network structure (Fig. 8-14). By replacing PEM's DES and RSA cryptography with cryptography rated for protection of classified information, true user-to-user security can become available to the military networking community. All the necessary trusted computer and cryptographic components exist. What remains is the secure integration of the trusted cryptographic control functions into workstation hardware and evaluation of the resulting Information Security (INFOSEC) workstations. Cryptographic and trusted systems components of such systems have traditionally been evaluated separately. A system that truly provides user-to-user security must be evaluated as a single entity. However, the piecemeal evaluation tradition is likely to continue indefinitely unless the user community issues strong statements of operational requirements for evaluated integrated INFOSEC products.

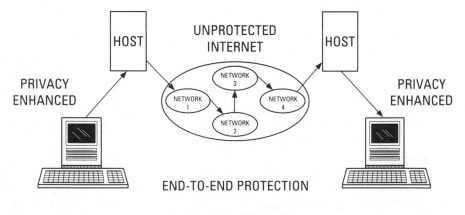

Fig. 8-14. End-to-end protection.

8.5 References

1. Barker, William C. "User-to-User Protection Enhances Network Security," *Signal, Journal of the Armed Forces Communications and Electronics Association*, Vol. 45, No. 5, January 1991, pp. 53–59.

2. Bosworth, Bruce. *Codes, Ciphers, and Computers*, Rochelle Park, NJ: Hayden Book Company, 1982.

3. *Computers at Risk: Safe Computing in the Information Age*, Washington, DC: National Research Council, 1991.

4. *Computer Security Requirements, Guidance for Applying the Department of Defense Trusted Computer System Evaluation Criteria in Specific Environments*, CSC-STD-003-85, also known as the Yellow Book, Fort George G. Meade, MD: National Computer Security Center, June 25, 1985.

5. Davies, Donald W. *Tutorial: The Security of Data in Networks*; IEEE Catalog EH0183-4, Los Alamitos, CA: The Computer Society Press, 1981. (Includes reprints of many of the historic articles in the development of cryptography.)

6. Denning, Dorothy. *Cryptography and Data Security*, Reading, MA: Addison Wesley Publishing Co., 1982.

7. Diffie, Whitfield and Martin E. Hellman. "Privacy and Authentication: An Introduction to Cryptography," *Proceedings of the IEEE*, Vol. 67, No. 3, March, 1979, pp. 397–427.

8. *Information Technology Security Evaluation Criteria (ITSEC)*, Draft, Version 1, May 2, 1990.

9. Landwehr, C.E. and H.O. Lubbes. *An Approach to Determining Computer Security Requirements for Navy Systems*, Washington, DC: Naval Research Laboratory Report 8897, May, 1985.

10. *Trusted Computer System Evaluation Criteria*, DoD 5200.28-STD, also known as the Orange Book, Fort George G. Meade, MD: National Computer Security Center, (superseded CSC-STD-001-83 dated August 15, 1983), December, 1985.

11. *Trusted Database Management Systems Interpretation of the Trusted Computer System Evaluation Criteria (Draft)*, NCSC-TG-021, Fort George G. Meade, MD: National Computer Security Center, October, 1989.

12. *Trusted Network Interpretation Environments Guideline, Guidance for Applying the Trusted Network Interpretation*, NCSC-TG-011, Version 1, also known as the Red Book or TNI, Fort George G. Meade, MD: National Computer Security Center, August 1, 1990.

13. Voydock, V.L. and Stephen T. Kent. "Security Mechanisms in High-Level Network Protocols," *Computing Surveys*, Vol. 15, No. 2, June, 1983.

14. Walker, Stephen T. "Network Security: The Parts of the Sum," *Proceedings of the 1989 IEEE Computer Society Symposium on Security and Privacy*, Los Alamitos, CA: IEEE Computer Society Press, 1989.

8.5.1 Additional Reading

1. *Advances in Cryptology: Proceedings of Crypto 82*, New York: Plenum Press, 1983.

2. Diffie, Whitfield and Martin E. Hellman. "New Directions in Cryptography," *IEEE Transactions on Information Theory*, Vol. IT-22, No. 6, November, 1976, pp. 644–654.

3. Kahn, David. *The Codebreakers*, New York: Macmillan, 1967.

4. Meyer, Dr. Carl and Stephen Matyas. *Cryptography—A New Dimension in Computer Data Security*, New York: Wiley, 1983.

5. Rivest, R.L., A. Shamir, and L. Adleman. "A Method for Obtaining Digital Signatures and Public Key Cryptosystems," *Communications of the ACM*, Vol. 21, No. 2, February, 1978, pp. 120–126.

Local Area Network Standards

John H. Carson and David C. Wood

Dr. John H. Carson is a Professor of Management Science in the School of Business and Public Policy at The George Washington University in Washington, DC. Dr. Carson is currently the Program Director of the Information Systems Technology program. He has published numerous articles on all aspects of computing and has lectured throughout the world on local area networks. His previous experience includes employment by the Software Productivity Consortium and The MITRE Corporation.

Dr. Carson is a member of IEEE, ACM, Eta Kappa Nu, and Sigma Xi. He holds a B.S.E.E., and an M.S. and Ph.D. in Information Science from Lehigh University, Bethlehem, Pennsylvania.

Dr. David C. Wood is a Consulting Scientist at The MITRE Corporation in McLean, Virginia. He is responsible for defining research and advanced technology work in networking and distributed systems, as well as for integration with related work across the corporation. For many years, Dr. Wood has led MITRE's support to the government in networking, including pioneering the development of local area networks incorporating TCP/IP and planning the development of the Defense Data Network based on ARPANET.

Dr. Wood has published numerous articles on networking and has taught courses on networks and protocols for The Johns Hopkins University, The George Washington University, the ACM, and the IEEE. Dr. Wood has held numerous offices in the Association for Computing Machinery (ACM), having served as Secretary, Council Member, and Chairman of the Special Interest Group on Data Communication (SIGCOMM). Dr. Wood holds a B.Sc. and Ph.D. in Mathematics from the University of Manchester, United Kingdom.

9.1 Introduction

The purpose of this chapter is to describe current and proposed standards for Local Area Networks, also known as *LANs*. The protocols used within a LAN are placed in the context of the Open Systems Interconnection (OSI) reference model. The evolution of LAN standards is described as starting with Ethernet, evolving to the IEEE 802 standards, and continuing with the development of the ANSI fiber-based FDDI standard. The various local network standards encompassed by IEEE 802 and ANSI FDDI are defined. In terms of the OSI reference model (see Chapter 5), the internal protocols to a local network occupy the two lower layers: the data link layer and the physical layer.

The first major step in the evolution of LAN standards occurred in 1980 with the publication of the Ethernet specification by DEC, Intel, and Xerox. The published Ethernet specification was derived from many years of research and development at the Xerox Palo Alto Research Center. An experimental Ethernet was first publicly described in 1976.[19]

The 1980 Ethernet specification encompasses the two lower protocol layers. At the data link, the specification defines a contention-based channel-access protocol known as *Carrier-Sense Multiple Access with Collision Detection* (CSMA/CD). This layer also defines a frame structure for messages similar to that used in *High-Level Data Link Control* (HDLC). At the physical layer, the specification defines the medium as a particular type of shielded coaxial cable with a topology known as a branching nonrooted tree. Baseband signaling is employed at a data rate of 10-million bits per second (Mbps). This contrasts with the earlier experimental Ethernet that used 3-Mbps signaling.

Ethernet configurations are illustrated in Figs. 9-1 and 9-2. Figure 9-1 shows a minimal configuration consisting of a single segment of coaxial cable that is up to 500 meters in length. User devices, or stations, such as workstations or host computers, are connected to the main cable by an access or transceiver

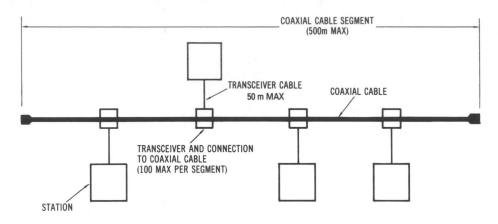

SOURCE: ETHERNET SPECIFICATION

Fig. 9-1. Minimal Ethernet configuration.

cable that can be up to 50 meters in length. The transceiver cable connects to the main cable via a transceiver, a small box that essentially performs the signal transmission and reception. Most of the Ethernet protocol logic is implemented in the workstation. A single segment can contain up to 100 stations.

For a local network extending more than 500 meters, multiple segments are required. These are interconnected by repeaters, as shown in Fig. 9-2. A repeater is connected as a regular station to two segments. However, every transmission on one segment is automatically retransmitted by the repeater onto the second segment with a small delay and, conversely, in the other direction. The repeaters essentially overcome the distance limitation of a single segment that results from the baseband signaling employed. Up to 100 stations can be on the local network. All the interconnected segments are one space as far as the CSMA/CD contention protocol is concerned. At most, two repeaters can be in the path between any two stations.

However, this allows for large configurations. For example, in a high-rise office building, one segment could be vertical up a utility shaft, with segments off on each floor. To connect segments that may be some distance away in adjacent buildings a point-to-point link is allowed. This can be up to 1000 meters in length and will appear as a repeater divided into two parts.

The rationale for many of the design decisions for the Ethernet specification is contained in *Evolution of the Ethernet Local Computer Network* by J.F. Shoch.[22] Xerox Corporation's goal in publishing the specification was to have it accepted as a *de facto* standard for LANs that other vendors would adopt, thus leading to open systems (i.e., interoperability among different vendor's equipment). Ethernet was widely accepted and as a result, board-level implementations of Ethernet controllers became available in about 1982 from vendors such as Intel, Interlan, and 3Com. Chip-set implementations, using very large-scale integration, started to come on the market in 1983 from Intel and Fujitsu.

Ethernet was incorporated as one of the options within the IEEE 802 local

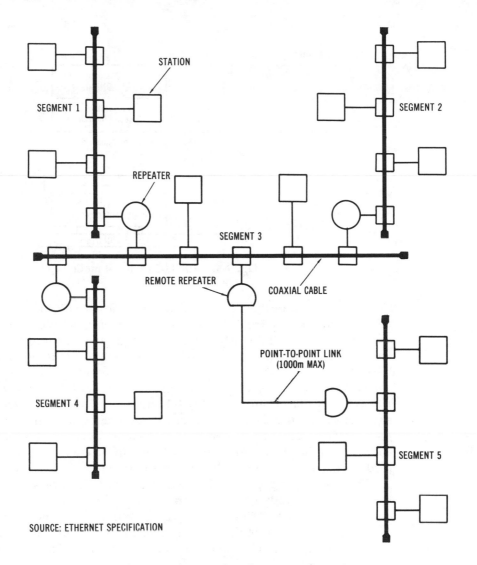

Fig. 9-2. Large-scale Ethernet configuration.

area network standards with just a few changes from the 1980 specification. Xerox Corporation agreed to these changes and revised their specification accordingly. The final Ethernet-based specification is described in more detail in the next section as part of the IEEE 802 standard.

9.2 IEEE 802 Local Area Network Standards

The IEEE established Project 802 on LAN standards in 1980. Since then, numerous working groups have been created within the 802 project. A starting point in

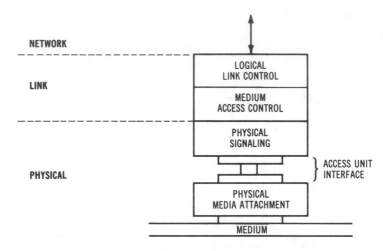

Fig. 9-3. IEEE 802 protocol model.

the development of the IEEE standards was the specification of the protocol model[17] illustrated in Fig. 9-3. The IEEE 802.1 Committee addresses the overall architecture of the IEEE LAN systems and, thus, extends from OSI Layer 1 up into OSI Layer 3. The remainder of the IEEE 802 committees address the two lower layers of the OSI reference model and provide an interface to the network layer. The data link layer is divided into two sublayers: a *logical link control* (LLC) sublayer similar to HDLC and a *medium access control* (MAC) sublayer such as the CSMA/CD protocol used in Ethernet. An *access unit interface* (AUI) is defined between the component containing both the link layer and physical signaling, and the physical medium attachment to the transmission media. This is analogous to the Ethernet transceiver cable.

Due to differing points of view, different application domains, and the influence of various corporate strategies, a family of LAN standards has emerged from the 802 Committee. As shown in Fig. 9-4, the standard consists of a common portion at the LLC sublayer together with three major options encompassing the MAC sublayer and physical layer. These options are: the CSMA/CD access protocol on a bus topology, a token access protocol on a bus topology, and a token access protocol on a ring topology. (A token access protocol is one in which permission to transmit, called the "token," is system-

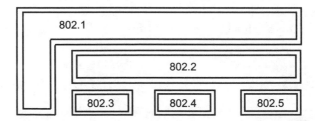

Fig. 9-4. Major components of the IEEE 802 model.

atically passed from node to node around the network. A particular node may transmit only when it possesses the token.)

At this time, there are four completed IEEE standards documents:

- IEEE 802.2 Logical Link Control
- IEEE 802.3 CSMA/CD
- IEEE 802.4 Token Bus
- IEEE 802.5 Token Ring

The IEEE 802.2 specification and portions of the IEEE 802.3 specification have been approved as International Standards. Portions of the 802.1 specification have also been completed.

9.2.1 Logical Link Control Sublayer (IEEE 802.2)

The scope of the LLC sublayer[17] consists of an interface service specification to the network layer above, LLC procedures, and an interface service specification to the MAC sublayer below (Fig. 9-5).

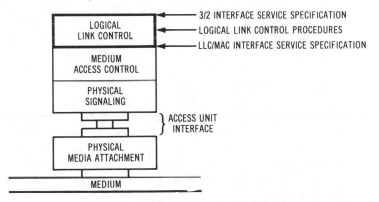

Fig. 9-5. Logical link control sublayer.

The IEEE 802.2 specification defines two forms of service for the network layer. The most commonly used is an unacknowledged connectionless service (i.e., a datagram style of service in which stations exchange data units without establishment of a data link connection and without acknowledgements). This is appropriate where the high-level protocols provide reliability and sequencing support. Additionally, the connectionless mode supports multicast and broadcast in addition to point-to-point communications. The other option is a connection-oriented service that, of course, only supports point-to-point operation.

The LLC procedures are based on HDLC and ADCCP (ANSI X3.66)[1] and, in particular, the *asynchronous balanced mode* (ABM) of those standards. However, HDLC/ADCCP is extended for the multistation, multiaccess environment of a local network. In a local network, a logical data link is possible between any pair of stations. This contrasts with the point-to-point or multipoint configurations supported by HDLC/ADCCP in which all transmissions are to and from a primary station. Moreover, in the local network, a single station can be simultaneously included in multiple data exchanges with many different stations. Within a single station, these multiple exchanges are identified by a *service access point* (SAP) which can be viewed as a port address to a higher-level protocol within that station.

The format of the LLC protocol data unit is shown in Fig. 9-6. The *destination service access point* (DSAP) and *source service access point* (SSAP) represent individual addresses as previously described. The DSAP is also usable as a group address.

DEST SAP	SOURCE SAP	CONTROL	INFO
1 OCTET	1	1	0 – M

Fig. 9-6. Logical link control frame format.

The *control field* may be either 8 or 16 bits long and is used for commands and responses in the sense of HDLC/ADCCP. Connectionless data exchanges use the *unnumbered information* (UI) 8-bit command. Connection-oriented data exchanges use the *information* (I) command and response, together with the *receive-ready* (RR), *reject* (REJ), and *receive not ready* (RNR) 16-bit commands and responses.

Two types of operation are defined using the LLC procedures: Type 1 (connectionless operation) and Type 2 (connection-oriented operation). In the Type 1 operation, there is no need for establishing a logical data link; acknowledgements, flow control, and error recovery are not provided, and either individual or group addressing may be used. In the Type 2 operation, a logical data link is established, acknowledgements are provided, and individual addressing only is supported.

Two classes of LLC are defined: Class I (which consists of the Type 1 operation only) and Class II (which consists of both the Type 1 and Type 2 operation.) Thus, all stations support the connectionless operation. Whereas, Class II stations can support both connectionless and connection-oriented operation.

IEEE 802.2 was approved as ISO Standard 8802-2 in 1989.

9.2.2 CSMA/CD Bus (IEEE 802.3)

The CSMA/CD access protocol[15] for use on bus topologies is one of the three major options within the IEEE 802 LAN standards. Although 802.5, the token ring protocol, is rapidly increasing in popularity, the most popular LAN standard is 802.3. The scope of the CSMA/CD option is shown in Fig. 9-7. It consists of the MAC service specification, the MAC sublayer using CSMA/CD, a *physical signaling* (PLS) sublayer service specification, the *attachment unit interface* (AUI) specification, and the *medium attachment unit* (MAU) consisting of the *physical medium attachment* (PMA) and the *medium dependent interface* (MDI).

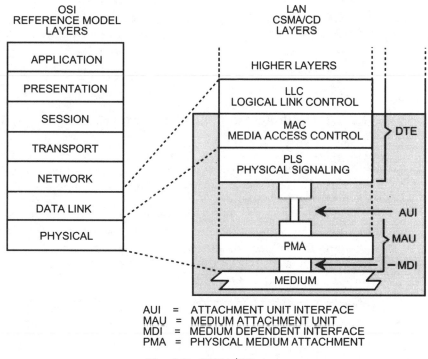

AUI = ATTACHMENT UNIT INTERFACE
MAU = MEDIUM ATTACHMENT UNIT
MDI = MEDIUM DEPENDENT INTERFACE
PMA = PHYSICAL MEDIUM ATTACHMENT

Fig. 9-7. CSMA/CD scope.

The MAC sublayer, together with the LLC specification, forms the OSI data link layer. The PLS provides the service primitive commands and operations necessary for the MAC. The AUI provides a mechanism for the *data terminal equipment* (DTE) to be separated from the medium. In some cases, the AUI may not be externally visible. The MAU provides a means of attaching devices, through the AUI, to a LAN. It addresses the electrical and mechanical issues specific to the medium and isolates these from the remainder of the system via the AUI. For the 802.3 or Ethernet standards, the MAU is known in the industry as a transceiver.

Within the IEEE 802.3, many suboptions concerning media and data rate exist. These options are listed in Table 9-1.

The options are named using the data rate followed by the transmission technique (*base*band or *broad*band), and then either the maximum segment length or "-T" for the 10-megabit twisted pair option.

The 10BASE5 and 10BASE2 options have been adopted as International Standard ISO 8802-3:1989.[16] It can be expected that some, if not all, of the other options will be adopted (perhaps with modifications) in the future.

Table 9-1. Options in IEEE 802.3

Name	Data Rate Mbps	Medium	Maximum Segment Length (Meters)
10BASE5	10	Thick Wire Coax	500
10BASE2	10	Thin Wire Coax	200
1BASE5	1	Twisted Pair	500
10BASE-T	10	Twisted Pair	100
10BROAD36	10	Broadband Coax	3600

9.2.2.1 Media Access Control Sublayer

The services provided by the *media access control* (MAC) sublayer allow the local LLC sublayer entity to exchange LLC data units with peer LLC sublayer entities. The MAC sublayer defines the MAC frame structure and the procedures of CSMA/CD protocol.

The MAC frame format is shown in Fig. 9-8. The preamble is a 7-octet field of alternating *1s* and *0s* that are used both for synchronization and to allow the PLS circuitry to reach its steady-state condition. The start frame delimiter field is the sequence 10101011; it immediately follows the preamble pattern and indicates the start of a valid frame.

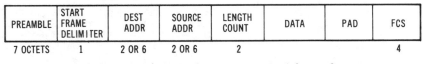

PREAMBLE	START FRAME DELIMITER	DEST ADDR	SOURCE ADDR	LENGTH COUNT	DATA	PAD	FCS
7 OCTETS	1	2 OR 6	2 OR 6	2			4

Fig. 9-8. CSMA/CD media access control frame format.

Next follows the destination and source addresses for the frame. The address fields can contain either two or six octets. Only the six octet form is allowed in the implementation guidelines, and the two octet form is likely to disappear in the future. This is an implementation option; however, the source and destination addresses must be the same size for all stations on a particular local network. The destination address can designate either an individual or a group address. There are two kinds of group address: a multicast group address associated with a group of logically related stations and a broadcast address denoting the set of all stations. Six-octet addresses may be locally or globally administered. Global addresses will be unique among any local network conforming to the standard. To insure this, the IEEE assigns global address bands upon request. It remains the responsibility of the assignee to insure that addresses are not duplicated within their assigned bands.

The length field is a two-octet field whose value indicates the number of LLC octets in the data field. The data field itself contains an LLC protocol data unit (i.e., DSAP, SSAP, control, and information) shown previously in Fig. 9-6. If the length of the data unit is less than a minimum required by a particular implementation of the protocol, then the data field is extended by extra octets known as *pad*. In the case of a 10-Mbps baseband system, the minimum frame size is 512 bits (64 octets). Finally, the *frame check sequence* (FCS) field contains a 32-bit *cyclic redundancy check* (CRC) computed as a function of the destination address, source address, length, LLC data, and pad fields.

The MAC frame format is similar, but not identical, to the original Ethernet specification. The addresses are always six octets in the Ethernet specification. Instead of the length field, there is a two-octet type field which is used to identify a higher-level protocol in the Ethernet specification.

The functions provided by the MAC sublayer are equivalent to the major functions provided in a data link layer protocol. The MAC sublayer provides data encapsulation (i.e, framing, addressing, and error detection). It also provides medium access management wherein medium allocation is performed using collision avoidance mechanisms and a contention resolution capability that handles collisions.

The CSMA/CD protocol operates as follows. The MAC sublayer constructs the frame from the LLC-supplied data. The carrier-sense signal provided by the physical layer is monitored. If there is passing traffic, then transmission is deferred. When the medium is clear, frame transmission is initiated after a brief interframe delay (9.6 microseconds for a 10-Mbps system) to provide recovery time for other stations. During transmission, the physical layer also monitors the collision-detect signal in the event of a collision.

A *collision* occurs when multiple stations attempt to transmit at the same time and their signals interfere with each other. A given station can experience a collision only during the initial part of its transmission (the collision window), before its transmitted signal has the time to propagate to all stations on the CSMA/CD medium and have the effects of that signal propagate back. Once the collision window has passed, the station is said to have acquired the medium. (Subsequent collisions are avoided since it can be assumed that all other stations have noticed and deferred to the signal.) Thus, the time to acquire the medium is based on the round-trip propagation time of the physical layer.

In the event of a collision, the physical layer of the transmitting station notices the interference on the medium and turns on the collision-detect signal. This is noticed by the MAC sublayer and collision handling begins. First, the collision is allowed to continue for a minimal time interval. A bit sequence called the *jam* (32 bits for a 10-Mbps system) is transmitted to ensure that the duration of the collision is sufficient to be noticed by the other transmitting stations. After the jam is sent, transmission is terminated and a retransmission attempt is scheduled after a randomly selected delay. In the event of repeated collisions, retransmission is still attempted. However, the interval in which the random delay is selected is doubled with each attempt. This is known as *binary exponential backoff*. However, the retransmission attempt is abandoned after 16 consecutive unsuccessful attempts and an error condition is signaled.

The retransmission delay is controlled by a parameter known as the *slot time* which exceeds the round-trip propagation and jam time. For a 10-Mbps baseband system, the slot time equals 512-bit times. The *backoff delay* is always an integral number of slot times. The number of slot times to delay before the nth retransmission is a random integer r, where

$$0 \leq r \leq 2^k$$

and

$$k = \min(n, 10)$$

In other words, the delay interval is doubled for the first ten retransmissions. Afterwards, it remains constant up to the 16th retransmission.

9.2.2.2 Physical Signaling and Attachment Unit Interface

The MAC sublayer communicates with the PLS sublayer using primitives defined in the PLS service specification. The DTE containing the data link and higher-level protocols may be physically separate from the MAU that connects to the transmission medium. The DTE and MAU are connected by a cable whose specifications are known as the AUI. This was previously illustrated in Fig. 9-7. The AUI also enables the DTE to be independent of the transmission media (e.g., baseband coaxial cable, unshielded twisted pair, or broadband coaxial cable).

The AUI is capable of supporting data rates of 1, 5, 10, or 20 Mbps and the AUI cable may be up to 50 meters long. The interface permits the DTE to test the AU interface, the AU interface cable, the MAU, and the medium. The AUI uses a standard 15-pin connector and consists of four signal circuits providing separate data and control circuits in each direction, together with power and ground.

Manchester encoding (Fig. 9-9) is used for the transmission of data across the AUI. It is a binary signaling mechanism that combines data and clock into a single-bit stream. The signal state during the first half of the bit period indicates the data value; a transition to the inverse state always occurs in the middle of each bit period.

Fig. 9-9. Manchester encoding.

9.2.2.3 Thick Wire Baseband (10BASE5)

The MAU is specific to the transmission medium. The MAU, for a baseband coaxial transmission system, closely follows the original Ethernet specification. Signaling is at a data rate of 10 Mbps with a maximum cable segment length of

500 meters. Multiple segments may be coupled together using repeater units to form a bus topology as described previously for Ethernet. Up to two repeater units may be in the path between any two MAUs. Allowing for a point-to-point link, the maximum cable connection path is 2500 meters. The data propagation delay for a repeater unit is specified to be less than 7.5 bit times.

The MAU detects a collision on the coaxial cable when the signal level on the cable equals or exceeds that produced by two transmitters. The coaxial cable has a 50-ohm characteristic impedance and may have a jacket of polyvinyl chloride or fluoropolymer. The cable jacket is marked with annular rings in a contrasting color every 2.5 meters. MAUs should only be attached at these 2.5-meter marks to ensure that signal reflections do not add in-phase to a significant degree. The total number of MAUs on a segment cannot exceed 100. The MAU-to-cable connection may be designed such that MAU is installed by either severing the cable or using a piercing tap connector that does not sever the cable. The shield of the trunk coaxial cable should be effectively grounded at only one point along the length of the cable.

9.2.2.4 Thin Wire Baseband (10BASE2)

The 10BASE2 option, often, called *thin wire*, is similar in concept to the 10BASE5 option above with two exceptions:

1. The use of a thinner coaxial cable and associated shorted cable lengths.
2. The AUI is typically invisible with the cable running directly to the equipment.

Most equipment connects to a 10BASE2 system by way of a tee-tap with the coaxial cable routed directly to the equipment. The AUI, although present, is embedded inside the interface and is essentially invisible.

9.2.2.5 Twisted Pair Baseband (1BASE5 and 10BASE-T)

The newest option in the IEEE 802.3 family is the 10BASE-T option, which was approved in September, 1990. The 10BASE-T option provides for 10-Mbps over *unshielded twisted pair* (UTP) and has attracted great attention. This option uses the same MAC as other 802.3 options but has four significant differences from the coaxial-based options:

1. 10BASE-T uses a star topology.
2. The MAU uses separate conductors for transmission and reception.
3. A link integrity test is included as part of the standard.
4. The use of multiport repeaters is an integral and necessary part of system design.

The AUI is the same as with other 802.3 options but is typically invisible with only the medium connection being visible. The separate conductors change the way collisions are detected. With this option, simultaneous activity on both transmit and receive conductors indicates the presence of a collision.

A minimal system would simply have two stations connected by a twisted pair cable. However, when more than two stations are required, a multiport repeater is used to create a star topology (Fig. 9-10). Such a topology is easier to handle from installation and maintenance points-of-view since the multiport repeaters provide a centralized location for wiring changes. The 100-meter maximum cable length also dictates the use of repeaters or bridges for medium- and large-scale systems.

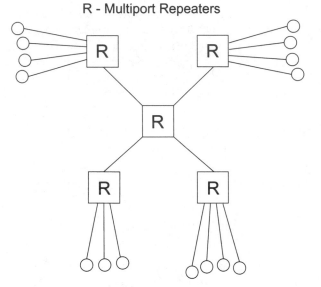

Fig. 9-10. 10BASE-T star topology.

The 1BASE5 option is a precursor to the 10BASE-T standard and has not experienced the popularity of the other 10BASE standards.

9.2.2.6 Broadband (10BROAD36)

Broadband LANs use the same types of coaxial cable and components used in community antenna television (CATV) systems used for TV distribution in towns and apartment buildings. Such cable systems can carry analog signals over a wide range of frequencies up to 300 MHz and, for newer systems, up to 400 MHz.

Broadband systems use a tree-like topology employing splitters (Fig. 9-11). The root of the tree is known as the *headend*. Signals are applied to the cable at directional taps and travel in a single direction. Broadband LANs may use either a dual- or single-cable system. In a dual-cable system, two parallel cables are used throughout the tree-like structure and looped together at the headend.

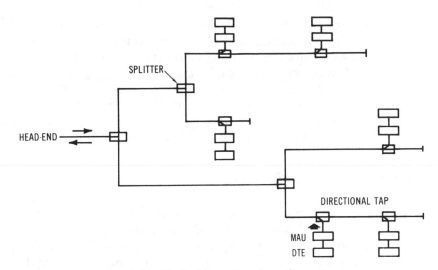

Fig. 9-11. Typical broadband configuration.

A MAU transmits on the inbound cable toward the headend where the signal loops onto the outbound cable and broadcasts to all MAUs.

In a single-cable system each transmission direction uses a different frequency.

With the midsplit system, inbound transmissions use the lower half of the frequency range and outbound transmissions use the upper half of the spectrum. A frequency translator at the headend shifts all inbound signals up in frequency and retransmits them on the outbound cable. Thus, the transmitter and receiver of a MAU will be on separate frequencies for a single-cable system.

Broadband systems use a 75-ohm coaxial cable. The trunk cable is generally aluminum sheathed. During the design of a broadband system, signal levels are calculated based on the attenuation of the cable, taps, and splitters. Amplifiers are inserted periodically in the cable system to maintain signal levels. With appropriate amplifiers, cable systems can be designed with a maximum length of several kilometers from the headend. IEEE 802.7-1989[15] provide guidelines for design of broadband systems for both 802.3- and 802.4-based systems.

Collision detection, based on signal levels, cannot be performed in broadband systems because of the variation in signal level at different points on the cable. Therefore, collision detection is usually performed using a bit comparison. That is, a transmitting MAU keeps a copy of its transmitted frame and compares this with the received frame. If they match for the duration required to acquire the cable, it is assumed no other MAU is transmitting. Due to differences in signal levels, a separate collision enforcement channel must be used to guarantee that all stations are reliably notified of a collision.

The current standards call for a 10-Mbps system with a maximum segment length of 3600 meters. A 25-meter drop from the cable to AUI is allowed and the AUI cable may be up to 50 meters long. Both single- and dual-cable systems are defined in the standard with a number of frequency options. The 10-Mbps system requires 18 MHz of bandwidth, 14 MHz for the data channel, and 4 MHz for the collision enforcement channel.

Besides the longer cable length, an advantage to the broadband option is the ability to use frequency division multiplexing (FDM) to incorporate additional channels on the cable plant. This is especially cost efficient where large cable plants are installed. Channels can be allocated for purposes such as closed circuit video, dedicated point-to-point connections, and voice channels.

9.2.3 Token Bus (IEEE 802.4)

The use of a token access protocol on a bus topology is the second of the three major options within IEEE 802. This is the option selected for the Manufacturers Automation Protocol (MAP). The scope of IEEE 802.4 (Fig. 9-12) is similar to the CSMA/CD option but without a distinct MAU physically separate from the DTE.[11]

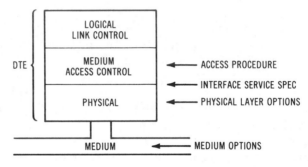

Fig. 9-12. Token bus option.

9.2.3.1 Media Access Control Sublayer

The frame format used in the token bus MAC sublayer (Fig. 9-13) is similar to that used in the CSMA/CD bus. The receiving modem uses the preamble to acquire signal level and phase lock. The preamble pattern depends on the modulation scheme and data rate; the duration must be at least two microseconds. The start delimiter consists of one octet that is distinguishable from frame data. The frame control octet determines the class of frame being sent: MAC control frames concerned with the token, LLC data frames, and MAC management data frames.

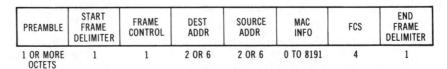

PREAMBLE	START FRAME DELIMITER	FRAME CONTROL	DEST ADDR	SOURCE ADDR	MAC INFO	FCS	END FRAME DELIMITER
1 OR MORE OCTETS	1	1	2 OR 6	2 OR 6	0 TO 8191	4	1

Fig. 9-13. Token bus media access control frame format.

Each token frame contains two address fields: the *destination address field* and the *source address field*. Addresses are either two or six octets in length; all addresses used on a given LAN are the same length. Six-octet addresses may be globally administered. The destination address may be an individual, group, or broadcast address. The source address is always an individual address.

Depending on the bit pattern specified in the frame's frame-control octet, the MAC data unit field can contain an LLC protocol data unit, MAC management data, or a value specific to one of the MAC control frames. The FCS is the same field as the ones used in other IEEE 802 options. Finally, there is an end delimiter that is always distinguishable from data and determines the position of the FCS.

The right to transmit, the token, passes among all the stations in a logically circular fashion. Each participating station knows the address of its predecessor (the station it got the token from), its successor (who the token should be sent to next), and also its own address. These predecessor and successor addresses are dynamically determined and maintained.

The token passes from station to station in numerically descending station-address order. Fig. 9-14 illustrates token passing for a simple 6-node configuration. Note that the numerical address of a station does not necessarily bear any relationship to its physical position on the bus. After each station has completed transmitting any data frames it may have, and has completed other

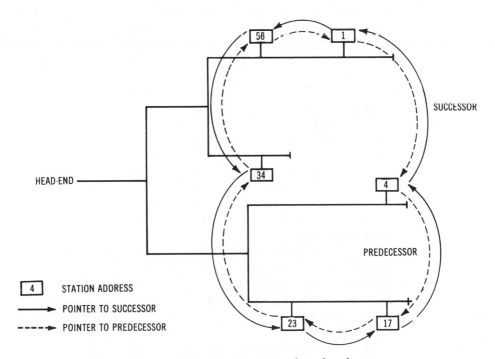

Fig. 9-14. Token passing in the token bus.

maintenance functions, the station passes the token to its successor frame and the station listens to make sure that its successor is active. If the sender hears a valid frame following, it assumes that its successor has the token and is operating correctly. If the token sender does not hear a valid frame after sending the token the first time, successive fall-back steps are taken to recover the token. First, the token-pass operation is repeated a second time. If the successor still does not respond, the sender assumes its successor has failed.

The sender now sends a *who_follows* broadcast frame containing its successor's address in the data field of the frame. Each station compares the address received with the address of its predecessor. If only one station has failed, the failed station's successor should recognize the who_follows frame and then send its address in a *set_successor* frame. The station holding the token then sets its successor the address contained in the set_successor frame, and the failed station has been spliced out of the logical ring.

If the sending station hears no response to a who_follows frame, it sends one more who_follows frame and, if it still doesn't receive a response, it assumes a more severe network failure has occurred. At this time, the station holding the token attempts to reestablish the logical ring by adding stations through the response-window technique. This technique is also used to splice stations back into the ring as required.

Solicit_successor frames are used to allow stations to join the ring. Stations must periodically issue solicit_successor frames and listen for a period of time called a *response window* that is one slot time in length. A *solicit_successor_1* frame offers an opportunity to join the ring to any station with an address between the current node's address and the address of its successor (remember, the stations are ordered in descending order.) A *solicit_successor_2* frame is used for the situation where the next frame has a higher address than its successor (when the "last" station loops back to the "first"). During normal operations, this is when stations join or rejoin the ring. When a station responds to a solicit_successor frame, it joins immediately behind the station that issued the frame. Set_successor frames are used to splice the new station into the logical ring. When more than one station responds to a single solicit_successor frame, a contention process is used to force the respondents to join one by one. When multiple stations respond to a solicit_successor frame, the issuing station sends a resolve_contention frame. The competing stations then select a 2-bit back-off delay (multiplied by a slot time) from bits within their address and try again. The back-off process repeats until each competing station has responded individually and joined the ring.

For a total network failure, the station holding the token issues a solicit_successor_2 frame with its own address as both the destination and source addresses. This special case indicates that any station may join the ring. Then a single station is selected through a contention process and a two-station ring is established. From then on, the process is the same as adding stations to a stable ring through use of solicit_successor_1 and solicit_successor_2 frames.

Ring initialization occurs in a similar manner except that a *claim_token* frame is used to establish the initial station for the ring. When a station(s) decides that ring initialization is required (by hearing no activity), it sends a claim_token frame with an information-field length that is a multiple of slot-times based on bits within its address. After sending the claim_token frame, the station listens to the medium. If activity is detected, that station loses and resigns from the initialization process. If silence is heard, the process is repeated until all the address bits of the station have been employed. The station that remains in the contest is the winner and begins adding stations using solicit_successor frames.

Stations are prohibited from monopolizing the bus through the *hi_pri_ token_hold_time* parameter. This limits the time that a station may hold the token before passing it on to the next station.

An optional priority mechanism provides for four priority classes. Stations not requesting a specific priority class default to the highest priority. Priority is implemented by allocating network bandwidth to the higher priority frames and only sending lower priority frames when there is sufficient bandwidth. Bandwidth utilization is determined by a station measuring the token rotation time for that station. The priority classes are assigned a *target_token_rotation time*. The frames are sent in priority order until the measured token-rotation time for that station plus the delay due to sending frames is higher than the *target_token_rotation time* for the highest priority frame class remaining.

9.2.3.2 Physical Layer and Medium

There are three particular types of physical layer and medium that are specified for the token bus.

1. Single-Channel Phase-Continuous FSK operating at 1 Mbps.
2. Single-Channel Phase-Coherent FSK operating at 5 and 10 Mbps.
3. Broadband bus operating at 1, 5, and 10 Mbps.

Guidelines for using these options are contained in IEEE 802.7-1989.

9.2.4 Token Ring (IEEE 802.5)

The third major option within IEEE 802 is the token ring.[14] That is, the use of a token MAC with a ring topology in contrast to the bus topology of the other options. This approach has several advantages over the CSMA/CD bus and is rapidly approaching the 802.3 options in popularity. One of the reasons for the popularity is that token-passing protocols are deterministic while contention-based protocols (such as IEEE 802.3) are probabilistic. Thus, IEEE 802.4 and IEEE 802.5 can be used in real-time systems while IEEE 802.3 should not.

The scope of the token ring is illustrated in Fig. 9-15. It encompasses a MAC service specification, MAC, and physical layer and medium options. The trunk-coupling unit is inserted in the trunk cable.

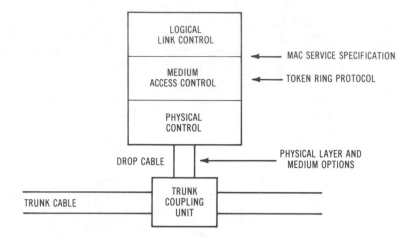

Fig. 9-15. Token ring option.

9.2.4.1 Media Access Control Sublayer

There are two basic formats used in the 802.5 standard: tokens and frames. Both formats begin with a *starting delimiter* (SD), which is a unique bit pattern indicating the start of the token or frame. Then an *access control field* (ACF) indicates whether the remaining bits contain a token or frame. Both tokens and frames also end with an *ending delimiter* (ED). The token contains only the SD, the ACF, and the ED while the frame also contains a frame control field, source and destination addresses, zero or more octets of data, an FCS, and a frame status field. The frame is very similar to that used by the token bus.

Like all the IEEE frame formats, the destination and source addresses may be two or six octets, but all stations on a local network must have the same address length. Six-octet addresses may be globally or locally administered. The destination address may be an individual or group address. The information field contains either LLC data or parameters in the case of a control frame. The FCS uses the same 32-bit CRC as the other 802 options. The frame status field contains two fields to indicate the intended recipient's response to the frame. When the frame is repeated by a station whose address matches the destination address, then the *address recognized bit* in the ending frame delimiter is turned on. If the frame is copied successfully at the destination address and the FCS balances, then the *frame-copied bit* is turned on.

The operation of the token ring is illustrated in Fig. 9-16. The physical connectivity of the medium establishes the logical connectivity of active stations on the ring. The token gives a station the opportunity to transmit frames. Each station around the ring repeats the data that it receives. Thus, a frame travels the full circle of the ring back to the source station which then removes the frame. A station passes the token to its physical successor when it has no more data to transmit, or when a token-holding timer has expired. The token

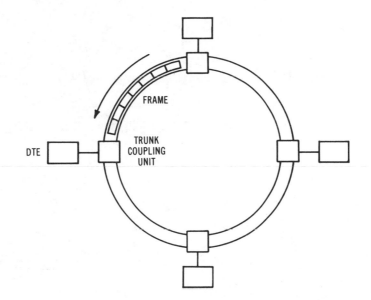

Fig. 9-16. Token ring operation.

may be reinserted either directly after the frame has been transmitted (early token release) or when the frame has traveled full circle and has been completely removed from the ring.

Priority is handled on the IEEE 802.5 token ring by attaching a priority value to both tokens and frames. Stations wishing to send priority PDUs *reserve* the ring by setting the reservation bits in the ACF as it repeats a frame. Then, only stations having PDUs of equal or higher priority than the reservation may claim the token. When the station that made the reservation completes its transmission, it lowers the token's priority to its original value before replacing it on the ring. Stacks are used to maintain order when one station increases the priority of a previous reservation. The station that makes the reservation is always charged with returning the reservation and priority to the value recorded when the reservation is made.

Ring maintenance is handled by designating one of the stations as *ring monitor*. This station is then responsible for dealing with lost and distorted tokens, orphan frames, priority failures, etc. The monitor station informs the other stations of its presence by transmitting *active monitor present frames* periodically. Timers are used throughout error monitoring and will cause a new active monitor to be established should the current active monitor fail.

9.2.4.2 Physical Layer and Medium

The original IEEE 802.5 specification (IEEE 802.5-1985)[12] defined 1- and 4-Mbps data rates. However, the current standard (IEEE 802.5-1989)[14] defines only 4- and 16-Mbps data rates. Transmission is over shielded twisted pair using differential Manchester encoding.

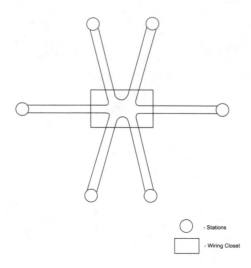

Fig. 9-17. Token ring wiring closet.

Although physically a ring, most configurations expect to use a "wiring closet" approach where the ring is formed at a central location and cables are extended to each of the stations (Fig. 9-17). This simplifies wiring and maintenance activities.

One interesting note, for IEEE 802.5, the bits of the information field are transmitted *most* significant bit first. The other IEEE 802 options, 802.3 and 802.4, transmit the information field *least* significant bit first.

9.2.5 IEEE Bridges (IEEE 802.1)

In addition to defining an overall architecture for LANs, the IEEE 802.1 Committee is developing standards for LAN bridges. Bridges are devices that allow LAN segments to be interconnected without the use of a higher-level protocol. Bridges differ from repeaters because their frames are regenerated in a store-and-forward manner. Therefore, bridges do not enter into any limitation specification within the standards. Thus, a LAN may be logically extended beyond the limits set forth in IEEE 802.X by using bridges to connect properly constrained segments. Further, bridges can serve as "firewalls" to prevent media failures from affecting all portions of the network. Bridges can also be used during system design to partition traffic for performance optimization.

The effort at developing a bridge standard has not proceeded smoothly because of two different approaches being vigorously supported by different factions. The solution has been to first consider both as options. Then, to modify one option to insure compatibility with the other. The two options will be briefly discussed here.

One option, the *spanning tree* option, is completely transparent to all stations and requires no modification of existing systems. This option is proposed for the IEEE 802.3 networks. The bridges interact with each other and, after selecting a "root," create a logical tree which can provide a path between any two LAN segments. Any paths that are redundant with the logical tree are deactivated to avoid loops. It is possible, and perhaps probable, that many spanning trees will not be optimal for certain wiring configurations. No active redundancy is allowed, but fault recovery is provided by activating redundant paths if necessary.

The other option, the *source routing* option, requires the transmitting station to embed routing information in the frame. In this case, the bridges follow the instructions received from the originating station and do not know anything about the overall network topology. In this way, redundancy can be employed with the stations deciding on alternative routes. This approach has been proposed for the IEEE 802.5 token ring system.

The final compromise has been to develop a *source routing transparent* (SRT) bridge that supports source routing when it is present and otherwise acts as a transparent bridge. In this manner, 802.5 LANs may be interconnected with 802.3 and 802.4 LANs.

9.2.6 Other IEEE 802 Standards

In addition to the three main groups of LAN standards, 802.3, 802.4, and 802.5, the IEEE 802 Standards Committee has numerous other LAN-standards activities underway in eleven subcommittees, 802.1 through 802.11. Some of these activities are briefly summarized in this section.

The IEEE 802.6 standard is for metropolitan area networks up to and exceeding 50 kilometers in diameter. The standard, also known as *distributed queue dual bus* (DQDB) *metropolitan area network* (MAN), defines a high-speed, shared medium access protocol for use over a dual unidirectional bus subnetwork. DQDB subnetworks may be interconnected via bridges, routers, and gateways to form a MAN. The 802.6 standard forms the basis for the Switched Multimegabit Data Service (SMDS) which is expected to be offered as a service by Local Exchange Carriers.

DQDB is based on a distributed queue access mechanism developed in Australia known as *queued packet and synchronous switch* (QPSX).[20] The dual bus architecture of a DQDB subnetwork consists of two unidirectional buses that provide full duplex communications between a linear set of nodes. The basic concept is that a node, wishing to transmit, issues a request on the upstream bus in order to access a slot on the downstream bus. Each node, by counting the number of requests it receives and unused slots that pass, can determine the number of segments queued ahead of it. This counting operation establishes a single-ordered queue across the subnetwork of segments queued for access to each bus.

A DQDB subnetwork supports connectionless data transfer, connection-oriented data transfer, and isochronous communications such as voice. The physical layer is defined to allow the use of different underlying transmission systems. The proposed standard includes support for DS3 channels (44.736 Mbps) and CCITT specified transmission systems operating at 34.368 Mbps, 139.264 Mbps, and 155.520 Mbps.

The IEEE 802.7 Committee has completed its work and developed "802.7-1989 IEEE Recommended Practices for Broadband Local Area Networks."[13] This set of guidelines applies to 802.2 and 802.4. The IEEE 802.8 Committee is working on a fiber-optics-based standard and serves as an advisory group to other committees using fiber optics (such as 802.3). The IEEE 802.9 is concerned with ISDN issues.

The IEEE 802.10 Committee is developing security standards for the various LANs. The security services will provide users with integrity, confidentiality, or both. Encryption and key management mechanisms are being defined. Finally, the IEEE 802.11 is exploring the use of wireless LANs using media such as radio and infrared.

9.3 Fiber Distributed Data Interface (FDDI)

The *fiber distributed data interface* (FDDI) is a 100-Mbps LAN using a token ring architecture with optical fiber as the transmission medium. FDDI was developed by Subcommittee X3T9 of the Accredited Standards Committee on Information Processing Systems, X3. In 1983 the FDDI effort was initiated to meet the need for a network with a much higher data rate than the LANs which were being developed by IEEE Project 802. The FDDI is intended to be used both among and between processors as well as for their high-performance peripherals. IEEE 802.5 formed the basis for the FDDI protocol.

FDDI adopts the same protocol architectural model as IEEE 802. It encompasses the lower half of the data link layer and the physical layer; the IEEE 802.2 LLC protocol can be used as the upper half of the data link layer. The basic FDDI consists of four component standards (Fig. 9-18).

1. *Medium Access Control (MAC)*—specifies access to the medium, addressing, data checking, and frame generation/reception (ANSI X3.139-1987).
2. *Physical Layer Protocol (PHY)*—specifies the encode/decode, clocking, and data framing (ANSI X3.148-1988).
3. *Physical Layer Medium Dependent (PMD)*—specifies the optical fiber link and related optical components (ANSI X3.166-1989).
4. *Station Management (SMT)*—specifies the control required for proper operation of stations in an FDDI ring.

The basic FDDI consists of a set of stations serially connected by a dual optical-fiber transmission medium to form a closed-loop comprising two counterrotating logical rings. The fiber links between stations may normally be up to 2 km in length; configurations of up to 500 stations and a total fiber

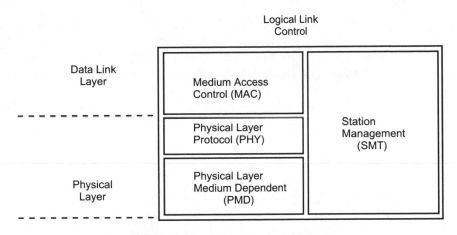

Fig. 9-18. FDDI protocol architecture.

path length of 100 km are supported by the default values of FDDI parameters. Two classes of stations are defined: a dual attachment station that connects directly to the dual rings, and a dual attachment concentrator to connect multiple stations in a tree topology that, while logically part of the ring, are physically connected at a single point. Thus, an FDDI network topology consists of one dual ring with multiple trees attached to it as shown in Fig. 9-19.

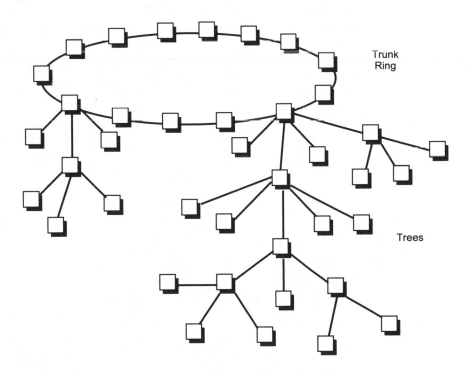

Fig. 9-19. FDDI ring of trees topology.

A station may insert information onto the ring only when it captures the token. Information is transmitted from station to station round the ring, with each station generally regenerating the signal. The addressed destination station copies the information as it passes; the station that originated the information removes it from the ring.

The four components of the standard are described in the remainder of this section.

9.3.1 Media Access Control

The MAC sublayer provides fair and deterministic access to the medium, address recognition, and generation and verification of FCSs. Its primary function is the delivery of frames, including frame insertion, repetition, and removal.[6]

A station gains the right to transmit its information onto the medium when it detects a token passing on the medium. The token is a control signal comprised of a unique symbol sequence that circulates on the medium following each information transmission. Any station, upon detection of a token, may capture the token by removing it from the ring. The station may then transmit one or more frames of information. At the completion of its information transmission, the station transmits a new token, which provides other stations the opportunity to gain access to the ring.

MAC data is transmitted as variable length frames containing up to 4500 octets of information. The token is represented by a specific, short fixed-length frame. The format of the frame and token is shown in Fig. 9-20. The preamble consists of eight or more octets used for establishing and maintaining clock synchronization between frames. The SD immediately following the preamble indicates the start of a valid frame. The frame control field distin-

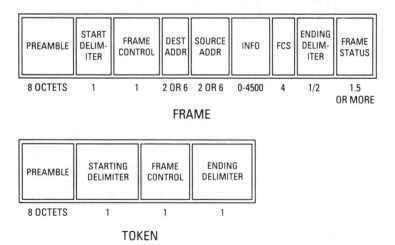

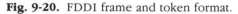

Fig. 9-20. FDDI frame and token format.

guishes a token or frame. It also defines the service class (synchronous or asynchronous) for frames, the length of the address fields (16 or 48 bits), and the MAC service access point. A token is completed with an ED. For frames, the frame control is followed by the destination address and source address, the information field, the FCS, the ED, and the frame status. The destination address may identify an individual, group, or broadcast address. The 48-bit address may be locally or universally administered; they use the same address structure as IEEE 802 LANs, and the universal addresses are administered by the IEEE Standards Office. The FCS uses the same CRC as IEEE 802 LANs. The frame status field is used to indicate when an error has been detected in the frame, when the addressed station has recognized its address, and when the frame has been copied by the station.

Two classes of service are supported: synchronous and asynchronous. The synchronous class of service is used for those applications whose bandwidth and response time limits are predictable in advance, thus permitting them to be preallocated. The asynchronous class of service is used for those applications whose bandwidth requirements are less predictable or whose response time requirements are less critical. The bandwidth required for synchronous traffic is allocated from the total available for FDDI traffic. Asynchronous bandwidth is instantaneously allocated from the pool of remaining ring bandwidths that are unallocated, unused, or both.

9.3.2 Physical Layer

The physical layer is divided into two sublayers: a physical layer protocol which specifies the upper sublayer, and a physical layer media-dependent standard which specifies the lower sublayer. The physical layer protocol specifies the data encode/decode, framing, and clocking requirements.[7] The physical layer media-dependent standard specifies the power levels and characteristics of the optical transmitter and receiver, interface optical signal requirements including jitter, the connector receptacle footprint, the requirements of conforming FDDI optical fiber cable plants, and the permissible bit-error rates.[3]

The MAC conveys information to the physical layer by a continuous stream, or sequence, of symbols. Symbols are used to convey three types of information: *line status* (such as quiet, halt, or idle), *control symbols* (used with SD, ED, or control indicator sequences), and *data symbols* (each representing four data bits). Each symbol is transmitted on the medium as a code group of five code bits. FDDI uses coding to combine data and clock in a serial baseband transmission. In the coding technique, known as *nonreturn-to-zero-invert* on ones (NRZI), a polarity transition represents a logical one and the absence of a transition denotes a logical zero. Only 24 of the 32 possible five-code bit sequences are required to represent the data, control, and line status symbols. These are assigned so that the code bit stream on the transmission medium contains at least two transitions for each transmitted symbol and is thus self clocking; the assignment also avoids an unacceptable number of consecutive zeros on the transmission medium and also avoids an unacceptable DC component.

A receiver recovers the clock used by the transmitter of the upstream station. Since the local clock used to control outgoing bits may differ slightly from the incoming frequency, an elasticity buffer is used to compensate for the difference. Idle symbols, which make up the preamble, are inserted or deleted to compensate for the difference in frequencies.

Stations are connected by a 62.5/125 micrometer multimode optical fiber up to 2 km in length. That means the nominal core diameter is 62.5 μm and the cladding diameter is 125 μm. Light-emitting diodes are used, transmitting at a nominal frequency of 1325 nm. As an FDDI option, any station may have a bypass. When the station's power is off, the station is automatically in the bypass mode and the in-bound medium is connected to the out-bound medium.

9.3.3 Station Management

The station-management standard covers connection management, station insertion and removal, station initialization, configuration management, fault isolation and recovery, and collection of statistics.[5] It is concerned with establishing and maintaining the physical and logical topology of the FDDI network.

The most general physical topology of an FDDI network is a dual ring of trees. All physical connections in an FDDI topology are duplex links. In a fully connected trunk ring, a duplex link supports counterrotating rings; and in a tree, the duplex link provides transmit and receive paths for one of the dual rings. Thus, two independent token/data paths may exist in a single, fault-free FDDI, one in each direction around the ring. If a station or link in the ring fails, the stations on either side of the failure automatically reconfigure, making use of their links in the reverse direction to create a single ring. The ring is then said to be *wrapped*. The maximum of 500 stations and a complete, dual fiber-path length of 100 km corresponds to up to 1000 physical connections and a path length of 200 km between the two rings.

9.3.4 Status and Evolution

Three of the components' standards of the basic FDDI were approved as the American National Standards in 1987–1989. The fourth component, station management, is likely to be approved in 1991. FDDI is also being processed as an International Standard. Commercial products based on the FDDI standard started to appear in the marketplace in 1989 from companies that include Communication Machinery Corporation, Digital Equipment Corporation, Fibronics, and Sun Microsystems. Most of these products use an FDDI chip set from Advanced Micro Devices (AMD).

Several proposed extensions to FDDI are under development. A single-mode fiber version of the physical layer medium-dependent standard will increase the permissible fiber links from 2 km to 60 km.[4] FDDI II adds the capability for circuit-switched services in addition to the packet services of the basic FDDI.[2] FDDI II employs a cycle structure to multiplex packet data and circuit-switched data on the same ring. FDDI II also provides synchronized channels at fixed data rates where a channel is identified by the location of its time slot. The bandwidth is divided into 16 wideband channels, each with a data rate of 6.1444 Mbps and a minimum of 768 kbps available for packet service. Any wideband channel not assigned for circuit service is available for use by the packet service.

9.4 Other Related Protocols

Most IEEE 802 LAN installations utilize the TCP/IP Protocol (Transmission Control Protocol/Internet Protocol) Suite.[8,9] The OSI protocols[18] are now emerging and can be expected to take their place along with the TCP/IP Suite for a period of several years. A number of protocols have been developed specifically for LAN systems. For example, two protocols specific to LAN systems have been specified within the TCP/IP Suite.

The *Address Resolution Protocol* (ARP) is designed to allow stations on a LAN to determine the LAN physical address of a station, given its IP internet address.[21] The LAN broadcast option is used to broadcast an ARP-based message asking all stations if any of them have the named internet address. The station actually assigned that address responds with a packet and the source address in the response identifies the station corresponding to the named IP internet address.

The *Reverse Address Resolution Protocol* (RARP) is used by diskless workstations to learn their IP internet address.[10] Again, a broadcast message is employed and a name server translates the LAN physical address to an IP internet address and responds.

These are just two examples of several protocols that are dependent on the LAN broadcast message capability. Broadcast messages provide the capability to query all stations on the LAN for many reasons. Unfortunately, broadcast messages cause difficulties for bridges and routers and these protocols often will not function properly on large concatenated LANs.

9.5 References

1. American National Standards Institute. *American National Standard, Advanced Data Communications Control Procedures*, ANSI X3.66-1979.

2. ———. *American National Standard (Draft Proposed), Fiber Distributed Data Interface (FDDI)—Hybrid Ring Control (HRC)*, ASC X3T9.5, Rev 6, May 1990, (FDDI-II, ANSI X3.186-199x).

3. ———. *American National Standard, Fiber Distributed Data Interface (FDDI)—Physical Layer Medium Dependent (PMD)*, ANSI X3.166-1989.

4. ———. *American National Standard (Draft Proposed), Fiber Distributed Data Interface (FDDI)—Single-Mode Fiber Physical Layer Medium Dependent (SMF-PMD)*, ASC X3T9.5, Rev 4.2, May 1990, (ANSI X3.184-199x).

5. ———. *American National Standard (Draft Proposal), Fiber Distributed Data Interface (FDDI) Station Management (SMT)*, ASC X3T9.5, Rev 6.2, May 1990.

6. ———. *American National Standard, Fiber Distributed Data Interface (FDDI)—Token Ring Media Access Control (MAC)*, ANSI X3.139-1987.

7. ———. *American National Standard, Fiber Distributed Data Interface (FDDI)—Token Ring Physical Layer Protocol (PHY)*, ANSI X3.148-1988.

8. Defense Communications Agency. *Military Standard Internet Protocol*, MIL-STD 1777, August 12, 1983.

9. ———. *Military Standard Transmission Control Protocol*, MIL-STD 1778, August 12, 1983.

10. Finlayson, R., T. Mann, J.C. Mogul, and M. Theirmer, *Reverse Address Resolution Protocol*, RFC 903, June, 1984.

11. Institute of Electrical and Electronic Engineers. *ANSI/IEEE Standard, Token-Passing Bus Access Method*, ANSI/IEEE Std 802.4-1985.

12. ———. *ANSI/IEEE Standard, Token Ring Access Method*, ANSI/IEEE Std 802.5-1985.

13. ———. *IEEE Recommended Practice, Broadband Local Area Networks*, IEEE Std 802.7-1989.

14. ———. *IEEE Standard, Token Ring Access Method*, IEEE Std 802.5-1989.

15. ———. *Supplements to Carrier Sense Multiple Access with Collision Detection*, ANSI/IEEE Std 802.3a, b, c, and e-1988.

16. International Organization for Standardization. *ANSI/IEEE Std 802.3-1988, Information Processing Systems—Local Area Networks—Part 3: Carrier Sense Multiple Access With Collision Detection (CSMA/CD)*

Access Method And Physical Layer Specifications. ISO 8802-3 : 1989 (E), 1989.

17. ———. *IEEE Std 802.2-1989, Information Processing Systems, Local Area Networks—Part 2, Logical Link Control*, ISO 8802-2: 1989 (E), 1989.

18. ———. *International Standard ISO 8073, Open Systems Interconnection—Connection-Oriented Transport Protocol Specification*, 1986.

19. Metcalfe, R.M. and D.R. Boggs. "Ethernet: Distributed Packet Switching for Local Computer Networks", *Communications of the ACM*, July, 1976, pp. 395–404.

20. Newman, R.M., Z.L. Budrikis, and J.L. Hullett. "The QPSX MAN," *IEEE Communications Magazine*, April 1988, pp 20–28.

21. Plummer, D.C. *Ethernet Address Resolution Protocol: Or Converting Network Protocol Addresses to 48 Bit Ethernet Addresses for Transmission on Ethernet Hardware*, RFC 826, November, 1982.

22. Shoch, J.F. et al. "Evolution of the Ethernet Local Computer Network", *Computer*, August 1982, pp. 10–26.

Error Control

Joseph P. Odenwalder

Joseph P. Odenwalder is an Assistant Vice-President at Titan Linkabit, Corp., San Diego, CA. At Linkabit, he is responsible for the system engineering and analysis for several military and commercial communication systems. Since joining Linkabit in 1972, Dr. Odenwalder has been involved in the selection, analysis, and development of error-control systems for applications with many different performance requirements and channel characteristics. He has also been involved in developing approaches for obtaining code synchronization, resolving modem phase ambiguities, obtaining received symbol quality information, dispersing the symbols in channel error bursts, and performing other operations associated with the application of error-control coding.

Before joining Titan Linkabit Corp., Dr. Odenwalder worked for Hughes Aircraft Co. where he did analysis and simulation studies of radar systems.

Dr. Odenwalder received a B.S. degree in electrical engineering from Rose-Hulman Institute of Technology in 1963, the M.S. degree in electrical engineering from Purdue University in 1964, and the Ph.D. degree from the University of California, Los Angeles, in 1970. His Ph.D. dissertation concerned Viterbi decoding of convolutional codes and concatenated coding with a Viterbi-decoded convolutional inner code and a Reed-Solomon outer code.

10.1 Introduction

A primary concern in any digital communication system is the reliability with which transmitted data sequences can be received at the destination. Whenever the destination data is not the same as the source data over some measurement interval, quite often one bit, an error is said to have occurred. If the number of errors over some time period, or the average error rate, is greater than what can be tolerated, some means of improving the reliability of the data transfer is required. One approach to improving the communication reliability is to improve the transmission medium. For example, if the communication link was from a satellite to a terrestrial terminal, the satellite radiated power or the terminal antenna gain could be increased. Usually a less costly approach is to add error-control processing at the transmit and receive terminals. This chapter addresses these error-control processing approaches.

Fig. 10-1 gives a block diagram of a digital communication system with a channel encoder and a channel decoder added for error-control processing. The digital source represents a digital source device or an analog source that has been digitized, i.e., analog-to-digital (A/D) converted to a digital sequence. Ideally, the source data will also have been source encoded,[51] if necessary, to minimize the number of bits that are required to describe the source information. Source decoding would be used to recover an estimate of the original source data. This *source encoding* and *decoding* should not be confused with the channel encoding and decoding, which is used for error control.[10]

Everything between the channel encoder and the channel decoder is, as far as the error-control coding is concerned, the *channel*. This channel includes the physical channel and the modulator and demodulator. An important step in selecting a good error-control approach is a careful characterization of this channel.

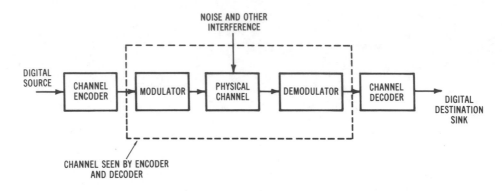

Fig. 10-1. Digital communications system with channel encoding and decoding for error control.

The *channel coding* provides error control with signal-processing approaches. The encoder adds redundancy in a manner that makes it easier for the decoder to select the correct sequence even in the presence of channel-induced errors. This redundancy is added in such a way that the decoder decision on any information symbol can be based on several received channel symbols rather than only one, as is usually the case in uncoded systems.

This chapter provides a description of a variety of error-control approaches with the emphasis on those approaches that are most likely to be encountered in present and future (especially satellite communication) applications. The approaches are described from a system engineering point of view that stresses performance, implementation complexity, and other system issues, such as synchronization, which must be considered in selecting an error-control approach.

Section 10.2 provides an overview of the fundamental concepts of coding with a discussion of the issues that should be considered in selecting an error-control approach and a summary of the characteristics and limits of the basic approaches.

Sections 10.3 and 10.4 cover linear block- and convolutional-coding approaches, respectively. Particular attention is given to a description of Viterbi decoding of convolutional codes because this approach is so widely used and because an understanding of the issues addressed there is also important in understanding other decoding approaches.

Section 10.5 covers error-control approaches for burst-noise channels.

10.2 Fundamental Concepts of Coding

Before attempting to select an error-control approach, a review of the performance expected of the approach, the channel environment in which it must operate, and any implementation or system issues that could affect the approach in the particular application must be considered.

10.2.1 Issues Affecting the Selection of an Error-Control Approach

Ideally an engineer should be familiar with the applicable following items before selecting an error-control approach:

1. The required information throughput rate.
2. The allowed throughput delay for the channel encoding and decoding.
3. The acceptable bandwidth expansion.
4. The modem modulation, symbol-rate, tracking-accuracy, phase ambiguity, and bit-slip characteristics.
5. The characteristics of the bursts on bursty channels in terms of the duration and attenuation of the bursts, their periodic or random nature, the guard space between bursts or their duty cycle, and the availability and reliability of information on the occurrence of a burst that could be given to the decoder.
6. The burst rate and duty cycle of the received data and the suitability of using a decoder at the smoothed average rate, rather than the burst rate.
7. The characteristics of any mutual-user or hostile jamming.
8. The robustness that is required of the error-control approach in the presence of channel variations.
9. The availability and characteristics of a return channel.
10. The availability of soft receiver decisions (quality information) for the decoder and the accuracy of the automatic gain control (AGC) that is used to obtain such information.
11. The decoder synchronization-time and loss-of-sync requirements.[52]
12. The bit, symbol, or message error probability (or rate)* or other measure of performance that is required versus some system parameter such as the information bit energy-to-noise ratio (E_b/N_0), the carrier power-to-noise density ratio (C/N_0), or the channel bit error rate (p).
13. The allowed rate of accepting incorrect messages.
14. The suitability of using a coding approach that uses more redundancy for a few disadvantaged users in the system than for other users who already have an adequate link performance.
15. The number of separately encoded sequences that must be simultaneously decoded.
16. The vulnerability of the destination data sink to bursts of errors from the decoder.
17. The cost, size, weight, and power restrictions.

---

* The terms *error probability* and *error rate* are used interchangeably here and in practice. Both terms refer to the average number of errors over some long measurement interval.

Most of these items are self-explanatory or will be discussed later. However, comments are warranted here on a few items. In Item 3, the *bandwidth expansion* refers to the fact that channel encoders add redundancy which, for a fixed source symbol rate, means a higher channel symbol rate and hence, in general, a larger bandwidth is required.[21] In bandwidth-limited situations, only a small amount of redundancy is acceptable. Higher-order modulation alphabet sizes, along with channel coding, can also sometimes be used in such a situation.[20]

In Item 4, the *phase-ambiguity characteristics*, in particular, should be noted. If the modem can lock up to a signal that is 180° or ±90° out of phase, *differential encoding* or *decoding* can be used with some codes, but much better performance is achieved when the differential coding is placed outside, rather than inside, the channel coding. Channel codes can also be selected such that the decoder is capable of resolving phase ambiguities without the need for differential coding. This is discussed further in Section 10.4 under Viterbi decoding of convolutional codes.

The concept of *soft receiver quantization* noted in Item 10, as opposed to *hard quantization*, is important and will be discussed further later. However, as an example, consider a system with *binary phase-shift keying* (BPSK) *modulation*. With hard receiver quantization, the demodulator merely tells the decoder if the demodulator output for each symbol was positive or negative. With soft receiver quantization, the demodulator also provides one or more additional bits of information describing the degree of confidence the demodulator had in the sign decision. In this case, the confidence level just depends on the magnitude of the demodulator output.

10.2.2 Coding Approaches and Characteristics

Error control can be approached using *forward-error-control* (FEC), *automatic-repeat-request* (ARQ), or *hybrid FEC-ARQ* approaches. With an FEC approach, the decoder automatically corrects as many channel errors as possible, or more precisely, it makes an estimate of the transmitted sequence based on hard- or soft-decision inputs without the aid of a communication link back to the transmitting terminal. With an ARQ approach, the decoder merely detects errors and makes use of a communication link back to the transmitting terminal (a *reverse link*) to ask to have the incorrectly received frame, or group of symbols sent again. These requests can be repeated until, hopefully, the frame is received correctly. Of course, for a fixed channel symbol rate, the repeated transmissions reduce the information throughput rate of the system.

In an ARQ system, an error occurs whenever the error-detection decoder incorrectly accepts a frame of data with errors. Usually the probability of such undetected errors can be made small by adding enough redundancy in the *error-detecting code*. These error-detecting codes are discussed in Section 10.3.3.

Another measure of performance for an ARQ system is its *throughput effi-*

ciency, which is defined as the ratio of the total number of information bits accepted by the decoder per unit time to the total number of bits that could have been transmitted in the same amount of time if the ARQ approach had not been used. This efficiency depends upon the channel error characteristics, the data rate, the propagation delay time, the frame length, and the characteristics of the ARQ protocol that is used. Three basic types of ARQ protocols are used: stop-and-wait ARQ, go-back-*N* ARQ, and selective repeat ARQ.

With the *stop-and-wait* ARQ approach, the transmit terminal sends one frame at a time and waits for an acknowledgment from the receive terminal* that the frame was accepted by the error-detection decoder before the next frame is sent. If the error-detection decoder at the receive terminal detects an error, it responds with a negative acknowledgment, and the transmit terminal sends the same frame again. Since this approach only requires that information be sent in one direction at a time, a half-duplex channel would suffice. The simplicity of this approach makes it attractive for some applications where the inefficiency involved in waiting for an acknowledgment is not excessive. This approach is usually not suitable for systems that use satellite links where, typically, the product of the propagation time times the data rate is large compared to the frame length. The use of larger frame lengths would reduce the idle-time inefficiency up to some point, but as the frame length is increased further, each frame becomes more likely to have an error and the retransmission of these frames begins to reduce the throughput efficiency.

Another approach to reducing the idle-time inefficiency in the stop-and-wait ARQ approach is to use a *continuous ARQ* approach. That is, have the transmit terminal send frames continuously without waiting for an acknowledgment that the frame was accepted and to have the receive terminal notify the transmit terminal of any missed frames on a simultaneously available reverse channel. Since the transmit terminal would have sent additional frames before it knows that the receive terminal missed a particular frame, it could go back some number of frames, depending on the round-trip delay in frame time delay intervals, and begin transmitting the frames again in sequence from that point. This is called a *go-back-N ARQ* approach. It is more effective than the stop-and-wait ARQ approach, but it becomes inefficient when *N* becomes large. The inefficiency can be overcome by asking to have only the specific frames that were missed retransmitted. That is, by using a *selective-repeat ARQ* approach. The disadvantage of the selective-repeat ARQ approach compared to the go-back-*N* approach is that if data must be presented to the user in the correct sequence, as is usually the case, then the selective-repeat ARQ approach requires extra buffering in the receive terminal for this frame reordering.

ARQ systems provide a good approach to reliable communication in some applications, especially those where channel errors occur in bursts. However, when random errors are also an important factor, the throughput efficiency of those approaches falls rapidly with increasing channel error rates.[40] A good

---

* The transmit and receive terminals referred to here are the source and destination points, respectively, for the forward-direction data frames.

approach in such an application is to use a hybrid ARQ approach where some FEC coding is used to correct the more common (especially randomly distributed) errors and then an ARQ scheme is used to drive the error rate down to the desired level. In such a hybrid approach, powerful random-error-correcting codes that take advantage of soft receiver decisions can be used; then, the hard-decision FEC-decoded data can be used with standard ARQ protocols. The FEC and ARQ approaches can also be combined in hybrid ARQ schemes where the ARQ protocol does not operate independently outside the FEC coding operations. S. Lin and D.J. Costello[25] give a good summary of such hybrid ARQ approaches.

FEC codes can be classified as block or convolutional. Block codes process data in blocks that are independent of one another.[37] A block encoder accepts data in blocks of k symbols, usually binary, and provides output encoded data in blocks of n symbols. Since redundancy is added, n will be larger than k. The ratio k/n is called the *code rate*, or usually just *rate* (R). That is, $R = k/n$ where $0 < R < 1$. This code rate should not be confused with the data rate of the code, which is the rate at which information is given to the encoder and which is typically measured in bits per second (bps). Note that the rate out of the encoder, referred to as the *channel data rate*, is $1/R$ times larger than the data rate.

Convolutional codes can also be described as providing n output symbols for each group of k input symbols. The difference is that any n-symbol convolutional encoder output depends not only on the last set of k input symbols but also on several preceding sets of input symbols. Also, with convolutional codes, k and n are much smaller than with block codes. As with block codes, the code rate is defined as $R = k/n$.

The reciprocal of the code rate is sometimes called the *bandwidth expansion* since adding coding increases the required channel symbol rate by this amount. Low-rate codes have a greater error-detection-and-correction potential than high-rate codes,[36] but they also have a larger bandwidth expansion.

10.2.3 Channel Characterization

Determining the characteristics of a communication channel can be a difficult task because these characteristics are very dependent on the properties of the particular communications medium, the equipment that is used, and even the effect of the other users on the communications medium.

One type of channel interference that is always present is that due to the thermal noise resulting from the random electron motion in the communication medium and equipment. This noise can be characterized by an additive uniform distribution of energy over a wide frequency range with a Gaussian level distribution. More precisely, the model for this type of interference is called *additive white Gaussian noise* (AWGN). It is a good model for most satellite communication links and for other high-quality links where other sources of interference do not become the dominant factor affecting the link.

On telephone channels used for the transmission of digital data, other sources of interference with impulse, or bursty, characteristics are usually the dominant type of interference. These impulses on the line typically have a duration of about 10 ms.[43] The papers listed in References 2 and 11 give some results of a 1969/1970 survey that was performed to measure the characteristics of a variety of telephone channels.

An important characteristic of channels, for the purpose of error control, is the burst, or memory, properties of the channel. Section 10.5 describes error-control approaches that can be used on bursty channels, or channels with memory. The majority of the rest of the chapter is concerned with memoryless channels or channels that can be made approximately memoryless, as far as the coding is concerned, with the use of the interleaving approaches discussed in Section 10.5.

A particularly simple, but important, channel is the binary input, binary output, channel for which the probability of receiving the symbol "1" when the symbol "0" was transmitted is equal to the probability of receiving a "0" when a "1" was transmitted. Such a channel is called a *binary symmetric channel* (BSC) and it can be represented by the channel transition probability diagram of Fig. 10-2. In this case, the transition probability (p) is the probability of a channel error, and it completely describes the channel. This transition probability depends on the type of modulation and the noise characteristics. For example, when BPSK modulation is used on a physical channel with additive white Gaussian noise (AWGN), p is given by

$$p = Q(\sqrt{2E_s/N_0}) \tag{10-1}$$

where,

$$Q(x) = (1/\sqrt{2\pi}) \int_{-x}^{\infty} \exp(-y^2/2)\,dy \tag{10-2}$$

is the Q-function

E_s/N_0 is the channel symbol energy-to-noise power spectral density ratio.

When soft receiver quantization with, say, q bits is available, the demodulator can quantize its output to any one of 2^q output intervals. Fig. 10-3 illustrates

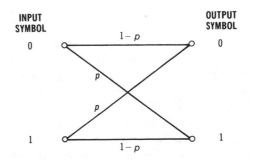

Fig. 10-2. Binary-symmetric-channel (BSC) transition-probability diagram.

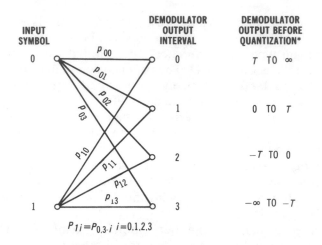

INPUT SYMBOL

DEMODULATOR OUTPUT INTERVAL

DEMODULATOR OUTPUT BEFORE QUANTIZATION*

0 p_{00} 0 T TO ∞

p_{01}

p_{02} 1 0 TO T

p_{03}

p_{10} 2 $-T$ TO 0

p_{11}

p_{12}

1 p_{13} 3 $-\infty$ TO $-T$

$$P_{1i} = P_{0,3-i} \quad i = 0,1,2,3$$

*T IS A QUANTIZATION THRESHOLD PARAMETER THAT IS CHOSEN TO OPTIMIZE THE PERFORMANCE OF THE SYSTEM.

Fig. 10-3. Channel transition-probability diagram for an AWGN channel with BPSK modulation and 2-bit soft receiver quantization.

the channel transition-probability diagram for such a case. This example is for an AWGN channel with BPSK modulation and 2-bit soft receiver quantization. In general, a *discrete memoryless channel* with an arbitrary number of inputs and outputs can be defined by giving the transition probabilities that specify the probability of receiving each output for each possible transmitted symbol.

The decoder output error-rate performance of error-control coding approaches on discrete memoryless channels is usually accomplished using analysis, simulation, or hardware test-set measurements based on these transition probabilities. For example, in a hardware test set-up or a computer simulation, random input data would be encoded and this encoded data would be modified in a pseudo-random manner, as indicated by the channel transition probability diagram, to obtain a q-bit input for the decoder. The decoder output would then be compared with a delayed copy of the encoder input sequence to see if errors occurred.

10.2.4 Coding Limits

C.E. Shannon[42] has shown that for any input-discrete finite-memory channel it is possible to find a code that achieves any arbitrarily small probability of error if the code rate (R) is less than some quantity called the channel capacity (C), and conversely, it is not possible to find such a code when the code rate is greater than the channel capacity. Unfortunately, this result is based on considering the ensemble of all possible codes; thus, it is only an existence theorem. Engineers are still faced with the task of finding a code with a reasonable implementation complexity that satisfies their error-probability requirements. While Shannon's result is an existence theorem, it is helpful to compare the channel quality (e.g.,

E_b/N_0, or channel error rate) required to achieve a given performance for a particular coding technique and code rate with the limiting channel quality possible for arbitrarily small output error rates at that code rate.

Another quality that frequently arises in describing the performance of coded communication systems is the *computational cut-off rate* (R_0). Upper bounds on the error-rate performance of randomly selected block and convolutional codes used on discrete memoryless channels show that for $O < R < R_0$, it is possible to achieve arbitrarily small error probabilities by increasing the complexity of the code.[55] With large-constraint-length sequential-coded convolutional codes (which will be discussed later), R_0 is the upper limit of code rates where the average amount of decoding computation per information bit is finite. This function also provides a useful measure for quickly comparing the potential benefits of coding on channels with different (e.g., quantization) characteristics.

For the binary symmetric channel (BSC) of Fig. 10-2, R_0 and C are given by[55]

$$R_0 = -\log_2\left[1/2 + \sqrt{p(1-p)}\right] \tag{10-3}$$

and

$$C = 1 + p\log_2 p + (1-p)\log_2(1-p) \tag{10-4}$$

where,
 p is the channel error rate.

Fig. 10-4 gives plots of the maximum channel error rate possible for $R \leq C$ and for $R \leq R_0$ from these equations versus the coding bandwidth expansion. This illustration shows, for example, that with a bandwidth expansion of 2 (i.e., $R = 1/2$), error-correcting coding is only useful (i.e., $R < C$) when the channel error rate (or probability) is less than 0.11. It also shows that with this bandwidth expansion, most coding techniques will require a channel error rate of less than 0.045 (i.e., $R \leq R_0$).

At the opposite extreme from the hard-decision channel represented by the BSC, consider an AWGN channel with BPSK or quadrature phase-shift keying (QPSK) modulation and no quantization.* In this case R_0 and C are given by[55]

$$R_0 = 1 - \log_2\left[1 + \exp\left(-R\frac{E_b}{N_0}\right)\right] \tag{10-5}$$

and

$$C = \left(\frac{1}{2}\right)\log_2\left(1 + 2R\frac{E_b}{N_0}\right) \tag{10-6}$$

---

* No *quantization* means the decoder works with unquantized demodulator outputs. It can also be considered as the limiting case with soft quantization where an infinite number of quantization bits are allowed. Hence, it is sometimes referred to as the infinitely soft receiver quantization case.

where,

E_b/N_0 is the information (i.e., encoder input) bit energy-to-noise density ratio.

The units of R_0 and C used throughout this chapter are bits per binary channel use. That is, for nonbinary channels, such as a channel with QPSK modulation, R_0 and C are normalized by the number of bits per channel use so that they are always between 0 and 1 and can easily be compared with the code rate.

For the binary-input, output-symmetric, q-bit soft-quantized channel, as in Fig. 10-3, R_0 and C are given by[51]

$$R_0 = 1 - \log_2 \left[1 + \sum_{i=0}^{2^q-1} \sqrt{p_{0i}p_{1i}} \right] \tag{10-7}$$

and

$$C = \sum_{i=0}^{2^q-1} p_{0i} + \log_2 \left[\frac{2p_{0i}}{p_{0i} + p_{1i}} \right] \tag{10-8}$$

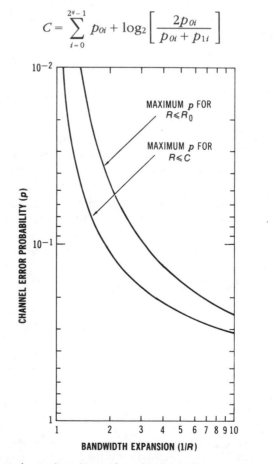

Fig. 10-4. Coding limits for a binary symmetric channel.

where,

p_{ki} ($k = 0$ or 1) is the probability of the demodulator output being in interval i given that the kth input symbol was sent.

Fig. 10-5 shows graphs of the minimum E_b/N_0 for which the condition $R \leq R_0$ is satisfied on an AWGN channel with BPSK or QPSK modulation and different amounts of quantization. These curves were obtained using Equations 10-3, 10-5, and 10-7 and the optimum uniform quantizer threshold-level spacings. These optimum quantizer thresholds are given in Table 10-1. Fig. 10-5 and Table 10-1 both show that there is approximately a 2-dB E_b/N_0 difference between the hard-quantization and the no-quantization curves for low code rates and approximately a 2.4-dB difference for the high code rates of Table 10-1. Also, 3 bits of quantization is seen to obtain most of this potential soft-decision decoding improvement.

In the limit as the bandwidth expansion becomes infinite, the minimum E_b/N_0 ratios for which $R < C$ and $R < R_0$ are −1.59 dB and 1.42 dB, respectively. For different channels, the characteristics of the curves of the type shown in Fig. 10-5 vary. Typically, with noncoherent or differentially coherent demodulation approaches, the curves have a minimum at some code rate and performance degrades for large bandwidth expansions.[32]

It should be noted that, while Fig. 10-5 shows that for this channel lower rate codes potentially improve performance, the incremental improvement for rates less than 1/4 is small. Also, the performance improvements become more difficult to achieve in practice since the lower code rates result in smaller channel symbol energy for tracking purposes.

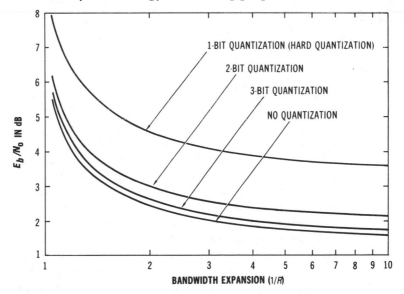

Fig. 10-5. Minimum E_b/N_0 for which $R \leq R_0$ on an AWGN channel with BPSK or QPSK modulation.

Table 10-1.   Minimum E_b/N_0 for Which $R \leq R_0$ on an AWGN Channel
with BPSK or QPSK Modulation

Code Rate (R)	Hard Receiver Quantization		2-Bit Soft Receiver Quantization		3-Bit Soft Receiver Quantization		No Receiver Quantization
	E_b/N_0 in dB for $R = R_0$	Channel Error Rate for $R = R_0$	E_b/N_0 in dB for $R = R_0$	Optimum Quantization Threshold $(T/\sigma)^*$	E_b/N_0 in dB for $R = R_0$	Optimum Quantization Threshold $(T/\sigma)^*$	E_b/N_0 in dB for $R = R_0$
1/1000	3.390	0.4737	1.96	0.983	1.58	0.564	1.420
1/4	3.890	0.1342	2.41	1.004	2.01	0.571	1.853
1/3	4.096	0.09536	2.59	1.013	2.19	0.573	2.031
1/2	4.590	0.04492	3.03	1.034	2.62	0.577	2.462
2/3	5.260	0.01718	3.64	1.060	3.22	0.586	3.056
3/4	5.713	9.033×10^{-3}	4.05	1.077	3.63	0.590	3.463
4/5	6.052	5.559×10^{-3}	4.37	1.090	3.94	0.596	3.770
5/6	6.320	3.764×10^{-3}	4.62	1.103	4.18	0.599	4.014
6/7	6.541	2.715×10^{-3}	4.82	1.114	4.39	0.601	4.215
7/8	6.727	2.053×10^{-3}	5.00	1.122	4.56	0.604	4.386
8/9	6.889	1.604×10^{-3}	5.15	1.127	4.71	0.606	4.534
9/10	7.030	1.289×10^{-3}	5.28	1.135	4.84	0.607	4.664
10/11	7.156	1.058×10^{-3}	5.40	1.140	4.95	0.609	4.780
11/12	7.269	8.843×10^{-4}	5.51	1.146	5.06	0.610	4.884
12/13	7.371	7.504×10^{-4}	5.60	1.151	5.15	0.612	4.979
13/14	7.465	6.441×10^{-4}	5.69	1.156	5.24	0.614	5.065
14/15	7.550	5.598×10^{-4}	5.77	1.159	5.32	0.614	5.144
15/16	7.630	4.902×10^{-4}	5.85	1.163	5.39	0.616	5.218
16/17	7.704	4.330×10^{-4}	5.92	1.167	5.46	0.617	5.287

* T is the quantization threshold-level spacing for a uniform quantizer with a cut point at zero, and σ is the standard deviation of the demodulator output to be quantized.

10.3 Linear Block Codes

Block codes are a class of codes in which data are presented to the encoder in blocks of k symbols, usually binary, and the encoder responds with a block of n symbols that are dependent on only those k input symbols. In this section, only linear block codes will be treated since they are, with few exceptions, the only block codes of practical interest. A code with these characteristics is called an (n, k) *linear block code*. The n-symbol encoder output block is called a codeword, and the code rate is $R = k/n$.

The more successful block coding techniques are based on finite-field algebraic concepts and a background in this area is necessary to fully understand some of the approaches. References 3, 6, 9, 26, 28, and 34 are some good sources for more detailed information on linear block codes. The emphasis here will be on the performance and implementation complexity of codes that are likely to be encountered in practice.

10.3.1 Fundamental Concepts and Characteristics

Linear block codes can be described by a $(k \times n)$-dimensional generator matrix **G**. If the k-symbol encoder input is represented by a k-dimensional vector **u** and the encoder output by an n-dimensional vector **v**, the encoder input-output relationship is given by

$$\mathbf{v} = \mathbf{uG} \qquad (10\text{-}9)$$

where the arithmetic is over some, not necessarily binary, finite field. To simplify this description, the remainder of this chapter will address binary codes unless specifically stated otherwise. In the binary case, all the elements in the generator matrix and the encoder input and output vectors are "0" or "1" and arithmetic is performed using ordinary multiplication rules and bit-by-bit module-2 addition.* Then, the code words are bit-by-bit modulo-2 sums of the rows of **G**. To guarantee that there are 2^k distinct codewords, the rows of **G** must be linearly independent.

Usually linear block codes are decoded using algebraic or table-lookup techniques based on hard-decision demodulator outputs. Several soft-decision approaches are available,[7,9] but the implementation complexities of these systems are greater, sometimes much greater, than those corresponding hard-quantized systems. In general, when soft decisions are available, a convolutional coding technique, which easily accommodates soft decisions, should be considered.

Another disadvantage of block codes compared to convolutional codes is that with block codes, an n-way ambiguity, which is much larger than required with convolutional codes, must be resolved to determine the start of a block.

Block codes are sometimes a good choice on channels where only hard receiver decisions are available and the data is already in a blocked format. A common application of block codes is for error detection.

The selection of block codes for use on discrete memoryless channels is usually based on the block distance properties of the code. The distance (sometimes called Hamming distance) between two codewords (or sequences) with an equal number of symbols is defined as the number of positions in which the symbols differ. The *code minimum distance* (d_{min})* is defined as the minimum distance between any two different encoder output codewords. Also the performance and distance properties of linear block codes are independent of the encoder input sequence, so for analysis purposes, without loss of generality, the all-zero sequence is usually assumed to have been transmitted.

---

* With binary arithmetic, addition and multiplication are defined as $0 + 0 = 0$, $1 + 0 = 1$, $1 + 1 = 0$, $0 \times 0 = 0$, $0 \times 1 = 0$, $1 \times 0 = 0$, and $1 \times 1 = 1$. Also, since $1 + 1 = 0$, $1 = -1$ and substraction is equivalent to addition.

* Reference 18 gives a table showing the largest code minimum distances that can be achieved for a wide range of binary (n, k) codes.

A block code with a minimum distance of $d_{\min}$ is capable of correcting any combination of $\lfloor(d_{\min} - 1)/2\rfloor$ or fewer channel errors or detecting any combination of $d_{\min} - 1$ or fewer channel errors, where $\lfloor x\rfloor$ is the integer part of x. However, while the minimum distance of the code may be sufficient to guarantee the detection or correction of a certain number of errors, the particular decoding algorithm may not be capable of such operation.

A block decoder that is capable of correcting any combination of t, $t \leq \lfloor(d_{\min} - 1)/2\rfloor$ or fewer channel errors and no combination of more than t errors is called a *bounded-distance decoder*. On a binary symmetric channel (BSC) with channel error-rate p, the block error probability, P_{block}, of such a coding system is the probability that more than t errors occurred. Since there are different ways of having i errors in n symbols, the block error probability is

$$P_{block} = \sum_{i=t+1}^{n} \binom{n}{i} p^i (1 - p)^{n-i} \qquad (10\text{-}10)$$

In general, decoders can be designed to correct all error patterns of t or fewer errors in the n-symbol block and some error patterns of more than t errors. With such a decoder, Equation 10-10 becomes an upper bound on the probability of a block error.

The bit error probability depends on the particular code and decoder. Usually block codes are selected to have given codeword distance properties, and codes are called *equivalent* if they have the same set of codeword distances. As noted previously, we may assume that the all-zero codeword was transmitted and can compare the other codewords to it. The distances in this case are equal to the number of nonzero symbols in the codewords. The number of nonzero symbols in a codeword is called the *weight* of the codeword. Then, two codes are called equivalent if they have the same set of codeword weights. Equivalent codes have the same block error probabilities on binary-symmetric channels; but, the bit error probabilities of these codes may vary. To determine this error probability, assume that the decoder can correct up to t channel errors. These errors are then corrected in the received sequence. The final step is to determine the encoder input block corresponding to the corrected received sequence. This step can be simplified by using a *systematic code*. Such a code has the property that all the k information symbols are sent unchanged along with $n - k$ parity symbols. For every linear block code, there exists a linear systematic block code with the same distance properties. Therefore, systematic block codes are commonly used.

The bit error probability for a systematic linear block code can be estimated by assuming that the error rate of the corrected received sequence is equal to the error rate of the corrected information-symbol sequence. Then, the bit error probability can be expressed as

$$P_b = \left(\frac{1}{n}\right) \sum_{i=t+1}^{n} \beta_i \binom{n}{i} p^i (1 - p)^{n-i} \qquad (10\text{-}11)$$

where β_i is the average number of symbol errors remaining in the corrected received sequence given that the channel caused i symbol errors. Of course,

$\beta_i = 0$ for $i \leq t$. When $i > t$, β_i can be bounded by noting that when more than t errors occur, a decoder that can correct no more than t errors would correct t errors in the best case and add t errors in the worst case. So β_i is bounded by $i - t \leq \beta_i \leq i + t$. For most decoder implementations, $\beta_i = i$ is a good approximation.

When a block code is used on a BSC for error detection only, the decoder fails to detect an error in a block code only when the error sequence transforms the encoded sequence into another valid codeword. By the linearity of the code, this implies that the error sequence is equal to a valid codeword. This probability of an undetected error can be expressed as

$$P_u = \sum_{i = d_{min}}^{n} A_i \, p^i (1 - p)^{n-i} \tag{10-12}$$

where A_i is the number of codewords of weight i (i.e., the number of codewords with i nonzero symbols). The performance and characteristics of error-detecting codes are discussed in more detail later in this section.

Before proceeding to a discussion of specific block codes, it is helpful to describe a simple and increasingly common decoding approach for codes where $n - k$ is small. Let $\mathbf{e}$ be an n-dimensional vector representing the channel error pattern.* Then, from Equation 10-9, the received codeword is

$$\mathbf{r} = \mathbf{uG} + \mathbf{e} \tag{10-13}$$

where, again, the arithmetic is bit-by-bit modulo-2.

The first step in the decoding procedure is to compute an $(n - k)$-dimensional syndrome vector defined by

$$\mathbf{S} = \mathbf{rH}^T = \mathbf{uGH}^T + \mathbf{eH}^T = \mathbf{eH}^T \tag{10-14}$$

where,

$\mathbf{H}$ is a $(n - k) \times n$ parity-check matrix with the property that $\mathbf{GH}^T = \mathbf{0}$ and $\mathbf{H}^T$ is the transpose of $\mathbf{H}$.

For systematic codes, the generator and parity check matrices can be expressed as $\mathbf{G} = [\mathbf{I}_k, \mathbf{P}]$ and $\mathbf{H} = [\mathbf{P}^T, \mathbf{I}_{n-k}]$, where $\mathbf{I}_k$ denotes the $(k \times k)$-dimensional identity matrix and $\mathbf{P}$ is a $k \times (n - k)$ matrix that specifies the particular block code.

For a system where all the codewords are equally likely, the probability of a block decoding error can be minimized by using a decoder that chooses its estimate of the transmitted codeword based on maximizing the probability of receiving the particular received word over all possible transmitted codewords. Such a decoder is called a *maximum likelihood decoder*. When the encoder input symbols are equally probable, a linear block code used on a

---

* The elements of the error vector in this BSC case are "0" or "1," where a "1" represents a channel-induced error and a "0" represents no error in the channel bit represented by that element.

discrete memoryless channel produces equally likely codewords. If the inputs are not at least approximately equally probable, source encoding should be considered to reduce the data rate that needs to be transmitted. In practice, the statistics to the input symbols are usually not known accurately enough to take advantage of small variations in the input probabilities. Therefore, maximum likelihood decoding is still a good approach.

For the BSC, a maximum likelihood decoder is equivalent to one that selects the codeword that differs from the received codeword in the fewest number of positions. Such a decoder is called a *minimum-distance decoder*. The syndrome of Equation 10-14 is sufficient to perform this decoding; that is, to estimate the error pattern **e**. In fact, when only systematic codes are considered, only the error bits corresponding to the k information bits of the received codeword need to be estimated. This estimate can be obtained using a table-lookup read-only memory (ROM). This ROM would have $(n - k)$ syndrome bits as an input address and k correction bits as its output. These k correction bits are then bit-by-bit modulo-2 added to the corresponding received codeword bits to obtain an estimate of the k-bit information block.

This approach is called *syndrome* or *table-lookup decoding*, and with the faster and denser ROMs that are continually being developed, it is becoming a common approach for implementing the high-code-rate block codes, which are of primary interest. When more powerful coding is needed for very noisy channels, low-rate Viterbi-decoded convolutional codes are usually a better choice.

The contents of the table-lookup ROM can be determined with a simple computer program. If the codes are capable of correcting all error patterns with t or fewer errors, the syndrome for each of these error patterns can be computed and the ROM output for that syndrome address set to the correct error pattern. After all of these error patterns have been accounted for, some error patterns corresponding to $t + 1$ or more bit errors can be included. Some of the error patterns with $t + 1$ errors produce syndrome sequences that have already been used for an error pattern of t or fewer errors and, thus, are not correctable.

10.3.2 Cyclic Codes

Cyclic codes are an important class of linear block codes in which every end-around cyclic shift of any codeword is also a codeword. In order to define the properties of cyclic codes, let the components of the code vector $\mathbf{v} = [v_0, \ldots, v_{n-1}]$ be the coefficients of a *codeword polynomial* $v(x) = v_0 + v_1x + \ldots + v_{n-1}x^{n-1}$. Then, mathematically, an end-around shift of a codeword $v(x)$ by i positions can be represented by $x^i v(x)$ modulo-$(x^n - 1)$. If the information bits to be encoded are also expressed in a similar polynomial form, then every codeword polynomial can be expressed in terms of a unique $(n - k)$-degree *generator-polynomial* $g(x)$ by $v(x) = u(x)g(x)$. This generator polynomial also satisfies the relationship

$$g(x)\, h(x) = x^n - 1 \tag{10-15}$$

where,

   $h(x)$ is a k-degree *parity polynomial.*

The generator and parity-check matrices of cyclic codes can be expressed in nonsystematic form in terms of the coefficients of the generator and parity polynomials as

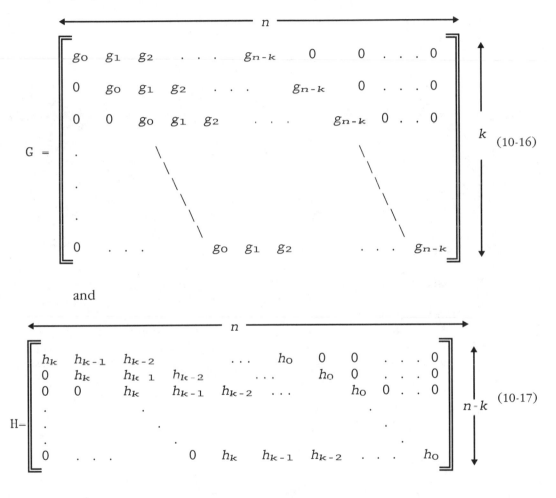

$$ (10\text{-}16) $$

and

$$ (10\text{-}17) $$

where,

   $g_0 = g_{n-k} = h_0 = h_k = 1,$

   the other coefficients of $g(x)$ and $h(x)$ are 0 or 1.

The generator matrix for an equivalent code in a systematic form can be obtained by bit-by-bit modulo-2 adding the appropriate rows of Equation 10-16.

Fig. 10-6 illustrates a circuit for encoding a cyclic code in the systematic form, which is almost always used in practice. This circuit uses a k-stage feedback shift register with the feedback tap multipliers based on the coefficients of the generator polynomial. These codes can also be generated using a

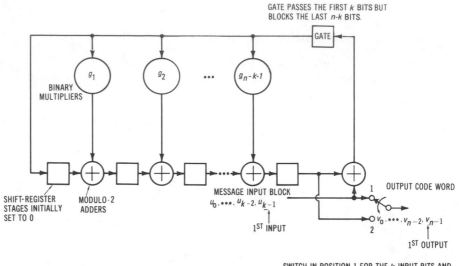

Fig. 10-6. Encoder for a systematic (n, k) cyclic code with generator polynomial $g(x) = 1 + g_1 x + g_2 x^2 + \ldots + g_{n-k-1} X^{n-k-1} + X^{n-k}$.

slightly different feedback shift-register implementation with tap multipliers based on the k parity-polynomial coefficients.[25] This is a more useful form than that of Fig. 10-6 when the parity polynomial has fewer coefficients than the generator polynomial; that is, when the code rate is less than 1/2. This is rarely the case in practical applications of these codes.

The first step in decoding a cyclic code is to compute the syndrome, $\mathbf{S} = [s_0, s_1, \ldots, s_{n-k-1}]$. For a cyclic code in systematic form, this calculation can be accomplished using the circuit of Fig. 10-7. This circuit is almost the same as the circuit of Fig. 10-6.

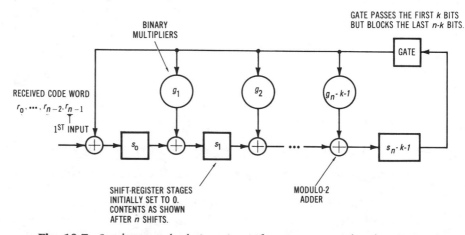

Fig. 10-7. Syndrome calculation circuit for a systematic (n, k) cyclic code with generator polynomial $g(x) = 1 + g_1 x + g_2 x^2 + \ldots + g_{n-k-1} x^{n-k-1} + x^{n-k}$.

A major advantage of cyclic codes is that their cyclic properties lead to simple encoder and syndrome calculation circuits. After the syndrome is calculated, a table-lookup approach or a variety of more sophisticated approaches can be used to estimate the error pattern and, ultimately, the k-bit information block. Some of these approaches are discussed in later subsections. More complete discussions can be found in the references noted at the beginning of this subsection. Good lists of generator polynomials for (n, k) binary cyclic codes with a wide range of n and k values and error-correcting-and-detecting capabilities are given in References 25 and 26.

10.3.3 Error-Detecting Codes

A common application of cyclic codes is for error detection. Such a code is called a *cyclic-redundancy-check* (CRC) code. Since virtually all error-detecting codes in practice are of the CRC type, only this class of codes will be discussed.

Define a *CRC error-burst* of length B in the n-bit received codeword as a contiguous sequence, or an end-around shifted version of a contiguous sequence, of B bits in which the first and last bits and any number of intermediate bits are received in error. Then binary (n, k) CRC codes* are capable of detecting the following n-bit channel error patterns:[25,34]

1. All CRC error bursts of length $n - k$ or less.

2. A fraction $1 - 2^{-(n-k-1)}$ of the CRC error bursts of length $B = n - k + 1$.

3. A fraction $1 - 2^{-(n-k)}$ of the CRC error bursts of length $B > n - k + 1$.

4. All combinations of $d_{min} - 1$ or less errors.

5. All error patterns with an odd number of errors if the generator polynomial had an even number of nonzero coefficients.

On a binary symmetric channel (BSC), the probability of an undetected error can be expressed in terms of the number of codewords (A_i) of each weight (i) as shown in Equation 10-12. Sometimes, especially for smaller channel error rates, a good approximation of the probability can be obtained using only the first few terms in the summation of Equation 10-12, so that only a few of the A_i quantities need to be determined. Also, in some cases, the probability can be upper bounded by $2^{-(n-k)}$. However, this last bound is not true for all binary cyclic codes.[24,54]

Usually the basic cyclic codes used for error-detection are selected to have very large natural block lengths (n). Then, this basic code, in a systematic form, is shortened by deleting the first few information bits. For example, an (n, k) cyclic code shortened by ℓ information bits produces an $(n - \ell, k - \ell)$ code. The resulting code is no longer a cyclic code; however, such modified codes are still referred to as CRC codes. All of the standard CRC codes use this

---

* The notation (n, k) denotes a block code with n channel bits and k information bits.

approach so that the same generator polynomial applies to the block lengths of interest. These *shortened* cyclic codes have at least the same minimum distances as the basic cyclic codes.

The encoder for these shortened CRC can be implemented as shown in Fig. 10-6. The decoder computes the syndrome, or an end-around shifted version of the syndrome, and only passes the block of data when the syndrome has all zero bits. A shifted version of the syndrome can be computed using the circuit shown in Fig. 10-7. Another error-detection implementation approach is to re-encode the information portion of the received codeword and only pass the block of data when the newly computed parity bits are all equal to the corresponding received parity bits.

Three standard CRC codes are commonly used:[14]

CRC-12 code with $g(x) = 1 + x + x^2 + x^3 + x^{11} + x^{12}$

CRC-16 code with $g(x) = 1 + x^2 + x^{15} + x^{16}$

CCITT CRC code with $g(x) = 1 + x^5 + x^{12} + x^{16}$

These codes have $n - k = 12$, 16, and 16 parity bits, respectively, and natural block lengths of $2^{n-k-1} - 1$.

More powerful 24-bit and 32-bit CRC codes (i.e., codes with 24 and 32 parity bits) are given in Reference 53. This reference also gives another 16-bit CRC that has a smaller probability of an undetected error than the two standard 16-bit CRC codes noted before for a wide range of shortened block lengths. The generator polynomials for these codes are

$$g(x) = x^{16} + x^{15} + x^{12} + x^{11} + x^8 + x^6 + x^3 + 1 \qquad \text{for the 16-bit CRC}$$
$$g(x) = x^{24} + x^{23} + x^{18} + x^{17} + x^{14} + x^{11} + x^{10} + x^7 + x^6 + x^5 + x^4 + x^3 + x + 1$$
$$\text{for the 24-bit CRC}$$
$$g(x) = x^{32} + x^{31} + x^{24} + x^{22} + x^{16} + x^{14} + x^8 + x^7 + x^5 + x^3 + x + 1$$
$$\text{for the 32-bit CRC}$$

10.3.4 Binary Error-Correcting Codes

A wide variety of binary linear error-correcting codes have been studied. Here we discuss three of those most likely to be encountered in practice. These are the Hamming, Golay, and BCH codes.

Hamming codes are a simple class of codes with the following parameters:

$$n = 2^m - 1 \qquad\qquad m = 3,4,5, \ldots$$
$$k = 2^m - 1 - m$$
$$n - k = m$$
$$d_{\min} = 3$$

Since these codes have a minimum distance of 3, they are capable of correcting all single errors or detecting all combinations of 2 or fewer errors. Although Hamming codes are not very powerful, they belong to a very limited class of linear block codes called *perfect codes*. A *t*-error-correcting code is called a perfect code if, with a table-lookup decoding based on using the $n - k$ syndrome bits as address bits, every error pattern of t or fewer errors can be corrected and no error pattern with more than t errors can be corrected.

Hamming codes are usually described in terms of their $(m \times n)$-dimensional parity-check matrix, which can be expressed in a form where the n columns are equal to all positive nonzero m-bit sequences.[15] With this representation, the m-bit syndrome specifies the location of any single error, which can then be corrected. If the syndrome is zero, the decoder assumes no errors occurred.

A parity bit can be added to the Hamming code to form an *extended Hamming code* with the following parameters:

$$n = 2^m$$
$$k = 2^m - 1 - m$$
$$n - k = m + 1$$
$$d_{min} = 4$$

This code is capable of correcting any single error and simultaneously detecting double errors or of detecting any combination of 3 errors. Usually a table-lookup approach is the easiest way of decoding these codes.

The $(23, 12)$ *Golay code** is another perfect code. The code has a d_{min} of 7 and, thus, is capable of correcting any combination of 3 or fewer errors or detecting any combination of 6 or fewer errors. The Golay code is a cyclic code generated by either

$$g(x) = 1 + x^2 + x^4 + x^5 + x^6 + x^{10} + x^{11}$$

or

$$g(x) = 1 + x + x^5 + x^6 + x^7 + x^9 + x^{11}$$

An *extended* $(24,12)$ *Golay code* can be formed by adding a parity bit to the $(23,12)$ Golay code. This extended code has a minimum distance of 8 with 1 code word of weight 0, 759 of weight 8, 2576 of weight 12, 759 of weight 16, and 1 of weight 24. In general, the minimum distance of any binary linear block code with an odd minimum distance can be increased by one by adding an overall parity bit.

The block, bit, and undetected error probabilities can be determined from Equations 10-10 through 10-12 for a decoder capable of correcting up to the maximum guaranteed error-correcting capability of the code, which is 3 here. The results are shown in Fig. 10-8 for the extended Golay code on a binary symmetric channel. Fig. 10-9 gives similar error-probability results for an AWGN channel with BPSK or QPSK modulation versus the information-bit-

---

* The values in the notation (n, k) denote a block code with n channel and k information bits.

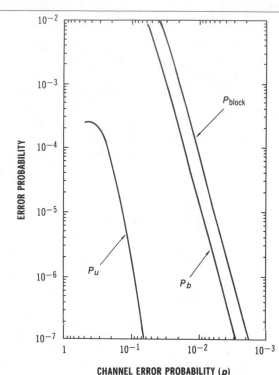

Fig. 10-8. Block, bit, and undetected error probabilities versus channel error rate with extended Golay coding.

energy-to-noise density ratio, E_b/N_0. This illustration also shows the bit-error-rate performance of a soft-decision (no quantization) maximum likelihood decoder.[32] The E_b/N_0 difference between the soft- and hard-quantization curves is about 2 dB, which is what was expected based on the curves of Fig. 10-5, As noted previously, several algorithms have been developed to provide soft-decision decoding for block codes,[7,9] but it is usually better to use Viterbi- or sequential-decoded convolutional codes in these applications.

One of the most important and powerful classes of linear-block codes is that of *BCH codes*. BCH codes are cyclic codes with a wide variety of parameters. The most common type, called *primitive BCH codes*, have the following parameters:

$$n = 2^m - 1$$
$$n - k \leq mt$$
$$d_{\min} \geq 2t + 1$$

where,

t is the error-correcting capability of the code,
m is a positive integer greater than or equal to 3.

A detailed description of BCH codes requires some algebraic developments that are beyond the scope of this chapter. S. Lin and D.J. Costello[25] give a good description of these codes and their algebraic decoding algorithms.

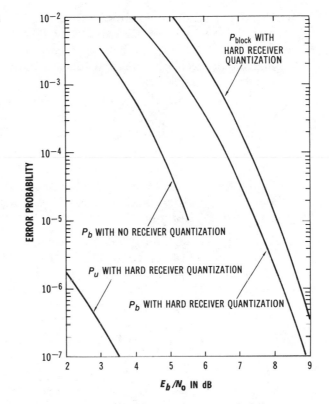

Fig. 10-9. Block, bit, and undetected error probabilities versus E_b/N_0
with extended Golay coding on an AWGN channel
with BPSK or QPSK modulation.

Appendix C of Reference 25 gives a large table of the generator polynomials for primitive BCH codes of length up to $2^{10} - 1$.

BCH decoders use an algebraic approach with arithmetic over a finite field of 2^m elements to estimate the channel error pattern. This error pattern is then subtracted from the received codeword to obtain an estimate of the transmitted codeword. An inverse coder mapping is used to provide an estimate of the original encoder input vector. This last step, of course, is trivial for codes generated in a systematic form.

In general, four basic steps are involved in determining the error pattern. For a primitive t-error-correcting code, these steps are:

1. Calculate $2t$ m-bit syndrome symbols. These symbols are calculated by multiplying the received codeword vector by the transpose of an appropriately defined $(2t \times n)$-dimensional parity-check matrix of m-bit symbols. In the binary-code case, this can be reduced to finding t m-bit syndrome symbols by multiplying by the transpose of a $(t \times n)$-dimensional parity-check matrix of m-bit symbols.

2. Using the syndrome symbols, find the coefficients for an e-degree error-locator polynomial where e, $e \leq t$, is the number of channel errors. The technique for doing this is referred to as the *Berlekamp Algorithm*.[3,15] This polynomial has the significance that its roots give the locations of the channel errors in the received block of symbols.

3. Find the roots, and thus the location of the errors, of the error-locator polynomial. The usual technique for doing this is referred to as the *Chien Search*.[15] It involves checking each of the n code-symbol locations to see if that location corresponds to a root of the error-locator polynomial.

4. Find the values of the errors. With binary codes, this step isn't needed since binary errors correspond to "1" elements. With nonbinary symbols, a simple formula is available.[15]

Fig. 10-10 gives the bit-error rate performance of 5-, 10-, and 15-error correcting BCH codes of block length 127.[32,35] This drawing also shows the performance of an *expurgated* (127, 112) *BCH code* used on some INTELSAT satellite channels.[29,56] The generator polynomial of the expurgated code is

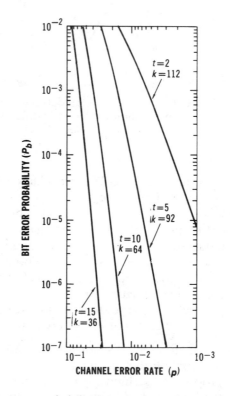

Fig. 10-10. Bit-error-probability-versus-channel-error-rate performance of several block-length 127 BCH codes.

formed from the (127, 113), $d_{\min} = 5$, BCH code by multiplying the generator polynomial of the basic (127, 113) code by $x + 1$. This expurgated code consists of the even-weight codewords of the basic code and has a minimum distance of 6. This approach can be used to increase the minimum distance of any odd-minimum-distance binary cyclic code by one.

The curves in Fig. 10-10 were all obtained using Equation 10-11 with $\beta_i = i$. Since the (127, 112) code only has 15 syndrome bits, it could be implemented with a table-lookup decoding approach. If such an approach is used, in addition to being able to correct all error patterns with 2 or fewer errors, some 3-error patterns could also be corrected and the resulting error rate would be slightly better than that shown in Fig. 10-10.

10.3.5 Reed-Solomon Codes

Reed-Solomon codes are a class of *nonbinary BCH codes* that achieve the largest possible code minimum distance for any linear block code with the given encoder input and output block lengths. For nonbinary codes, the distance between two codewords is defined as the number of nonbinary symbols in which the sequences differ. The minimum distance for these codes is given by

$$d_{\min} = n - k + 1 \qquad (10\text{-}18)$$

The most common Reed-Solomon codes are primitive codes with 2^m-ary symbols. These codes have the following parameters:

Symbol alphabet size = 2^m, m-bit symbols
$n = 2^m - 1$ symbols = $m(2^m - 1)$ bits
$n - k = 2t$ symbols = $2mt$ bits
$d_{\min} = 2t + 1$

where,
  t is the symbol-error-correcting capability of the code.

A code which achieves the minimum distance of Equation 10-18 is called a *maximum-distance-separable* code. The number of codewords of each weight, i, in such a code can be expressed as

$$A_k = \binom{2^m - 1}{k} (2^m - 1) \sum_{i=0}^{k-2t-1} (-1)^i \binom{k-1}{i} 2^{m(k-i-2t-1)} \; for \; k \geq 2t + 1 \quad (10\text{-}19)$$

where,
  $A_0 = 1$,
  $A_k = 0$ for $1 \leq k \leq 2t$.

These codes are particularly good as outer codes in concatenated coding systems.[30] In such a system, the inner code provides some error control by, typically, operating on soft-decision demodulator outputs. Then, the outer decoder processes the hard-decision data provided by the inner decoder to reduce the error rate to the desired level. Binary inner-code symbols are grouped to form the 2^m-ary Reed-Solomon code symbols. These codes are also sometimes used on jamming or fading channels with noncoherent demodulation and 2^m-ary orthogonal signal modulation. In summary, Reed-Solomon codes are sometimes a good selection when channel errors occur in short bursts that approximately match the number of bits in a Reed-Solomon symbol. These codes are not a good choice for binary channels with random errors.

The performance of a system with this type of coding on a memoryless channel can be specified in terms of the channel symbol error rate (p_s) using equations similar to those for a binary system. For channels with 2^m-ary orthogonal signal modulation, the bit error rate is a fraction $2^{m-1}/(2^{m-1})$ of the symbol error rate.[48]

Fig. 10-11 shows the bit-error-probability versus channel-symbol-error-probability performance for $n = 31$ codes capable of correcting various numbers of symbol errors. Fig. 10-12 gives similar curves versus E_b/N_0 for a system with 32-ary *multiple frequency-shift keying* (MFSK) *modulation*, noncoherent demodulation, and AWGN.[29]

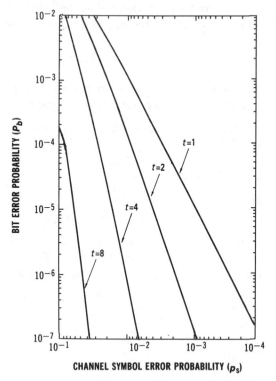

Fig. 10-11. Bit-error-probability versus channel-symbol-error-probability performance for several $n = 31$, t-error-correcting Reed-Solomon coding systems on a channel with 32-ary orthogonal signal modulation.

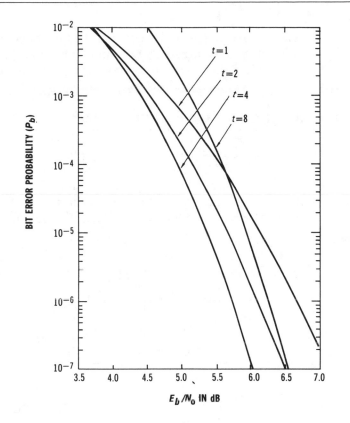

Fig. 10-12. Bit-error-probability versus E_b/N_0 performance of several $n = 31$, t-error-correcting Reed-Solomon coding systems on an AWGN channel with 32-ary MFSK modulation.

10.4 Convolutional Coding

Convolutional codes are a class of codes in which the encoder accepts data in small groups of k symbols (quite often $k = 1$) and provides encoded output data in small groups of n ($n > k$) symbols with the property that each output group depends not only on the k inputs at that time but also on several preceding input groups.* That is, the encoder has memory.

*This definition of convolutional codes assumes that the encoding is performed with feedforward logic. Convolutional codes can also be defined to include codes generated by encoders with feedback logic. G.D. Forney[12] has shown that for any linear convolutional code generated by an encoder with feedback logic, there exists an encoder with only feedforward logic that generates the same set of encoder output sequences. For this reason, and since most convolutional encoder implementations use linear feedforward logic, the discussion presented here is restricted to linear feedforward codes unless specifically stated otherwise. An example of a nonlinear code with feedback logic in the encoder is given in Section 10.3.4.

The large coding gains and the availability of decoding algorithms that can take advantage of soft receiver decisions and yet be simply implemented have led to a widespread use of these codes in communication systems.

10.4.1 Structure of Convolutional Codes

Fig. 10-13 gives a block diagram of a simple binary convolutional encoder that illustrates many of the fundamental concepts of convolutional coding. In this example, two output bits are generated for each input bit. A convolutional encoder that accepts k input bits and generates n output bits in this manner is called an $R = k/n$ encoder. In this example, the code rate is $R = 1/2$.

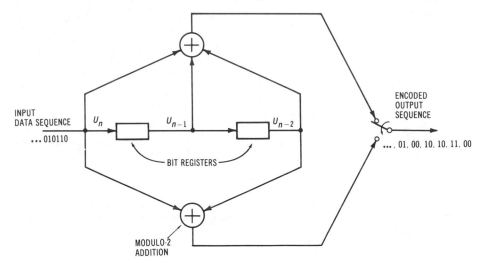

Fig. 10-13. $R = 1/2$, constraint-length-3 convolutional encoder example.

The two output sequences in this example are shown multiplexed into a single output sequence at twice the bit rate of the input sequence. The two output bits generated for a particular input are seen to depend on that input bit and on the two previous bits as well as on the modulo-2 adder input connections. The two previous inputs are called state bits in this finite-state-machine representation. The total number of bits that are needed to specify each set of n output bits (that is, the number of state bits plus the number of input bits k) is called the *constraint length, K.* In the example of Fig. 10-13, the constraint length is equal to 3. Sometimes the constraint length is defined to be the number of state bits v, where $v = K - k$. The first definition is used here.

The particular convolutional code is specified by giving the bit register-to-adder tap multipliers. For an $R=1/n$ code, the code can be specified by n K-bit generators $\mathbf{g}^{(1)}, \mathbf{g}^{(2)}, \ldots, \mathbf{g}^{(n)}$, which give the tap multipliers for the first through the nth output sequences. In this case, the code is specified by the generators

$$\boldsymbol{g}^{(1)} = \left[\begin{array}{ccc} g_0^{(1)} & g_1^{(1)} & g_2^{(1)} \end{array} \right] = [111]$$

and

$$\boldsymbol{g}^{(2)} = \left[\begin{array}{ccc} g_0^{(2)} & g_1^{(2)} & g_2^{(2)} \end{array} \right] = [101]$$

where,

$g_0^{(1)}$ and $g_0^{(2)}$ correspond to the tap multipliers for the current input bit.

The *generator matrix* for an $R = 1/n$ convolutional code with a single multiplexed output sequence can be expressed as in Equation 10-20.

$$G = \left[\begin{array}{cccccccc} g_0^{(1)} \cdots g_0^{(n)} g_1^{(1)} \cdots g_1^{(n)} & & \cdots & g_{k-1}^{(1)} \cdots g_{k-1}^{(n)} & & & \\ & g_0^{(1)} \cdots g_0^{(n)} g_1^{(1)} \cdots g_1^{(n)} & & \cdots & & g_{k-1}^{(1)} \cdots g_{k-1}^{(n)} & \\ & & g_0^{(1)} \cdots g_0^{(n)} g_1^{(1)} \cdots g_1^{(n)} & \cdots & & & g_{k-1}^{(1)} \cdots g_{k-1}^{(n)} \\ & & & & & & \\ & & & & & & \end{array} \right]$$

This form of the generator matrix assumes that the encoder state was initially zero and that the input sequence is arbitrarily long. If the input has some finite length of L, then **G** has L rows and $n(L + v) = n(L + \boldsymbol{K} - 1)$ columns. So the code rate is actually $R = L/(nL + nv)$. Such a code is still referred to as an $R = 1/n$ code, however, since, typically, L is much larger than v, and thus, the difference in the code rates is very small. The extra sequence, of in this case $n(\boldsymbol{K} - 1)$ channel bits, is called a *tail* or *flush sequence*. For an $R = 1/n$ code of the type shown in Fig. 10-13, it is generated by shifting a sequence of $\boldsymbol{K} - 1$ zero symbols into the encoder.

The generators can also be expressed in a polynomial form in terms of a unit delay element, D. For example, the generator polynomial for the ith generator of a $R = 1/n$ code can be expressed as

$$g^{(i)}(D) = g_0^{(i)} + g_1^{(i)} D + \ldots + g_v^{(i)} D^v.$$

All convolutional encoders can be implemented using a shift-register approach similar to that shown in Fig. 10-13. For an $R = k/n$, $k \neq 1$, code there are, in general, k tapped shift registers, rather than just one, and the tap multipliers from each point of each register to the modulo-2 adder associated with each output must be specified. These tap multipliers are specified by the $(k \times n)$-dimensional generators $\mathbf{G}_0, \mathbf{G}_1, \ldots, \mathbf{G}_m$, where $\mathbf{G}_0$ specifies the tap multipliers for the current k-bit input and $\mathbf{G}_m$ specifies the tap multipliers for the oldest set of inputs that still affect the current n-bit output. The generator polynomial for an $R = k/n$ code is $\mathbf{G}(D) = \mathbf{G}_0 + \mathbf{G}_1 D + \ldots + \mathbf{G}_m D^m$, and the code generator matrix can be expressed as

$$
\mathbf{G} = \begin{bmatrix}
\mathbf{G}_0 & \mathbf{G}_1 & \mathbf{G}_2 & . & . & . & \mathbf{G}_m & & & & \\
& \mathbf{G}_0 & \mathbf{G}_1 & \mathbf{G}_2 & . & . & . & \mathbf{G}_m & & & \\
& & \mathbf{G}_0 & \mathbf{G}_1 & \mathbf{G}_2 & . & . & . & \mathbf{G}_m & & \\
& & & & . & & & . & & & \\
& & & . & & & & & . & & \\
& & & & . & & & & & . & \\
\end{bmatrix} \tag{10-21}
$$

An $R = k/n$ *systematic convolutional code* is a code in which the encoder provides each of the k input sequences directly as outputs. It would then also provide $n - k$ parity output sequences. Such a code has the advantage that in applications where blocks of data are transmitted, the tail sequence that needs to be transmitted is shorter than for nonsystematic codes, since there is no need to send known tail bits. Also with some decoding approaches, the decoder implementation is simplified. However, for a given rate and constraint length, the *sequence maximum likelihood-decoding** performance of feedforward systematic codes is much inferior to that of nonsystematic codes. An equivalent feedforward nonsystematic code cannot be found as with block codes.† If the implementation complexity of the decoder is only weakly dependent on the constraint length, it is sometimes reasonable to use a larger-constraint-length systematic code to achieve the same performance as a shorter-constraint-length more-difficult-to-implement nonsystematic code. This is quite often the approach used with sequential-decoded convolutional coding systems. However, Viterbi-decoded convolutional coding systems, which have an implementation complexity that increases approximately exponentially with increasing constraint length, are usually implemented using nonsystematic codes.

As with linear block codes, particular convolutional codes are selected such that the codewords, or code sequences, out of the encoder are as different as possible. If the convolutional code is not selected carefully, it can ex-

---

* A sequence maximum likelihood decoder is a decoder that selects the most likely encoder input sequence based on the particular received sequence.

† G.D. Forney[12] has shown that if feedback logic is allowed in the encoder, then for every nonsystematic code there is a systematic code that is equivalent to the nonsystematic code in the sense that it generates the same set of encoder output sequences. However, as noted with block codes, the bit error rates of equivalent codes are not the same. In general, a code generated with feedback logic can be expected to have a higher bit error rate that an equivalent code generated using only feedforward logic.

hibit what is called *catastrophic error propagation*. Such a code is called a *catastrophic code*. A catastrophic code is defined as a code for which there exist two encoder input sequences that differ in an arbitrarily large number of bit positions which are encoded into sequences that differ only in a finite number of bit positions. With such a code, a channel that causes a finite number of channel symbols to be received unreliably can cause an arbitrarily large number of decoder output errors with a sequence maximum likelihood decoder. For an $R = 1/n$ code, a necessary and sufficient condition for it to be noncatastrophic is that the greatest common divisor of the generator polynomials be equal to D^ℓ for some $\ell \geq 0$. For an $R = k/n$ code, a similar condition is that the greatest common divisor of the determinants of the $\binom{N}{K}$ $(k \times k)$-dimensional submatrices of the $(k \times n)$-dimensional generator polynomial $\mathbf{G}(D)$ be equal to D^ℓ for some $\ell \geq 0$.[27] Systematic codes are noncatastrophic. An example of a catastrophic code is the $R = 1/2$ code with generator polynomials $g^{(1)}(D) = 1 + D^2$ and $g^{(2)}(D) = 1 + D$, which has a common factor of $D + 1$ with modulo-2 arithmetic.

The structure and characteristics of convolutional codes can be illustrated using tree, trellis, and state-diagram representations. Fig.10-14 illustrates the tree representation for the $R = 1/2$ code of Fig. 10-13 with a tail sequence inserted after four inputs bits. An encoder output sequence is determined by tracing a path through this tree representation from left to right. At each junction or node, the encoder input along with the state represented by that node specifies whether the upper or lower branch should be used. Each branch between nodes is labeled with the output symbols that are generated in that state transition. The tree representation for an $R = k/n$ encoder would have 2^k n-bit branches coming from each node.

The *tree representation* from the decoder's point of view replaces the n bits on each branch by a quality measure called a *branch metric*. The decoder's job is to use these branch metrics as a basis for finding the most likely path through the tree. More precisely, a path (or sequence) maximum likelihood decoder is one that compares the conditional probabilities, called *likelihood functions*, that the particular received sequence was received given each possible transmitted sequence and then selects as its output the sequence corresponding to the largest (most likely) likelihood functions. On a discrete memoryless channel, these sequence (or path) probabilities are equal to the product of similar symbol conditional probabilities or symbol likelihood functions. Usually it is more convenient to work with the log of these conditional probabilities. Then the log of the path conditional probabilities, called the *path log-likelihood functions*, can be computed by adding the corresponding symbol log-likelihood functions. Since the logarithm is a monotonic function of its argument for positive arguments, comparing the log-likelihood functions and selecting the largest also leads to a maximum likelihood decoder. If the branch metrics are chosen to be the branch log-likelihood functions, which are just the sum of the n channel-symbol log-likelihood functions (i.e., symbol metrics) for that branch, and the decoder selects the path through the tree with the largest metric, then the decoder is a maximum likelihood decoder.

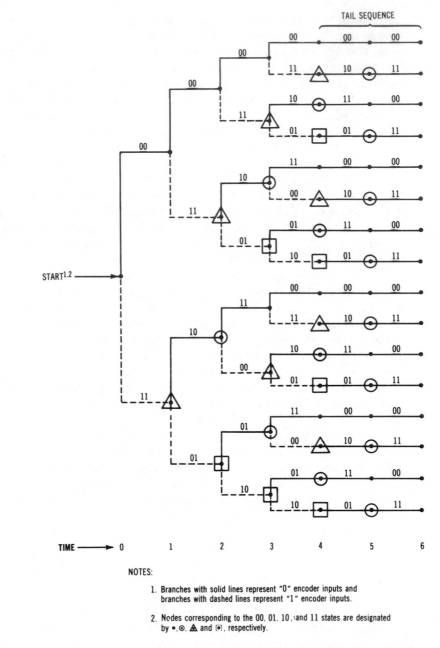

NOTES:

1. Branches with solid lines represent "0" encoder inputs and branches with dashed lines represent "1" encoder inputs.

2. Nodes corresponding to the 00, 01, 10, and 11 states are designated by •, ⊙, ▲ and ▣, respectively.

Fig. 10-14. Tree representation for the encoder of Fig. 10-13 with a tail sequence inserted after four input bits.

For the binary symmetric channel (BSC) with a channel error rate of p, the branch log-likelihood function or branch metric, is equal to[49]

$$\text{(Branch Metric)}_{\text{BSC}} = -\alpha_1 d_n \beta_1 \tag{10-22}$$

where,

> a_1 and β_1 are positive constants, with a_1 being greater than zero,
>
> d_n is the number of bit positions in which the received n-bit sequence disagrees with the n-bit encoder tree representation for that branch.

Since a_1 and β_1 do not affect the outcomes of the path metric comparisons, their exact values are not important. In fact, the metrics can always be scaled by adding (or subtracting) some quantity from all the metrics or by multiplying (or dividing) all of the metrics by a positive quantity.

For an AWGN channel with BPSK modulation and no quantization, the branch log-likelihood functions (or branch metrics) are:[49]

$$(\text{Branch metric})_{\text{BPSK,AWGN}} = a_2 \sum_{k=1}^{n} r_k v_k - \beta_2 \qquad (10\text{-}23)$$

where,

> a_2 and β_2 are constants, with a_2 being greater than zero,
>
> r_k is the demodulator output for the kth symbol of the branch,
>
> $v_k = \pm 1$ is the normalized tree representation for the kth bit of the branch in question.

In referring to the tree representation of Fig. 10-14, it is clear that after a few branches the structure becomes repetitive. In particular, the set of paths emanating from nodes that correspond to the same encoder state are identical. This leads to a *trellis diagram* in which the identical paths coming from the same state are merged into a single branch. Fig. 10-15 shows such a trellis diagram for the encoder of Fig. 10-13 with a tail sequence added after four encoder input bits, as in the tree representation of Fig. 10-14. As with the tree representation, metrics can be assigned to each branch of the trellis to obtain a

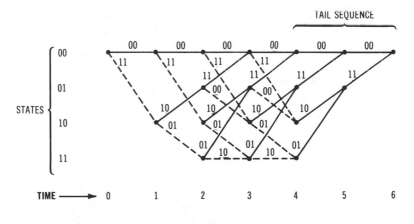

NOTES: Branches with solid lines represent "0" encoder inputs and branches with dashed lines represent "1" encoder inputs.

Fig. 10-15. Trellis representation for the encoder of Fig. 10-13 with a tail sequence inserted after four input bits.

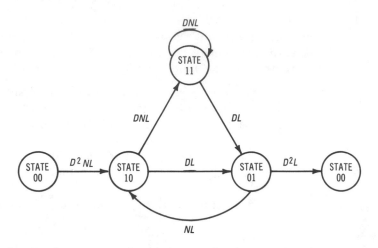

Fig. 10-16. Augmented state diagram for the encoder of Fig. 10-13.

decoder trellis. This representation is especially useful for Viterbi decoding of convolutional codes.

Another representation, which is useful for determining the code distance properties for linear convolutional codes, is the *augmented state-diagram* representation of Viterbi.[49] The purpose of this representation is usually to determine the complete weight structure of the code, as specified by a *code generating function*, $T(D,N,L)$. This state diagram has the all-zero state split into two parts and the transitions between states labeled with terms of the form $D^i N^j L$, where i $(0 \leq i \leq n)$ represents the number of channel symbols in which the branch differs from the all-zero path, j $(0 \leq j \leq k)$ represents the number of information (i.e., encoder input) bits in which that path differs from the all-zero input, and the power of L represents the length of the path in branches. Fig. 10-16 illustrates such a representation for the encoder of Fig. 10-13.

Based on the augmented state diagram, a generating function, $T(D,N,L)$, can be determined. For the diagram of Fig. 10-16, the result is

$$
\begin{aligned}
T(D,NL) &= \frac{d^5 NL}{1 - DNL - DNL^2} \\
&= D^5 NL^3 + D^6 N^2 (L^4 + L^5) + D^7 N^3 (L^5 + 2L^6 + L^7) + \ldots
\end{aligned}
\tag{10-24}
$$

This generating function represents all of the nonzero paths that become un-merged from the all-zero path at some node and then remerge at a later time. For example, Equation 10-24 means the minimum weight path has a weight of 5, it is 3 branches long, and, of the 3 information bits that this path represents, only one bit is a one. This weight (or distance with respect to the all-zero sequence) of the minimum-weight path among all arbitrarily long paths is called the *free distance* (d_{free}) of the code.

10.4.2 Viterbi Decoding for $R = 1/n$ Binary Codes

Viterbi decoding is a path maximum likelihood decoding approach for convolutional codes that takes advantage of the remerging path structure illustrated in the trellis representation.

The easiest way to describe the Viterbi decoding algorithm is by referring to an example. Figs. 10-17 through 10-20 illustrate the Viterbi decoding algorithm for the $K = 3$, $R = 1/2$ code of Fig. 10-13. These figures illustrate the progression through the decoder trellis diagram for a hard-decision decoder and a particular received sequence. The branches in the trellis diagrams are labeled with the normalized branch metrics, which are equal to the number of bits in which the received symbols at that branch differ from the encoder output symbols that are noted on the corresponding encoder trellis representation of Fig. 10-15.

For the first two (or in general $K-1$) branches, the decoder merely accumulates branch metrics to obtain 2^{K-1} path metrics. Then, after three (or in general K) branches, the paths begin to remerge as noted in Fig. 10-17. A Viterbi decoder compares the path metrics of the two paths entering each node and eliminates the path with the worst (largest in this sample) metric.

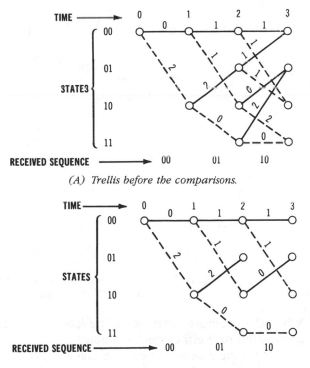

(A) Trellis before the comparisons.

(B) Trellis after the comparisons.

Fig. 10-17. Viterbi-decodong example for the encoder
of Fig. 10-13 after three branches.

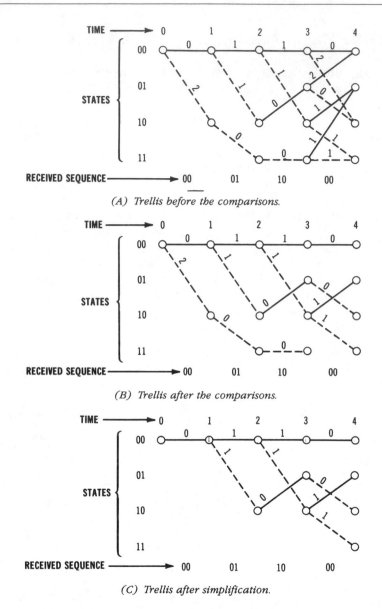

(A) Trellis before the comparisons.

(B) Trellis after the comparisons.

(C) Trellis after simplification.

Fig. 10-18. Viterbi-decoding example for the encoder of Fig. 10-13 after four branches.

When the remerging paths have the same path metrics, the decoder can arbitrarily eliminate either one of them.

Each time a new branch of n channel symbols is received, a Viterbi decoder computes 2^K path metrics by adding the branch metrics to the 2^{K-1} previously computed path metrics. Then, 2^{K-1} comparisons are made between the two paths entering each state, and only the path with the best metric at each

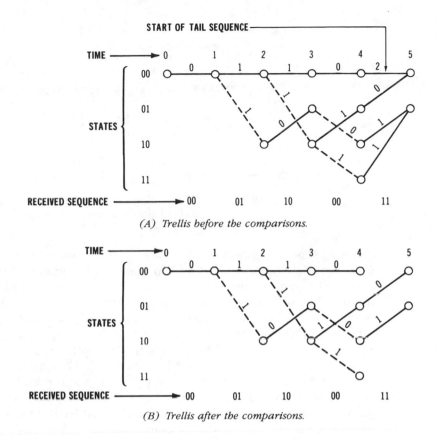

(A) Trellis before the comparisons.

(B) Trellis after the comparisons.

Fig. 10-19. Viterbi-decoding example for the encoder
of Fig. 10-13 after five branches.

node is retained. This procedure is illustrated in Fig. 10-18. This example also illustrates how after a few branches the paths tend to remerge. In this case, all the paths have remerged at the first branch, and the decoder can make a decision on the bit corresponding to that branch. Here the decoder would provide a "0" output bit.

Fig. 10-19 illustrates how a tail sequence of $K-1$ all-zero information bits is processed. Since the encoder input for the tail sequence is known to be zero, only branches corresponding to "0" inputs are extended.

Fig. 10-20 shows the trellis at the end of this short tailed-off Viterbi-decoding example. In this case, the upper path is selected and the complete decoder output sequence is 001000.

Eventually, as illustrated in this example, if a tail sequence is used, the paths all merge into the all-zero-state node and the Viterbi decoder is left with a single most likely path. In practice, convolutional codes are usually used with arbitrarily long sequences of data without a tail sequence. In such an application, whenever the decoder is given a new branch of n quantized

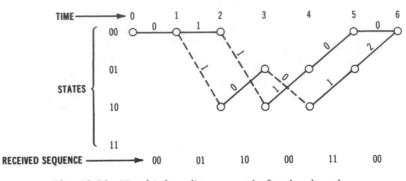

Fig. 10-20. Viterbi-decoding example for the decoder
of Fig. 10-13 after six branches.

received symbols, it provides an estimate of the information bit that corresponds to some branch that is a fixed number of branches in the past. This is accomplished by picking the current state that corresponds with the path with the best metric, tracing this path back through the trellis for some number of branches m (called the *path memory*), and finally providing as an output the information bit that corresponds to that branch. This approach means that only m bits need to be retained for each of the 2^{K-1} paths. Since the retained paths tend to remerge a few constraint lengths of branches back, a memory larger than this has little impact on performance. It is also possible to achieve the same performance by tracing back from an arbitrary current state if a larger path memory is provided. When paths are traced back from the current maximum likelihood state, a path memory of about five constraint lengths of branches is a good choice for $R = 1/2$ codes. Slightly smaller path memories are suitable with lower rate codes and larger memories are required with higher rate codes.

As noted previously, the symbol metrics should be equal to the symbol log-likelihood functions or normalized versions of these functions. However, it is usually more convenient to use positive or zero integer metrics with smaller metrics being best. This can be accomplished by using a metric that is equal to the log-likelihood function multiplied by some negative value and, then, looking for the smallest, rather than the largest metric. In addition, with Viterbi decoding, it has been found that a very coarse metric quantization has little impact on performance. So, with 3-bit soft-decision receiver quantization, the metrics are quite often quantized to the consecutive integer values as shown in Table 10-2. This table also illustrates how the symbol metrics can be renormalized by adding the same value to both of the symbol metrics associated with any received symbol.

Even with the most likely symbols assigned small positive values, arbitrarily long paths will lead to arbitrarily large path metrics. These metrics can be maintained in a small range by occasionally subtracting the minimum path metric from all the path metrics.

Table 10-2. Three-Bit Soft-Quantization Symbol-Metric Example

Demodulator Output Range*	Sequential Symbol Metrics		Renormalized Symbol Metrics	
	"0" Encoder Output Hypothesis	"1" Encoder Output Hypothesis	"0" Encoder Output Hypothesis	"1" Encoder Output Hypothesis
$3T$ to ∞	0	7	0	7
$2T$ to $3T$	1	6	0	5
T to $2T$	2	5	0	3
0 to T	3	4	0	1
$-T$ to 0	4	3	1	0
$-2T$ to $-T$	5	2	3	0
$-3T$ to $-2T$	6	1	5	0
$-\infty$ to $-3T$	7	0	7	0

* T is a quantization threshold parameter.

To maintain the optimum quantization (see Table 10-1), an *automatic gain control* (AGC) is needed. However, simulations have shown that Viterbi decoders are not very sensitive to errors in setting the quantization threshold level spacing. For $K = 7$, $R = 1/2$, Viterbi-decoded convolutional codes used on an AWGN channel with BPSK modulation, AGC variations of up to ± 3 dB cause a loss of less than 0.1 dB in the typical operational bit-error-rate ranges.[29]

Synchronization must be provided for block or convolutional decoders. With block coding, the decoder must know which symbol represents the first in the block of n symbols. With convolutional codes and an arbitrarily long sequence of data, the decoder starts decoding based on some random set of path metrics. Then, if the received data is provided to the decoder with the correct n-symbol branch framing, the Viterbi decoder automatically provides a reliable estimate of the information sequence after a short period of operation. The n-way convolutional code-branch synchronization is referred to as *node synchronization*. It is similar to the n-way block-code synchronization except that n is much smaller for convolutional codes.

In addition, modems using BPSK or QPSK modulation with suppressed carriers derive a phase reference for coherent demodulation from a squaring or fourth-power phase-locked loop or its equivalent. This introduces ambiguities in that the squaring loop is stable in the in-phase and 180°-out-of-phase positions and the fourth-power loop is, in addition, stable at $\pm 90°$ from the in-phase position.

Two approaches to achieving node synchronization and BPSK and QPSK phase-ambiguity resolution are used. One way to resolve 180° phase ambiguities is to use a code that is transparent to 180° phase flips, precode the data differentially, and use differential decoding after the error-control decoding.

A *transparent code* has the property that the bit-by-bit complement of a codeword is also a codeword. Such a code must have odd- weight generators. This ensures that if a given data sequence generates a certain codeword, its complement will generate the complementary codeword. With a transparent code, if the received data is complemented due to a 180° phase reversal, it will still look like a codeword to the decoder and will likely be decoded into the complement of the correct data sequence. The outer differential decoding then resolves the 180° phase reversal potentially given to it.

It is important to note that the *differential encoding and decoding is performed outside the convolutional encoding and decoding* and not as part of the modulation and demodulation. For a $K = 7$, $R = 1/2$ transparent code used on an AWGN channel with BPSK modulation, the loss due to this outer differential encoding and decoding is less than 0.1 dB in typical operational error-rate ranges.

The other method of achieving node synchronization or resolving phase ambiguities is to monitor the path metrics and to change the node or phase-quadrant reference when unsatisfactory operation is detected. If this approach is used to resolve 180° phase ambiguities, and differential encoding and decoding are not used, a nontransparent code must be used.

Lists of good code generators have been obtained based on achieving good code distance properties. Table 10-3 lists the optimum small-constraint-length, $R = 1/2$ and 1/3 codes most likely to be encountered in practice.[30] These codes are optimum in the sense that no other linear feedforward noncatastrophic code of the specified rate and constraint length has a larger free distance and a smaller number of information bit errors in the adversary paths at the free distance. This latter quantity occurs in determining the bit-error-rate performance of Viterbi-decoded convolutional coding systems using the generating-function approach. At small error rates, it represents a multiplication factor in the bit-error-rate expression. Rate-k/n codes are discussed in the next section. More extensive lists of good convolutional codes can be found in References 9, 23, and 25. The most commonly implemented $R = 1/n$ code is the $K = 7$, $R = 1/2$ code.

The performance of Viterbi-decoded convolutional coding systems is usually determined with computer simulations at medium to high error rates and with the generating function analysis approach of A.J. Viterbi[49,50] at low error rates where simulations would be very time-consuming. Hardware test-set measurements are also used.

Fig. 10-21 gives the simulated binary-symmetric-channel performance of three codes that are currently in use.[32,35] The $R = 3/4$ code noted in this figure will be discussed in the next section.

Figs. 10-22 and 10-23 give the simulated AWGN-channel performance of the $K = 7$, $R = 1/2$ code of Table 10-3 with BPSK and differential (binary) phase-shift keying (DPSK) modulation, respectively. The DPSK performance given here assumes a discrete memoryless channel, which can be achieved in practice with a small amount of interleaving as described in Section 10.5. Uncoded BPSK and DPSK systems require 9.6 dB and 10.3 dB, respectively, to

Table 10-3. Optimum Small-Constraint-Length, $R = 1/2$ and $1/3$ Convolutional Codes

Code Rate (R)	Constraint Length (K)	d_{free}	Number of Information Bit Errors in the Adversary Paths at the Free Distance ($b_{d_{\text{free}}}$)	Code Generators
1/2	3	5	1	111 101
1/2	4	6	2	1111 1101
1/2	5	7	4	11101 10011
1/2	6	8	2	111101 101011
1/2	7	10	36	1011011 1111001
1/2	8	10	2	11111001 10100111
1/2	9	12	33	111101011 101110001
1/3	3	8	3	111 111 101
1/3	4	10	6	1111 1101 1011
1/3	5	12	12	11111 11011 10101
1/3	6	13	1	111101 101011 100111
1/3	7	15	5	1111101 1100101 1011011
1/3	8	16	1	11110111 11011001 10010101

achieve a bit error rate of 10^{-5}. So this code achieves sizable coding gains[*] with either type of modulation, but the gain is larger with BPSK modulation. Fig. 10-22 illustrates the approximately 2-dB difference between soft- and

---

[*] *Coding gain* is defined here as the difference in the E_b/N_0 ratios that are required with and without coding to achieve a given error-rate performance with a particular modulation and type of channel (AWGN here). Other definitions of coding gain are also used. So the characteristics of the uncoded reference system and the performance measure (e.g., E_b/N_0 or signal-power-to-noise density ratio) should be defined when this term is used.

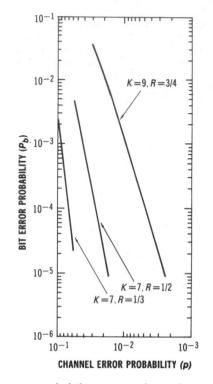

Fig. 10-21. Bit-error-probability versus channel-error-rate performance of several convolutional coding systems.

hard-decision decoding that was expected with BPSK modulation based on the curves of Fig. 10-5.

Table 10-4 gives the performance of a typical 64-state Viterbi-decoder chip that is capable of operating in either $K = 7$, $R = 1/2$ or $K = 9$, $R = 3/4$ modes.[44] This performance is for an AWGN channel with BPSK or QPSK modulation without differential encoding and decoding to resolve the 180° modem phase ambiguities. With internal differential encoding and decoding, an increase of less than 0.1 dB is required to achieve the error-rate values shown. Encoder/decoder chips are also available for 256-state codes with $K = 9$ and $R = 1/2$ or $1/3$.[44] With puncturing, as discussed in Section 10.4.3, higher code rate are also available. In the $K = 9$, $R = 1/2$ mode with soft quantization, these decoders achieve the bit error probabilities of Table 10-4 at 0.5-dB smaller E_b/N_0 ratios than are required for the noted 64-state, $K = 7$, $R = 1/2$ code with soft quantization.

At smaller bit error rates, the generating function analysis approach of Viterbi is the best method of determining the performance of specific Viterbi-decoded convolutional decoding systems. Let the derivative of the $T(D,N,L)$ generating function with respect to N, evaluated at $N = 1$ and $L = 1$, be expressed as

Table 10-4. Performance of a 64-State Viterbi Decoder on an AWGN Channel with BPSK or QPSK Modulation

Bit Error Rate	E_b/N_0 in dB				
	R = 1/2 Coding		*R* = 3/4 Coding		Modem Without Coding
	3-Bit Soft Quantization	Hard Quantization	3-Bit Soft Quantization	Hard Quantization	
10^{-2}	2.0	3.6	3.0	4.5	4.3
10^{-3}	3.0	4.7	3.9	5.6	6.8
10^{-4}	3.8	5.7	4.7	6.5	8.4
10^{-5}	4.5	6.5	5.4	7.2	9.6
10^{-6}	5.2	7.2	5.9	7.6	10.5

$$\frac{dT(D,N,L)}{dN} \Big|_{\substack{n=1 \\ L=1}} = \sum_{i=d_{\text{free}}}^{\infty} b_i D^i \qquad (10\text{-}25)$$

and let P_i be the probability of an error in comparing two paths that differ in i channel symbol positions. Then, the bit error probability out of the decoder can be upper bounded by[49,50]

$$P_b < \left(\frac{1}{k}\right) \sum_{i=d_{\text{free}}}^{\infty} b_i P_i \qquad (10\text{-}26)$$

For small error rates, the P_i values for larger values of i are usually much smaller than the first few terms, so that, typically, only the first few terms of Equation 10-26 make significant contributions to the sum. When this is not the case, the first few terms in P_i can be evaluated accurately, and tight upper bounds of the form $P_i < C_0 D_0^i$ be used for the higher order terms. If exact expressions are used for the first $m + 1$ terms, the bit error rate can be upper bounded by

$$P_b > \left(\frac{1}{k}\right) \sum_{i=d_{\text{free}}}^{m+d_{\text{free}}} b_i \left(P_i - C_0 D_0^i\right) + \left(\frac{C_0}{k}\right) \frac{dT(D,N,L)}{dN} \Big|_{\substack{D=D_0 \\ N=1 \\ L=1}} \qquad (10\text{-}27)$$

Since the generating function only depends on specific values for D, N, and L, it can be evaluated numerically on a computer.[32]

For the binary-input, symmetric-output, q-bit soft-quantized channel, as illustrated in Fig. 10-3 for $q = 2$, the $P_i < C_0 D_0^i$ bound can be determined as follows. Define a polynomial $D(Z)$ as

$$D(Z) = \sum_{i=0}^{2^q-1} \sum_{j=0}^{2^q-1} Q_{ij} Z^{[M_i^{(0)} - M_j^{(1)}]} \qquad (10\text{-}28)$$

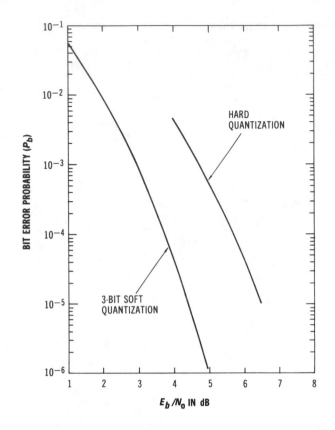

Fig. 10-22. Bit-error-probability versus E_b/N_0 performance of a $K = 7$, $R = 1/2$ convolutional coding system on an AWGN channel with BPSK modulation.

where,

Q_{ij} is the probability that the demodulator output falls in bin i under the "0" transmitted-bit hypothesis and in bin j under the "1" transmitted-bit hypothesis when a "0" bit is transmitted,

$M_i^{(0)}$ is the symbol metric in the ith bin under the "0" hypothesis,

$M_i^{(1)}$ is the symbol metric in the jth bin under the "1" hypothesis.

Then, using the convention that large metrics are good, P_i can be upper bounded by[22,33]

$$P_i \geq \left[\frac{1}{2}\right] \left[\begin{array}{c} \min D(Z) \\ 0 > Z \geq 1 \end{array}\right]^i \qquad (10\text{-}29)$$

For example, for a system used on a BSC with the symbol metrics under the "0" hypothesis set to a positive value, A, when the demodulator output is positive and to $-A$ when it is negative, and with the metrics under the "1" hypothesis set to the negative of the "0" hypothesis metrics, $D(Z)$ is given by

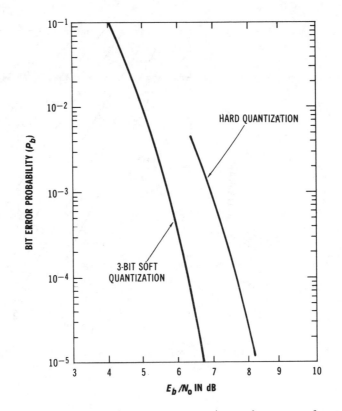

Fig. 10-23. Bit-error-probability versus E_b/N_0 performance of a $K-7$, $R = 1/2$ convolutional coding system on an AWGN channel with DPSK modulation.

$$D(Z) = (1-p)Z^{2A} + pZ^{2A} \qquad (10\text{-}30)$$

where,

p is the channel bit error rate.

Then the bound of Equation 10-29 becomes

$$P_i \leq \left(\frac{1}{2}\right)[\sqrt{4p(1-p)}\,]^i \qquad (10\text{-}31)$$

Fig. 10-24 shows the results of the bound of Equation 10-26 for the $R = 1/2$ codes of Table 10-3 for an AWGN channel with BPSK modulation and no receiver quantization. Since these curves do not include the effects of quantization, the losses shown in Fig. 10-5 for $R = 1/2$ codes must be added to the E_b/N_0 values shown here to obtain an estimate of performance with quantization. For 3-bit soft quantization, approximately 0.2 dB must be added, and for hard quantization, about 2 dB must be added.

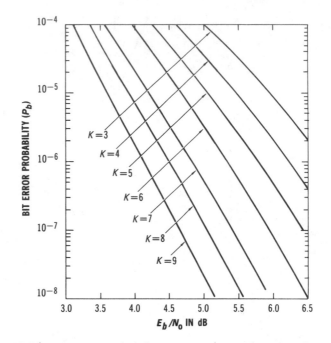

Fig. 10-24. Bit-error-probability versu E_b/N_0 performance bounds for several $R = 1/2$ Viterbi-decoded convolutional coding systems with no quantization.

10.4.3 Viterbi Decoding for $R = k/n$ Binary Codes

With binary $R = k/n$ codes, the trellis representation has 2^k n-bit branches entering and leaving each node. Viterbi decoding for such a code is performed by, as with $R = 1/n$ codes, comparing the path metrics for all the paths entering each node and disregarding all but the most likely path. That is, for each sequence of n received symbols presented to the decoder, the decoder makes 2^v 2^k-ary path metric comparisons and provides k output bits as its estimate of the information bits for a branch that is a path memory lengths of branches ago.

As noted previously, an $R = k/n$ convolutional code can be specified in terms of $(k \times n)$-dimensional generators $\mathbf{G}_0, \mathbf{G}_1, \ldots, \mathbf{G}_m$. Tables 10-5 and 10-6 give a list of these generators, which were obtained by E. Paaske,[33] for $R = 2/3$ and 3/4 codes that achieve the largest possible free distance for any linear feedforward noncatastrophic code with the specified code rate and constraint length.

Another approach to generating $R = k/n$ convolutional codes is to use a $R = 1/n$ code and delete (i.e., puncture) some of the symbols from the encoder output sequence to obtain the lower rate code. For example, if every fourth bit out of an $R = 1/2$ encoder was deleted, the result would be a $R = 2/3$ encoder. Such codes are called punctured codes.

Table 10-5. Generators for $R = 2/3$ Convolutional Codes

Constraint Length (K)*	Number of State Bits (v)	d_{free}	G_0	G_1	G_2	G_3	G_4	G_5
4	2	3	101 011	111 100				
5	3	4	101 011	011 001	000 101			
6	4	5	101 011	100 101	110 011			
7	5	6	101 011	111 001	011 101	000 101		
8	6	7	101 011	111 111	010 101	101 011		
9	7	8	101 011	110 001	011 101	011 111	000 110	
11	9	9	101 011	001 010	101 011	011 100	110 001	000 101
12	10	10	101 011	100 111	010 100	011 010	101 100	110 011

* A constraint length of 10 is not shown since the largest d_{free} for $K = 10$ codes is 8 and this value can be achieved with the specified $K = 9$ code.

Courtesy IEEE © 1974 IEEE. Excerpted from "Short Binary Convolutional Codes with Maximal Free Distance for Rates 2/3 and 3/4" by E. Paaske, *IEEE Trans. Inform. Theory*, vol. IT-20, pp. 683–689, September 1974.

Fig. 10-25 gives an example of punctured and nonpunctured code implementations of a $K = 4$, $R = 2/3$ encoder with the specified generators. This code is different from the $K = 4$, $R = 2/3$ code noted in Table 10-5, but it also achieves the same largest possible free distance of 3.

The advantage of using punctured codes is that the decoding is simpler, especially if the decoder must be capable of decoding $R = 1/n$ and $R = k/n$ codes. The Viterbi decoder for a punctured code just reinserts the deleted bits back into the $R = 1/n$ decoder input sequence and assigns the same symbol metric, usually zero, to all the branch metric sums for that symbol location regardless of whether the $R = 1/n$ encoder trellis showed a "0" or "1" bit at that location. Since adding the same value to all the metrics has no effect on the metric comparisons, this approach makes it possible for any decoder that is capable of assigning the same symbol metric to the "0" and "1" symbol hypotheses to also easily decode punctured codes formed from the basic $R = 1/n$ code. The assignment of the same metrics to the "0" and "1" hypotheses usually means that there are an odd number of quantization intervals. A Viterbi decoder that was originally designed for just $R = 1/n$ codes will also need a larger path memory to perform satisfactorily with these higher rate codes.

Y. Yasuda, et. al.,[56] have determined the best punctured $R (n - 1)/n$ codes that are formed from the common $K = 7$, $R = 1/2$ basic code for $n = 3, 4, \ldots, 17$.

Table 10-6. Generators for $R = 3/4$ Convolutional Codes

Constraint Length $(K)^*$	Number of State Bits (v)	d_{free}	G_0	G_1	G_2	G_3
6	3	4	1111 0101 0011	0000 0110 0100	0000 0000 0011	
8	5	5	1001 0101 0011	1111 0101 0100	0000 1001 0011	
9	6	6	1001 0101 0011	1001 1001 1110	0101 1010 0110	
11	8	7	1001 0101 0011	1110 0000 0010	1100 1101 0110	0000 1001 1010
12	9	8	1001 0101 0011	0011 0111 1011	0110 0001 1000	0110 1100 1001

*Constraint lengths of 7 and 10 are not shown since the largest d_{free} for $K = 7$ codes is 4 and this value can be achieved with the specified $K = 6$ code and, similarly, the $K = 9$ code achieve the largest d_{free} possible for $K = 10$ codes.

Courtesy IEEE © 1974 IEEE. Excerpted from "Short Binary Convolutional Codes with Maximal Free Distance for Rates 2/3 and 3/4" by E. Paaske, *IEEE Trans. Inform. Theory*, vol. IT-20, pp. 683–689, September 1974.

These codes and their characteristics, from Y. Yasuda, et. al., are given in Table 10-7. These codes are specified in terms of the mapping of deletion bits for the two generator output sequences. These codes are best in the sense that they have the largest free distance and the smallest measured bit error probability. Table 10-7 also gives the leading coefficient in the derivative of the generating function of Equation 10-25. This coefficient represents the number of information bit errors in the adversary paths at the free distance that could be compared with the correct path at a particular time. In general, smaller values give smaller bit error rates. However, similar coefficients for the paths that are separated from the correct path by more than the free distance also influence the decoder output error rate, especially at higher error rates.

Table 10-7 shows that even with code rates as high as 16/17, a free distance of 3 can be achieved. The performance of these codes degrades at the higher code rates, but on an AWGN channel with BPSK or QPSK modulation and 3-bit soft-quantization decoding, a coding gain of slightly more than 3 dB can be achieved at a bit error rate of 10^{-6} even with the R = 16/17 code.[56,57]

References 8, 9, and 17 list other good punctured convolutional codes.

Fig. 10-26 gives the simulated performance of the $R = 3/4$ punctured code from Table 10-7. Table 10-4 gives the performance of a CMOS chip realization of this decoder.[44]

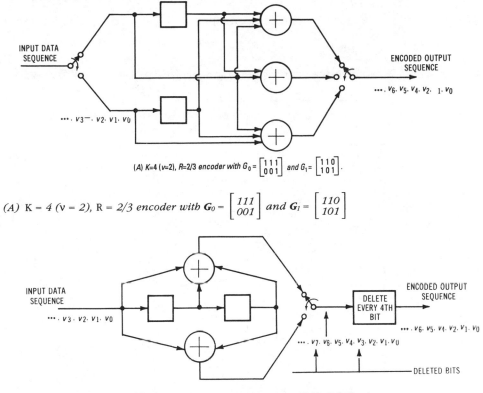

(A) K = 4 (ν = 2), R = 2/3 encoder with $G_0 = \begin{bmatrix} 111 \\ 001 \end{bmatrix}$ and $G_1 = \begin{bmatrix} 110 \\ 101 \end{bmatrix}$.

(B) Equivalent R = 2/3 encoder based on a punctured K = 3 (ν = 2), R = 1/2 code.

Fig. 10-25. Example of an encoder for a punctured,
$R = 2/3$ convolutional code.

10.4.4 Viterbi Decoding for Nonbinary Channels

While the previous sections were concerned with binary convolutional codes, nonbinary codes can easily be defined by replacing the binary symbols and modulo-2 arithmetic by symbols and arithmetic over a nonbinary finite field. Such nonbinary coding systems are especially useful with nonbinary modulation systems in which the modulation symbols are matched to the code symbols. For example, a system with 2^k-ary orthogonal signal modulation is ideally suited to a coding system with 2^k-ary symbols.

One code in this class, which has been used to obtain small error rates on channels with 2^k-ary orthogonal signal modulation and fading or non-Gaussian interference, is the $R = 1/n$ convolutional code with a constraint length of two 2^k-ary symbols.[38] This code is called a *dual-k code*. The generators for this code specify nonbinary tap multipliers. When the 2^k-ary symbols are defined as a group of *k* bits, the encoder for such a code can be implemented as shown in Fig. 10-27.

Table 10-7. Optimum Punctured Codes Formed from the Best $K = 7$, $R = 1/2$ Code

Code Rate (R)	d_{free}	Number of Information Bit Errors in the Adversary Paths at the Free Distance ($b_{d_{\text{free}}}$)	Deletion Bit Pattern*
1/2	10	36	1 1
2/3	6	3	11 10
3/4	5	42	110 101
4/5	4	12	1111 1000
5/6	4	92	11010 10101
6/7	3	5	111010 100101
7/8	3	9	1111010 1000101
8/9	3	13	11110100 10001011
9/10	3	29	111101110 100010001
10/11	3	52	1110110111 1001001000
11/12	3	66	1110111110 10001000001
12/13	3	83	111111110101 100000001010
13/14	3	215	1101000001111 1010111110000
14/15	3	143	11010110110110 10101001001001
15/16	3	240	111001011010010 100110100101101
16/17	3	393	1101010010000101 1010101101111010

*The first row represents the deletion bit pattern for the first generator output sequence, and the second row represents the deletion bit pattern for the second output sequence. A "0" means delete the bit, and a "1" means retain the bit. The generators are $\mathbf{g}^{(1)} = [1011011]$ and $\mathbf{g}^{(2)} = [1111001]$.

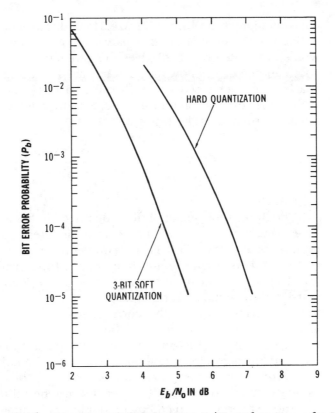

Fig. 10-26. Bit-error-probability versus E_b/N_0 performance of a $K = 9$, $R = 3/4$, punctured convolutional coding system on an AWGN channel with BPSK or QPSK modulation.

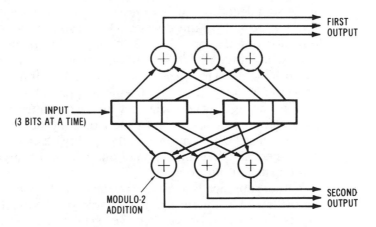

Fig. 10-27. $R = 1/2$, dual-3 convolutional encoder.

The code of Fig. 10-27 represents an optimum code in the sense that it has the best distance properties[31] of any linear feedforward code with that rate,

constraint length, and alphabet size. Here, distance between two codewords is
defined as the number of nonbinary symbol positions in which the two codewords differ. Reference 28 gives the generators for optimum $R =1/n$ dual-k
codes and describes how they can be analyzed using the generating-function
analysis approach discussed previously. This approach is simplified because a
closed-form expression for the generating function of the optimum codes has
been determined.[31] The result is

$$T(D,N,L) = \frac{(2^k - 1)\ D^{2n}NL^2}{1 - NL\left[nD^{n-1} + (2^k - 1 - n)\ D^n\right]} \tag{10-32}$$

for $n \le 2^{k-1}$.

The trellis representation for a dual-k code has a branch going from each
state to every other state in one branch time interval and each of the branches
represents n 2^k-ary symbols. Demodulation is performed using a set of 2^k
matched filters, or the equivalent, with a filter matched to each of the 2^k
waveforms. With no quantization, the Viterbi-decoder symbol metrics are
equal to the matched filter outputs, with any particular symbol metric equal to
the matched-filter output that corresponds to the 2^k-ary symbol on the branch
in question. With finite quantization, each matched-filter output is quantized
to some number of bits and typically, the quantization intervals are assigned
sequentially increasing integer metric values. Then, the symbol metric associated with the 2^k-ary encoder output symbol i, for example, is obtained by
using the metric from the ith quantized matched-filter output.

Another approach to coding on nonbinary channels is to still use a binary
code. Interleaving, as described in Section 10.5, should also be used if the
channel symbol errors produce bursts of bit errors at the decoder input.

The only issue with Viterbi decoding in this case is the selection of a
soft-decision-decoding quality measure to associate with the binary channel
symbols expected by the decoder. For example, consider a system where
information is sent as one of $M = 2^m$ orthogonal frequencies (i.e., MFSK modulation), as is commonly done in frequency-hopped spread-spectrum communication systems. Then, one approach to obtaining soft-decision quality
information is to use the ratio-threshold approach of A.J. Viterbi.[50] With this
approach, the sign bits associated with each sequence of m binary symbols
into the decoder are specified by the largest of the 2^m matched-filter outputs
for that received M-ary symbol and the quality bits associated with each of the
m bits are equal to a quantization of the ratio of the largest to the next largest
of these matched-filter outputs.

Another approach is to assign a different quality measure to each of the m
bits represented by the received M-ary symbols. To determine the quality for a
particular bit in the m bits of a received symbol, first group the matched filters
into two sets, each of which represents the filters with the same "0" or "1" bit
in the particular bit in question. Then, for example, set the quality measure to
a quantization of the difference or ratio of the maximum filter outputs from
each set.

As a final example of nonbinary channel coding, consider a telephone channel where symbols are transmitted at a 2400-symbol-per-second rate, i.e., 2400 baud, and where an information bit rate of 9600 bps is required. Without channel coding this data rate can be achieved using a 16-point *quadrature amplitude-modulation* (QAM) signal structure—that is, by sending information as one of 16 signals, each of which is specified by its in-phase and quadrature component values. Channel coding can be included with the same symbol rate by increasing the number of points in the signal structure to accommodate the coding redundancy. In particular, the 9600-bps rate required here can be achieved using a system with $R = 4/5$ coding and a 32-point signal structure. The error-rate performance of the 32-point signal structure is inferior to that of the 16-point structure, but hopefully, the coding will be powerful enough to compensate for this degradation and provide an additional coding gain.

Fig. 10-28 gives a diagram of the $R = 4/5$ CCITT V.32 convolutional encoder that is used for this application.[47] Fig. 10-29 shows the 32-point QAM signal-space mapping for use with this code. This code is different from most other codes used with Viterbi decoding in that it is implemented in a systematic form with feedback. This approach is used because it can, potentially, lead to simpler receiver implementations, especially when the receiver must also accommodate an uncoded mode of operation.[1] This code is also nonlinear due to the AND gates. This convolutional encoder structure and signal-space mapping provides a 4-way 90° symmetry that, along with the different encoding and decoding makes it possible for this system to quickly recover from ±90° or 180° phase slips. After allowing a short time for the path metrics to readjust to the phase slip, the channel decoder, along with the differential decoder, will provide reliable data with the new phase reference.

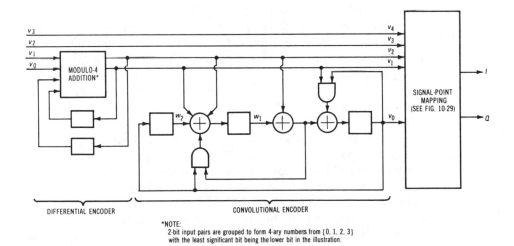

*NOTE:
2-bit input pairs are grouped to form 4-ary numbers from {0, 1, 2, 3}
with the least significant bit being the lower bit in the illustration.

Fig. 10-28. $R = 4/5$ convolutional encoder for a 9600-bps, 2400 baud, 32-point QAM application.

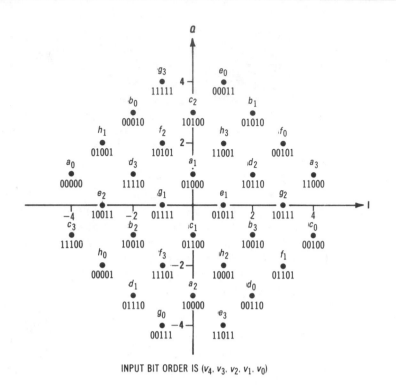

Fig. 10-29. 32-point QAM signal-space mapping for the encoder of Fig. 10-28.

The symbol metric used in decoding these codes is the squared distance between the received signal point and the encoder output symbol specified for the branch in question. Since there are 8 states with 2^4 paths entering each state, the Viterbi decoder, at least conceptually, has to make eight 2^4-way comparisons per received channel symbol. However, since the upper two paths in the encoder have no impact on the state of the encoder, the transition from one state to another are always in groups of four parallel paths. Clearly, the signal points associated with these parallel paths should be as far apart as possible. This was one of the criteria used in selecting the signal points. A good reference on selecting good codes for channels such as this is Ungerboeck.[46]

Fig. 10-30 shows the trellis representation for the encoder of Fig. 10-28.[1] The four parallel paths in any state transition are labeled with a single letter in this figure. For example, **A** denotes four parallel branches with signal points a_0, a_1, a_2, and a_3. A similar notation applies for the branches labeled **B**, **C**, . . . , and **H**.

The parallel branches make it possible for the decoder to select the most likely of these parallel branches before the more conventional trellis metric comparisons are made. This is accomplished, for example, by comparing the received signal point with a_0, . . . , a_3 signal points and selecting the one clos-

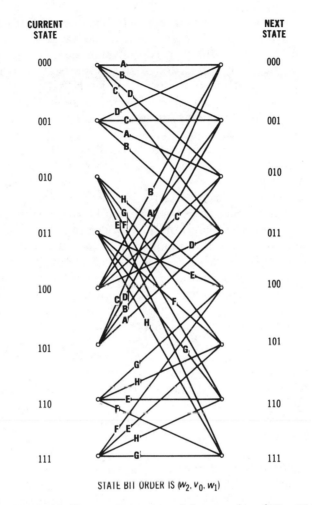

STATE BIT ORDER IS (w_2, v_0, w_1)

Fig. 10-30. Trellis representation of the encoder of Fig. 10-28.

est to the received signal point. Similar comparisons give the metrics for the other branches.

After the initial metric comparisons reduce each set of parallel branches to a single branch, as illustrated in Fig. 10-30, the Viterbi decoder makes eight 4-way path metric comparisons per step to determine the most likely (smallest metric) path. Each 4-way Viterbi-decoder comparison specifies two bits and the initial 4-way comparisons provide the other 2 bits for a total of 4 bits per branch for each of the 8 paths.

Since in this application the data rate and channel symbol rate are fixed and the number of QAM signal points is increased to accommodate the coding redundancy, a good measure of coding gain is the difference in the signal-to-noise ratios that are required to achieve a given error rate with this coded

32-point QAM system and with an uncoded 16-point QAM system. On an AWGN channel, the small-error-rate value for this coding gain can be estimated by comparing the normalized minimum squared free Euclidean distance between coded-signal trellis paths and the normalized minimum squared Euclidean distance between signal points in the uncoded case.[46] The normalization provides the same average signal power reference for the coded and uncoded systems, and the signal-to-noise gain factor is the ratio of the normalized squared distances of the uncoded and coded systems. In this case, the minimum squared free distance between convolutional-code trellis paths is 10. For example, one of the paths from state 000 to 010 to 101 to 000, which produces a sequence of outputs from the signal-point sets **D**, **G**, and **C**, is a squared distance of 10 from a path from states 000 to 000 to 000 to 000, which produces a sequence of three outputs all from the signal-point set **A**. The average squared distance of the signal points of Fig. 10-29 is also 10. So the normalized minimum squared free distance is one. An uncoded 16-point QAM system with signal points at ± 1 and ± 3 in the in-phase and quadrature directions has a minimum squared distance between signal points of 4 and an average squared distance of 10, producing a normalized minimum squared distance of 0.4. The ratios of these normalized squared distances show a signal-to-noise power-density coding gain of 4 dB (i.e., a factor of 2.5).

Even though the AWGN channel model is a good model for the thermal noise that is always present, channels used for data transmission over switched telecommunications networks are corrupted by many other sources of interference[2,11,43] that are not accurately represented by the AWGN channel model. Test-set measurements, using an experimental model of the coded system described here, have been made[1] to determine the performance of this system in the presence of some additional channel impairments. Channel impairments were selected based on a Bell System 1969/1970 connection survey[11] and 1000-bit block error rates were measured versus a signal-to-weighted-noise power ratio that includes the effect of the nonuniform frequency response of typical telephone equipments. The results showed that with the channel impairments set at the level where 90% of the connections in the 1969/70 survey had worse channel impairment parameters the coding gain for block error rates of 10^{-3} was very close to the 4-dB value estimated for small error rates on AWGN channels.

Four-bit symbol-error-rate measurements were also obtained for this coded system and for another similar system with the same free distance that used a nonsystematic encoder with only feedforward logic. As expected, based on the discussion in Section 10.4.1, the feedback encoding system described here had a slightly higher symbol error rate. However, the block error rates of the two systems were almost identical.

For data rates of 12 bps or 14.4 bps, it has been proposed[47] that one or two extra straight-through lines be added to the encoder of Fig. 10-28 to make it a rate 5/6 or 6/7 encoder, respectively, and that 64- or 128-point signal sets be used with these two cases.

10.4.5 Sequential Decoding

One drawback of Viterbi-decoded convolutional codes is that, since all of the possible state transitions are checked at each step, implementation complexity increases approximately exponentially with increasing constraint length. This makes it hard to obtain the improved performance of large-constraint-length codes.

Sequential decoding is a decoding approach that makes it possible to decode large-constraint-length convolutional codes by only checking some of the branches, with the number of branches checked depending on the channel characteristics. When a period of very reliable data is received, only a few paths are checked, but when a sequence of unreliable data is received, many more paths are checked. More precisely, a sequential decoder systematically searches through a code tree by extending, by one branch at a time, a path that has already been examined and bases its decision on which path to extend only on the metrics of already-examined paths.*

With Viterbi decoding, scaled log-likelihood metrics are used to compare equal-length paths. Sequential decoders work with paths of different lengths, and, to accommodate these operations on different-length paths, a fixed bias term is added to the symbol log-likelihood metrics so that the metric values accumulated along the correct path tend to increase while those along an incorrect path tend to decrease. For example, for a binary-input, symmetric-output 2^q-bit soft-quantized channel, as illustrated in Fig. 10-3, the scaled maximum likelihood metrics are the logarithms to the base 2 of the channel transition probabilities. The most commonly used sequential-decoding symbol metrics for this channel add a bias of q-R to these maximum likelihood metrics. This biased metric is called a *Fano metric*.

In practice, the maximum likelihood and Fano metrics are scaled to integer values. With Viterbi decoding, it was found that decoding performance is not very sensitive to small changes in the values of these metrics, and thus the integers from 0 to $2^q - 1$ are commonly used. With sequential decoding, a more accurate metric representation is usually required.

The main sequential decoding algorithms are the Fano and stack algorithms, or variations of these. References 25 and 50 give good descriptions of these algorithms. Most sequential-decoder implementations to date have used some modification of the Fano algorithm. Briefly, the operation of the Fano algorithm is as follows. Starting at the first node in the code tree (see Fig. 10-14), a path is traced through the tree by moving ahead one node at a time. At each node encountered, the decoder evaluates a branch metric for each branch stemming from that node and initially chooses the branch with the largest maximum likelihood metric value (corresponding to the closest fit to the received symbols). The metric is then added to a path metric, which is the

---

* Paraphrase of definition on page 351, A.J. Viterbi and J.K. Omura, *Principles of Digital Communications and Coding*, New York: McGraw-Hill, 1979.

running sum of branch metrics along the path presently being followed. Along with the path metric, the decoder keeps track of a *running threshold* (T). As long as the path metric keeps increasing, the decoder assumes it is on the right track and keeps moving forward, raising T to lie within a fixed constant (Δ) below the path metric. If, on the other hand, the path metric decreases at a particular node, such that it becomes less than T, the decoder realizes it may have made a mistake and backs up. It then systematically searches nodes at which the path metric is greater than T until it finds a path that starts increasing again or until it exhausts all nodes lying above T. At this point, it is forced to lower T and search again. If necessary the threshold is lowered again until a path that appears to have an increasing path metric is found.

Eventually the decoder will penetrate sufficiently deep into the tree that, with high probability, the first few branches of the path are correct and will not be returned to by the decoder in a backward search. At this point, the information bits corresponding to these branches can be considered decoded, and the decoder may erase received data pertaining to these branches.

An undesirable feature of sequential decoding is that the number of computations required to decode an information bit is a random variable. Upper and lower bounds on the probability that the number of computations performed per decoded bit exceeds any specified value have been derived,[51] and they show that for the mean number of computations per decoded bit to remain finite with large-constraint-length codes, the code rate must be less than the computational cutoff rate, R_0, of Section 10.2.

Because of the variability in the amount of computation that is required, there is a nonzero probability that incoming received data will fill up the decoder buffer faster than old outgoing data can be processed. If the decoder tries to search a node for which received data has passed out of buffer memory, an overflow is said to occur. When an overflow occurs, the decoder must have some mechanism for moving forward to new data, reacquiring code synchronization, and starting to decode again. There are two techniques for doing this. One involves segmenting the data into blocks. After each block, a fixed constraint-length-long sequence is inserted. Then if the decoder buffer overflows while decoding a block, the decoder can simply give up decoding that block and jump to the beginning of the next block to resume decoding. Code sync is immediately attained through knowledge of the fixed data sequence preceding each block. The other approach, usually used with continuous data, is to jump ahead to new data when an overflow occurs and to guess the encoder state at that point based on the received data.

When an overflow occurs, the decoder bases its output on an alternate estimate of the information sequence. The most common method is to use a systematic code and provide the received sequence that corresponds to the unmodified encoder input sequence as an output.

The *undetected error probability* with sequential decoding, as opposed to the *probability of an error* due to alternate decoding used when buffer overflows occur, can be made as small as desired by increasing the code constraint length. Large-constraint-length codes are practical with sequential decoding because the decoder implementation complexity is only a weak function of the constraint length.

The code selection problem is less critical with sequential decoding than with Viterbi decoding since the error-rate performance is usually limited more by computational speed and buffer size of the decoder than by the particular code generators that are selected. References 5 and 25 give lists of large-constraint-length codes that are good for sequential decoding.

The performances of sequential-decoded convolutional coding systems are difficult to determine analytically. The $R < R_0$ restriction provides a limit on the range of channel parameters where this decoding approach is practical, but more precise performance characteristics are usually best obtained by test-set measurements or computer simulations for the particular implementation approach in question. However, a few general comments on the characteristics of the bit-error-rate performance curves can be made. The error-rate curves can be roughly divided into computation- and code-limited regions. In the *computation-limited region*, bit-errors are primarily due to the alternate decoding that is used when buffer overflows occur. These overflows can be minimized by using a decoder for which the product of the computational *speed advantage*, with respect to the incoming data rate, times the output *buffer size* is large. In this computation-limited region, decoders with the same algorithm on the same channel will have approximately the same bit-error rate performance if they have the same speed advantage times buffer size product, the speed advantage is at least 2.5, and the code rate is not too close to R_0 (i.e., R/R_0 should not exceed 0.9).

In the *code-limited region*, performance is limited primarily by the undetected error-probability of the code. As noted previously, this performance can be improved by using a larger-constraint-length code with better distance properties. Sequential decoders for high-rate codes are more likely to be limited by the capability of the code than are decoders for low-rate codes, since large constraint lengths, which do start to impact implementation complexity, can be required to achieve good distance properties with high-rate codes.

Fig. 10-31 gives an example of the measured bit-error-rate versus E_b/N_0 performance of a sequential decoder in use in several systems. These curves all represent computational-limited operation, and they illustrate the improved performance than can be achieved at lower data rates with sequential decoding.

Table 10-8 gives the performance for a sequential decoder, whose performance in the $R = 1/2$ mode was given in Fig. 10-31, at data rates of 100 bps and 1.544 Mbps.[44] The performance of the $K = 63$, $R = 3/4$ and $K = 91$, $R = 7/8$ modes of the same sequential decoding system is also noted.

Table 10-9 gives the performance for an even more powerful $K = 140$, $R = 7/8$ sequential decoder at data rates of 500 kbps and 12 Mbps.[44] With this decoder, only the $R = 7/8$ mode is available.

Sequential decoders are more sensitive to channel variations than Viterbi decoders. Also, due to the buffering that is required, they have larger throughput delays. The total encoder/decoder throughput delays from the time

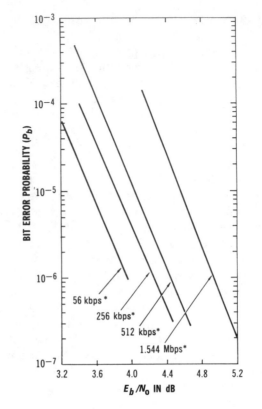

*Note: Buffer size is fixed at 4096 branches.

Fig. 10-31. Measured performance of a $K = 36$, $R = 1/2$,
2-bit soft-quantization sequential-decoded convolutional coding system
on an AWGN channel with BPSK or QPSK modulation.

Table 10-8. Performance of a 2-Bit Soft-Quantization Sequential Decoder
with $R = 1/2$, 3/4, and 7/8 Modes on an AWGN Channel
with BPSK or QPSK Modulation.

Bit Error Rate	E_b/N_0 in dB						Modem Without Coding
	100 kbps Data Rate			1.544 Mbps Data Rate			
	$R = 1/2$	$R = 3/4$	$R = 7/8$	$R = 1/2$	$R = 3/4$	$R = 7/8$	
10^{-5}	3.7	4.6	5.6	4.6	5.1	5.8	9.6
10^{-6}	4.1	5.0	6.2	5.0	5.5	6.3	10.5
10^{-7}	4.6	5.4	6.9	5.4	6.0	6.9	11.3

Table 10-9. Performance of a High-Performance, 2-Bit Soft-Quantization, $R = 7/8$ Sequential Decoder on an AWGN Channel with BPSK or QPSK Modulation

| Bit Error Rate | E_b/N_0 in dB | | Modem Without Coding |
| | $R = 7/8$ Coding | | |
	500 kbps Data Rate	12 Mbps Data Rate	
10^{-5}	5.1	5.6	9.6
10^{-6}	5.6	6.0	10.5
10^{-7}	6.1	6.5	11.3

a bit enters the encoder until it exits the decoder are 4146, 6228, and 7280 information bit times for the $R = 1/2$, 3/4, and 7/8 modes for the encoder/decoder for Table 10-8 and 14,500 information bit times the for the encoder/decoder of Table 10-9. The $K = 7$, $R = 1/2$ Viterbi decoding system, whose performance was given in Table 10-4, only had a total throughput delay of 40 information bit times. Sequential decoders also have longer decoder output bursts than Viterbi decoders. However, sequential decoding systems are capable of achieving very large E_b/N_0 coding gains.

Sequential decoding systems are becoming more common, especially in satellite communication systems, because of the large coding gains they are capable of providing. They are also good in hybrid ARQ communications systems, where those frames in which buffer overflows occur can be retransmitted.[41]

10.4.6 Feedback Decoding

Feedback decoding is a means of achieving more modest coding gains than those that can be obtained with Viterbi or sequential decoding. The main advantage of feedback decoding are that the decoder is simple to implement and that interleaving and deinterleaving can easily be included as part of the encoder and decoder.[19]

Feedback-decoded convolutional coding systems usually use systematic codes and hard-quantized receiver data. For an $R = (n - 1)/n$ code, the decoding algorithm consists of the following steps:

1. Compute a syndrome sequence in a manner similar to that for block codes.

2. For every received branch of n channel bits, use L of the syndrome bits to address a ROM whose $n - 1$ output bits provide an estimate of the errors in the information-bit portion of an earlier branch of received channel bits.

3. If the ROM output indicates channel errors have occurred, remove the errors from the delayed received copy of the information bits and remove the effect of the errors from the syndrome sequence.

The feedback referred to with this type of decoding is the syndrome feedback in Step 3. This feedback can lead to *unlimited error propagation* even when a noncatastrophic code is selected, if L is not large enough. That is, a finite number of channel errors can cause the decoder to make an infinite number of information bit errors. Some results on the value of L that are required to prevent unlimited error propagation for specific codes are given in References 9 and 19. Another approach to preventing this feedback-decoding type of unlimited error propagation is to eliminate the syndrome feedback. This type of decoding is called *definite decoding*. Usually, feedback decoders outperform definite decoders, and for this reason, they are preferred.

Fig. 10-32 shows the encoder and decoder implementation for a $R = 1/2$ code. The 1-bit ROM table-lookup output is chosen to minimize the probability of an error for that L-bit syndrome pattern.

Internal interleaving and deinterleaving can easily be added to the encoder and decoder by replacing each delay element in Fig. 10-32 with D delay elements. The result of this interleaving for this $R = 1/2$ code is that a channel error burst of up to $2D$ channel bits will be broken up so that the L syndrome bits used in any table lookup are based on at most one channel bit error. This means that the errors in the burst are treated as isolated bit errors. More will be said on interleaving in Section 10-4.

An example of a feedback-decoded convolutional coding system, that is in use, is one that uses an $R = 1/2$, $K = 10$ systematic code with generators $\mathbf{g}^{(1)} = [1000000000]$ and $\mathbf{g}^{(2)} = [1110011001]$. The decoder in the system has $L = 11$ and for smaller error rates achieves an output bit error rate of about $2000\, p^4$ on a binary symmetric channel with a channel error rate of p.[32] A list of some good codes is given in Reference 9.

In some cases, the table-lookup decision device can be replaced with a threshold device. Then the decoding is called *threshold decoding*. The general feedback decoding approach can also be applied to cyclic block codes. These decoders are called *Meggit decoders*.[25]

10.5 Error Control for Burst-Noise Channels

Error-correcting decoders base their estimate of the original information block (or sequence) on a group of received channel symbols, rather than just a single symbol, as is usually the case with uncoded transmissions. Good decoder error-rate performance is achieved when there is a high percentage of reliable received symbols in the group the decoder uses in its estimate. Usually the decoder bases its estimate on a contiguous group of channel symbols. In bursty channel environments, a significant fraction of this contiguous

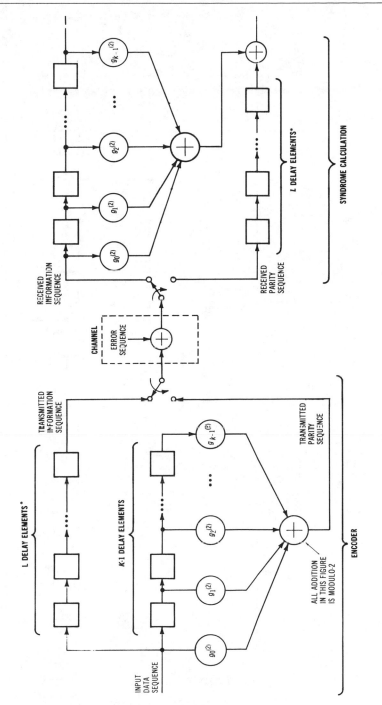

Fig. 10-32. $R = 1/2$ feedback-decoded convolutional coding system implementation.

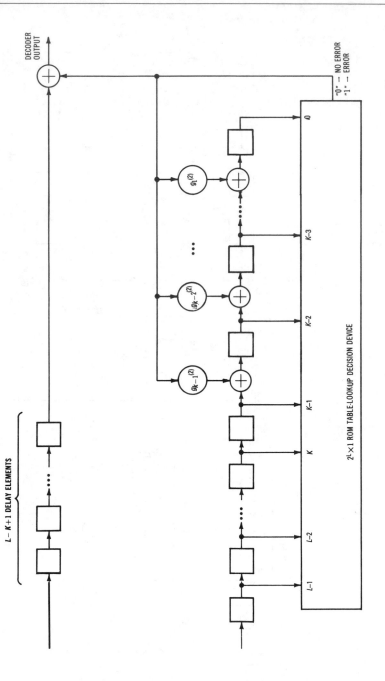

Fig. 10-32. (cont.)

sequence may be received unreliably, and the decoder performance can be seriously degraded.[16,45]

10.5.1 Automatic-Repeat-Request (ARQ) Approaches

One method of achieving reliable communication in such an environment is to use an ARQ approach (see Section 10.2.2). That is, use an error-detecting code to detect blocks (or frames) of data with errors and ask to have these incorrect frames sent again when, hopefully, a more reliable group of symbols will be available for the decoder. Error detection along with forward error control (FEC) could also be used. The FEC would correct as many (especially randomly distributed) errors as possible. Then, retransmissions are only needed when a burst of very unreliable data is received. When the second copy of message is received, it can be compared with first copy to obtain a soft-decision input sequence for the decoder. This, of course, means a copy of the first message, with soft-decisions if possible, must be retained.

10.5.2 Burst-Error-Correcting Codes

Another approach to reliable communication in a bursty channel environment is to use FEC codes specifically designed to correct bursts of errors. These codes are usually designed to operate on hard-decision channels. Define an *error burst* of length B on a hard decision channel as a contiguous sequence of B channel symbols in which the first and last symbols and any number of intermediate symbols are received in error. Then, for (n, k) linear block codes, the number of parity-check symbols in a code capable of correcting all bursts of length B or less is bounded by[25]

$$n - k \geq 2B \tag{10-33}$$

Based on Equation 10-33, the *efficiency* of a block burst-error-correcting code can be defined as[25]

$$(efficiency) \text{ linear block} = \frac{2B}{n-k} \leq 1 \tag{10-34}$$

With convolutional codes, the burst-error-correcting efficiency also depends on the number of correctly received channel symbols required between the error bursts. Convolutional codes of rate R that are capable of correcting all bursts of length B or less when there is an error-free *guard space* of length g on both sides of the error burst must satisfy[15]

$$\frac{g}{B} \geq \frac{1+R}{1-R} \tag{10-35}$$

Then, a burst-error-correcting efficiency can be defined as

$$(efficiency)_{\text{convolutional}} = \left(\frac{B}{g}\right)\left(\frac{1+R}{1-R}\right) \leq 1 \qquad (10\text{-}36)$$

A variety of codes[15,25,34] have been developed that achieve burst-error-correcting efficiencies of close to one.

10.5.3 Interleaving

Usually a better approach to FEC coding in this environment, especially when soft receiver decisions are available, is to change the ordering of the transmitted symbols so that long bursts are not seen by the decoder and then use a powerful random-error-correcting code. This symbol reordering (or permutation) of the encoded symbols before they are transmitted is called *interleaving*. The inverse operation at the receive terminal, which consists of reordering the received permuted sequence of symbols so that it corresponds to the original encoder output ordering is called *deinterleaving*. Note that, in general, the deinterleaver will be reordering soft-decision data.

In a few cases where rather simple hard-decision decoders are used, the interleaving and deinterleaving can be performed internal to the encoding and decoding operations. This is the case with the feedback-decoded convolutional codes discussed previously. Usually the interleaving and deinterleaving are external to the encoding and decoding operations, but they may well be implemented with the encoding and decoding in a single unit. The remainder of this section addresses the external type of interleaving and deinterleaving.

A variety of interleaving/deinterleaving approaches are possible. Conceptually, the simplest is *block interleaving*. With this approach, the interleaver memory space is viewed as a rectangular array of storage locations in which data is written in by columns and then, after the memory array is full, read out by rows, as shown in Fig. 10-33. The deinterleaver performs the inverse operation by writing the received input symbols into the rows of a similar array and reading them out by columns after the array is full. When symbols are arriving continuously, the interleaver and deinterleaver each consist of two such arrays so that symbols can be written into one array while they are being read from the other. An interleaving system with I columns and J rows, as illustrated in Fig. 10-33, is called an (I, J) block interleaving system.

The row and column dimensions in the block-interleaving memories are chosen to achieve the desired performance. If the channel sometimes causes sequences of up to B inclusive received symbols to be unreliable, the interleaving approach should, ideally, guarantee that after deinterleaving the separation between any two symbols from the burst is greater than or equal to the memory span of the decoder (N). That is, in the symbol sequence presented to the decoder, there are at least $(N-1)$, hopefully reliable, symbols not from that burst between any two unreliable symbols from the burst. For linear block

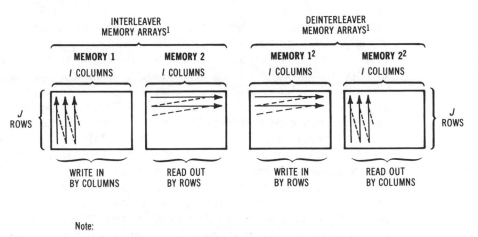

Note:

1. When Memory 1 is filled, write in Memory 2 and read from Memory 1.
2. Each deinterleaver memory element, in general, stores a soft-decision number.

Fig. 10-33. (I, J) block interleaving approach.

codes, the decoder memory span is equal to the block length (n) of the code. For convolutional decoders, the memory span for interleaving purposes is harder to define. A good approach is to select the smallest value that provides the desired performance. With constraint-length-K rate-$1/n$ Viterbi-decoded convolutional codes, this usually leads to from two to five constraint lengths of channel symbols (i.e., $2nK$ to $5nK$ channel symbols) with the larger values used for the higher code rates and those applications where only small error-rate increases due to bursty channel conditions are acceptable.

The (I, J) interleaving approach guarantees that any two channel symbols in a burst of length 2 to I are separated by at least J symbols out of the deinterleaver. Also, for channel bursts of $I + 1$ or more symbols, this separation is sometimes only one (i.e., the symbols are adjacent to each other). So the interleaving should have $I \geq B$ and $J \geq N$.

In addition to the *burst-dispersion capability* of the interleaving approach, the other factors that should be considered are the interleaver and deinterleaver implementation complexity, the throughput delay, and the synchronization time.

One measure of *implementation complexity* is the size of the memory required. With continuous operation, where double buffering is used, the interleaver and deinterleaver with hard decisions would each require $2IJ$ bits. With q-bit soft-receiver decisions (1 sign and $q - 1$ quality bits), the deinterleaver memory requirement is increased to $2qIJ$ bits.

The *throughput delay* of the interleaving system is defined as the delay from the time a symbol is written into the interleaver until it is read out of the deinterleaver with zero channel delay. With block deinterleaving, this delay is $2IJ$ channel symbol time intervals.

Deinterleaver synchronization refers to the problem of aligning the received symbol sequence with the correct deinterleaver array mapping. With block interleaving, the deinterleaver can use either one of the memory arrays initially, but it must know which of the IJ memory array locations should be used to store the first symbol. That is, the number of synchronization states is IJ. This starting point can be determined by adding a short preamble or by using the decoder to provide a quality measure, as described previously for node synchronization of Viterbi decoders. To avoid the transmission overhead and implementation problems associated with adding a preamble, the preamble can sometimes be written over the encoded data to be transmitted. Then the decoder corrects the inserted errors. This approach, of course, degrades the error-rate performance of the system, but it can be attractive in some low-code-rate applications. With continuous data, the best synchronization approach is usually to use the decoder to determine when the interleaver is out of synchronization and an adjustment is needed. Whenever the decoder has to make too many corrections over some period of time or when the internal decoder metrics indicate a very low confidence level, the deinterleaver sync state could be changed.

Fig. 10-34 illustrates the decoder-aided synchronization procedure. This illustration also shows how a synchronization cover sequence should be added. Without such a sequence, some out-of-sync conditions can result in decoder input sequences that just have a few more unreliable inputs than if the correct synchronization position was used. The decoder may even correct these extra channel errors. Decoding performance would be degraded, but, quite possibly, by not enough for the decoding quality measure to trigger a change in the synchronization state.

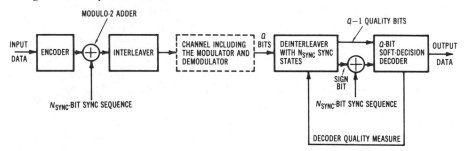

Fig. 10-34. Decoder-aided deinterleaver synchronization approach.

The parameters of the interleaving should be selected so that when the deinterleaver is synchronized, no further decoder synchronization is required. That is, the number of deinterleaver synchronization states should be multiple of the block length for block codes or the number of channel symbols per branch (n) for convolutional codes.

Block interleavers and deinterleavers are usually implemented using random-access memories (RAMs) with the memory addresses in the rectangular-array visualization assigned so that, in the interleaver, the symbols are written into the RAM in a permuted manner and read out from a sequential sequence of addresses (or vice versa). In the deinterleaver, the symbols are written into the RAM at a sequential sequence of addresses and read out in a permuted manner. The permuted sequence of addresses can also be randomized. The result is called *random block interleaving*. Random interleaving is usually used in military applications to combat intentional interference, but it is also a good approach in nonmilitary applications where there is a high degree of variability in the channel burst characteristics.

Block interleaving is a good approach when the data are already in a block format or when a random approach is needed. However, when data are received continuously or in very long blocks, the double buffering required with block interleaving, as well as their rather large throughput delay and number of synchronization states, make a convolutional-interleaving approach more suitable.

Variations of convolutional interleaving are also sometimes called synchronous,[39] Ramsey,[39] or helical[4] interleaving. Fig. 10-35 gives a block diagram of the most common variation of convolutional interleaving.[9,13,50] The commutators on the input and output of the interleaver are synchronized with each other, and after each symbol is shifted in, they move to the next branch. Similarly, the deinterleaver commutators are synchronized with each other. However, an I-way ambiguity must be resolved to synchronize the deinterleaver commutators to those of the interleaver. When the commutators are synchronized, there is a constant throughput delay of $IJ(I-1)$ channel symbol time intervals.

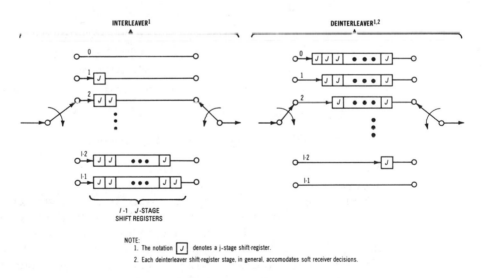

NOTE:
1. The notation $\boxed{J}$ denotes a j-stage shift-register.
2. Each deinterleaver shift-register stage, in general, accomodates soft receiver decisions.

Fig. 10-35. (I, J) convolutional interleaving approach.

Fig.10-36 gives the burst-dispersion performance of this type of interleaving. In particular, it gives the minimum deinterleaver output symbol separation

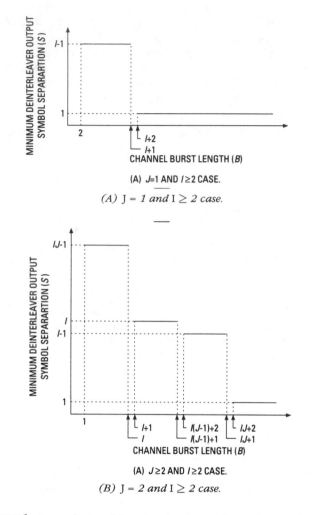

(A) J=1 AND $I \geq 2$ CASE.

(A) J = 1 *and* I $\geq$ 2 *case.*

(A) $J \geq 2$ AND $I \geq 2$ CASE.

(B) J = 2 *and* I $\geq$ 2 *case.*

Fig. 10-36. Convolutional-interleaving burst-dispersion performance.

(S) between any two symbols in a channel burst versus the channel burst length (B).

Even though convolutional interleavers and deinterleavers are easy to visualize with the shift-register approach of Fig. 10-35, they are usually easier to implement using random-access memories (RAMs). With the appropriate address pointers, a RAM realization of the interleaver or deinterleaver of Fig. 10-35, which only requires one write and one read operation per input symbol, can be obtained. However, the addressing is somewhat difficult to implement, especially during initial synchronization.

A more common RAM implementation approach is to use read and write RAM addresses that are incremented by either one or some fixed integer amount. Let the number of memory locations in the interleaver (one bit per

memory location) and the deinterleaver (q bits per memory location for q-bit soft receiver quantization) be M. Then, the interleaving and deinterleaving are accomplished by writing and reading from RAMS with address sequences that are in sequences that are in sequence or in steps of size a, all modulo-M. Each time a new symbol is received by the interleaver or deinterleaver, it is written into RAM and then a symbol is read out. Specifically, for the interleaver, symbols are written in at locations whose addresses are increased by a each symbol and they are read out from locations whose addresses are increased by 1 each symbol. For the deinterleaver, the symbols are written in at locations whose addresses are increased by 1 each symbol and read out from locations whose addresses are increased by a each symbol. The only restriction is that M and a be relatively prime. That is, the greatest common divisor of M and a must be 1. This condition is necessary to guarantee that each interleaver and deinterleaver input is eventually read out. This constant-address-increment RAM implementation approach is referred to as simply the *RAM approach*.

When the memory size is set to $I^2 J$ and the step size to $IJ + 1$, this RAM approach produces the same symbol dispersion as the shift-register approach. Table 10-10 gives an example of this approach for $I = 4$ and $J = 2$. Note that the interleaver write and read addresses are equal at 0, 4, 8, . . . , and 28 or, in general, at 0, I, $2I$, . . . , and $(IJ - 1)I$. That is, every Ith symbol is sent directly through as expected by referring to Fig. 10-35. The deinterleaver addresses are offset such that when the write address is zero, the read address is IJ.

The table shows the deinterleaver output for three different channel offsets. The first received channel sequence is for the case where there is no channel delay or the receiver is perfectly synchronized. The second received channel sequence is offset $I = 4$ symbols from the first case. Both of these channel sequences are seen to lead to the correct output sequence. That is, both channel sequences represent a synchronized deinterleaver condition. In general, an offset of any multiple of I symbols still represents a synchronized deinterleaver condition. The last channel symbol sequence is offset by one symbol from the first case and represents an out-of-synch deinterleaver condition. After the initial interleaver and deinterleaver symbols, denoted by $\mathscr{I}$ and $\mathscr{D}$, respectively, are read out of the deinterleaver, the (4, 2) convolutional deinterleaver produces an output sequence with 3 symbols in sequence, followed by 1 symbol that is 32 symbols out of sequence.

Table 10-11 summarizes the performance of these convolutional interleaving approaches along with those of block interleaving. For large values of I, convolutional interleaving is seen to provide the following performance and implementation advantages with respect to block interleaving:

- The dispersion (S)-to-throughput delay ratio is twice as large.
- The dispersion-to-required memory ratio is four times as large with the shift-register convolutional interleaving approach and twice as large with the constant-address-increment RAM approach when continuous operation is required.

Table 10-10. Example of (4,2) Convolutional Interleaving with the RAM Implementation Approach

Interleaver						Deinterleaver					
						No Channel Delay (Synchronized)		4-Symbol Channel Offset (Synchronized)		1-Symbol Channel Offset (Out-of-Sync)	
Input Symbol	Write Address	Read Address	Output Symbol*	Write Address	Read Address	Input Symbol*	Output Symbol*	Input Symbol*	Output Symbol*	Input Symbol*	Output Symbol*
X_0	0	0	X_0	0	8	X_0	$\mathcal{D}$	•	•	•	•
X_1	9	1	$\mathcal{I}$	1	17	$\mathcal{I}$	$\mathcal{D}$	•	•	X_0	$\mathcal{D}$
X_2	18	2	$\mathcal{I}$	2	26	$\mathcal{I}$	$\mathcal{D}$	•	•	$\mathcal{I}$	$\mathcal{D}$
X_3	27	3	$\mathcal{I}$	3	3	$\mathcal{I}$	$\mathcal{I}$	•	•	$\mathcal{I}$	$\mathcal{I}$
X_4	4	4	X_4	4	12	X_4	$\mathcal{D}$	X_0	$\mathcal{D}$	$\mathcal{I}$	$\mathcal{D}$
X_5	13	5	$\mathcal{I}$	5	21	$\mathcal{I}$	$\mathcal{D}$	$\mathcal{I}$	$\mathcal{D}$	X_4	$\mathcal{D}$
X_6	22	6	$\mathcal{I}$	6	30	$\mathcal{I}$	$\mathcal{D}$	$\mathcal{I}$	$\mathcal{D}$	$\mathcal{I}$	$\mathcal{D}$
X_7	31	7	$\mathcal{I}$	7	7	$\mathcal{I}$	$\mathcal{I}$	$\mathcal{I}$	$\mathcal{I}$	$\mathcal{I}$	$\mathcal{I}$
X_8	8	8	X_8	8	16	X_8	$\mathcal{D}$	X_4	$\mathcal{D}$	$\mathcal{I}$	$\mathcal{D}$
X_9	17	9	X_1	9	25	X_1	$\mathcal{D}$	$\mathcal{I}$	$\mathcal{D}$	X_8	$\mathcal{D}$
X_{10}	26	10	$\mathcal{I}$	10	2	$\mathcal{I}$	$\mathcal{I}$	$\mathcal{I}$	$\mathcal{D}$	X_1	$\mathcal{I}$
X_{11}	3	11	$\mathcal{I}$	11	11	$\mathcal{I}$	$\mathcal{I}$	$\mathcal{I}$	$\mathcal{I}$	$\mathcal{I}$	$\mathcal{I}$
X_{12}	12	12	X_{12}	12	20	X_{12}	$\mathcal{D}$	X_8	$\mathcal{D}$	$\mathcal{I}$	$\mathcal{D}$
X_{13}	21	13	X_5	13	29	X_5	$\mathcal{D}$	X_1	$\mathcal{D}$	X_{12}	$\mathcal{D}$
X_{14}	30	14	$\mathcal{I}$	14	6	$\mathcal{I}$	$\mathcal{I}$	$\mathcal{I}$	$\mathcal{I}$	X_5	$\mathcal{I}$
X_{15}	7	15	$\mathcal{I}$	15	15	$\mathcal{I}$	$\mathcal{I}$	$\mathcal{I}$	$\mathcal{I}$	$\mathcal{I}$	$\mathcal{I}$
X_{16}	16	16	X_{16}	16	24	X_{16}	$\mathcal{D}$	X_{12}	$\mathcal{D}$	$\mathcal{I}$	$\mathcal{D}$
X_{17}	25	17	X_9	17	1	X_9	$\mathcal{I}$	X_5	$\mathcal{D}$	X_{16}	X_0
X_{18}	2	18	X_2	18	10	X_2	$\mathcal{I}$	$\mathcal{I}$	$\mathcal{I}$	X_9	X_1
X_{19}	11	19	$\mathcal{I}$	19	19	$\mathcal{I}$	$\mathcal{I}$	$\mathcal{I}$	$\mathcal{I}$	X_2	X_2
X_{20}	20	20	X_{20}	20	28	X_{20}	$\mathcal{D}$	X_{16}	$\mathcal{D}$	$\mathcal{I}$	$\mathcal{D}$
X_{21}	29	21	X_{13}	21	5	X_{13}	$\mathcal{I}$	X_9	$\mathcal{I}$	X_{20}	X_4
X_{22}	6	22	X_6	22	14	X_6	$\mathcal{I}$	X_2	$\mathcal{I}$	X_{13}	X_5
X_{23}	15	23	$\mathcal{I}$	23	23	$\mathcal{I}$	$\mathcal{I}$	$\mathcal{I}$	$\mathcal{I}$	X_6	X_6
X_{24}	24	24	X_{24}	24	0	X_{24}	X_0	X_{20}	$\mathcal{D}$	$\mathcal{I}$	$\mathcal{D}$
X_{25}	1	25	X_{17}	25	9	X_{17}	X_1	X_{13}	$\mathcal{I}$	X_{24}	X_8
X_{26}	10	26	X_{10}	26	18	X_{10}	X_2	X_6	$\mathcal{I}$	X_{17}	X_9
X_{27}	19	27	X_3	27	27	X_3	X_3	$\mathcal{I}$	$\mathcal{I}$	X_{10}	X_{10}
X_{28}	28	28	X_{28}	28	4	X_{28}	X_4	X_{24}	X_0	X_3	$\mathcal{I}$
X_{29}	5	29	X_{21}	29	13	X_{21}	X_5	X_{17}	X_1	X_{28}	X_{12}
X_{30}	14	30	X_{14}	30	22	X_{14}	X_6	X_{10}	X_2	X_{21}	X_{13}
X_{31}	23	31	X_7	31	31	X_7	X_7	X_3	X_3	X_{14}	X_{14}
X_{32}	0	0	X_{32}	0	8	X_{32}	X_8	X_{28}	X_4	X_7	$\mathcal{I}$
X_{33}	9	1	X_{25}	1	17	X_{25}	X_9	X_{21}	X_5	X_{32}	X_{16}
X_{34}	18	2	X_{18}	2	26	X_{18}	X_{10}	X_{14}	X_6	X_{25}	X_{17}
X_{35}	27	3	X_{11}	3	3	X_{11}	X_{11}	X_7	X_7	X_{18}	X_{18}
X_{36}	4	4	X_{36}	4	12	X_{36}	X_{12}	X_{32}	X_8	X_{11}	$\mathcal{I}$
X_{37}	13	5	X_{29}	5	21	X_{29}	X_{13}	X_{25}	X_9	X_{36}	X_{20}
X_{38}	22	6	X_{22}	6	30	X_{22}	X_{14}	X_{18}	X_{10}	X_{29}	X_{21}
X_{39}	31	7	X_{15}	7	7	X_{15}	X_{15}	X_{11}	X_{11}	X_{22}	X_{22}
•	•	•	•	•	•	•	•	X_{36}	X_{12}	X_{15}	$\mathcal{I}$
•	•	•	•	•	•	•	•	X_{29}	X_{13}	•	•
•	•	•	•	•	•	•	•	X_{22}	X_{14}	•	•
•	•	•	•	•	•	•	•	X_{15}	X_{15}	•	•

* $\mathcal{I}$ and $\mathcal{D}$ represent initial symbols in the interleaver and deinterleaver, respectively.

Table 10-11. Characteristics of Block and Convolutional Interleaving Approaches

	(I, J) Block Interleaving	(I, J) Convolutional Interleaving	
		Shift-Register Approach	RAM Approach
Restrictions	$I \geq 2, N \geq 2$	$I \geq 2, J \geq 1$	$I \geq 2, J \geq 1$ Memory Size $= I^2 J$ Step Size $= IJ + 1$
Minimum Deinterleaver Output Symbol Separation (S) for a Channel Burst Length	$S \quad \begin{cases} J \text{ for } 2 \geq B \geq I \\ 1 \text{ for } B \geq I + 1 \end{cases}$	For $J = 1$ $S = \begin{cases} I - 1 \text{ for } 2 \leq I + 1 \\ 1 \quad \text{for } B \geq I + 2 \end{cases}$ For $J \geq 2$ $S = \begin{cases} IJ - 1 \text{ for } 2 \geq B \geq I \\ I \quad \text{for } I + 1 \leq B \leq I(J - 1) + 1 \\ I - 1 \text{ for } I(J - 1) + 2 \leq B \leq IJ + 1 \\ 1 \quad \text{for } B \geq IJ + 2 \end{cases}$	For $J = 1$ $S = \begin{cases} I - 1 \text{ for } 2 \leq I + 1 \\ 1 \quad \text{for } B \geq I + 2 \end{cases}$ For $J \geq 2$ $S = \begin{cases} IJ - 1 \text{ for } 2 \geq B \geq I \\ I \quad \text{for } I + 1 \leq B \leq I(J - 1) + 1 \\ I - 1 \text{ for } I(J - 1) + 2 \leq B \leq IJ + 1 \\ 1 \quad \text{for } B \geq IJ + 2 \end{cases}$
Throughput Delay in Channel Symbol Periods	$2IJ$	$IJ(I - 1)$	$IJ(I - 1)$
Number of Synchronization States	IJ	I	I
Interleaver Memory Size in Bits	IJ for a Single Block. $2IJ$ for Continuous Operation.	$IJ(I - 1)/2$	$I^2 J$
Deinterleaver Memory Size in Bits with q-Bit Soft Receiver Decisions	qIJ for a Single Block. $2IJ$ for Continuous Operation.	$qIJ(I - 1)/2$	$qI^2 J$

10.6 References

1. AT&T Information Systems. "A Trellis-Coded Modulation Scheme That Includes Differential Encoding for 9600 Bit/Sec, Full-Duplex, Two-Wire Modem," *CCITT COM XVII*, August, 1983.

2. Balkovic, M.D., H.W. Klancer, S.W. Klare, and W.G. McGruther. "High-Speed Voiceband Data Transmission Performance on the Switched Telecommunications Network," *Bell System Technical Journal*, vol. 50, pp. 1349–1384, April, 1971.

3. Berlekamp, E.R. *Algebraic Coding Theory*. New York: McGraw-Hill, 1968.

4. ———. "Helical Interleaving," *Workshop Record for University of Southern California—Army Research Office Workshop on Research Trends in Military Communications*, May, 1983, pp. 169–183.

5. Bhargava, V.K., D. Haccoun, R. Matyas, and P.P. Nuspl. *Digital Communications by Satellite: Modulation, Multiple Access and Coding*, New York: Wiley, 1981.

6. Blahut, R.E. *Theory and Practice of Error Control Codes*. Reading, MA: Addison-Wesley, 1983.

7. Chase, D. "A Class of Algorithms for Decoding Block Codes with Channel Measurement Information," *IEEE Transactions on Information Theory*, vol. IT-18, pp. 170–182, January, 1972.

8. Clark, G.C., J.B. Cain, and J.M. Geist. "Punctured Convolutional Codes of Rate $(n - 1)/n$ and Simplified Maximum Likelihood Decoding," *IEEE Transactions on Information Theory*, vol. IT-25, pp. 97–100, January, 1979.

9. Clark,G.C., Jr. and J.B. Cain. *Error-Correction Coding for Digital Communications*. New York: Plenum Press, 1981.

10. ———. *Error-Correction Coding for Digital Communications*," New York: Plenum Press, 1988.

11. Duffy, F.P., and J.W. Thatcher, Jr. "Analog Transmission Performance on the Switched Telecommunications Network," *Bell System Technical Journal*, vol. 50, pp. 1311–1347, April, 1971.

12. Forney, G.D., Jr. "Convolutional Codes I: Algebraic Structure," *IEEE Transactions on Information Theory*, vol. IT-16, pp. 720–738, November, 1970.

13. ———. "Burst-Correcting Codes for the Classic Bursty Channel," *IEEE Transactions on Communications Technology*, vol. COM-19, pp. 772–781, October, 1971.

14. Freeman, R.L. *Telecommunication Transmission Handbook, 2nd Ed.* New York: Wiley, 1981.

15. Gallager, R.G. *Information Theory and Reliable Communication.* New York: Wiley, 1968.

16. Geist, J.M., and J.B. Cain. "Viterbi Decoder Performance in Gaussian Noise and Periodic Erasure Bursts," *IEEE Transactions on Communications*, vol. COM-28 Part II, pp. 1417–1422, August, 1980.

17. Haccoun, D., and G. Bégin. "High-Rate Punctured Convolutional Codes for Viterbi and Sequential Decoding," *IEEE Transactions on Information Theory*, vol.37, pp.1113–1125, November, 1989.

18. Helgert, H.J., and R.D. Stinaff. "Minimum-Distance Bounds for Binary Linear Codes," *IEEE Transactions on Information Theory*, vol. IT-19, pp. 344–356, May, 1973.

19. Heller, J.A. "Feedback Decoding of Convolutional Codes," *Advances in Communication Systems, Vol. 4*, A.J. Viterbi, Ed., New York: Academic Press, 1975, pp. 261–278.

20. Hideki, I., editor. *Essentials of Error-Control Coding Techniques*, New York: Academic Press, 1990.

21. Jiří, A. *Foundations of Coding: Theory Applications of Error-Correcting Codes with an Introduction to Cryptography and Information Theory*, New York: John Wiley & Sons, 1991.

22. Jacobs, I.M. "Probability of Error Bounds for Binary Transmission on the Slowly Fading Rician Channel," *IEEE Transactions on Information Theory*, vol. IT-12, pp. 431–441, October, 1966.

23. Larsen, K.J. "Short Convolutional Codes with Maximal Free Distance for Rates 1/2, 1/3 and 1/4," *IEEE Transactions on Information Theory*, vol. IT-19, pp. 371–372, May, 1973.

24. Leung-Yan-Cheong, S.K., and M.E. Hellman. "Concerning a Bound on Undetected Error Probability," *IEEE Transactions on Information Theory*, vol. IT-22, pp. 235–237, March, 1976.

25. Lin, S., and D.J. Costello, Jr. *Error Control Coding: Fundamentals and Applications.* Englewood Cliffs, NJ: Prentice-Hall, 1983.

26. MacWilliams, F.J., and N.J.A. Sloane. *The Theory of Error-Correcting Codes.* Amsterdam: North-Holland, 1977.

27. Massey, J.L., and M.K. Sain. "Inverses of Linear Sequential Circuits," *IEEE Transactions on Computers*, vol. C-17, pp. 330–337, April, 1968.

28. McEliece, R.J. *The Theory of Information and Coding.* Reading, MA: Addison-Wesley, 1977.

29. Muratani, T., H. Saitoh, K. Koga, T. Mizuno, Y. Yasuda, and J.S. Snyder. "Application of FEC Coding to the INTELSAT TDMA System," *Proceedings of the 4th International Conference on Digital Satellite Communications*, October, 1978, pp. 108–115.

30. Odenwalder, J.P. "Optimal Decoding of Convolutional Codes," Ph.D. dissertation, University of California, Los Angeles, 1970.

31. ———. "Dual-k Convolutional Codes for Noncoherently Demodulated Channels, *ITC Conference Record*, 1976, pp. 165–174.

32. ———. "Error Control Coding Handbook," Final Report under Contract No. F44620-76-C-0056 for USAF, Linkabit Corp., July, 1976.

33. Paaske, E. "Short Binary Convolutional Codes with Maximal Free Distance for Rates 2/3 and 3/4," *IEEE Transactions on Information Theory*, vol. IT-20, pp. 683–689, September, 1974.

34. Peterson, W.W., and E.J. Weldon, Jr. *Error-Correcting Codes, 2nd Ed.* Cambridge, MA: MIT Press, 1972.

35. Pettit, R.H. *ECM and ECCM Techniques for Digital Communications Systems.* Belmont, CA: Lifetime Learning Pub., 1982.

36. Piret, P. "Convolutional Codes: An Algebraic Approach," Cambridge, MA: MIT Press, 1988.

37. Pless, V. *Introduction to the Theory of Error-Correcting Codes*, 2nd ed., New York: John Wiley & Sons, 1989.

38. Proakis, J.G. *Digital Communications.* New York: McGraw-Hill, 1983.

39. Ramsey, J.L. "Realization of Optimum Interleavers," *IEEE Transactions on Information Theory*, vol. IT-16, pp. 338–345, May, 1970.

40. Rhee, M.Y. *Error Correcting Coding Theory*," New York: McGraw-Hill, 1989.

41. Shacham, N. "Performance of ARQ with Sequential Decoding over One-Hop and Two-Hop Radio Links," *IEEE Transactions on Communications*, vol. COM-31, pp. 1172–1180, October, 1983.

42. Shannon, C.E. "A Mathematical Theory of Communication," *Bell System Technical Journal*, vol. 27, pp. 379–423 (pt. I) and 623–656 (pt. II), 1948.

43. Tanenbaum, A.S. *Computer Networks.* Englewood Cliffs, NJ: Prentice-Hall, 1981.

44. Titan Linkabit Corp. "Error Control Product Brochures," San Diego, CA: Titan Linkabit Corp.

45. Trumpis, B.D., and P.L. McAdam. "Performance of Convolutional Codes on Burst Noise Channels," *NTC '77 Conference Record*, December, 1977, pp. 36:3-1 to 36:3-14.

46. Ungerboeck, G. "Channel Coding with Multilevel/Phase Signals," *IEEE Transactions on Information Theory*, vol. IT-28, pp. 55–67, January, 1982.

47. United States of America. "Draft Recommendation for 14,400 Bits per Second Modem," *CCITT COM XVII*, October, 1983.

48. Viterbi, A.J. *Principles of Coherent Communication*. New York: Mc-Graw-Hill, 1966.

49. ———. "Convolutional Codes and Their Performance in Communication Systems," *IEEE Transactions on Communications Technology*, vol. COM-19, pp. 751–772, October, 1971.

50. ———. "A Robust Ratio-Threshold Technique to Mitigate Tone and Partial Band Jamming in Coded MFSK Systems," *MILCOM '82 Proceedings*, vol. 1, October, 1982, pp. 22.4-1 to 22.4-5.

51. Viterbi, A.J., and J.K. Omura. *Principles of Digital Communication and Coding*. New York: McGraw-Hill, 1979.

52. Wiggert, D. *Codes for Error Control and Synchronization*, Norwood, MA: Artech House, 1988.

53. Wolf, J.K., and R.D. Blakeney, II. "An Exact Evaluation of the Probability of Undetected Error for Certain Shortened Binary CRC Codes," *MILCOM '88 Proceedings*, vol.1, October, 1988, pp.287–292.

54. Wolf, J.K., A.M. Michelson, and A.H. Levesque. "On the Probability of Undetected Error for Linear Block Codes," *IEEE Transactions on Communications*, vol. COM-30, pp. 317–324, February, 1982.

55. Wozencraft,J.M., and I.M. Jacobs. *Principles of Communication Engineering*. New York: Wiley, 1965.

56. Yasuda, Y., Y. Hirata, K. Nakamura, and S. Otani. "Development of Variable-Rate Viterbi Decoder and Its Performance Characteristics," *Proceedings of the Sixth International Conference on Digital Satellite Communications*, September, 1983, pp. XII-24 to XII-31.

57. Yasuda,Y., K. Kashiki, and Y. Hirata. "High-Rate Punctured Convolutional Codes for Soft Decision Viterbi Decoding," *IEEE Transactions on Communications*, vol. COM-32, pp. 315–319, March, 1984.

Index

C

F

K-L

M

Q

R

Sams—Covering The Latest In Computer And Technical Topics!

Audio

Advanced Digital Audio	.$39.95
Audio Systems Design and Installation	.$59.95
Compact Disc Troubleshooting and Repair	.$24.95
Handbook for Sound Engineers:	
The New Audio Cyclopedia, 2nd Ed.	.$99.95
How to Design & Build Loudspeaker	
& Listening Enclosures	.$39.95
Introduction to Professional	
Recording Techniques	.$29.95
The MIDI Manual	.$24.95
Modern Recording Techniques, 3rd Ed.	.$29.95
OP-AMP Circuits and Principles	.$19.95
Principles of Digital Audio, 2nd Ed.	.$29.95
Sound Recording Handbook	.$49.95
Sound System Engineering, 2nd Ed.	.$49.95

Electricity/Electronics

Active-Filter Cookbook	.$24.95
Basic Electricity and DC Circuits	.$29.95
CMOS Cookbook, 2nd Ed.	.$24.95
Electrical Wiring	.$19.95
Electricity 1-7, Revised 2nd Ed.	.$49.95
Electronics 1-7, Revised 2nd Ed.	.$49.95
How to Read Schematics, 4th Ed.	.$19.95
IC Op-Amp Cookbook, 3rd Ed.	.$24.95
IC Timer Cookbook, 2nd Ed.	.$24.95
RF Circuit Design	.$24.95
Transformers and Motors	.$29.95
TTL Cookbook	.$24.95
Understanding Digital Troubleshooting, 3rd Ed.	$24.95
Understanding Solid State Electronics, 5th Ed.	$24.95

Games

Master SimCity/SimEarth	.$19.95
Master Ultima	.$16.95

Hardware/Technical

First Book of Modem Communications	.$16.95
First Book of PS/1	.$16.95
Hard Disk Power with the Jamsa Disk Utilities	$39.95
IBM PC Advanced Troubleshooting & Repair	$24.95
IBM Personal Computer Troubleshooting	
& Repair	.$24.95
Microcomputer Troubleshooting & Repair	.$24.95
Understanding Fiber Optics	.$24.95

IBM: Business

10 Minute Guide to PC Tools 7	.$ 9.95
10 Minute Guide to Q&A 4	.$ 9.95
First Book of Microsoft Works for the PC	.$16.95
First Book of Norton Utilities 6	.$16.95
First Book of PC Tools 7	.$16.95
First Book of Personal Computing, 2nd Ed.	.$16.95

IBM: Database

10 Minute Guide to Harvard Graphics 2.3	.$9.95
Best Book of AutoCAD	.$34.95
dBASE III Plus Programmer's	
Reference Guide	.$24.95
dBASE IV Version 1.1 for the First-Time User	$24.95
Everyman's Database Primer Featuring dBASE IV	
Version 1.1	.$24.95
First Book of Paradox 3.5	.$16.95
First Book of PowerPoint for Windows	.$16.95
Harvard Graphics 2.3 In Business	.$29.95

IBM: Graphics/Desktop Publishing

10 Minute Guide to Lotus 1-2-3	.$ 9.95
Best Book of Harvard Graphics	.$24.95
First Book of Harvard Graphics 2.3	.$16.95
First Book of PC Paintbrush	.$16.95
First Book of PFS: First Publisher	.$16.95

IBM: Spreadsheets/Financial

Best Book of Lotus 1-2-3 Release 3.1	$27.95
First Book of Excel 3 for Windows	$16.95
First Book of Lotus 1-2-3 Release 2.3	$16.95
First Book of Quattro Pro 3	$16.95
First Book of Quicken In Business	$16.95
Lotus 1-2-3 Release 2.3 In Business	$29.95
Lotus 1-2-3: Step-by-Step	$24.95
Quattro Pro In Business	$29.95

IBM: Word Processing

Best Book of Microsoft Word 5	$24.95
Best Book of Microsoft Word for Windows	$24.95
Best Book of WordPerfect 5.1	$26.95
First Book of Microsoft Word 5.5	$16.95
First Book of WordPerfect 5.1	$16.95
WordPerfect 5.1: Step-by-Step	$24.95

Macintosh/Apple

First Book of Excel 3 for the Mac	$16.95
First Book of the Mac	$16.95

Operating Systems/Networking

10 Minute Guide to Windows 3	$ 9.95
Best Book of DESQview	$24.95
Best Book of Microsoft Windows 3	$24.95
Best Book of MS-DOS 5	$24.95
Business Guide to Local Area Networks	$24.95
DOS Batch File Power	
with the Jamsa Disk Utilities	$39.95
Exploring the UNIX System, 2nd Ed.	$29.95
First Book of DeskMate	$16.95
First Book of Microsoft Windows 3	$16.95
First Book of MS-DOS 5	$16.95
First Book of UNIX	$16.95
Interfacing to the IBM Personal Computer,	
2nd Ed.	$24.95
The Waite Group's Discovering MS-DOS,	
2nd Edition	$19.95
The Waite Group's MS-DOS Bible, 4th Ed.	$29.95
The Waite Group's MS-DOS Developer's Guide,	
2nd Ed.	$29.95
The Waite Group's Tricks of the UNIX Masters	$29.95
The Waite Group's Understanding MS-DOS,	
2nd Ed.	$19.95
The Waite Group's UNIX Primer Plus, 2nd Ed.	$29.95
The Waite Group's UNIX System V Bible	$29.95
Understanding Local Area Networks, 2nd Ed.	$24.95
UNIX Applications Programming:	
Mastering the Shell	$29.95
UNIX Networking	$29.95
UNIX Shell Programming, Revised Ed.	$29.95
UNIX: Step-by-Step	$29.95
UNIX System Administration	$29.95
UNIX System Security	$34.95
UNIX Text Processing	$29.95

Professional/Reference

Data Communications, Networks, and Systems	$39.95
Handbook of Electronics Tables and Formulas,	
6th Ed.	$24.95
ISDN, DECnet, and SNA Communications	$49.95
Modern Dictionary of Electronics, 6th Ed.	$39.95
Reference Data for Engineers: Radio, Electronics,	
Computer, and Communications, 7th Ed.	$99.95

Programming

Advanced C: Tips and Techniques	$29.95
C Programmer's Guide to NetBIOS	$29.95
C Programmer's Guide	
to Serial Communications	$29.95
Commodore 64 Programmer's	
Reference Guide	$24.95

Developing Windows Applications	
with Microsoft SDK	.$29.95
DOS Batch File Power	.$39.95
Graphical User Interfaces with Turbo C++	.$29.95
Learning C++	.$39.95
Mastering Turbo Assembler	.$29.95
Mastering Turbo Pascal, 4th Ed.	.$29.95
Microsoft Macro Assembly Language	
Programming	.$29.95
Microsoft QuickBASIC	
Programmer's Reference	.$29.95
Programming in ANSI C	.$29.95
Programming in C, Revised Ed.	.$29.95
The Waite Group's BASIC Programming	
Primer, 2nd Ed.	.$24.95
The Waite Group's C Programming	
Using Turbo C++	.$29.95
The Waite Group's C: Step-by-Step	.$29.95
The Waite Group's GW-BASIC Primer Plus	.$24.95
The Waite Group's Microsoft C Bible, 2nd Ed.	$29.95
The Waite Group's Microsoft C Programming	
for the PC, 2nd Ed.	.$29.95
The Waite Group's New C Primer Plus	.$29.95
The Waite Group's Turbo Assembler Bible	.$29.95
The Waite Group's Turbo C Bible	.$29.95
The Waite Group's Turbo C Programming	
for the PC, Revised Ed.	.$29.95
The Waite Group's Turbo C++Bible	.$29.95
X Window System Programming	.$29.95

Radio/Video

Camcorder Survival Guide	.$ 14.95
Radio Handbook, 23rd Ed.	.$39.95
Radio Operator's License Q&A Manual,	
11th Ed.	.$24.95
Understanding Fiber Optics	.$24.95
Understanding Telephone Electronics, 3rd Ed.	$24.95
VCR Troubleshooting & Repair Guide	.$19.95
Video Scrambling & Descrambling	
for Satellite & Cable TV	.$24.95

**For More Information,
See Your Local Retailer
Or Call Toll Free**

1-800-428-5331

*All prices are subject to change without notice.
Non-U.S. prices may be higher. Printed in the U.S.A.*

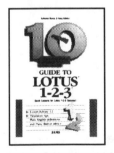